DATE DUE

GAYLORD   PRINTED IN U.S.A.

D1158363

ECONOMICS

ECONOMICS

The Culture of a Controversial Science

MELVIN W. REDER

The University of Chicago Press
CHICAGO AND LONDON

MELVIN W. REDER is the Isidore and Gladys J. Brown Professor Emeritus in the Graduate School of Business at the University of Chicago. He is the author of *Studies in the Theory of Welfare Economics* and *Labor in a Growing Economy.*

THE UNIVERSITY OF CHICAGO PRESS, CHICAGO 60637
THE UNIVERSITY OF CHICAGO PRESS, LTD., LONDON

© 1999 by The University of Chicago
All rights reserved. Published 1999

06 05 04 03 02 01 00 99 98 99   5 4 3 2 1

ISBN (cloth): 0-226-70609-5

LIBRARY OF CONGRESS CATALOGING-IN-PUBLICATION DATA

Reder, Melvin Warren, 1919–
  Economics : the culture of a controversial science / Melvin W. Reder.
    p.   cm.   ˙
  Includes bibliographical references and index.
  ISBN 0-226-70609-5
  1. Economics. 2. Economists. I. Title.
HB71.R348   1999
330—dc21   98-8640
                                                          CIP

♾ The paper used in this publication meets the minimum requirements of the American National Standard for Information Sciences—Permanence of Paper for Printed Library Materials, ANSI Z39.48-1992.

To my wife, Edna

CONTENTS

PREFACE

This book attempts to describe the salient features of the culture of economics. As this culture is centered on the social activity of generating, discussing, appraising, and amending ideas about the functioning of economies, its characteristics are inseparable from the intellectual folkways that structure this activity. Among other things these folkways prescribe the language, research techniques, and theory characteristics required by the culture as a condition of general approval.

Prescriptive interpretations of such folkways are usually considered to be the subject matter of methodology. Consequently, in various places throughout the book I have felt compelled to make comments that touch on methodological issues. However, these remarks are only incidental: this is not a book about methodology. Its purpose is to describe the intellectual practices of economists rather than to appraise them. But because one very important reason for adopting or retaining a particular practice is that it appears to have led to satisfactory results, it is unavoidable that description should spill over into appraisal whenever an attempt is made to explain why practices are what they are. Nevertheless, in describing intellectual practices, I have tried hard to avoid placing weight on methodological considerations.

The description of the culture of economics that I offer is only partial. Ideas, regardless of their importance, are not the only constituent of this culture: not less than others, economists are concerned with loaves and fishes. However, along with mating practices and other aspects of daily life, I consider this concern a minor one and treat it accordingly. Like members of other scientific cultures, economists pursue fame and fortune by seeking recognition of their contributions to the ideas that characterize their subject. Therefore I shall assume that economists behave as if wealth were a by-product of a quest for the acclaim of their disciplinary peers, and consideration of its motivating power accordingly otiose.

Let me qualify: once past their dissertations, many—possibly most—economists are intellectual freelancers, available for work on whatever problem offers the best prospect for pecuniary reward. Hope of making an "important contribution to the field"—if ever it existed—diminishes to the vanishing point. As is generally recognized, research effort follows the funds available for its support. Consequently, in its choice of subject matter the bulk of economic writing closely follows popular interest.

Nevertheless, the ideas and techniques that fledgling economists are taught do not closely track either research funding or popular interest. And this book is concerned with the vicissitudes of such ideas. The primary sensitivity of such ideas is to currents of intradisciplinary discourse, and their protagonists would feel it infra dig to offer popular support as evidence of merit. In short, the ideas we shall discuss are appraised by the criteria of a more or less self-contained culture which provides its own rewards to successful members.

Although the book is focused on the characteristics of a disciplinary culture, or subculture,[1] it does not ignore the larger culture within which that discipline functions. Indeed, providing an analysis of the interaction of the larger culture with the economics subculture is a major objective of this book, whose purpose is to induce recognition of the several faces of economics and an understanding of how they are interrelated. Among economists, I hope to increase cultural self-awareness. While such self-awareness might also help to improve the manner in which they do research, and the topics they select, I am incapable of doubting that self-awareness is a good in itself. Among the general public, I hope to improve understanding of the various things economists do, and of how their diverse interests interrelate. From this improved understanding, they may learn how better to appraise the arguments of economists, both vis-à-vis one another, and against those emanating from strangers to their culture.

For books of this sort, there is always a proper concern as to how much knowledge of the subject the author supposes the reader to possess. While it is always true that more knowledge will not hurt, the main argument of this book can be readily followed by any college undergraduate having an active interest in the economic aspects of public affairs. The broad outline of the argument, which is summarized in the first chapter, does not involve any technical economics. In part 1, I discuss the relation of the social function of the economist as a member of a recognized community of experts to the problematic status of economics as a science: this discussion is developed and extended in part 3. Neither of these parts make any use of technical economics.

1. See chapter 1, note 1.

Part 2 is a hiatus in the general argument that is needed to provide support for the critical view of economics as a science taken in parts 1 and 3. Part 2 contains some technical argument (though not a great deal), and it is offered with a minimum of theoretical fireworks. Interest in the subject matter should suffice to overcome any occasional gap in background knowledge and enable the general reader to follow the broad argument without difficulty.

Much as I hate to encourage skimming, I confess that at some places in part 2 a reader who is already persuaded of the point at hand may be able to glide over an argument that I would prefer he or she read carefully. However, in any case, lack of technical background will rarely—if ever—be a serious obstacle to following the argument.

However infelicitous the final product, it is far superior to the first draft read by Robert Flanagan and Jules Theeuwef, and two anonymous referees for the University of Chicago Press. Adrian Throop provided valuable criticism of chapters 4 and 5, and Mark Granovetter greatly improved my perspective on the boundaries of the subject. Though I have not always been able to accept the advice of these critics, the alterations induced by their comments have greatly improved the final product. While I cannot believe this product is free of expository blemishes, their number and salience has been greatly reduced by the meticulous editing of Claudia Rex: Reder and readers are heavily indebted to her.

More generally, conversations with Moses Abramovitz, Tibor Scitovsky and Gavin Wright over many years have left their imprint on the way I think about the subject matter of this book. Proper recognition of the debt to my wife, Edna, would involve a lengthy discourse on the interface of love and obligation which I am not ready to publish. Inadequate though it is, a dedication must suffice.

PART ONE

CULTURE AND SCIENCE

ONE

OVERVIEW

conomics consists of a number of interrelated branches and an
associated trunk. This book is an attempt to describe the characteristics of the conceptual network that they support. Economics
is a culture or, more precisely, a subculture;[1] it is also a discipline, a science, and a profession. Further, it is an important ingredient of statecraft
or public policy formation, where it serves as a source both of ideology
and technical support.

It is convenient to begin with the cultural facet, because, properly
speaking, our primary focus is upon economists rather than economics.
As Jacob Viner put it, "Economics is what economists do."[2] This definition
has (at least) one implication: the boundaries of economics are set by the
proclivities of its practitioners and not by a specified subject matter. To
be sure, exercise of the skills that distinguish economists from others usually takes place in connection with the study of a particular subject matter
(i.e., the production and exchange of goods, services, and claims thereto)
where they find their primary use. However, application of these skills is
not circumscribed by a traditional subject matter and, as we shall see, their
field of application has been expanding during the past quarter century.
In any case, defining economics in this way provides a convenient entry
point to a discussion of the culture of its practitioners.

Like many other academic disciplines, economics is the product of a
particular culture whose members constitute a profession that is coexten-
sive with the domain of the culture. Such professional cultures are characterized by (1) a matrix of professional associations; (2) culturally speci-

1. Economists constitute a subculture which is a part of the general culture of the whole
society. As the interrelations of the general culture and the subculture are very important I
shall take pains to distinguish between them. However, for brevity, except where necessary
to avoid confusion I shall refer to the subculture as the "culture of economics."

2. As Lee Hansen (1991, p. 1054, n. 1) has noted, there is no particular citation that can
be offered for this remark. I seem to recall hearing Viner make this—or a similar—remark
in class, but memories of events more than half a century in the past are subject to discount.
In any case, the attribution to Viner is now part of an oral tradition.

fic media of communications (e.g., specialized journals); (3) a specialized language (jargon) which is easily misunderstood by the uninitiated; (4) criteria and tokens of achievement and status that have general recognition within the culture (e.g., degrees and prizes); and (5) recognized centers of activity and associated training programs that initiate and indoctrinate (acculturate) neophytes.

As often noted, and protested, the effect of these characteristics is to insulate a discipline from external currents of opinion. However, such insulation is essential to a function that the subcultures perform for society as a whole. This function is the provision of expertise within the domain of its competence.[3] The expertise sought is for guidance in the making of practical decisions. Though in economics the major source of this demand derives from the conduct of public business, there is an important and growing use for economic expertise in private decision making as well.

The need for expertise is rooted in the specialization of functions and the associated compartmentalization of knowledge that exists in any reasonably well-developed society. A major problem in procuring expert advice is identifying those who are competent to give it. Such identification is greatly facilitated by the existence of generally accepted credentials: establishing a subculture in which membership and, even more, high status betoken specific expertise is an effective and commonly used method for establishing such credentials.

The meaning of expertise has varied from society to society: oracles, shamans, sages, rabbis, wizards, and the like, have all functioned as experts in one context or another. And the credentials of expertise have varied similarly: claims of supernatural sources of information have been a frequent rationale for claims of expertise. But in the modern Western societies to which our interest is restricted the only acceptable rationale for a claim of expertise has been, for several centuries, possession of scientific knowledge. This is not to suggest that in all sections of a modern Western society science is considered as the only acceptable basis for valid esoteric knowledge. Many, perhaps most, members of such societies concede the status of expert, in one context or another, to persons who can make no valid claim to a scientific foundation for their statements—and often do not even try to do so. Astrologers, faith healers, gurus, and religious au-

---

3. The boundaries of these domains are rarely precise or generally accepted. This remark applies especially to the case of economics, where the specification of disciplinary turf has provoked considerable dispute (described in chapter 14).

thorities of all kinds continue to attract large numbers of convinced adherents. Nevertheless, in practical decision making, both in the public sector and in large private organizations having some measure of public accountability, there is virtually unanimous acceptance of the notion that expert advice must rest upon scientific findings.

For example, when it was revealed that then First Lady Nancy Reagan had been guided by an astrologer concerning the timing of possible presidential actions, the White House, with evident embarrassment, took great pains to issue assurance that no public business had been affected by such advice.[4] For good reasons or bad, the effective makers of policy in organizations with public responsibility—who are overwhelmingly graduates of secular institutions of higher learning—require that, wherever available, scientific advice must serve as the basis for the making of decisions, or at least appear to do so.[5]

Even more to the point, most economists take great pride in the scientific character of their field and reject suggestions that its claims to merit are other than those of a science. Obviously, the significance of this statement depends upon the definition of science. But, as this definition is a major topic of chapter 2, I shall defer extended discussion.

Like any culture of experts, economics is greatly concerned with maintaining an effective monopoly of authority over the validation of statements about matters falling within its domain. While the authority of every science has been challenged in one connection or another, the authority of economics has been and continues to be more subject to questioning than most natural sciences. Moreover, economists feel more vulnerable to such challenges than the practitioners of more secure sciences, notably physics and microbiology, and accordingly are highly sensitive both to aspersions upon the scientific status of their subject, and to behavior that might reflect unfavorably upon that status. As we shall see, the uneasiness of economists with the scientific status of their discipline, and their attempts to defend it, lie at the root of many of the distinctive characteristics of their culture.

4. For Nancy Reagan's dependence on her astrologer see Donald T. Regan (1988), especially pp. 70–74 and 367–70. Regan makes it very clear that White House insiders were embarrassed and highly secretive about the role played by astrology in the scheduling of the President's activities.

5. Though it is no part of this argument, I conjecture that the attitude of the courts has been an important factor in generating this disposition. A heavy burden of proof would be placed upon any agent who claimed to have acted without obtaining (and heeding) conventional scientific advice.

An illustration of the insecure status of economics in an area that is close to the heart of its domain is provided by some recent discussion of international trade policy. Paul Krugman (accurately) describes this literature:

> the view of trade as a quasi-military competition is the conventional wisdom among policymakers, business leaders, and influential intellectuals. . . . It's not just that economists have lost control of the discourse; the kinds of ideas that are offered in a standard economics textbook do not enter into that discourse at all. . . .

> [O]ne gets nowhere in making sense of the debate on international "competitiveness," among people who regard themselves and are regarded by others as sophisticated, unless one realizes that their views are based on a failure to understand even the simplest economic facts and concepts.[6]

Authors whose writings are thus castigated by Krugman include Lester Thurow, Robert Reich, Jeffrey Garten, Clyde Prestowitz, Edward Luttwak, Ira Magaziner, Paul Kennedy, and Sir James Goldsmith. What these writers have in common is an image of international trade in which the participants are engaged in a quasi-military struggle. In this image, the gains of one participant must be the losses of others: it is impossible for all participants to benefit. The intended effect of propagating this image is to persuade the public of the need to pursue trade policies aimed at achieving victory in the entailed struggle. The details of the various proposed policies need not concern us: in general, they involve government intervention in international trade for reasons and in situations that most economists would agree are inappropriate.

Yet as Krugman says, "the vision of international trade as a competition with winners and losers, a competition America had better win, *is* the conventional wisdom. The stuff that is in the college textbooks is a contrarian view, with hardly any real influence."[7] That this conventional wisdom is rooted in a number of crude fallacies is not to the present point, which is that the economist's claim to a monopoly of expertise is parlous and conceded only under particular circumstances.

In general, where an issue is restricted to the finding and/or the interpretation of "facts" that incorporate an analytical construction of econo-

6. Paul Krugman (1995), pp. 9–18. Also see Krugman's invited review article of this literature in *The Economist,* 29 April–5 May 1995, pp. 99–100.

7. Krugman (1995), p. 12.

mists (e.g., national accounts, cost-of-living indices, indicators of business conditions), the authority of the discipline is respected. But where an issue involves determination of a causal relationship among prices and quantities, especially if the distinction between real and nominal values is salient, the economist is likely to find his turf invaded by untutored outsiders, as reflected in Krugman's discussion of international trade policy. Although expressed with greater vehemence than is usually found in published statements, Krugman's remarks typify the reaction of economists to such invasions of their disciplinary turf.

Though rarely acknowledged, defining and defending the disciplinary turf is an important objective of most graduate training programs in economics. Courses in economic theory and econometrics teach—well or badly—how an economist is supposed to analyze an economic problem and (less carefully) what problems should be considered as properly economic. That the emphasis is placed on technique (how to do economics) rather than on content (what to do with it) is an important characteristic of the disciplinary culture, and the focus of much controversy; this will be discussed later. In teaching how to analyze an economic problem—which concepts and vocabulary to use, characteristics required of acceptable models, criteria to apply in appraising solutions—the training program indoctrinates recruits to the discipline. This indoctrination is a large part of the process of acculturation that creates the mindset described by the title, "economist."

This mindset is characterized by a strong preference for certain methodological procedures and a correlative aversion to others. (Krugman's philippic, quoted above, is a striking expression of such aversion.) The procedures and ancillary skills entailed will be described later. For the moment it will suffice to note that the pressure to use these procedures, and acquire the necessary ancillary skills, greatly influences the selection of recruits by training institutions and induces self-selection among prospective candidates, which is to say that the selection process is slanted toward those with taste and aptitude for the implied course of study.[8]

An important consequence of this training bias is its effect upon the intellectual characteristics of the typical member of the culture. For example, with few exceptions, economists learn nothing about the techniques of laboratory experimentation and are insensitive to the nuances

---

8. While it is easy to exaggerate, it is safe to say that at the present time a lack of aptitude for mathematics and quantitative reasoning generally imposes a severe handicap—if not an absolute bar—to successful participation in a Ph.D. program in economics.

of its procedures.[9] Similarly, they are rarely trained in the procedures of collecting data and are inclined to undervalue the skills it requires, and the contribution to economic knowledge made by those engaged in data collection. This is not to suggest that economists ignore data, but to say that typically they are content to use data gathered by others, and to focus effort and ingenuity upon the construction of models that can be applied to it. In so doing, they are reflecting not only the cultural values which they have internalized, but also the rewards of prestige and esteem—and sometimes cash—that are largely determined by the standards of the economics culture. Economists, in short, typically value clever theoretical ideas—especially when they can be applied to explain salient economic phenomena—over the assiduous gathering, careful preparation and lucid presentation of data (a preference which has been widely noted and much deplored). As I shall argue, this pattern of relative valuation is not adventitious, but the direct consequence of the insecure status of economics as a science.

Temporarily withholding comment on its desirability, let us consider some of the consequences of this trait. One of these is a bias in the selection of the culture's heroes. With few if any exceptions, graduate training in economics begins with the learning of techniques, both theoretical and econometric. Emphasis is placed on learning the best—i.e., the newest—techniques, which are pejoratively compared with their predecessors. The individuals credited with the innovations are immediately identified as meritorious, and those making the most and/or the biggest innovations are cultural heroes. As these innovations often involve utilizing a previously unexploited mathematical wrinkle, possession of mathematical skill quickly becomes a major criterion for ranking students. Contrary to much recent comment, mathematical talent is not the sole criterion by which graduate students in economics are judged; conceptual originality is at least as important. But without the capacity for mathematical implementation, conceptual originality is heavily discounted: full credit is not given for an original idea that is not given a formal (i.e., mathematical) presentation. And, unaccompanied by conceptual originality or mathematical skill, breadth of knowledge relevant to understanding the functioning of an actual economy, and/or an aptitude for hard and careful work with empirical materials, is considered as meritorious, but nothing more.[10]

9. The exceptions arise from the existence of a few programs in experimental economics which will be discussed in chapter 7.

10. For further argument in support of the view of the profession expressed in this paragraph and its predecessor, and some supporting empirical evidence, see David C. Colander

The tropism for theory is one, but not the only, defining characteristic of the economics culture. Any research that finds practical application is a source of kudos within the culture. If the research embodies a new theoretical idea, that is cause for special celebration. However, even without a headdress of theoretical innovation, sound empirical work that finds practical application is a reliable source of esteem within the profession. Conversely, theoretical ideas that have practical impact but do not meet with cultural acceptance are resisted—and resented—within the profession.[11] The one prominent exception to this last statement is Keynes's General Theory, which will be discussed below (in chapters 4 and 5) in some detail.

A very important practical application of economics is in the field of welfare economics. Broadly defined, welfare economics attempts to devise and appraise the performance of economies and the actions of public authorities[12] in terms of criteria of social propriety. In recent years, the term "welfare economics" has come to be reserved for esoteric and often highly mathematical studies of the efficiency properties of economic models. However, such studies are not as central to economic thinking as more traditional exercises in measuring economic performance that may be termed "applied welfare economics." As defined here, applied welfare economics includes the construction of national accounts and cost-of-living indices and measures of productivity, business activity, economic progress, and income distribution.[13] These measurements are intellectual constructions that function as data for appraising the economic performance of a community and measuring the distribution of its fruits.

So far as I am aware, no other science has a social responsibility analogous to that born by economics in providing the means for quantitative description and appraisal of the economic performance of societies. So long as governments assume some responsibility for aggregate economic performance, or have it thrust upon them, the instruments by which such

---

and Arjo Klamer (1987), pp. 95–111. This work contains references to other articles and books that are more or less supportive of the same view.

11. The remarks of Krugman, quoted above, exemplify this attitude.

12. In principle, these applications can be—and are—made to the behavior of private organizations and individuals as well. However, as the typical application is to the actions of governmental bodies, except where otherwise specified, our discussion will be restricted to the public sector.

13. As is discussed in chapter 11, economics is also responsible for intellectual constructions having wide practical use in the private sector. These include financial instruments for measuring, managing, pricing, and transferring risk, and for pricing the right to pollute.

performance is measured will be of potential concern to participants in the political process. As we shall see, often the choice of economic yardsticks has more or less predictable consequences for the political slant of the resulting measurements, and therefore is a matter for political concern.

It is a fundamental tenet of economics that the units of measurement of wealth, income, value, and so on may not be chosen arbitrarily, but must be justified by an economic theory in which the resulting concepts are embedded. Taken together with the political concern about measurement procedures, this tenet creates a link between economic theory and political argument that gives an ideological dimension to the culture of economics. As will be discussed in chapter 12, in economics the relations of science and ideology are complex and not susceptible of facile treatment. At this point, the only remark to be made on these relations is that their impact upon economic thought arises from the possibility that they may conflict with the obligations of an economist in his function as expert.

In discussing the manner in which the economics culture generates ideas and applies them, I shall pay but little attention to the role played by financial support. The rationale for this neglect is an assumption, here made explicit, that there is relatively little to say—that is not obvious—about the possible effect of variations in the magnitude of financial support upon the course of economic thought. This is not to suggest that making funds available to support research on a specific topic, or on the subject as a whole, will fail to generate an increased quantity of research output (i.e., journal articles, books, etc.) and probably of relevant factual information about the matters addressed. Like chicken soup, financial support can't hurt and might help. But it is very difficult to go beyond this (very) weak statement.

The presuppositions underlying these remarks are the same as those entertained by most authors of histories of economic thought. Despite large differences of emphasis and disagreements of interpretation, virtually all such histories are written as if economic ideas were a response either to currents of opinion—parochial or secular—or to perceived economic problems, but not to the availability of research funds. This proclivity of historians may be interpreted in (at least) two ways: (1) ideas are produced by creative individuals who are driven solely by intellectual interests which are not much influenced by the availability of support. Though an increase in research support may increase the volume of work done in developing and applying the ideas of a few creative economists, such work, done mainly by the noncreative majority, does not add much to the stock of ideas.[14] (2) Although the level of resources available for support and the style and outcome of the resulting research are, or might be, connected, at this time we are unaware of the characteristics of that connection.

To take a concrete example: since World War II research funds for the study of economic development have been widely available and have generated voluminous country reports, general works on development, and not a little theoretical speculation in professional journals. Without attempting to appraise the overall quality of this research, I will conjecture that if its quantity (measured in real dollars of input) had been halved, the contribution of its output to the history of economic ideas would not have been substantially affected. Implicit in this speculation is an "elitist" judgment that major ideas are a response to events and to currents of thought that will emerge regardless of the financial support available to their potential inventors. The level of resource support affects the extent to which such ideas will be elaborated and given empirical application, and the general attention they attract, but not their general configuration. This alleged disjunction of the basic structure of ideas from the extent of their elaboration and application is a largely untested hypothesis about whose validity I am far from certain.[15] However, faute de mieux, this hypothesis is maintained throughout the book.

Another neglected characteristic of the economics culture is the occupational and geographical composition of its membership. In the twentieth century, especially the second half, most contributors to the literature of economics were professors of the subject at a college or university, with civil servants and staff members of privately funded but not-for-profit research institutes constituting a significant minority.[16] Employees of profit-

14. The analogy of the dichotomy between the "creative minority" and other economists with Schumpeter's dichotomy between entrepreneurs and "the swarm of imitators" is obvious.

15. I would place far less credence in this hypothesis in the context of the natural sciences where the course of theoretical speculation is surely influenced by the economic feasibility of the implied experiments whose relative costs may differ greatly. Conceivably, if economics were to become a predominantly experimental science—which it never has been—this statement might apply there as well.

16. There is substantial mobility between academic positions and employment in government or not-for-profit research so that for our purposes the individuals involved constitute a single research community. Although not completely isolated from this community, economists employed by private firms constitute a separate community. It might be re-

seeking firms represented a much larger fraction of the culture's membership than of the authorship of its professionally oriented research output.[17] This is because a very substantial part of the research output of
business economists is directed to problems of particular interest to their
employers who, in any case, frequently restrict publication of their employees' research. Especially in finance, jobs in private business provide a
significant and growing source of employment for holders of advanced
degrees in economics and add significantly to the resonance of ideas originating within the profession, but—again with the possible exception of
finance—those who fill them do not make a major contribution to its research output.

The focus of business economists on the particular problems of their
employers compels them to cultivate practically useful ideas and techniques regardless of their consonance with culturally approved preconceptions. For the business economist, and sometimes the civil servant, it
is usually sufficient that an idea should work in practice. But for academic
economists often the primary task is to find out whether and how what
seems—at least temporarily—to work in practice, can also be made to
work in theory.

This distinction between the criteria for success in theoretical and in
applied work exists in most, if not all, sciences. However, as we shall see,
the contrast is much sharper in economics than elsewhere. That is, in economics, the separation of theory from application is greater than in most
other sciences, with the result that much applied work has had to proceed
without close relation to theory—and sometimes in direct conflict with it.
The resulting tension is at the root of much of the acrimonious discussion
of methodology in which economic literature abounds.

Despite the numerical preponderance of business economists in the
economics profession,[18] the separation of theory and application, together
with the far greater publication rate of academics, has given a cast to economic writing that is different from that found in most natural sciences.
In economics, it is much more common for leading researchers in one of

marked that the integration of this latter group with the first two is much greater in the field
of finance (see chapter 8) than in other parts of the subject.

17. By "professionally oriented research output" I mean articles in professional journals, textbooks and books published for the general trade, and certain publications of governments and international agencies.

18. For an estimate of the relative numbers of business and other economists see Arjo
Klamer and David C. Colander, *The Making of an Economist* (1990).

its branches to write a textbook or a treatise on its subject—and for journal articles to amend and develop the arguments of a treatise—than is the case in a natural science. Although the causal arrow goes in both directions, I attribute this phenomenon mainly to the fact that in the teaching of economics the stress is upon getting the theory straight rather than upon applying it properly. While theory is not ignored in the training of natural scientists, success in its assimilation is judged more by proper use in applied research or, less frequently, by the making of culturally approved innovations than is the case in economics.

Although there are a number of reasons for this state of affairs, I shall argue that the salient factor is the relative weakness of the link between theory and application in economics. That is, economic theory has such weak implications for applied work that satisfactory application does not provide strong evidence about a researcher's command of economic theory. Hence mastery of theory, in the manner required for passage of a comprehensive examination, becomes a major objective in the training of an economist, and provision of assistance in acquiring this mastery—whether in the form of expository articles, textbooks or treatises—has come to constitute an important species of professional accomplishment.

Another dimension of the economics culture that I recognize but largely ignore is the geographical spread of its membership. While in one form or another economic matters probably have been thought about by participants in government everywhere and at all times, as commonly used, "economics" refers to the writings of western Europeans and emigrants therefrom during the past four centuries, with heavy emphasis on the period since 1776. While professing to be applicable anywhere, and open to all, economics has been done mainly—though not exclusively—by residents of English-speaking countries. Until World War II the major center of economics was in the British Isles, but since 1945 the subject has been dominated by residents of the United States. These residents include large numbers of European and, in recent years, Asian emigrants. The reason for this predominance of American residents would seem to lie in the heavy investment made there in the provision of training and research facilities which, inter alia, has created employment opportunities in staffing them.

As a result, the initial advantage of the English language that stemmed from the nineteenth-century predominance of British economics has been reinforced with the result that, at the end of the twentieth century, economic discussion is conducted primarily in English. Combined with the concentration of economic research in academic institutions, this has had the effect of heavily imprinting the culture of economics with the characteristics of American academia. While it is possible that a fuller account of the culture of economics would reveal significant traces of this imprinting, the focus of this book is inimical to an exploration of its consequences.[19]

19. Bruno S. Frey and Reiner Eichenberger (1991) is an interesting discussion of the differences between the career patterns and research foci of American and European economists. In terms of their distinctions, this book is focused on the American branch of the profession.

T W O

ECONOMICS AND OTHER SCIENCES

To put it mildly, outside the circle of professional economists, statements implying that economics is a science—and that its practitioners should be treated accordingly—do not meet with universal acceptance. Varying with the audience, such statements are met with comments alluding to failed predictions, mathematical models that do not facilitate useful results, lack of consensus among "certified" economists as to the probable effects of contemplated actions by public authorities, and so on. Generous observers will sometimes suggest that the shortcomings of economics reflect the relative youth of the discipline; those less kind strike at the jugular by asserting that the nature of the subject matter, the relation of the investigator to the phenomena under study, or both, will always prevent economics from functioning as a proper scientific discipline.

Because the validity of such negative judgments depends critically upon the definition of science, I ask the reader to bear with some definition and clarification of concepts. To argue, as I shall, that economics has a valid claim to scientific status requires proposal of a criterion that demarcates science from nonscience. At the outset I concede that such a criterion must be arbitrary: all that can be offered in defense of any specific proposal is that it is—more or less—conventional, or that it should be appealing to the reader and serve to advance the discussion in which it is to be used.

Although from a logical point of view a definition may be arbitrary, for the purposes of this book the definition of "science" must be such that economics can fit within it. For, as argued above, the community of economists claims a monopoly of expertise over a particular domain of phenomena, and such claims will be accepted in a modern Western society only if the expertise is based on possession of "scientific knowledge." It is not sufficient merely to call a subject a science: justification for use of the term must be provided. Despite its name, Creation Science would not be accepted as a science in circles where the argument of this book might hope to find an audience. Accordingly, this chapter must offer a justification for designating economics as a science.

PARADIGMS AND SCIENTIFIC SUBCULTURES

In spirit the criteria used here for distinguishing a science from other bodies of knowledge are similar to those used by Thomas S. Kuhn (1970) in *The Structure of Scientific Revolutions*. According to these criteria a science is a body of knowledge associated with a subculture whose members communicate with one another in a specialized language. Such a body of knowledge is organized around one or more paradigms whose characteristics give it structure. Inter alia, paradigms serve to distinguish research whose results will be considered acceptable (within the subculture) from research whose outcomes will not be so considered. Further, when spelled out, a paradigm enables researchers to distinguish phenomena that it claims to explain or account for from those that constitute anomalies that challenge its validity.

Still further, typically a paradigm generates a rough ranking of outstanding anomalies in order of their salience, and an implicit status ranking of members of the subculture based on past and prospective contributions to the dispelling of anomalies or the proposal of acceptable modifications of paradigms. The history of a science, and of its heroes, is a history of the establishment of paradigms, the perception of anomalies, and the reconstruction (or replacement) of paradigms to accommodate recalcitrant observations.

In recent philosophy of science literature, "paradigm" has been variously defined, and its proper use much debated.[1] What I shall mean by the term is a set of interrelated propositions that are currently accepted, together with a specification of the procedures by which they may be altered. The proposition-altering procedures associated with a given paradigm constitute the exclusive means by which acceptable amendments to that paradigm can be made.

Typically, a paradigm is associated with an exemplar—a worked example, like a completed crossword puzzle—that serves to characterize proper research procedure. Often a paradigm is identified by a particular set of interrelated concepts (a Conceptual Organization, or CO) with which it is associated. (Later I shall distinguish between complete para-

1. For a full discussion of the problems associated with this concept see M. Masterman (1970).

digms, which have both an exemplar and a CO, and incomplete paradigms, which lack an exemplar.)[2]

Although I would not insist that every science be associated with at least one paradigm, all of those discussed in this book possess that characteristic. In addition, each of these sciences is associated with a scientific subculture (such as described in chapter 1) and often with an academic discipline and a related university department. It should be noted, however, that there are academic disciplines that are not and do not claim to be sciences (e.g., the Humanities).

SCIENTIFIC METHOD

At the risk of repetition, in a science proffered contributions are judged in accordance with whether the procedures used and the results achieved are compatible with a subculturally accepted set of interrelated propositions and techniques. However, and very important: though limited by the commitments of its community to previous findings and approved research procedures, the paradigm(s) of a science must be such as to accommodate new propositions. A body of knowledge that does not provide for the possibility of new discovery is not a science. No matter how learned they may be, mandarins, brahmins, and Talmudic scholars are not scientists.

Further: all arguments of a science must satisfy the twin canons of *openness* and *replicability*. 'Openness' refers to the right of anyone to examine the evidence upon which an assertion of fact is based, and the correlative duty of the asserter to provide access to the evidence.[3] One effect of openness is to preclude acceptance of assertions based solely on authority or on information not publicly accessible. Accordingly, theories or propositions that are in any way dependent upon claims of revelation or pronouncements of authorities, living or dead, are denied scientific standing.

As any layman can testify, openness and accessibility are not synonymous. The facts that provide support for a physical theory may consist of photographs of wavy lines whose interpretation and pertinence to the the-

2. George Argyrous (1992) presents a good discussion of the paradigm concept as it applies to economics. Despite some differences of detail, his use of the paradigm concept is generally similar to mine. Also see the further discussions of Sheila C. Dow (1994) and Argyrous (1994) on this subject.

3. Similarly, the basis for assertions about the logical implications of propositions (e.g., mathematical proofs) must be made available for scrutiny and challenge.

ory can be understood only by a well-trained physicist. Without undergo-
ing the requisite training, one must accept the *interpreted* facts on faith.
In consequence, it is conceivable that laymen could be deceived by a conspiracy of initiates (i.e., physicists) to propagate a false view of the world.
Thus, for laymen, belief in the validity of a scientific theory does not rest
upon direct examination of the supporting evidence, but is conditional
upon a judgment of the mores of the relevant scientific subculture. To
believe that a science is 'open,' one must believe either (1) that a sufficient
fraction of its initiates is committed so irrevocably to the pursuit and publication of "scientific truth" as to render ineffective any conspiracy to the
contrary, or (2) that rivalry among the initiates is sufficiently strong as to
cause proponents of a false claim to be challenged by many others. Further, for a science to be truly open, the prevailing attitude among its practitioners toward the instruction of aspirants should be one of helpfulness;
there should be no tendency to impede access to "professional secrets"
from those seeking to become initiated. With few exceptions, most sciences adhere consistently to the canon of openness.

Nevertheless, tension exists between this canon and the requirements
of expertise. To the extent that expertise can be acquired easily, it loses
its mystery and invites laypeople to dispense with the services of experts.
Although openness is an essential characteristic of a scientific attitude, its
importance derives largely from its being ancillary to replicability. The
judgment of a scientific community on the credibility of a research report
depends critically upon whether the events reported can be replicated by
other members of the community. Replicability requires openness in the
sense that if a scientific result is to be replicated, the conditions under
which the relevant observations can be made must be fully specified.
However, openness is not synonymous with replicability.

Taken literally, no sequence of events is ever replicable. Two sequences
of seemingly identical events must differ in respect of time, location, or
both: otherwise the sequences could never be distinguished. In what
sense, then, is it possible ever to replicate an event sequence, such as a
specific experiment or a series of astronomical observations?

The possibility of replication depends upon a set of conventions as to
the irrelevance of certain characteristics of an event sequence. Although a
complete description of the event sequence that constitutes a report of a
scientific finding must include a specification of the place and time of the
relevant observations, the conventions of replication are such as not to

require repetition of the relevant event sequence at exactly the same place and time. (If this were not the case, replication would never be possible.) Indeed, if an event sequence that constituted a scientific finding could not be repeated at a wide variety of (suitable) times and places, the report of its occurrence would be suspect and the finding deemed to be either an artifact of defective research procedure, or the result of inaccurate reporting (or both). For example, a laboratory result that applied only to a given city in a given month would be considered either as invalid or (much less likely) of such limited applicability as to be of negligible scientific interest.

Consequently, it is customary in many sciences to say that a laboratory experiment has been replicated, even though the sequence of events that constitutes replication differs both in time and location from the original experiment. In effect, in these sciences, it is conventional to require that a satisfactory description of an experiment should be independent of time and place. As will be seen, the capability of satisfying this requirement is an important reason for the greater success of the natural sciences as compared with social sciences. In economics, many propositions are offered as valid only for certain times and places (e.g., for developed economies in the latter part of the twentieth century), and the conditions necessary and/or sufficient for their proper application are the subject of serious professional debate.[4]

These criteria for distinguishing sciences from other bodies of knowledge are strictly ad hoc, and I do not suggest that they are useful for any purpose other than to get our discussion off the ground. However, the criteria do reflect conventions to which every scientific subculture adheres, albeit implicitly. These conventions are characteristic, not only of scientific subcultures, but also of the broader culture of a highly and secularly educated class from which each of the subcultures draws membership and material support.

The values, especially the intellectual standards, of this class are shared by all scientific subcultures and operate so as to cause immediate rejection of any proposition or procedure that is seemingly in conflict with them. For example, any proposition that implied acceptance of any of the distinctive tenets of (say) astrology, or of faith healing, or of Creation Science

---

4. In the context of relativity theory, some experimental results are sensitive to spatio-temporal specification. However, in most situations in the natural sciences such sensitivity does not arise.

would be rejected out of hand by any "respectable" science and by a consensus of the "educated class."

Similarly, any proposition (or procedure) that is in seeming conflict with what is accepted within the domain of a culturally recognized field of expertise will be paid little heed. Should any science have the temerity to give serious consideration to "notions" that conflicted with what was "known" within the recognized domain of another science, the offending science would quickly lose status (and support) within the broader scientific community. Individual sciences, particularly economics, generally recognize this fact and behave accordingly.

For example, about a half century ago, the statistical practices of economists were often at variance with those approved by mathematical statisticians.[5] After a relatively brief struggle, such variance became unacceptable, and for at least the last quarter century any relevant discovery in (mathematical) statistics has been immediately reflected in the procedures demanded by editors of economics journals, with the economic content of published articles altered to comport with the new discoveries in statistics.

The point being made is that, in the struggle over the introduction of mathematical statistics into economics curricula, pressure from outside played an important role. This pressure came partly from the expressed preferences of granting institutions and the opinion of the "hard science" genre on university appointment committees, but also from the manifest preferences of students. In choosing among alternative fields of specialization, prospective recruits to economics were (and are) powerfully influenced by general opinion in the social class from which most of them come and where all of them desire to locate. This opinion was, and continues to be, overwhelmingly in favor of using statistical procedures consonant with what is taught in departments of statistics.

While openness would suggest that any science should be responsive to challenges emerging from discoveries in the domain of any other, in practice this is not the case. One can imagine—though barely—that economists in the 1940s and 50s might have resisted proposed innovations in statistical procedures on the ground that use of the new procedures would

---

5. For the benefit of younger and/or ahistorical readers, I note that until well into the 1950s (if not later) most Ph.D. programs in economics required a demonstration of competence in statistics, but permitted this to be discharged by courses and/or examinations that did not require knowledge of calculus. Mathematical statistics was a separate option, taken by only a small minority of Ph.D. candidates.

lead to results that contradicted established propositions of economics, and must therefore be considered invalid. The nature of empirical propositions of economics is such as to render absurd any such argument, and none to this effect was ever suggested. Analogously, propositions of chemistry are not permitted to conflict with those accepted in nuclear physics, and so chemists must be attentive to innovations in the latter field, though physicists are not subject to a reciprocal admonition.

Similarly, propositions in the life sciences must be sensitive to innovations in the domain of chemistry, though the arrow of influence does not point in the reverse direction. Whether a possible hierarchy of the sciences more closely resembles a pecking order or a food chain, or how many dimensions it might have, or if it would represent a complete ordering does not much concern us. What is important is that economists fear, and with reason, that the rank of their subject in such a hierarchy would be rather low. This fear, which has a great influence on the functioning of the economics culture, arises from its performance in respect of two essential criteria of merit: prediction and control.

PREDICTION AND CONTROL

In any context, the ultimate rationale for expertise is the ability to predict and control. Ability to predict does not always accompany ability to control—astronomy and meteorology provide cases in point—but ability to control implies ability to predict.[6] In a scientific context, ability to predict and/or control implies knowledge of a law.

Discovery of a law is the height of scientific achievement, and those responsible (often) become heroes of their subculture. Varying with their salience, finding new applications of (previously established) laws may also constitute significant scientific achievements. The important point is that capability of successful prediction unrelated to a law is not considered to be scientific. Seeming examples of ability to predict without reference to a covering law are regarded by the scientific culture as anomalies to be dispelled: it must be shown either that such predictions involve misrepresentation of the facts of the prediction, or that the prediction was an accident and not replicable.

The unwillingness of the scientific culture to accept the possibility of a capability to predict without a specifiable covering law follows directly

---

6. As usually defined, ability to control without ability to predict would be indicative of some sort of psychological malfunction.

from the canon of openness. If one or a limited number of persons could "reliably" predict some class of events without being able to explain how they did it, they would possess secret knowledge, which is precluded by openness.[7]

Typically a scientific law does not stand alone, supported only by a particular body of empirical evidence, but is related to a family of other laws by a network of conceptual relations which arise from a common paradigm. Evidence for the validity of any one law consists not only of its own performance in prediction and control, but also of its consonance with the laws and other propositions contained in its paradigmatic network. The criteria for appraising such consonance are critical to explaining the status of economics as a science.

But before discussing the criteria for consonance, it will be useful briefly to consider the more general question of what the criteria should be for determining the validity of propositions in economics generally. If, as proposed at the beginning of chapter 1, economics is defined as what economists do, it follows that what is valid in economics is what the consensus of economists so declares. Of course, as has already been noted, this consensus is constrained by the views of the broader scientific community, which requires adherence to the general conventions of scientific method.[8]

A major theme of this book is that, although economists generally recognize the validity of the criteria of prediction and control as standards for judging the performance of a science and strive to satisfy these standards, thus far their success in doing so has been quite limited. As the *Economist*—a bit uncharitably—put it, "an economist, it is said, is an expert who will know tomorrow why the things he predicted yesterday did

7. Where ability to predict without knowledge of a valid covering law appears to exist (e.g., premodern knowledge of astronomical regularities), the scientific posture is to treat the ability as a phenomenon in need of explanation.

8. At this point it is appropriate to recognize that there has developed within economics, as in many other disciplines during the past two decades, a tendency to deprecate the authority of science and scientific method and to encourage consideration of other validity criteria on a par with those of scientific method. In economics this work has been strongly associated with the Rhetorical Movement, especially the writings of Deirdre (né Donald) McCloskey. The bearing of these contentions on this book is discussed below in Chapters 11 and 12.

For a report on the state of these struggles—"Science Wars"—see the *Economist*, 13–19 December 1997, pp. 77–79. I assume throughout the book that attacks on the status of science have so far, at least, had negligible impact on the standing of science with the general public.

not happen today."[9] While this adverse appraisal of their forecasting capabilities is not seriously disputed, no consensus exists as to the appropriate response. In an important sense this book is an attempt to propose such a response. A necessary first step in framing such a proposal is to indicate the relation of prediction and control to other possible criteria of performance by which a science may be judged.

I begin by remarking that, like other sciences, economics attempts to establish the validity of its propositions by testing them empirically, and/or by showing that their logical implications are consistent with (other) established propositions in the network associated with an accepted paradigm. In general, these procedures of validity establishment are consonant with the criteria of prediction and control. But in applying these criteria economics is far less successful than most natural sciences, and as a result must place greater reliance upon another criterion, i.e., consistency with an accepted paradigm.

Before considering the more demanding criterion of control, let us briefly discuss the performance of economics in the sphere of prediction. Predictions or forecasts may be dichotomized as absolute and conditional. While economists are not successful at either, they find conditional predictions much more congenial. These generally take the form, if conditions x, y, and z obtain then some set of economic variables, x', y', and z' will behave in a specified manner. Absolute predictions involve no 'if' clause: they simply assert that x', y', and z' will occur at some more-or-less specific time and place.

The archetypical absolute prediction is a weather forecast: the vicissitudes attending such forecasts are painfully similar to those associated with forecasts of business conditions. And, for a long time, students of both types of phenomena have attempted to increase forecasting accuracy by observing behavior in greater detail and over longer periods of time, by improving statistical techniques, and by learning more about the structure of the processes generating the behavior to be forecasted. While in both fields such efforts have materially increased knowledge of the processes involved, the gain in forecasting accuracy has been at best somewhat limited.

In the case of business conditions, three factors are responsible for this limitation: (1) much economic activity, notably investment, depends upon expectations of future activity. Such expectations are strongly influenced

9. *The Economist,* 18–24 April 1998.

by available forecasts. Hence altering the forecasts—improving them or otherwise—would be likely to alter the behavior being forecasted. While this would not preclude the possibility of improving the quality of forecasts (see later in this chapter), it does complicate the task. Such complication does not arise in weather forecasting. (2) A forecast of business behavior is not a direct forecast of behavior as such but a forecast of behavior as *recorded*. It is a forecast of future records from past records. Consequently, changes in recording and/or accounting procedures might disturb an otherwise accurate forecasting technique, even though behavior had been unchanged.[10] While in principle such changes in observational technique might also affect predictions of the weather, or of other phenomena studied by natural scientists, they are much more salient to economic forecasting. (3) Although weather patterns may be affected by changes in the physical environment, the changes are slower and probably less disruptive of the relationships upon which forecasting depends than those occurring in the institutions and technology that bear upon economic forecasting.

In any case, the difficulties of making satisfactory absolute predictions about economic phenomena are of far less concern than those associated with conditional forecasts. The status and prestige of a science depends upon its capability of making the if-then statements that reflect the operation of a law. Thus the prestige of physics rests upon the many cases where it can, on demand, produce unusual phenomena provided only that it be allowed to require that certain conditions be satisfied. The most famous demonstration of this capability is the production of nuclear fission by processing a radioactive substance in a specified way. Analogous examples of prediction and control can be offered by each of the various branches of chemistry and microbiology. Typically, such conditional predictions may be translated into if-then statements that are quantitatively precise and capable of expression in mathematical notation.

While science does not consist exclusively of disciplines capable of such performance, clearly economics aspires to perform in this manner, and its failure to do so has been a continuing cause for concern. A half century ago, one marked difference between economics and the natural sciences, especially physics, was the greater and more effective use of mathematics by the latter. After much effort, this relative deficiency of economics has been largely (arguably completely) eliminated. Yet the pal-

10. Such changes occur frequently because of changes in technology, input prices, and taxes.

pable difference in performance remains. This difference is most apparent in comparisons of the quantitative precision of laws presented in a natural science—and their stability over time and space—with the imprecise statements of covariation generated by economics the validity of which are notoriously variable with time and place.

While there are many reasons for the difference in the performance of economics from that of the natural sciences, I shall focus upon only one: the difference between the manner in which economics and the more successful natural sciences explain the behavior of complex entities by reference to the behavior of simpler entities that constitute them. Analogous to the natural sciences, economics conceives of behavior at higher levels of complexity—the economy as a whole or the industry—as resulting from the behavior of simpler entities, ultimately individuals.

However, economics does not contain, or propose, an explanation of individual behavior in terms of constituent parts of individuals. To obviate the need for such explanation it offers a generalized characterization of individuals (i.e., by their tastes and endowed wealth) but does not attempt to probe deeper. So represented, individuals are complex and heterogeneous, with characteristics subject to frequent change without much notice.

To probe beneath the individual's tastes, economics would have to enter the domain of psychology. While from time to time such expeditions have been suggested, the strong consensus of the economics community has been to avoid them in the hope of insulating its own subject matter from turbulence originating in the other discipline. Whatever the overall cost to economics of such an insular attitude, it has not involved a sacrifice of opportunity to explain tastes in terms of the behavior of component parts of the individual. This is because, with the exception of its physiological branch, psychology itself has made no attempt to construct such explanations. Although economics and psychology have had important and continuing disputes about the analysis of choice behavior, and other matters as well, these debates suggest no controversion of this statement.

On a number of fronts (e.g., abnormal behavior and cognitive processes generally), physiological psychologists are seriously at odds with disciplinary colleagues otherwise disposed as to whether and/or how to explain human behavior in terms of neurons, synapses, etc. that might ultimately relate the behavior of the human organism to biochemical phenomena. If a research program in physiological psychology were to generate a successful explanation of (say) choice behavior such that differences in risk aversion across individuals could be related to differences in hormonal balance, and ultimately to differences in body chemistry, the effect on ideas and research programs in both economics and psychology would be enormous.[11]

It should occasion no surprise that the likelihood of such a development in the foreseeable future would be heavily discounted by nonphysiological psychologists and, so far as I am aware, hope of such a development has not been held out by psychologists of any variety. However, such results are what the public would like psychology to deliver, and what psychologists would like to provide, if only they could. A similar and possibly even stronger statement would hold for economics and its practitioners.

In all social sciences, both the dissatisfaction of the laity with the results and the practitioners' feelings of methodological inadequacy are greatly exacerbated by comparison with the performance of such natural sciences as physics, chemistry, microbiology, and genetics. The hallmark of these sciences is the provision of prediction and especially control by procedures associated with explanations of more complex phenomena by the behavior of their simpler components. While not all natural sciences can be so characterized (think of geology, seismology, paleontology, or meteorology), it is such achievements that attract public acclaim and arouse the (misguided) emulative desires of economists.[12]

Consider the situation in physics and chemistry where the behavior of what can be observed directly is everywhere explained as the consequence of the behavior of atomic particles that are not directly observable. These in turn are explained by the behavior of subatomic particles and so on through a succession of "layers of simplification" to the behavior of elementary particles that constitute the "ultimate units of explanation."[13] To explain an observed phenomenon or, even better, to make it appear on demand, a physicist or chemist formulates a procedure describable in terms of operations upon molecules, atoms, and subatomic particles, along with precisely specified instructions as to the scale on which the procedure must be performed in order to obtain the predicted result.

11. If this led to the capability of altering behavior (say) toward risk in a purposive manner—i.e., facilitating control—the impact would be magnified even further.

12. Philip Mirowski (1989) has argued strongly that, to its detriment, economic theory has borrowed improperly from physics. This is discussed briefly in chapter 6.

13. Notoriously, attempts at a general definition of "explanation" encounter problems. As used here, an explanation of an observed phenomenon (or behavior) consists of (somehow) relating the phenomenon to be explained to a "covering law."

It is important to add that, not only are such procedures describable in terms of operations upon microscopic or submicroscopic particles, but the conceptualization of the relevant phenomena involves such particles in an essential way. Inter alia, one effect of such involvement is that change in an accepted theory of behavior at one level of complexity entails reconsideration and possible alteration of accepted theories about behavior at higher levels of complexity.[14]

Similar situations exist in biochemistry and microbiology. In biochemistry, diagnosis of a disease in an organism involves identifying its malfunction with the presence of particular microorganisms and relating symptoms to their presence and/or behavior. In turn, the interaction of these microorganisms with the host organism is related to the chemical interaction of elements of the host with the microorganisms: treatment consists of introducing the host to other chemicals so as to alter the preexisting process. Discovery of the chemicals needed in the cure is made by analyzing their molecular characteristics together with those of the offending microorganisms and of the host organism.

In microbiology, especially genetics, characteristics of larger organisms are traced to those of its microscopic and submicroscopic components, that is, genes and chromosomes. Here, control is demonstrated by generation of prespecified changes in larger organisms (both animal and vegetable) that result from (prespecified) alteration of the characteristics of their submicroscopic components.

However much economists may eat their hearts out they cannot do this sort of thing, and there is no prospect that they will be able to do it in the foreseeable future.[15] Accordingly, to defend their subject's right to be considered a science it is necessary that they offer a broader conception of scientific performance than what is suggested by prediction and control. I shall argue that economists do have such a notion of science and that they operate with it. But because it is not explicit, it is not applied consistently, and its use is attended with much controversy.

But before discussing this criterion let us complete our discussion of prediction. In physics, laws usually gain credence by lending themselves

14. In principle, the arrow of influence from theories at a given level of complexity could go in either direction, from greater to lesser complexity or the reverse. However, for the purpose of this argument, it is sufficient to focus on the cases where the arrow goes from less to greater complexity.

15. Obviously, this assertion requires support. While this support is scattered throughout the book, it is most heavily concentrated in chapters 7 and 8.

to the making of valid conditional predictions. While this statement is generally true, it often happens that for a considerable period of time, the only available tests involve *retrodiction* rather than prediction.[16]

Retrodiction is essentially the explanation of past events in terms of a hypothesis proposed ex post facto. Obviously, the support given a hypothesis by a particular retrodiction varies with the availability of alternative explanations and the salience of the facts retrodicted. In physics, tests of hypotheses by retrodiction are considered to be provisional and temporary, and subject to later confirmation by appropriate predictions.[17]

But whether a hypothesis has been tested by prediction or retrodiction is of much less importance in physics (or other natural sciences) than it is in economics. This is because of the "uniformity of nature," or, the relative invariance of physical laws over time and space. Physical, chemical, and biological laws are expected to operate in the same manner regardless of the location of the laboratory or when they are tested, and generally do so.

However, as Weinberg points out, this invariance of laws may be limited, holding over only a restricted—though to us very large—segment of time and space.[18] In all parts of time and space of which the human race has knowledge, the laws of physics (as we know them) apply, though elsewhere they may not. In short, for most practical purposes the laws of physics may be assumed to have universal applicability.

So viewed, economics might be thought of as a science analogous to physics, with the critical difference being that in many circumstances the "laws" of economics hold only for very short intervals of space and time.[19] But a major consequence of the spatial and temporal instability of the laws of economics is that often they are inapplicable to the particular domain of space and time that is of practical concern. To compound the difficulty, only rarely would it be safe to assume that an economic "law" did apply to a particular situation without detailed and time consuming investigation that would be precluded by the time frame of the relevant decision-making process.

16. Retrodiction is the "forecasting" of events that have already occurred.

17. For an excellent discussion of prediction and retrodiction in physics, see Steven Weinberg (1992), pp. 96–97 and 123. My discussion above is greatly indebted to this reference.

18. Ibid., p. 38.

19. As used here, a scientific law is a quantitatively specific behavioral relation. Thus, relations whose quantitative strength may vary across time and space, albeit without change of sign—i.e., most economic "laws"—do not qualify.

Put differently, because the domain of a valid economic law is likely to be small, the domain from which proper data samples may be drawn is correspondingly restricted. This causes, in practice, inadvertent pooling of data from a multiplicity of domains across which economic laws may differ. One effect of such pooling is greatly to reduce the power of ordinary statistical procedures to distinguish valid from invalid hypotheses.

The argument of the previous paragraph says in effect that the Emperor's clothes are transparent; it is also consistent with perceiving him to be naked. Whether we decide that most laws of economics are of very limited applicability, or simply invalid, is of little practical or theoretical importance. What is wanted are laws comparable in scope and power to those delivered by the more successful natural sciences. Since these cannot be delivered within the foreseeable future, economists are compelled to ask—both in conscience and on behalf of those who provide them with support—what the scientific value is of what they do. As the answer to this question must be cognate with the criteria used to appraise the merits of research contributions, it is necessary to consider these criteria explicitly.

A convenient point of departure is to note the very different attitudes toward seemingly aberrant observations taken by economists and by natural scientists. In any science, hypothesis testing requires observations made under precisely specified conditions. Often, in the relevant natural sciences, such observations can be obtained through controlled experiments. In economics, however, this source of data is rarely available (but see chapter 7), and normally its hypotheses can be tested only through observation of "natural experiments," that is, by studying history. As a result economists must wait, often for long periods, to obtain observations that might constitute a reasonable approximation to the conditions specified in an hypothesis, and even then disputes about the closeness of the approximation frequently create disagreements among "reasonable" people as to the bearing of the test on the credibility of the hypothesis being tested.

These difficulties are conflated with the strong possibility that the structures of many economic relationships vary with time and place, with the result that—unlike physicists, chemists, and the like—economists rarely feel confident in dismissing a reported observation as incredible simply because its occurrence would imply violation of an established law. Because of this, economists are obliged to accept most reports of empirical phenomena at face value, appraising them as best they can by the standards of other disciplines (e.g., history) or by common sense, but rarely are they able to reject them because of their incompatibility with the laws of economics.[20]

THE METAPHOR OF THE JIGSAW PUZZLE

In all sciences hypotheses are tested, and the validity of propositions appraised, by procedures that can be placed under the rubric, "prediction and control." But in addition to these procedures, all sciences are concerned with the consonance of any candidate proposition both with other propositions that are considered to have been accepted and with an overall theoretical framework, the *paradigm*. Should a hypothesis deemed valid by the criteria of prediction and control be found inconsistent (or to have implications that are inconsistent) with the paradigm, its validity constitutes an anomaly, the dispelling of which is a matter of prime importance for the relevant scientific community.

In the natural sciences, such situations lead to attempts to show either that the new finding was accepted in error or that some previously accepted proposition was flawed: failing both, efforts will be made to alter the paradigm. But in economics, far less than in the natural sciences, test-

---

20. This statement may seem to conflict with the frequent accusations that economists are given to dogmatic denials of reports of behavior that appear to suggest failure of decision makers to maximize profits or utility, or to suggest that they have displayed money illusion, or otherwise violated the implications of (what we shall term) the resource allocation paradigm. However, despite appearances, such denials (by careful economists) are rarely absolute, but are usually subject to (often unstated) stipulations about the absence of transaction costs, or the presence of transitory disturbances of one kind or another, or of asymmetry in the information available to different transactors, etc. Whether one or another of such stipulations applies in a given situation is always a matter for judgment, so that it is rarely possible to rule out the possibility that seemingly anomalous behavior could be reconciled with accepted economic theory.

This is as good a point as any to acknowledge an expository difficulty and explain my resolution of it. There is a group of economists, (other) social scientists, and philosophers who are actively concerned with issues of prediction and control and methodological issues generally. I have been sorely tempted to comment on their work, but after several abortive attempts I have found that doing justice to their arguments would require a substantial departure from the main argument of the book. Accordingly and with reluctance, I refrain from comment and confine myself to urging the reader to acquaint him- or herself with the relevant literature. By way of guidance, I would suggest consulting two journals (*Economics and Philosophy* and the *Journal of Economic Methodology*) and any of a number of books and monographs on the subject. Among recent publications, I have found four to be especially pertinent to the theme of this book: Bruce Caldwell (1982), Daniel Hausman (1992), Tony Lawson (1997) and Alexander Rosenberg (1992).

ing a suspect hypothesis is difficult, and usually the results are indecisive. That is, in economics, attempts to replicate the test of a hypothesis by observing an allegedly similar process at work in a different place and at a different time usually confound the factors of interest with the effects of changing the time and place of observation. Consequently, far more than in the natural sciences, economics must rely on consonance with an accepted paradigm as the basis for appraising candidate propositions. The fact of this reliance is a major reason for the attention paid (in economics) to refining its paradigms, that is, creating and burnishing theories.

Comparison of economics with highly developed natural sciences will be facilitated by introducing the metaphor of a jigsaw puzzle. Each science may be considered as confronted with such a puzzle, and its dominant purpose defined as finding the solution (i.e., completion) of the puzzle as quickly as possible. The pieces of a puzzle consist of reports of empirical phenomena that are generated exogenously, and which each scientific community must fit together as best it can. Not all of the reports are accurate, and part of a community's task is to decide which pieces belong in the completed puzzle and which do not. None of the sciences is given a picture of its completed puzzle (i.e., its solution) but each must create one from the imaginings of its practitioners, aided by what is imprinted on the surfaces of the pieces. It is not stipulated to any science that its puzzle has an unique solution or, indeed, any solution at all.

Assembly of the pieces of a puzzle is guided by the image of its overall solution—a paradigm—and also by images of the local configurations of various parts of the solution, which are specific theories. The images of all local configurations must be incorporated in any solution of a puzzle, that is, the images of all local configurations must fit together to form a coherent whole. Empirical research consists of picking pieces of the puzzle from a large pile and inferring from their shapes and colors whether and how each piece fits into the contemplated overall solution.

Constructions of contemplated paradigms (solutions) and of specific theories (local configurations) are only loosely constrained by shapes and colors of the pieces drawn from the pile of experience, and are guided largely by the imaginings of their creators. The significance of any given piece at any given time depends both upon the partial assemblies into which it might be fitted at the moment when it is drawn, and upon the overall solution contemplated at that moment. Obviously, the apparent place of a given piece in a contemplated solution is subject to variation with changes in that contemplated solution.

Scientific research proceeds, not only by drawing pieces from the pile, but also by elaborating the imagined characteristics (both) of contemplated overall solutions and of relevant local configurations. Neither overall solutions nor local configurations are ever envisaged with complete clarity, and sharpening of the images (i.e., making theoretical elaborations and refinements) contributes to the process by which new pieces are assimilated to partially assembled puzzles and, occasionally, leads to revision of specific theories and even of entire paradigms. The jigsaw puzzle metaphor serves to remind us that in all sciences—and especially in economics—the criteria used to determine the validity of particular propositions include consonance with a contemplated overall picture of the world, as well as those associated with prediction and control.

But the main purpose of the jigsaw metaphor is to highlight the characteristics of economics that differentiate it from (some) natural sciences rather than to describe those shared by all sciences. One such characteristic is that economics must accept pieces from the pile as drawn, with no capability of prespecifying any of their features. This is in contrast to the capability of experimental natural sciences to call up pieces that are shaped so as to satisfy the requirements of a specified niche in a particular contemplated local configuration. If the surface pattern upon one of these selected pieces is consonant with the adjoining pieces, then the augmented configuration is "not disconfirmed" as part of the contemplated overall solution: otherwise it *would* be disconfirmed, which would entail abandoning either the contemplated solution or the local configuration (or both), or rejecting the piece as flawed (i.e., not belonging in the pile). But notice: all of this decision making has involved only the surface characteristics of the piece (i.e., its color pattern) but not its shape, which was preselected to fill the niche.

The capability of making such prespecification of the pieces to be selected (i.e., making controlled experiments) enables a fortunate natural science to eliminate many erroneous conjectures as soon as an appropriate experiment can be thought up. But economics must wait until history generates a suitable experiment (ejects a suitable piece from the pile). Moreover, the "natural experiments" provided by history never correspond precisely to the requirements of the puzzle solver, so that—unlike the natural scientist—the economist is usually faced with a difficult decision as to whether a given piece fills a proposed niche well enough to be considered supportive of a contemplated partial configuration (or of an overall solution), or the reverse. In addition, and far more often in economics than in natural sciences, the difficulty attending such judgment calls is aggravated by the presence of competing solutions, whose advocates are attempting to cope with similar difficulties.

The result of this cross-scientific difference in the puzzle-solving environment is that the natural sciences can, through trial and error, discriminate among proposed local configurations with much greater speed and accuracy than can economics. Consequently, in a puzzle-solving race among communities of scientists of equal ability, a natural science would fill its puzzle space with promising local configurations far more rapidly than economics. As a further consequence, at any given time, in the domain of a natural science the report of a new empirical finding must undergo careful vetting to establish its compatibility with the many other empirical findings that have already been accepted as valid. That is, the new finding must not only fill its prescribed niche, but also must not cause conflict between any of the contemplated relations of its local configuration with other local configurations and must, in addition, be compatible with the contemplated overall solution.[21]

In economics, the same tests of validity that apply to the natural sciences are used, but with different relative weights attached to them. Because of the inability to obtain precisely the data needed (and the consequent need to make do with what can be made available), together with (justified) uncertainty as to the invariance of observed empirical associations across time and space, the report of a new empirical finding is only rarely resisted on the ground that it is in conflict with previously accepted findings. An allegation that the appearance of an unexpected relationship—or the absence of an expected one—was due to the variability of "nature" with time and place is too plausible to reject casually, and is very resistant to detailed empirical refutation.[22] Consequently, although it is common practice to vet a report of a new empirical study for the manner in which it was conducted, once the research procedure has been accepted as "state of the art" there is a strong tendency to set its results into the "big picture" as well as possible, and not to reject them as unacceptable

21. This statement oversimplifies, but should not mislead. Often a new empirical finding entails "minor" revisions of local configurations and even of the overall picture, but without creating great theoretical problems. The entailed revisions are made fairly easily and without great controversy, so that the history of the subject records the gradual evolution of a theory rather than a revolution.

22. For example, tests to determine whether tastes or technologies—or the distributions of endowed resources—have (or have not) changed have usually been inconclusive.

because of their seeming incompatibility with previously accepted findings.[23]

The difficulty of rejecting reported empirical findings despite their potentially anomalous character is partially compensated for by placing greater reliance upon compatibility with the paradigm. For example, the reluctance of economists to reject (say) a report of events in Germany during the 1980s because it was incompatible with a report for the United States during the 1970s would be to some extent balanced by a proclivity for rejecting such a report on the ground that the implied behavior would be incompatible with an accepted paradigm. In other words, economics tends to accept statements as valid (or reject them as invalid) depending upon their consonance with a "big picture."

While the same proclivity can be observed in physics and biology, in these sciences the report of observations that appear to violate an accepted law are quickly resolved. Either the experiment on which the report was based is shown to be flawed (the usual case) or the relevant community sets to work to reconstruct the (now defunct) "law," and its supporting paradigm, so as to accommodate the new findings.

In economics, such resolution is rarely possible: the facts reported are never quite those required for testing a theory, and deciding whether the approximation is good enough to serve as the basis for rejecting some previously accepted proposition is usually a judgment call. In such cases, a major determinant of the economist's judgment is how strongly she adheres to the paradigm that would be threatened by acceptance of the report and/or how easily she thinks the paradigm could be repaired to accommodate it.

As a result, in economics, for long periods of time, controversial research results live on in a kind of limbo, attached to a disputed paradigm, neither being quite accepted nor completely rejected. While conflicts of ideology probably contribute to such situations, I shall argue that the principal factor is the inability of economists to obtain the empirical observations required for proper testing of the theories they entertain.

In terms of the jigsaw puzzle metaphor, empirical research in economics has not led to the creation of a plurality of local configurations, each of which could be envisaged—despite problems of imperfect resolution—as part of a complete solution.[24] Rather, it has led to a collection of dispa-

23. Typically, the findings previously accepted have no greater claim to credence than the new ones.

24. A complete solution would correspond to what Weinberg (1992), calls a Final Theory.

rate pieces, few of which offer promise of contributing to the formation of a useful local configuration. In contrast, the successful natural sciences contain numerous local configurations (specific theories) which serve to direct searches for adjacent pieces by preselecting the characteristics sought. Success in developing these local configurations acts both as part payment for the resources used and as psychological reinforcement to the scientists engaged in the work. Indeed, the construction of local configurations that generate practical applications is a major reason for the great prestige of science among nonscientists.

Both in the natural sciences and in economics making local configurations cohere with the contemplated overall solution is a matter of great concern, and the desire to maintain this coherence is an important determinant of research priorities.[25] Though similar concerns (about coherence) exist in all branches of science, economists have been far less successful than natural scientists in maintaining a tolerable approximation to coherence between specific empirical findings and the implications of overall solutions. Indeed, the discrepancy between empirical findings and the implications of theory is such that in most major subfields there is ongoing debate as to whether major empirical findings should be interpreted as the outcome of a disturbed and badly observed stochastic process governed by a broadly applicable theory, or would be better explained by a specific ad hoc theory whose major justification is its success in rationalizing a particular retrodiction (historical episode).

As will be argued, there is virtually no part of economics where the implications of an overall theory have been convincingly borne out by empirical observation.[26] Nevertheless, the dominant paradigm is accepted by the majority of economists, whose training leads them to approach problems by attempting to apply it, whatever the difficulties, and to explain away the resulting anomalies. A further consequence of this proclivity of economists is an uneasy reliance on the consonance of a paradigm's implications for the behavior of individuals with the "findings" of their

25. For example, in physics the purpose of Gravity Probe B is to test some implications of the general theory of relativity. Despite the cost of building and launching this space probe—about $500 million—apparently the experiment will be made. However, opinion within the physics community is divided as to whether the potential results warrant the entailed cost (see the *Economist,* 10–16 June 1995, pp. 73–74).

26. The quotations from Krugman (see above, pp. 5–6) are indicative of the situation in international trade. Chapter 8 presents detailed evidence of the situation in Labor Economics and in Finance, and the argument of chapters 3 and 4 contains many references to perceived deficiencies of price theory as an explanation of the behavior of product prices.

own introspection as a criterion of validation, as we shall see in chapter 7. Because of the abundance of evidence from experiments, the fruits of introspection are far less needed by natural scientists to whom, in any case, they are unavailable. (No one attempts to imagine what an atom is "trying to do.") Consequently, natural scientists—at least in their own fields—operate as behaviorists. And the desire to be "scientific" leads many economists to profess behavioristic criteria of validity that they find difficult to live with in (some) conditions of practice. But consideration of this difference between human and natural sciences will be left until later.

In short, it may be said that both economics and the natural sciences are engaged in similar puzzle-solving enterprises that entail, inter alia, the integration of the solutions to a set of often disparate problems with a (contemplated) overall theoretical framework. This integration has been distinctly more successful in the natural sciences in that there the overall framework(s) have been of great and continuing assistance in devising solutions to particular problems, while this has not been the case in economics. Despite this, and with exceptions to be noted, economists adhere to the framework of their choice with a tenacity that is not noticeably less than that displayed by natural scientists.

An important reason for such adherence is service provided by the framework other than assistance in the solution of particular problems. As we shall see, the dominant paradigm of economics has become an integral part of the intellectual framework within which major problems of economic policy are discussed by the *lay* public.[27] Pursuant to this, as we shall see, the dominant paradigm plays a vital role in the construction and measurement of numerical concepts relevant to the performance of a community's economy (e.g., national accounts, index numbers of production and of the cost of living, and indicators of technical progress).

Ability to operate within the framework of these quantitative concepts comprises a large part of the skill that identifies an economist as an expert. The utility of this framework is highly dependent upon the existence of stable empirical relationships among prices and quantities analogous to the relationships that serve as bases for if-then statements in the natural sciences. But although to the present economics has not been able to produce such relationships,[28] there has not yet appeared a successful chal-

27. While this remark refers primarily to public sector problems, increasingly it applies to matters of the private sector as well.

28. Invariably such ad hoc relations as have seemed, temporarily, to have given a good fit to a limited set of observations have broken down when extended across time or location.

lenger to the dominant paradigm as a source of valid, empirical price-quantity relationships.[29]

Both in economics and in the natural sciences, the relation of research findings to an accepted paradigm is of great concern. While perhaps a matter of degree, this concern is manifested differently in the two domains, especially in the teaching process. In the natural sciences, where students are taught by workbooks and salient examples, paradigms are allowed to emerge from the process of solving problems rather than inculcated as "principles." Typically, the reverse is the case in economics, where the student is drilled in the principles of the subject with applications introduced as illustrations.

In the natural sciences, the empirical—usually experimental—evidence bears the burden of convincing the student, with the paradigm presented as a convenient summary of what has been observed. But in economics, typically, the student is first persuaded of the validity of a paradigm with (problematic) empirical material sometimes presented as an admittedly imperfect illustration of an argument whose validity has already been established by deduction from principles. While indicative of an important difference between economics and successful natural sciences, this should not be taken to suggest that paradigms are unimportant in either domain.

To a practicing scientist, in either domain, much of the appeal of an accepted paradigm derives from the simplification it introduces to the research process. Applying an accepted paradigm to new problems is much easier, and entails less risk to professional esteem in the event of failure, than a failed attempt to create new concepts and tools. Hence it is not surprising that members of a scientific community should attempt to tackle new problems by seeking to apply established paradigms. By so doing, a researcher is guaranteed that any proposed solution to a problem will be regarded, at a minimum, as professionally respectable.

In contrast, departures from the format associated with an accepted paradigm create obstacles to professional communication that are not easily overcome. In part, the barriers reflect genuine difficulties of communicating outside a familiar conceptual framework. Attempts at such communication greatly increase the probability of misunderstanding and place

29. As will be seen, many economists who adhere to the dominant paradigm as a source of conceptual orientation depart from it, in one way or another, to accommodate empirical anomalies that prove resistant to reconciliation with the paradigm.

great demands on the innovator's expository skill.[30] But, in addition, the would-be innovator must contend with prejudice stemming from vested intellectual interests, and sometimes from ideological interests as well.

The deterrent effects of these obstacles would be quite sufficient to explain the inertial force of a paradigm: those who ignore them must be either foolhardy or strongly motivated to make a major alteration in the scientific culture. However, there is yet a further channel through which paradigms work to mold the ideas and research activities of their adherents: framing effects.

FRAMING EFFECTS

I have borrowed the notion of a framing effect from the literature of choice theory where it has been used to describe the effect of explanatory discussion on the answers given by experimental subjects to questions about their preferences among alternative gambles.[31] It is likely that decision theorists borrowed the notion of framing effect from other psychological literature where the effect of changing the frame was found to alter observers' perceptions of the picture being framed.

Treating paradigms as frames is an obvious extension of the basic idea of a paradigm. Adherence to a paradigm exerts pressure on an economist to interpret events in a manner consistent with that paradigm: recalcitrant observations may—and sometimes do—exert counterpressures, thereby generating anomalies. But the strength of such counterpressures varies with the confidence that the economist can place in the validity of the empirical findings that are their source. As will be seen, in economics the degree of this confidence is weak, so that the influence of the framing paradigm is correspondingly strong.

The capability of a paradigm to serve as a cognitive frame for research stems from the relation between the notions of a conceptual frame and Cognitive Dissonance.[32] In a nutshell: the theory of cognitive dissonance is that individuals have a tropism for maintaining consonance (i.e., avoiding

30. A prime example of this is Keynes's *General Theory* (discussed below in chapters 4 and 5).

31. A convenient entry to the large literature on framing effects is to be found in the volume, *Rational Choice: the Contrast between Economics and Psychology,* ed. R. M. Hogarth and M. W. Reder (1987). Among the most pertinent chapters are those of Einhorn and Hogarth and Tversky and Kahnemann. The notion of framing effects in the context of choice-decision theory was introduced in an earlier paper of Tversky and Kahnemann.

32. The locus classicus of cognitive dissonance is Leon Festinger (1957).

dissonance) among their various beliefs and, in particular, between any particular belief and the interpretation of empirical phenomena that bear upon its validity. When a paradigm adherent is confronted with phenomena that are anomalous to her conceptual frame, she is impelled to make a reconciliation. This might be done by any of a number of possible mutual adjustments of one to the other. What is stressed here is the possibility that in order to minimize cognitive dissonance, a scientist may be led either to misinterpret an observed phenomenon or to restate a theory so as to dispel a threatening anomaly.

Although the second possibility does arise in economics, it can be fairly well managed by cautious statement of the theory in question, and is of distinctly less importance than the first. The first possibility refers to the difficulties of deciding whether particular bits of evidence tend to support or to disconfirm a proposed theory. Aversion to cognitive dissonance offers a supplementary reason—beyond the sheer difficulty of assessing empirical information—for the effect of paradigm adherence in determining beliefs about the characteristics of an economy.[33]

Beyond its capability of helping to dispel cognitive dissonance among researchers, a paradigm also has the power to mobilize popular support for a particular way of viewing the world. One important way it does this is by suggesting convenient shortcuts to solutions to otherwise very difficult problems. While such shortcuts are appreciated by professional economists—sometimes more than they should be—their primary market is found among laymen concerned with public affairs. What this gens requires is an unambiguous guide through a maze of complex problems leading to solutions that can be explained simply and is capable of appealing to the sections of society from which they hope to draw support.

In this task metaphors are of very great assistance as expository devices, and ideologies act as reservoirs of sympathy—or antipathy—to patterns of thought that appear congenial or the reverse. The relation of metaphors and ideologies to paradigms will be discussed later.

33. In the course of writing this chapter, it has occurred to me that cognitive dissonance might be used as the basis for a "theory of theory choice." However, development of this idea would be a major digression from the theme of this book and, in any case, I have not done the considerable work necessary for such a venture.

PARADIGMS AND ANOMALIES

THE DOMINANT
PARADIGM: RAP

In every part of economics one finds applications of the idea that the phenomena of interest are the result of attempts to allocate scarce resources efficiently. For this and other reasons, I term the paradigm associated with the allocation of scarce resources the "dominant paradigm." Throughout the book this paradigm will be designated as RAP (short for Resource Allocation Paradigm). But despite its pervasiveness and survival capacity, RAP has always been beleaguered by the claims of various rivals, each citing alleged anomalies for which it fails to account. The characteristics of (some of) these "other paradigms" are discussed in Chapters 4 through 6. This chapter is devoted to the explication of RAP which, in addition to being widely—though not universally—accepted, has been elaborated to a far greater extent than any of its rivals.[1]

In a sense, the descriptions of various paradigms that constitute this and the next two chapters are a digression from the book's main argument. The purpose of this digression is to give specific examples of what is meant by the concept of an economic paradigm, and to identify some of the more important ones. An impatient reader who is reasonably well versed in economic theory might be able to skip chapters 3 through 6 without losing the thread of the argument. However, while making no claim to originality, to advance the argument of the book I have emphasized some points that are often neglected. Accordingly, I urge even the well-versed reader at least to skim these chapters.

A convenient way to begin the description of RAP is to paraphrase Lionel Robbins' definition of economics as the subject that deals with the "allocation of scarce resources among alternative uses for the maximization of want satisfactions."[2] While I do not accept it as a definition of economics (I prefer Viner's), Robbins' definition is a beautifully succinct

---

1. What I have termed RAP is obviously very close to what is usually called the neoclassical paradigm, and a reader might well question the need for a neologism. The explanation is that RAP is more abstract—e.g., it has no place for firms or a state—than the neoclassical paradigm, and the two should not be confused.

2. See Robbins (1935).

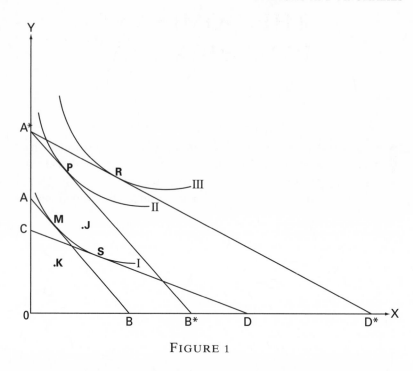

FIGURE 1

description of the exemplar of RAP. In effect, it states that the problem
that characterizes RAP is to find the allocation of scarce resources that
maximizes want satisfactions, that is, utility.

THE PROBLEM OF CONSUMER CHOICE: THE EXEMPLAR

We begin by analyzing the problem of consumer choice, sometimes called
the economics of Robinson Crusoe. This stylized example, or exemplar,
presents the essence of RAP and serves to define a number of its principle
concepts. Consider figures 1 and 2 (below on p. 50). The axes of either figure measure quantities of resources, variously denoted as goods, products,
commodities, outputs, objects of choice, and so on. Taken literally, these
figures would apply only to situations where there were exactly two objects of choice. However for most, though not all, purposes the argument
can be extended to the case of three or more choice variables without
need for further adumbration.

Initially, let us concentrate on figure 1, which refers to an individual
consumer or, more generally, choice maker. Each of the curves there represented is the locus of all pairs of quantities of two distinct choice objects,
x and y, that yield the individual some specified level of want satisfaction

or, synonymously, utility. Such curves are commonly called *indifference curves*, presumably because an individual would be indifferent as to which member of this set of (X,Y) pairs he obtained; i.e., he would derive equal utility from any of the pairs located on a given curve.

The common name for the set of curves in figure 1 is *indifference map*. Its construction is such that if any point, J, is either due north, due east, or northeast of some other point, K, J will correspond to an (X,Y) pair on a higher indifference curve than that of the (X,Y) pair to which K belongs. Accordingly, J corresponds to greater utility than K, and is said to be superior to K.

A given indifference map is said to reflect a particular state of tastes (for X and Y) of the relevant individual. Accordingly, a change in an individual's tastes is described as a shift of his entire indifference map, and the meaning of such expressions as "tastes unchanged" or "tastes given" is conveyed by saying that the relevant indifference map is unchanged. It is important to note that the locus of an indifference map is assumed to be independent of the resource constraint—the line AB—to which we now turn.

Each point on the straight line, AB (variously called a budget line, budget constraint, or resource constraint) represents the maximum amount of X that an individual would be able to obtain if he were also to obtain the corresponding quantity of Y. The negative slope of this line indicates that to obtain a larger quantity of X with a given resource constraint it is necessary to accept a smaller quantity of Y, and conversely. That AB is a line, rather than a curve, implies that the amount of X that an individual can obtain by relinquishing a given quantity of Y is independent of the quantities of X and Y already possessed; that is, the individual is limited in the quantity of anything she wishes to buy only by her resources and prices. There is no quantity rationing.

Simple though it is, this interpretation of AB serves to define some concepts essential to RAP.

1. The length of the line segment $0A$ measures the individual's resource command over Y (the maximum quantity of Y that he could obtain given his resource constraint) or, alternatively, expresses his wealth in terms of Y. Similarly, the line segment $0B$ measures wealth in terms of X. If Y is defined as all uses of resources other than X, then the line segment $0A$ measures the individual's wealth in terms of "other goods."[3]

---

3. Though often done, representation of a collection of heterogeneous "other goods" as a single (homogeneous) good involves a number of tricky problems commonly associated

2. The slope of $AB(= 0A/0B)$ is the rate at which X and Y may be substituted for one another. This rate is defined as the rate of exchange between X and Y or, alternatively, as the *price* of Y in terms of X.[4] This same idea is expressed by the statement that the rate of exchange between X and Y is the cost of Y in terms of X. Taken together, the preceding two sentences imply that, in the exemplar, cost and price are identical. This reflects a particular concept of cost, commonly called *alternative cost*.[5] That is, the cost of a unit of X is the amount of the alternative (i.e., Y) that must be foregone (sacrificed) in order to obtain it.[6]

3. The idea that resources are scarce is implicit in economic theories of all kinds, but only in RAP is the idea given center stage. Its centrality in RAP is conveyed by the role of AB in figure 1. AB divides all possible pairs of X and Y quantities into those attainable with the resources available to the choice maker (represented by points on or below AB) and those unattainable with those resources (represented by points above AB). The content of the idea that resources are scarce is conveyed by two properties of figure 1: (1) some levels of utility are unattainable with the specified resource limitation, and (2) that in order to obtain more X, within the given resource limitation, it is necessary to sacrifice some Y.

4. Crucial to RAP is the assumption that those who allocate resources behave *rationally*. The meaning of rationality has long been a matter of dispute, both within the economics profession and between economists and others.[7] However, figure 1 provides a simple interpretation of this concept that is consistent both with its role in RAP and with its general use among economists: a resource allocator is behaving rationally if she chooses the (X,Y) pair that places her on the highest indifference curve attainable, given the resources available to her. Thus, a rational individual will never choose a point southwest of AB, but will always opt for a position on the line itself. She will always use all of her scarce resources.

The particular point on AB that she selects, shown as M, will be one at which an indifference curve is tangent to the budget line. (N.B., This

---

with the construction of index numbers. However, these problems do not impair use of this convention for our limited expository purpose.

4. Conventionally, the price of Y in terms of X is defined as the reciprocal of the price of X in terms of Y.

5. In this context, "cost" should be interpreted as marginal cost.

6. This concept of cost is inconsistent with ordinary accounting definitions of cost. It is also inconsistent with definitions of "real cost" such as effort or disutility incurred in the process of production.

7. For some recent examples, see Hogarth and Reder (1987).

assertion requires that the indifference curves be convex from below.)[8] At any point other than M, (say) N, the slope of the indifference curve (called the marginal rate of substitution, or MRS) $A*B*$ will differ from the slope of AB. Such a difference implies that the amount of X required to hold utility constant despite the sacrifice of a small quantity of Y, will differ from the amount required to make such a trade (of Y for X) through the market. This means that, at N, the market would permit an individual to obtain a quantity of X large enough to increase her utility by trading a unit of Y. By definition, rationality requires that all such trades be made, which implies that the individual would move away from N. By a similar argument, it can be shown that rationality implies movement away from any position except M. This argument requires that the cost of trading, i.e., the transaction cost, be negligible.[9]

In a nutshell, in the context of RAP, rational behavior is identical with constrained maximization of utility (constrained optimization). The idea of constrained optimization is applied in many branches of science, all of which share (some of) the mathematical techniques used in economics. However, in economic applications, the constraint(s) are interpreted as resource limitations, while elsewhere they are interpreted differently.[10] In effect, figure 1 is a graphic representation of the resource allocation paradigm for the simple but important case of a single choice maker. Whenever a situation can be interpreted as presenting a choice problem for a single choice maker (whether a biological individual or an agent with authority to choose for a collection of individuals), RAP directs the economist to assume that the choice maker acts as a rational, resource-constrained utility maximizer proceeding in the manner suggested by figure 1.

Thus, to explain why the quantities of X and Y that are chosen varied

8. Although correct in the main, the assertion about the optimality of M is subject to qualification and amplification: (1) In order for M to be a point of maximum rather than minimum utility, it is necessary that the indifference curves be convex (and not concave) to the origin. (2) There are cases where the locus of the indifference map is such that M lies at either A or B, implying that one good or the other is consumed in zero quantity. Such cases, called corner solutions, have interesting implications for the theory of price but are of no concern in the present context. (3) It is assumed implicitly that both X and Y are economic (i.e., scarce) goods and therefore that the marginal utility of each is positive. Where this assumption does not hold, the intuitive power of RAP is greatly attenuated although the formal argument is not invalidated.

9. In RAP it is implicitly assumed that goods can be exchanged without cost, i.e., that the transaction cost is zero.

10. For a discussion of optimization principles outside of economics, see P. J. H. Schoemaker (1984).

from, say, M to S (in figure 1), an economist would say that their relative prices changed from $0A/0B$ to $0C/0D$. Similarly, he would explain a movement from M to P as the result of an increase in resources from AB to A^*B^*, and from M to R as the result of changes in both relative prices and available resources.[11]

Of course, it may happen that tastes change (indifference maps shift) in which case an explanation of behavior as resulting from (changes in) relative prices and/or available resources must be supplemented or, in the extreme, abandoned altogether. Thus, although RAP does not require that tastes be unchanging, the occurrence of such changes reduces the salience of the paradigm. Accordingly, economists who adhere to RAP prefer explanations of quantity behavior that emphasize changes in relative prices or in available resources (e.g., changes in income or wealth) and minimize the role of changes in tastes.[12]

In addition to the above characteristics, RAP requires that the utility level of any individual depend only upon the quantities of *real* goods and services that she consumes and not upon their *nominal* (or money) value. Thus if the prices of all goods and services consumed by an individual were to double together with a doubling of her money income, RAP implies that her utility level would be unchanged. Violation of this restriction upon utility functions is generally considered grounds for rejecting an argument as incompatible with RAP: such a violation is commonly termed a *money illusion*. Showing that an argument implies the existence of a money illusion is an effective means of discrediting the argument among RAP adherents.

Although I shall not labor the details, which are a staple of courses in beginning price theory, the implications of RAP for the behavior of (individual) producers are almost analogous to those for individual consumers. The problem of each producing unit is to maximize the output obtainable from resources (inputs) of any given value which are available at market determined prices.[13] Output maximization is accomplished by

11. It may be remarked that distinguishing the effect (on quantity consumed) of a change in resources from the effect of a change in relative prices, at one time presented a serious analytical problem. Now the distinction is made, and routinely applied, in elementary theory courses.

12. RAP explains changes in quantities used solely by changes in prices and resource quantities, with tastes and technology constant. When changes in the latter take place, their effects must be somehow allowed for.

13. The producing unit also has the problem of determining the level of output, a problem that has no analogue in the theory of the household. This is discussed later.

selecting the best combination of inputs attainable with a given "outlay budget" and given input prices: this also serves to minimize the cost of whatever is produced.

Analogous to the consumer's indifference map, the producing unit is assumed to possess a map of product isoquants, given exogenously, which is considered descriptive of the best technology (technique) available. Like changes in tastes, changes in technology are themselves unexplained and function as causal determinants of such changes in methods of production (input combinations) as occur with unchanged relative input prices.

A further proposition fundamental to RAP that is logically entailed by its axioms, but not readily interpreted in terms of figures 1 and 2, is that optimization by competitive producers requires producing (anything that is produced) in the quantity that makes its marginal cost of production equal to its price.[14]

In other words, RAP explains the behavior of individual choice makers as the selection of quantities in response to exogenously given prices and levels (quantities) of resource command guided by the intent to maximize an exogenously given objective function.[15] The paradigm directs the economist to create models that explain individual choice making in terms of these variables.

Application of the paradigm is not restricted to the behavior of individuals: it further directs the economist to explain the price-quantity behavior of such aggregates of individuals as industries, geographical areas, etc. on the maintained hypothesis that each of the individual decision makers is behaving in accordance with the paradigm. To accomplish this, the economist is directed to find or to create variables that represent aggregate behavior as quantities supplied or demanded by (many) individuals, each of whom is maximizing utility in the manner of figure 1.

The resulting price-quantity combinations are interpreted as the outcome of the interaction of the choice making of all resource owning individuals, as determined by *equilibrium conditions*. These conditions are: (1) the quantity supplied of each good, commodity, etc. must equal the quantity demanded and (2) the price paid in all transactions involving any specific good must be the same (see below, pp. 59–61). Changes in the price or quantity of any one good are then explained as the aggregate

---

14. This will be elaborated on below.

15. In the case of the consumer, the objective is utility; in the case of a producer it is output.

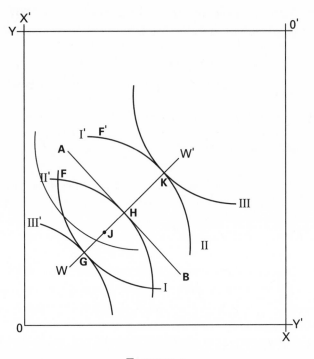

FIGURE 2

result of changes in the determinants of the behavior of rational individual choice makers. Ultimately, these determinants are tastes, techniques (technology), and resources.

TRADE AND EFFICIENCY

To analyze the notions of demand and supply and see how they relate to the exemplar of resource constrained optimization by individuals, let us move to the case where are two individuals whose behavioral possibilities include trade. To do this, we need to introduce the concept of efficiency.

The idea of an efficient economy, and related notions, is exemplified in figure 2, which presents the indifference maps and resources available to two individuals, 1 and 2. In this diagram the conventional axes, $0Y$ and $0X$, refer to 1 and the inverted axes, $0'Y'$ and $0'X'$, to 2. $0Y(= 0'Y')$ measures the amount of Y available to 1 and 2 combined: similarly, $0X(= 0'X')$ measures the amount of X available to both. (By construction, points X and Y' are identical, as are Y and X'.) The four coordinates of any point in the rectangle, $0X0'Y''$, measure the X and Y quantities possessed by 1 and 2, respectively; any point within the rectangle (or on the axes) represents a set of endowments of 1 and 2 that is consistent with the (two person) community's total endowments of X and Y. The indifference curves referring to 1 are convex to the $0Y$ and $0X$ axes and analogous to those of figure 1. The indifference curves referring to 2 are convex to $0'Y'$ and $0'X'$ (and therefore concave to $0Y$ and $0X$) and labeled with primed Roman numerals. The curve WW' is a locus of points where an indifference curve of 1 is tangent to an indifference curve of 2. (WW' is commonly called the *contract curve.*) At any point, F, off the curve WW' the indifference curves of 1 and 2 will intersect (as distinguished from being tangent), implying the existence of an opportunity for both parties to increase their utility by moving to some other point. Accordingly, it is only at points on WW' that an improvement (i.e., increase in utility) for one person will be impossible without reducing the utility of the other.

As figure 2 shows, at all points on WW' the indifference curves of the two individuals are tangent, implying the absence of opportunity for (further) utility gains for both. Thus if the "endowments" (of X and Y) for 1 and 2 were such as to place them at some point, F, off of WW', both could gain by trading appropriate quantities of X and Y so as to move on to WW' somewhere between G and H (e.g., J). Rationality implies that, in the absence of transaction costs, such a trade would be made. An efficient economy is defined as one where all such opportunities for improvement of both parties are fully utilized.

Clearly, it is in the interest of 1 to locate (on WW') as far to the northeast (and for 2 to locate as far to the southwest) as possible. However, with resource endowments and the rate of exchange between X and Y given exogenously, rationality uniquely determines their positions on the contract curve, WW'.[16] With different endowments (e.g., F' or F''), but the same rate of exchange between X and Y (given by the slope of AB), 1 and 2 would locate at different points on WW'.

Figure 2 vividly illustrates the possibility of mutually beneficial trade. Moreover, it explicates the meaning of the proposition, "if potential trading partners are rational, all opportunities for mutually beneficial trade will be utilized." In accordance with this exemplar, the paradigm directs

16. In the literature of economic theory, figure 2 is commonly known as the Edgeworth-Bowley box diagram after F. Y. Edgeworth (1845–1926) and A. L. Bowley (1869–1957); WW' is known as the contract curve.

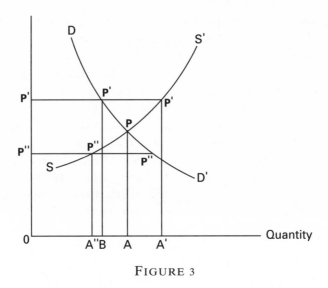

FIGURE 3

economists to construct models in which it is assumed that all possibilities of mutually beneficial exchange are utilized, and to reject those implying the contrary. Such "directions" have exerted an extremely powerful influence upon the characteristics of models that economists employ.

For example, such models imply that valuable resources are always fully employed, and that opportunities for increased efficiency in resource allocation are always exploited. Thus, as portrayed in figures 1 and 2, the exemplar displays many of the characteristics of RAP. The main characteristic that is missing is the determination of prices by Supply and Demand: let us now turn to this matter.

THE PARADIGM PROPER AND PARADIGM ADJUNCTS

In figures 1 and 2 the prices of X and Y are presented as arbitrary givens. However, in RAP prices are not arbitrary: every price is uniquely determined by the condition that the quantity supplied is equal to the quantity demanded. Conventionally, this condition is portrayed, as in figure 3, by a supply-and-demand diagram, on the vertical axis of which is measured price (in dollars), with quantity measured on the horizontal axis. The coordinates of the point of intersection of the supply curve, SS', with the demand curve, DD', give the equilibrium price and quantity.

In this diagram, the supply and demand curves are not arbitrary but are derived, for each possible price, by summing the utility maximizing quantities of all individuals. The equilibrium price, assumed to be unique, is the one that equates the total quantity supplied with the total quantity demanded; this price is also called the market clearing price. Only the market clearing price—so derived—can place all possible pairs of community members at points such as M in figure 2.

As the loci of the indifference maps of figures 1 and 2 generally depend upon the prices of other goods (i.e., goods other than X and Y), RAP requires that the prices and quantities of all goods be determined simultaneously. In order that all individuals in a community, acting rationally, generate a set of market clearing prices such that each arrives at a position such as M in figure 1 for every pair of goods that enters her utility function, it is necessary that certain stringent conditions be imposed upon the tastes, technology, and resources of the members of the community.

In essence, these conditions are mathematical extensions of the ideas underlying figures 1 and 2 and have been generally agreed upon since the early 1950s. An imaginary economy in which these and related conditions are satisfied may be said to possess an *efficient equilibrium;* an economy having such characteristics is often termed an Arrow-Debreu world (A-D).[17]

Existence of an Arrow-Debreu world requires satisfaction of some very restrictive conditions. Inter alia, these conditions require that (1) every argument of every utility function be associated with a commodity (good or service) having a competitively determined price;[18] (2) transaction costs be zero; (3) every individual know (with certainty) his own utility function, the prices associated with each of its arguments and his wealth; and (4) technology be public information. Stated less technically, an Arrow-Debreu world is one in which lack of knowledge, including uncertainty as to the future, does not influence anyone's behavior. It is also a world in which all "good things" can be bought or sold, without effort (cost), at competitive prices.[19]

Obviously, none of these conditions is ever completely satisfied in a

17. It was not until around 1950 that the conditions for an efficient equilibrium were established for an economy consisting of resource owners communicating with each other only by making offers to buy or sell. Establishment of these conditions is generally attributed to K. J. Arrow and Gerard Debreu. For an exposition of the formal properties of these conditions see K. J. Arrow and F. H. Hahn (1971).

18. This condition is sometimes expressed by saying that markets must be complete.

19. There is nothing in the notion of an efficient equilibrium that requires that it be reached with the aid of prices, competitive or otherwise. In principle, it could be attained by the commands of an omniscient dictator. However RAP is almost always described in terms of the actions of decentralized decision makers guided solely by competitive prices—the Invisible Hand—and I shall follow this convention.

real-world economy. In applied work, adherence to RAP is reflected in a tendency to minimize the significance of departures from A-D and in the proposal of paradigm preserving adjustments. Typically, nonadherents to RAP treat departures from A-D as grounds for abandoning the paradigm.[20]

I shall term the set of propositions that hold only in A-D the paradigm proper (RAP proper) to distinguish it from a swarm of *paradigm adjuncts*. (The "paradigm" includes both the paradigm proper and the adjuncts.) As all propositions in the paradigm proper refer to equilibrium positions, none can apply literally to behavior that is directly observable.[21]

Valid use of the paradigm proper is made in analyses at high levels of abstraction such as studies of long run equilibrium, comparative statics and theoretical welfare economics. It is this part of economics that is most completely formalized and where considerations of mathematical elegance and logical rigor have the greatest weight in appraising the quality of research contributions.

In short, the paradigm proper is the conceptual framework used in pure theory. It includes the corpus of theorems about marginal equivalences, total cost minimization and distribution of incomes in accordance with the marginal productivity of resources that are the staple of courses in price theory. In RAP proper, the implications of efficiency and competitive equilibrium always coincide: it is the world of Pareto optimality (see below, chapter 9).

But as will be seen, the impact of the paradigm proper is felt far beyond the domain of pure theory. The conceptual organization and, ultimately, the ideology often associated with the paradigm, is rooted in the paradigm proper. Accordingly, attacks on propositions of the paradigm proper arouse concern over a far wider section of the economics community, and are resisted with much greater intensity, than those directed at particular paradigm adjuncts. Stated differently, the paradigm proper pertains to every aspect of economics, while any particular adjunct relates only to one or a few aspects.

The function of paradigm adjuncts is to bridge the conceptual chasm

20. In an econometric context, adherence to RAP is expressed by impounding in disturbance terms the effect of the forces excluded from the paradigm. The validity of RAP depends upon the assumption that such disturbances are uncorrelated with variables operating within the paradigm.

21. By definition, analysis of real-world phenomena (i.e., directly observable behavior) must consider the effects both of observational errors and of disturbances arising from the operation of forces excluded from the paradigm.

between A-D and the real world of observable phenomena. The need for an adjunct arises wherever it is necessary to consider a disequilibrium position, a non-zero transaction cost, an observational error, or any other departure from the strict conditions of A-D.[22] But the most important of the adjuncts lies close to the heart of the paradigm proper: the law of supply and demand.

SUPPLY AND DEMAND

We begin by noting that the paradigm proper does not explain how equilibrium prices get established: it merely states that such prices must be consistent with the conditions that quantity supplied equals quantity demanded and that all transactions in a given commodity at a given time occur at the same price. To explain how an equilibrium price gets established requires a "story" that, although a basic part of elementary economics, is no part of the paradigm proper. This story is customarily told with the aid of figure 3.

In this diagram, the D curve (demand curve) presents quantity demanded as an (inverse) function of price and the S curve (supply curve) presents quantity supplied as an increasing function of price. (As is customary, it is assumed that the demand curve is downward sloping and the supply curve upward sloping.)[23] In interpreting figure 3, it is usually convenient to assume that the prices of all other goods are fixed at their equilibrium levels and that the quantity transacted by any individual has no effect on the price.[24]

The tropism of actual prices for their equilibrium level is usually ex-

22. Readers who are acquainted with methodological literature will note a resemblance of the distinction between the paradigm proper and paradigm adjuncts and that made by the late Imre Lakatos between the "hard core" of a scientific research program and its "protective belt." After some struggle, I have come to realize that the similarity raises issues that can best be addressed elsewhere. For those curious about such issues—which I find fascinating—a good introduction is Spiro Latsis (1976).

23. Except for the (unusual) case where the income effect of a price change exceeds the substitution effect, demand curves are considered to be downward sloping; arguments implying the reverse are suspect, and require special justification.

Although usually drawn as upward sloping, there is no general presumption that supply curves have this property. Rather it is considered that the shape of a supply curve—especially the direction of its slope—will vary from one problem to another. However, when a supply curve is negatively inclined, it is likely that application of RAP will encounter difficulty.

24. It is usually easier to interpret figure 3 if it is supposed that the supply curve refers to specialized producers rather than to consumers seeking to trade in order to move to the contract curve, as in figure 2.

plained in the following way: if, in figure 3, a price higher than the equilibrium, AP, (say AP') were somehow to prevail, then the quantity supplied
($0A'$) would exceed the quantity demanded ($0B'$); that is, there would be
excess supply. Conversely, at any price lower than AP (say AP''), there
would be excess demand.[25] The "law" of supply and demand asserts that
whenever there is excess supply (demand) the price will fall and, conversely, the price will rise whenever there is excess demand. Accordingly,
given that S and D are unchanged, any price other than AP will change,
and therefore only AP can persist. Hence, typically, it is asserted that the
actual or market price tends toward the equilibrium price, AP.

Although essential to the application of RAP, and to much of its intuitive appeal, the law of supply and demand is inconsistent with the paradigm proper. Consider: at some arbitrarily chosen disequilibrium price,
AP', the supply quantity, $0A'$, would exceed the demand quantity, $0B'$.
This implies that some suppliers would be unable to sell all that they desired at AP'; such sellers would be "quantity restricted." But both $0A'$
and $0B'$ are calculated on the assumption that every individual is on his
contract curve, which is inconsistent with the presence of quantity restrictions upon either suppliers or demanders.

To maintain the logical integrity of the paradigm without destroying
its empirical relevance it would be necessary to relax at least one of the
assumptions upon which both D and S are constructed. However accomplished, such relaxation must involve specification of a set of (non-price)
rationing rules to determine the allocation of "scarce" customers or scarce
suppliers in the presence of excess supply or demand and—if the law of
supply and demand is to hold—a set of associated rules relating changes
in price to the magnitude of excess demand or supply.

In other words, operation of the law of supply and demand implies the
possible existence of (at least temporary) disequilibrium in a market, and
exposes a need for rule(s) prescribing the allocation of goods in "short
supply" or in "deficient demand." Apparently, as usually stated the law is
quite vague: to make its meaning precise it is necessary to specify (i) the
relation of speed of price change to the magnitude and duration of excess

25. In figure 3, only the equilibrium point is consistent with the paradigm proper. At any
other price, the hypothetical quantities demanded and supplied are merely (counterfactual)
implications of the construction of the curves on the assumption that all other prices are set
at their equilibrium levels. It is to be emphasized that the paradigm proper says nothing
about the movement of prices from disequilibrium to equilibrium levels (or to other disequilibrium levels).

supply (demand) and (ii) associated non-price rationing rules that operate in the presence of excess supply. Such specifications are commonly termed "dynamic," and always involve elements extraneous to the paradigm proper.

Should the non-price rationing rules themselves be explicable as the outcome of individual optimization under conditions of limited information and/or non-negligible transaction costs, the augmented model of price determination could be considered as RAP conforming, with the augmenting rules serving as paradigm adjuncts. However, if the rules cannot bear such an interpretation, their operation constitutes an anomaly for RAP.

Provided that they are compatible with rationality, the behavioral rules describing non-price rationing and price movements in disequilibrium exemplify paradigm adjuncts. Paradigm adjuncts, such as these, are needed to remedy the consequences of using concepts, or accepting propositions, that are incompatible with one or another assumption of the paradigm proper. Appearance of such adjuncts indicates a "seam" where a theoretical innovation was made, or is needed, to reconcile the paradigm proper with the intuitive beliefs, empirical observations and conceptual conventions of working economists.

Wherever need for a paradigm adjunct appears, an opportunity is created for a theoretical innovation; an appreciable part of the history of RAP concerns the creation of such adjuncts. Indeed, a young economist seeking to make his mark in the culture would do well to find a phenomenon whose occurrence was anomalous to the paradigm proper and/or to an accepted adjunct and to provide a new adjunct to dispel the anomaly. But to accept the paradigm proper does not imply acceptance of a proposed adjunct. As we shall see in chapter 4, an adjunct demanding situation may lead to the proposal of a new paradigm as well as to an adjunct that preserves RAP. First, to fix ideas, let us consider a few further examples of paradigm adjuncts.

Some Further Paradigm Adjuncts

1. *Money.* In the paradigm proper the assumed absence of transaction cost leaves no reason for an individual to prefer one tradable item to another in effecting an exchange. Thus, at given prices, any good would be as acceptable as any other in exchange for a third, and a barter economy would function exactly like one in which money is used. In such case, it would be irrational to hold a cash balance. However, the use of money is

so nearly ubiquitous, and its advantages so obvious, that it has always been recognized that the paradigm proper must be augmented to allow for its use.

To reconcile the paradigm with the practice of holding cash balances it is necessary to assume that (1) the flows of receipts and payments are not perfectly anticipated, and (2) there is a penalty for being unable to make prompt payment in terms of what is accepted as cash. Given these assumptions, it is possible to construct a demand function for cash balances. In early attempts to construct such a function it was assumed that a choice maker's demand for a stock of cash was some constant (positive) fraction of his total real wealth; more recently, the rate of interest was added as a second determinant of the demand for cash balances.[26]

In the paradigm proper, only relative prices are determined. Augmenting the paradigm proper with a demand function for cash balances makes it possible to determine the level of money or (absolute) prices. Such determination of the level of money prices is at the root of the Quantity Theory of Money, an adjunct to RAP which will be discussed later.[27]

But whether a demand function for cash balances is consistent with RAP depends upon its rationale. If it is derived from the preference functions of rational individuals (relating their cash holdings to their wealth levels and the interest rate given the probability of "running out" of cash and the penalty for doing so), a demand function may be interpreted as paradigm consistent. In such case, the justification for the form and parameters assigned to the demand function constitutes a paradigm adjunct. In the event that the demand function is posited without rationalization, or a fortiori if the rationalization were inconsistent with the paradigm, its use would constitute an abandonment of the paradigm.

It is worth noting that the above remarks on the demand function for cash balances refer only to (simple) models in which claims (e.g., securities) are absent. In the presence of claims, which can serve as close substi-

26. A demand function for cash balances relates the desired stock of cash with the level of wealth (W) and the rate of interest (i): quantity demanded is assumed to increase with W (i constant) and to diminish with i, (W) constant. The form and parameters of such a function depend upon the probability distribution of the differences in current receipts and current payments and the penalty attached to having an insufficient stock of cash to meet commitments and/or to make desired purchases.

27. The reader may wonder why I discuss the demand for cash balances and omit consideration of its supply. The reason is that in RAP money is treated as "fiat money" whose supply is set arbitrarily by the authorities. The level of nominal (i.e., money) prices varies inversely with the quantity supplied but relative prices are left unaffected in the postulated absence of "Money Illusion." (see above, p. 48).

tutes for money, the problem of reconciling the demand for a cash balance with the requirements of rationality (i.e., providing a suitable paradigm adjunct) becomes more difficult. However, we need not enter into these complications.[28]

At this point it may be well to specify the criterion that distinguishes paradigm adjuncts from theories, models, conjectures, etc. that are incompatible with the paradigm. Define the criterion in terms of a hypothetical research paper explaining the observed variation of one or more economic variables in time or location where the observed behavior does not conform exactly with what is implied by the paradigm. A paradigm adjunct would purport to explain such movements by further variable(s), each of which reflected only the action of utility maximizing individuals plus random disturbances ("noise"). Since no one believes that the real world conforms literally to the paradigm proper, insistence upon use of such adjuncts, and avoidance of variables not capable of such characterization, is the primary basis for distinguishing models or theories that are compatible with RAP from others. Thus very many disagreements about the appropriate model to apply to a given problem turn on the question of whether or not the model to be applied is RAP-compatible.

2. *Markets.* No concept is more basic to RAP than that of "the market." Yet, as we have seen, the paradigm proper says nothing about how a market functions. All that it says is that (1) for every tradable item there may be only one price at any given time, (2) the price must be such as to make the quantity supplied equal the quantity demanded, and (3) every resource owner (trader) must be maximizing his utility. Nothing whatever is said about how a market operates to cause the satisfaction of these conditions, particularly (1) and (2).

Economists have offered many different stories purporting to describe the manner in which some particular price (or prices) is set, but none has been considered broadly applicable. For the present purpose, it is sufficient to note that wherever such stories are consistent with the paradigm, each price-setting procedure functions as a paradigm adjunct with a limited domain of application.[29] (The reason for the comparative neglect of the price-setting process is discussed below.)

28. For an excellent introduction to the subtleties of reconciling the demand for cash with the postulate of rationality in the presence of interest-bearing securities, see K. D. Hoover (1988), chapters 5 and 6.

29. One such story is that of Walras's imaginary auctioneer; another (with many variants) is that of the entrepreneur who charges a "markup" over unit costs; a third is that of many followers imitating the price behavior of a dominant leader. Each of these, and other,

In RAP, the concept of a market refers to a transaction locus in which all units of the same good are considered as interchangeable by every transactor: this is a sufficient condition for *the law of one price*.[30] To a close approximation, this state of affairs is approximated by an organized exchange (e.g., a security or commodity exchange) where units of a specific tradable entity are treated as interchangeable, and trades in them generate a series of transaction prices referring indifferently to all units. Although it is recognized that outside of organized exchanges the units of a single good or service may differ in quality, with corresponding differences in price, adherents of RAP nevertheless apply the notion of a single market very widely, treating the (allegedly minor) anomalies that result as errors of approximation.

To study this matter further, let us remind ourselves of the assumption (intrinsic to the paradigm proper) that any item affecting any individual's level of utility is associated with a market clearing (competitive) price. Let us also remark that outside of organized exchanges, any good or service may be heterogeneous: in principle, every unit of every good may differ somewhat from every other unit of the "same" good. So considered, every individual's utility function includes many varieties of goods that are consumed in zero quantity, together with a much smaller number of (other) goods each of which is consumed in a finite amount.

Without much argument, RAP assumes for all goods (products) located within a small region surrounding any of the positive quantity goods that (1) they may be treated as homogeneous, (2) they have a common price, and (3) their quantities may be summed to yield an aggregate quantity associated with that common price. Such assumptions underlie both the Marshallian theory of the (competitive) industry and the statistical practice of constructing aggregate quantities of output for empirically specified industries where any aggregate quantity is associated with an average price for the industry's output through both a supply curve and a demand curve.

So long as the relative prices of all product varieties within an industry vary proportionately, RAP proper will apply to the industry as a whole. But normally this condition is not satisfied well enough to avoid need for

---

stories is more-or-less plausible at particular times and for a limited number of cases. But none has had wide applicability and even among those that have appeared to be applicable under certain conditions at particular times, none has avoided numerous contradictions by the subsequent flow of events.

30. Succinctly, the law of one price states that at any given time all units of a given commodity are traded at the same price.

an adjunct. The precise form of the adjunct may vary from one industry to another, but however specified it must imply the absence of any correlation between differences in the relative prices of the industry's product varieties and differences in the relative quantities produced.[31]

On this maintained assumption, the RAP theory of the competitive industry is applicable to problems where it is considered proper to treat the output of an industry as though it were homogeneous. Where it is desired to analyze the price-quantity relations among the product varieties—or among the firms producing them—such treatment is inappropriate. Depending upon the number and differentia of the product varieties and the objectives of the analysis, application of a theory of Duopoly, Oligopoly or Monopolistic Competition may be required.[32]

The discussion of the last few paragraphs refers to industries whose output is not sold on organized exchanges. In such industries price-quantity behavior is qualitatively different from that on organized exchanges. For example, a good traded on an organized exchange is capable of generating a futures market where commitments to buy or sell said good (at a specified price at a specified date in the future) are traded. In addition, there may arise a variety of derivative markets for trading claims reflecting speculation on what such future prices will be.[33] Interrelations among the (spot) price of a good and the prices of all futures and derivative claims are supposed to conform to RAP. (This is discussed further in chapter 8.)

Both in popular discourse and in academic analyses, the behavior of these interrelated asset prices is discussed exclusively in terms of their response to new information about the future. No reference is made to such concepts as shortages, surpluses, availabilities, order backlogs, variations in product characteristics or payment terms, list prices versus transaction prices, all of which are vital elements in the description of any market except an organized exchange.[34] Further: on an organized ex-

31. Failing this assumption, the relation of an industry's average price and its aggregate output quantity will depend in part upon the factors responsible for the (assumed) correlation of prices and quantities among the industry's product varieties. There is no presumption that such factors would be compatible with RAP.

32. The idea that the analyst may vary the model used, competitive industry or otherwise, to suit the problem at hand derives from Milton Friedman's (1953) classic discussion of the subject.

33. Not all goods traded on organized exchanges actually generate a market in futures or other derivatives, but any of them could, provided there was sufficient trader interest.

34. This must be qualified: disequilibrium phenomena do appear on organized exchanges; for example, sometimes transaction orders cannot be executed. Indeed, the normal

change, typically transactions are "paper exchanges," involving no act of physical delivery. This makes it possible for such markets to be impersonal (i.e., buyers and sellers do not know the identities of their trading counterparts), and for purchases and sales to occur solely as a response to receipt of information or a change of opinion. This, in turn, generates a class of speculators who hold assets for no purpose other than to profit by transacting on the basis of information flows. It is the activity of such speculators that makes for the almost continuous flow of transactions—and moment-to-moment price movements—that distinguish organized exchanges from other markets.

Nevertheless, despite these qualitative differences between the price-quantity behavior of things traded on organized exchanges and of things traded otherwise, RAP purports to explain both types of behavior. To understand this claim, consider that the sector of organized exchanges is a close approximation to the domain of RAP proper, and that the sector of all other markets is—at best—a much rougher approximation. Imagine a partition between the two sectors. On the organized exchange side of the partition there is a large number of markets for trading securities and commodities. In each of these markets the characteristics of the asset traded have been carefully designed so as to make it capable of functioning as an object of transaction on an organized exchange.[35] In particular, all units of any given asset must be sufficiently similar as to induce transactors to think of them as interchangeable. The market for each of these assets is generally conceived as continuously clearing, with price fluctuating as required.[36] As was already remarked, price-setting mechanisms vary from one organized exchange to another and always involve considerable institutional machinery.[37]

---

operation of an exchange typically is regulated by rules intended to insure "orderly markets." Determining the efficiency of such rules (i.e., whether they are compatible with RAP) raises tricky analytical issues. Some of these matters are touched on in chapter 8. For the present purpose, we shall ignore such complications and adopt the conventional assumption that organized exchanges always clear.

35. For a fascinating account of the problems of creating a tradable asset capable of functioning as a vehicle for trading on an organized exchange (in this case, a futures contract for plywood), see Richard L. Sandor (1973).

36. Because transactions do not occur at every instant, the analyst must adopt a convention for measuring prices during intervals between transactions. Typically it is assumed that the price does not vary during such intervals.

37. As we are not concerned with the differentia of organized exchanges, but only with their common characteristic of (almost) continuous clearing, I shall not dwell on the details

On the organized exchange side of the partition, RAP contends that the price of each asset conforms to the law of one price. Price differences among transactions at a given moment and all aspects of quantity rationing (shortages, surpluses, delivery difficulties) are considered anomalous and alleged to be infrequent and/or unimportant. For markets on the organized side of the partition, the empirical content of RAP is adherence to the law of one price and its logical implications such as the absence of opportunities for profitable arbitrage (see chapter 8).

On the other side of the partition, where organized exchanges do not exist, a common characteristic of markets is the heterogeneity of traded units: such heterogeneity makes the law of one price inapplicable. In this context, the validity of RAP requires that such price differences as are found among apparently similar transactions must be explicable as resulting from differences in the cost of transacting (e.g., differences in delivery charges or in the method of payment) or in production cost variations associated with small differences in product specification. The anti-RAP interpretation of such price differences is to attribute them to differences in transaction profit that cannot be traced to such cost differences. But whether price differences are due to rational exploitation of a monopoly position, to irrational behavior, or to some other non-cost-associated cause is irrelevant: any failure to impute price differences among transactions to differences in marginal cost must be considered anomalous to RAP.

3. *Monopoly and Price Making.* In the paradigm proper, all markets are competitive. However, RAP adherents generally have been aware of the existence of monopolies and have constructed a paradigm adjunct to reconcile this fact with the view of the world presented by their paradigm.[38] In essence the adjunct consists of an assumption that whatever monopolies may exist are neither so prevalent nor so large as to destroy the equality of the equilibrium price of any resource among all of its alternative uses. That is, the adjunct limits RAP to situations where a large but finite number of "industries" uses inputs from a much smaller number of resources (termed factors of production) which are priced equally in all industries. If an industry is sufficiently small so that changes in the magnitude of its demand for any resource will not be sufficient to alter its price

---

of such institutional machinery. However, if RAP is to hold, each such mechanism must serve as a de facto paradigm adjunct with the required properties for achieving efficiency.

38. In this context, I use the term "monopoly" to refer indifferently to monopoly proper, and to duopoly and oligopoly.

to any industry, then the presence of monopoly in that industry will not undermine the validity of RAP. The adjunct asserts that all monopolies to be found in the real world satisfy this condition.

Were this not the case, it would be incorrect to interpret the marginal cost of output in a monopolized industry as the value of the resources that had to be drawn from some other industry in order to produce an additional unit of its output. As we shall see, inability to interpret marginal cost in this fashion precludes some of the most important practical applications of RAP. In brief, to paraphrase Sir Dennis Robertson, RAP envisages the economy as a huge bowl of competitive warm milk on which float a few lumps of monopolistic butter.

RAP is commonly associated with a particular theory of monopoly wherein the monopolist is a profit-maximizing seller. But it does not matter greatly whether actual monopolists behave in a manner compatible with this theory. The implications of RAP that give the paradigm its influence require the predominance of competition, but say nothing specific about price-quantity behavior in its absence.

The posture of RAP toward monopoly is closely related to its posture toward the process of price setting generally. In the paradigm proper, prices are determined by the condition that markets clear—that is, that quantity supplied equals quantity demanded—in all markets, but nothing is said about how such equality is brought about. Every transactor is envisaged as a "price taker"; the price taken is said to have been set by "the market."[39] But this is understood as shorthand for something like the following: "each price maker is so tightly constrained by the offers of competing transactors that her choice among possible prices is virtually nil. Consequently, she must take the same price as her competitors (i.e., act as a price taker)."[40]

In effect, RAP says that although a transactor is legally free to charge or offer whatever she pleases, the restrictions of competing offers and rationality together preclude the possibility of setting a price different from that set by the market. Problems of ascertaining the prices currently charged by competitors; of how to decide which price to react to if the prices of competitors' prices differ from one another; and others—i.e., the

39. The concept *price taker,* and the correlative *price maker,* were introduced by Tibor Scitovsky (1951).
40. It should be understood that a price taker could always charge more than her competitors on pain of making no sales, or charge less on pain of making less on each transaction than she need accept. Either option would imply a violation of rationality.

problems of price makers—are asserted to have but negligible effect upon actual transaction prices. Consequently, it is held that—in competition— only negligible error is caused by assuming that all transactors are price takers with prices set by unspecified impersonal forces called the market.[41] It follows that the details of price setting processes are a matter of—at most—secondary importance.

The remarks of the previous two paragraphs apply to competitive markets, but not to monopolies. While not impossible, it is implausible to suppose that a monopolist will be a price taker, and generally she is not portrayed as such. Hence, in RAP discussions, descriptions of price making tend to be conflated with the analysis of monopoly. This is unfortunate because the two phenomena are logically distinct; in some contexts, such as labor markets, it is often useful to consider competitors as price makers. However, for better or worse, the view of the world that leads RAP to treat the competitive industry as the standard type of market structure also causes it to consider the details of any price setting process as a matter of secondary importance.

4. *Paradigm Adjuncts in General.* The three foregoing examples are in no sense exhaustive of the stock of paradigm adjuncts, extant or potential. Where and whenever a new or previously unrecognized set of circumstances arises to which RAP is potentially applicable, it is likely that a new adjunct will be required to make the application successful.

In essence, RAP proper applies only to individuals, constrained only by their (lack of) resources. Thus any attempt to analyze the behavior of any entity that involves the coordination of the decisions of a plurality of individuals, such as a firm, a family, or a state, requires the creation of an adjunct. More generally, consideration of any entity involving "governance" requires an adjunct. Many of these adjuncts will appear, in one guise or another, in the following chapters. But first let us examine (some of) the other paradigms in the jungle of economics.

41. The validity of this assertion is, of course, a matter of fact to be decided case by case.

THE KEYNESIAN
PARADIGM: KP

In this and the next two chapters I shall discuss a few leading examples of "other" paradigms operative in economics: chapters 4 and 5 are devoted exclusively to the Keynesian Paradigm (KP). While I do not know whether it would be possible to compile a complete list of the paradigms used in economics, such a list would be unnecessary for our purposes: the examples to be presented here are intended as illustrative rather than exhaustive.

While not all economic paradigms use RAP as a point of departure, most of those discussed in this book do. Yet I do not agree with the (many) adherents of RAP who would identify economics—or "sound economics"—with their chosen paradigm. Despite their various problems, "other paradigms" are more than a tissue of errors.

In what follows I have tried as much as possible to avoid burdening the reader with analytical details. In this endeavor I have been less successful in the case of KP than in the others, but even here I have skimped drastically, as many readers will readily perceive.

An Overview of the Keynesian Paradigm

By making the degree of resource use a variable of the economic system— explicitly allowing for the possibility that the degree of resource use may be less than full (i.e., less than 100 percent)—the Keynesian Paradigm (KP) departs sharply from RAP which requires full use of resources in order that no choice maker be off of a contract curve. While it is not logically necessary that it do so, KP focuses on labor as the resource subject to underutilization, which is to say that KP focuses upon the possibility that there may be underutilization of labor, or involuntary unemployment. Involuntary unemployment implies economic waste, leaving open the possibility that government intervention might generate a larger net output from given resources than what would be attainable by the uncoordinated action of individuals working through competitive markets.

Since the publication of *The General Theory*[1] at the end of 1935 until the present, the validity of KP has been a major topic of debate among professional economists. While the major issues of this debate emanate from macroeconomics, there have been important and unavoidable spillovers to microeconomics, especially in the study of labor markets. *The General Theory* emerged as a response to the massive unemployment that accompanied the great depression of the 1930s. At the time, it was widely believed that "orthodox" economic theory could not satisfactorily account for the role of effective demand in causing unemployment, and that a new theory was required. The General Theory purported to fill this need, and it attracted enthusiastic support as well as stern opposition from within the economics profession, and from the interested public as well.

Historians of economic thought may disagree as to how well *The General Theory* would have fared in the debates of the late 1930s, had RAP been deployed with the sophistication commonly displayed a quarter-century later. But, as a matter of doctrinal history, there is no dispute that in the late 1930s and 40s the Keynesians were victorious, converting or neutralizing the major part of the economics profession, and leaving avowed defenders of RAP in a distinct minority.[2] The revival of RAP, in the guise of monetarism, did not become important until the late 1950s.[3]

The Keynesian Paradigm consists of three essential elements: (1) The degree of resource use is variable, with the level of effective demand being a major determinant. (2) There is at least one stable relation among variables representing components of aggregate expenditure. This relation is expressed as the aggregate consumption function: a transform of this relation, the famous multiplier, is its more familiar designation. (3) The rate of interest depends upon, inter alia, the desire of the public to hold cash balances (i.e., its *liquidity preference*) which makes it unavailable for the task of equating the supply and demand for savings.

Before commenting on each of these elements, let me make the obvious point that the focus of KP is much narrower than that of RAP: it does not seek to explain the determination of prices and quantities of individual commodities. Its purpose is to introduce the state of effective demand

---

1. J. M. Keynes (1936), hereafter referred to as *The General Theory*.

2. A very important part of this minority were the economists of the "Chicago School." See M. W. Reder, (1982).

3. Precise dating is difficult and unnecessary: I would suggest the publications of Milton Friedman (1956) and (1957) as a demarcation point.

as a variable required for a proper description of an economic system, and to make the entailed alterations to RAP. While these alterations are not trivial, they do not require a complete reconstruction of the theory of relative prices. But neither do they militate against such a reconstruction.

From the standpoint of RAP, a proper description of an economy should include a measure of its wealth (resources) including its labor force (human capital); its tastes, indicated perhaps by a survey of household expenditures; and its technology, indicated by one or more of the production functions in use. Varying with the problem at hand, such a description might or might not include specification of the distributions of the various wealth components (including human capital), but it would not include a variable to reflect the level of effective demand. This is because the postulate of rationality and the assumption of zero transaction costs together imply that resources will always be fully utilized in equilibrium.

This is not to say that acceptance of RAP necessarily implies rejection of the possibility of fluctuations in economic activity, the occurrence of which implies the possibility of *transitory* variations in the degree to which resources are utilized. But in RAP such variations are portrayed as the result of errors of anticipation, or as a lagging quantity response to (unanticipated) price changes, and may not be interpreted as the result of moving from one long-run equilibrium position to another in response to an exogenous change in the state of effective demand.

We need not tarry over the question of whether it might be possible to translate all statements about changes in the level of effective demand into statements about changes in expectations of prices and quantities.[4] Regardless of one's views on this matter, it is not disputed that, by making the level of effective demand an exogenous determinant of the degree of resource use, the Keynesian Revolution proposed a fundamental change in the frame within which an economy is perceived. In a nutshell, KP proposed to expand the list of necessary givens by adding to RAP's tastes, techniques, and resources an additional item—an indicator of the state of effective demand.

Although over the years Keynesians of various stripes have proposed differing characterizations of capitalist economies, the specification of an exogenously determined level of effective demand is common to all of them. As portrayed in *The General Theory,* the level of effective demand = aggregate income (Y) is defined as the sum of the levels of expen-

---

4. In my opinion, such a translation could be made, but it would be of uncertain utility.

diture on capital goods, investment (I), and on consumption goods, consumption (C).

I varies inversely with the rate of interest and positively with the state of "Animal Spirits" (see below), while C varies positively with the level of Aggregate Income.[5] The interaction of these three variables (Y, I, and C) constitute the exemplar of KP which is portrayed in figure 4 whose axes measure dollar amounts. Exogenously determined Investment is measured by $0I$: the ordinates of the 45-degree line through the origin, $0Y$, measure the aggregate dollar amount spent by purchasers of final goods and the abscissae measure the aggregate amount paid out by producers of these goods. (The construction of $0Y$ reflects the assumption that aggregate expenditure on final output is always equal to aggregate payments by the producers of that output.)

The consumption function, $C(Y)$, relates aggregate expenditure on consumption (C) to aggregate income. Keynes argued that although C always increases with Y, the effect of an increase in Y is to increase C by a lesser amount than the increase in Y. These two assumptions are reflected in figure 4 by making $C(Y)$ positively inclined throughout, but with a slope always less than unity. That the slope of $C(Y)$, called the marginal propensity to consume (MPC), at any point is less than unity assures that it will intersect $0Y$ from above thereby guaranteeing positions of stable local equilibrium at E and E'; E and E' are the points at which $C(Y) + I$ and $C(Y) + I'$ intersect $0Y$.

The effect on aggregate income of an exogenous increase in investment from $0I$ to $0I'$ is to raise aggregate income from $0E$ to $0E'$. It is important to note that $0E' - 0E > 0I' - 0I$. This difference is due to the increase in consumption that results from the increase in income that results from the increase in investment. The magnitude of this discrepancy reflects the operation of the famous investment multiplier (multiplier for short). The multiplier is equal to the reciprocal of one minus the MPC where the latter is defined as the slope of the tangent to $C(Y)$ at the relevant level of Aggregate Income.

Perceived from the side of purchasers, the working out of the multiplier process is a story about the generation of saving. The purchase of consumption goods is made with one part of household income (spend-

5. The relation of C and Y, the consumption function, is more intuitively appealing if Y is interpreted as anticipated income. However, in its simple form KP assumes that for short-run purposes anticipations of income are fairly accurate, so that anticipated income is equal to actual income.

ing) and the purchase of investment goods with the remainder (saving). In the Keynesian accounting scheme, now generally accepted, an increase in aggregate investment (production of investment goods) generates an addition to aggregate household income exactly equal to what would be required to generate the additional aggregate saving needed to consummate its purchase.[6] The multiplier process is the obverse side of the process of income enhancement that generates the savings.

The marginal propensity to consume determines the amount by which household income must increase in order to generate the necessary savings. But MPC is, by definition, the residual of the increment in aggregate household income that the community (i.e., all households taken together) chooses not to save. Therefore, decreasing the marginal propensity to save $(1 - MPC)$ will increase the magnitude of the increase in income (the multiplier effect) that results from a given increase in aggregate investment.

While no longer fashionable, in the late 1930s and 40s there were many attempts to construct and utilize multipliers of one kind or another, for example, foreign trade multipliers, government expenditure multipliers, industry expenditure multipliers, and so forth. The critical step in such constructions is to find a variable of interest whose aggregate dollar quantity is sufficiently large as to have an appreciable effect upon aggregate expenditure, and thereby to generate still further increases in aggregate income, and so on.

An important feature of this exemplar is its conflation of real and nominal values of the variables. Figure 4 says nothing about prices and quantities: it speaks only of dollar aggregates. For all that the diagram tells us, an increase in aggregate expenditure could reflect solely an increase in prices with no change in employment or output. But this would be contrary to its intention. The diagram is constructed on the assumption that both the wage rate and the level of product prices are "more or less" fixed so that variations of dollar magnitudes reflect variations in real quantities.[7] This means that for all points to the left of F, the levels of output and employment vary with the level of (exogenously determined) aggregate

6. In the Keynesian accounting system, saving necessarily equals investment; $S = I$. In the early days of the Keynesian Revolution, there was great difficulty in getting the economics community to accept the logical necessity of this identity, and the confusion was eliminated only after much debate in the professional journals.

7. N.B. Figure 4 is constructed on the assumption that there is one kind of labor and two final products: an investment good and a consumption good.

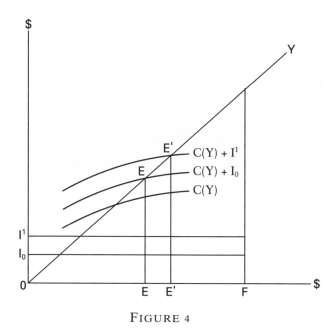

FIGURE 4

investment. It is assumed that aggregate employment increases with aggregate output; F corresponds to an output level at which a fixed supply of labor is fully employed.

Thus any level of output to the left of F will imply the existence of excess labor supply. In RAP this would lead to a reduction in the price of labor (the money wage rate) that would continue until the quantity demanded once again equalled the quantity supplied. But in KP, this reaction does not occur: for a variety of reasons the level of money wages is not free to balance supply and demand in the labor market. In KP the money wage rate is assumed to be fixed and (at all points to the left of F) the level of product prices is assumed to vary with the money wage rate and to be the same at all levels of output. In other words, figure 4 is constructed on the assumption that movements of the levels of wages and product prices have but a negligible affect on aggregate output and employment which (to the left of F) is governed by the interaction of Investment and the Consumption Function.[8] Whatever effect movements of wages and prices may have on the level of employment must be chan-

8. The rationale for this assumption is discussed below.

neled through their impact—if any—on the determinants of these variables.

For the entire range of Y values to the left of F the critical implication of RAP that all resources are employed—that every individual is on his resource constraint at equilibrium prices—is violated. There is unused productive capacity, especially unemployed labor. The RAP dictum, "there is no free lunch," does not apply. Everyone could have a higher (real) income if only Investment were increased, or if the Consumption Function were shifted upward.[9] What is scarce is not resources, but opportunities to use them, that is, employment opportunities. Attempts to save do not have the effect of increasing the capital stock, but, in the absence of sufficient demand for investment goods, are aborted through reductions in aggregate household income.

The establishment of these propositions, all contrary to RAP, was the objective of *The General Theory*. Keynes did not contend that they applied everywhere, but only to the left of F. He conceded, more or less, that RAP would apply at F—full employment—but insisted that his theory was more general than RAP in that it covered the area to the left of F where attempts to apply RAP would lead to incorrect results. What Keynes was trying to do was to supplement the conceptual organization of RAP with that of figure 4.

As can be readily perceived, KP is not rich in implications. Its relevance is limited to analysis of the implications of exogenously caused shifts in the general level of economic activity, with given resources, due to changes in the attitude of resource owners toward engaging in such activity. The significance of KP for this book derives from the fact that RAP precludes the possibility that such shifts of attitude could have this result.

So far as the general public was concerned, Keynes might well have stopped with the argument of figure 4. However, he wanted to persuade the economics community as well as the general public, and this required consideration of "details" that cannot be encompassed in that argument.

FULL EMPLOYMENT AND BOTTLENECKS

Even in the 1930s there was no denying that the economy sometimes got to full employment, and that a "general theory" must apply to that state

9. That is, if the propensity to save were reduced.

as well as to the points left of *F.* However, Keynes's insight and his paradigm had relatively little to contribute to the analysis of a fully employed economy. In effect he was willing to leave the full employment economy within the domain of RAP—or the version of it current in 1935—which he termed "classical economics."

However, it could not be pretended that possible states of the world could be dichotomized into those of full employment and those of underemployment. Clearly, there were intermediate states characterized by supply bottlenecks and temporary shortages of one thing or another that required analysis: here, KP would not apply without amendment.

Partly to avoid giving further offense to the ideas of the professional community he was seeking to persuade, and partly because he remained in many respects a Marshallian neoclassical, Keynes provided an analysis of states intermediate between full employment and underemployment that represented no major break with RAP. In particular, this analysis assumed that product prices were set by competition (price equals marginal cost), that marginal cost of production and supply price increased with the level of output, and that the marginal product of labor diminished with employment (and the level of output).[10] The structure of this argument, and its consistency with KP have been a source of continuing professional discussion, most of which is beside the present point.

Despite the problems associated with making a sharp dichotomy between states of full employment and states of underemployment, I shall continue to make it because it greatly simplifies the exposition without distorting the spirit of *The General Theory.*

INVOLUNTARY UNEMPLOYMENT AND EQUILIBRIUM

All points of figure 4 to the left of *F* are constructed on the assumption that the levels of wages and product prices are historically determined, that is, given. While it is convenient to interpret this assumption literally, and assume that they are invariant, the spirit of the argument does not require this. The spirit of the argument is that the economic forces of primary interest are those that determine the level of investment and the position of the consumption function. Any influence that wages and prices might have on aggregate output and employment must be channeled through their impact upon I and $C(Y)$. All that this argument requires is

10. The relevant argument is contained in *The General Theory,* chapters 20 and 21.

the less rigid assumption that even if wages and prices were to move, the effect of such movements *as are feasible* (see below) upon the positions of I and $C(Y)$ would be negligible.

The relation of figure 4 to unemployment is as follows: (1) to the left of F, aggregate employment varies in the same direction as Y so that (scaling problems aside) Y may serve as an indicator of employment. (2) The labor supply (i.e., the number of people seeking employment) is given by F and is the same at all levels of Y. Hence (to the left of F) the percentage of the labor force that is unemployed is always equal to 1 minus the percentage employed and is an inverse to the percentage employed. As this percentage is determined by the positions of I and $C(Y)$, and cannot be altered by the individual actions of those affected, the affected individuals are said to be *involuntarily* unemployed.

According to KP, the structure of the economy is like a game of musical chairs with the level of aggregate demand determining the number of chairs. If the number of chairs should be less than the number of players, some players must remain unseated, although the rules of the game do not enable us to predict which: figure 4 does not indicate which individuals will be unemployed; only their quantity.

Since it is assumed that all persons in the labor force (labor supply) would prefer to be employed at the going wage, it follows that those (somehow) selected for unemployment would desire to change places with those who have jobs, presumably by offering to work for less. The problem for KP is to explain why this does not happen. In *The General Theory,* and ever since, the problem of reconciling the appearance of involuntary unemployment with the assumption of a free labor market has exercised adherents of KP, and those of RAP. The issue has been a veritable cockpit of paradigmatic conflict, and a focal point for the development of economic theory.

For RAP there cannot be both involuntary unemployment (or involuntary anything) and equilibrium: equilibrium requires that every individual be at an optimum given his tastes and resources. The existence of involuntary unemployment is tantamount to the existence of a quantity restriction on the sale of labor services, which is precluded by RAP.

KP explanations of involuntary unemployment usually involve, in some way, the notion of "sticky wages." As we have already seen, apart from organized exchanges, all prices are more or less sticky: they do not vary with sufficient rapidity as to make markets clear continuously. Certainly there are no cases of labor markets that function like organized exchanges, and it is generally agreed that wage rates are among the stickiest of all prices. The particular causes of wage stickiness, and their effects on the speed of wage adjustment, vary greatly from one labor market to another, but such differentia are not to the present point.[11]

Keynesians argue that unemployment is involuntary because it results from institutional restrictions (customs, conventions, and union rules) on wage movements that are beyond the control of the individual wage earner.[12] (These restrictions define the "feasible movements" of wages referred to above.) Arguably, such restrictions may be the consequence of attempts to minimize the cost of labor turnover, as will be discussed in chapter 8. Moreover, as we shall see, it might even be rational for individual job seekers to observe such institutional restrictions despite their unemployment. But, regardless of possible rationalizations of wage stickiness, KP contends that the job seeking procedures of unemployed individuals—particularly offers to work for unusually low wages—are effectively constrained by conventions and customs as evidenced by the fact that such institutions are respected in the face of persisting unemployment. However, as we shall see below, RAP offers an alternative interpretation of the seeming involuntariness of unemployment.

INVESTMENT AND SAVING

In figure 4, the level of aggregate Investment (I) is taken as a datum: but this is for expository purposes only. In KP, I is functionally related to the rate of interest. Specifically, the level of I is the quantity at which the marginal efficiency of capital (mec) is equal to the rate of interest (r). The mec of any given investment is defined as the rate at which the stream of its anticipated returns must be discounted in order to equal the cost of making it. So long as this rate exceeds the rate at which money can be borrowed, or can be earned by lending it out, it will be advantageous to make the investment. Thus, arraying all possible investment projects available to members of a community from highest to lowest, it is possible to generate an mec schedule in which the quantity of I undertaken always

---

11. A good introduction to the subject of wage adjustments is Arthur Okun (1981), especially chapters 2 and 3. See also below, chapter 8.

12. In *The General Theory* it was also argued (Chapter 19) that in the absence of such restrictions an economy might become more unstable (i.e., in response to a given decline in aggregate demand output and employment might decline more than it actually does), but that is another issue.

increases as *r* decreases. That is, as the rate of interest declines, the number of projects that it will be profitable to undertake increases.[13]

The mec schedule (and its negative slope) is essentially an RAP notion that Keynes borrowed (with due acknowledgment) from Irving Fisher (1930). It had been generally understood before publication of *The General Theory* that the locus of this schedule was heavily dependent upon the state of opinion among investors about future profits, which Keynes termed "animal spirits." Thus the level of *I* was made dependent upon the relation of animal spirits—the state of business confidence—to the rate of interest. In itself this was nothing new. Novelty arose from the manner in which mec was integrated into the picture of the total economy.

This integration involved relating aggregate saving to aggregate investment. *I* was determined by mec and the rate of interest (*r*). Aggregate saving (*S*) depended primarily upon the level of aggregate income, and possibly, but to a much lesser degree, upon *r*. Thus the level of *S* generated by a given level of *Y*—call it desired savings—might greatly exceed the level of *I* called forth by the state of animal spirits.[14] In RAP, such a state of affairs would cause a decline in *r* which would equilibrate *S* and *I* without any change in *Y*. In KP the effect of "excess desired saving" upon *r* would be indirect and slow, but the reaction upon *Y* would be quick and powerful: the primary effect of excess desired saving would be to reduce both *S* and *C* through a negative effect upon *Y* powerful enough to swamp any countervailing effect that might come to *Y* through a decline in *r*.

Thus if at a hypothetical level of *Y* corresponding to full employment, desired *S* exceeded *I*—or what comes to the same thing, *C* was too small to absorb all available resources[15]—that level of *Y* could not be supported and *Y* would fall until it reached a level where *S* and *I* were equal. That is, desire to save too much, or consume too little, would cause a loss of potential income thereby generating involuntary unemployment.

13. There is yet a second reason for mec to decline as *I* increases: at any given capital stock the marginal cost of producing still further capital goods will increase as the rate at which they are produced increases. This is a conventional RAP (in this case Marshallian) proposition.

14. The distinction between desired and realized (actual) savings is essential to the coherence of the KP. The relation between these two concepts of savings caused great confusion and debate in the late 1930s. However, the issues involved have long since been laid to rest and there is no point in resurrecting them here.

15. Note that *C* is defined as *Y-S*.

This was the root of the Keynesian view that an economy might be too thrifty for its own prosperity, and that more rather than less saving might be desirable. Because it was believed that high income recipients tended to save a greater fraction of their income than recipients with lower incomes, this argument served not only as a basis for discouraging thrift generally, but also as ground for an ancillary redistribution of income to the advantage of lower income recipients.

While nothing in RAP should lead its adherents to favor more rather than less thrift or to oppose a more egalitarian distribution of income, this aspect of KP drew a great deal of adverse attention from economists who were favorably disposed to RAP. (The reason for this will be discussed in chapter 10.) In the depression of the 1930s, the antithrift message of *The General Theory* had great resonance both within the profession and in the general public, though this is no longer the case. Contemporary Keynesians rarely argue for measures to discourage thrift, and while they may retain a (faint) egalitarian bias, such bias is almost never rationalized by arguing that redistributing income is needed in order to prop up effective demand.

THE RATE OF INTEREST

In KP, there is but one rate of interest: the return on a riskless bond. The effect of default risk[16] on r is (de facto) subsumed under animal spirits and impinges on I through the mec schedule.[17] No distinction is made between long- and short-term bonds, so that there is but one rate of interest to consider. The asset owner is viewed as having to allocate his liquid assets between cash (which yields no interest) and bonds. Cash is assumed to have general acceptability in transactions while bonds do not. Therefore a rational person will hold bonds only if they yield interest; in other words, interest is a payment needed to offset the greater convenience of having cash (liquidity) to make transactions.

The quantity of cash that any individual (or all of them together) will wish to hold varies inversely with the premium paid (interest rate) for holding bonds, and with the inconvenience entailed by being "cash short." The amount of cash "needed" at any given time to avoid a given degree of inconvenience is assumed to increase with the volume of transactions. For the community as a whole, this is taken to imply that, at a given price

16. Default risk is the risk of nonrepayment by a borrower.

17. There is little discussion of this point in *The General Theory*. As will be seen later in this chapter, this omission has contributed to an overemphasis on the "liquidity trap."

level, the demand for cash will increase with the level of aggregate output. In addition to this transaction demand for cash, individuals may wish to hold more or less cash depending upon their expectations about future movements of interest rates (bond prices) or prices of goods.

The rate of interest is determined by the condition that the bond market clears and that all of the stock of money is held by willing owners. The stock of (nominal) money is determined by the fiat of the monetary authority (a central bank or other). All of this is very similar to the paradigm adjunct used to assimilate money to RAP.[18] But there are differences: (1) to the left of F the price level of goods (output) is assumed to be unrelated to the stock of money, but determined by the money wage rate which is historically given; (2) the demand for money varies both with the level of aggregate output and the level of product prices; (3) while the rate of interest depends upon the supply of money, it is unrelated to the rate of savings. To facilitate discussion of these differences, let us integrate the diverse parts of KP.

IS-LM

The customary way of presenting this integration is by means of the famous *IS-LM* diagram (figure 5).[19] The vertical axis of this diagram represents the rate of return on assets, and the horizontal axis the level of aggregate (real) output; the diagram is constructed on the assumption of a fixed money wage rate which is a historical datum. (Interpret this to mean that the wage rate is going to be whatever it has been in the immediate past, regardless of what happens to *IS* and *LM*.) The abscissae of the negatively inclined *IS* curve give the levels of aggregate income that would be generated by the interaction of a given mec schedule with a given consumption function at the corresponding rate of interest; each point on the *IS* curve corresponds to a position such as E' in figure 4.

The *LM* curve gives the interest rate and level of output couples at which a given stock of money would be (willingly) held. *LM* is drawn on the assumption of a given stock of nominal money (M) and of a given money wage rate (w). Increases in M will reduce r at any given level of output and decreases in w will also decrease r. The effect of w upon *LM*

18. See above, chapter 3.
19. The locus classicus of this exposition of The General Theory (and of *IS-LM*) is Hicks (1937). While figure 5 is an oversimplified version of the original diagram, it is useful for the present discussion.

works via its effect in lowering the level of product prices which reduces the demand for cash balances at any level of aggregate output. Thus increasing the money supply or lowering the money wage rate are equally efficacious means of increasing output and reducing unemployment by shifting *LM* downward.

Though it may have a horizontal section in figure 5, *LM* is assumed normally to slope upward, reflecting the underlying assumption that as aggregate output increases so does the (transaction) demand for cash at a given rate of interest, thereby making the equilibrium rate of interest rise with aggregate output at any given stock of money. The intersection of the *IS* and *LM* curves determines an equilibrium position, *G*, characterized by a level of aggregate output such that the rate of return from investing a dollar is equal to the rate of interest that could be earned by lending it to someone else to invest. As drawn, *G* represents a position of less than full employment.

In a nutshell, the *IS-LM* diagram determines the equilibrium levels of output and employment and the rate of interest given the money wage rate, the stock of money, the determinants of the mec schedule and the consumption function, and the assumption that the product price level is determined by the money wage rate.

Apart from a possible "liquidity trap" (see below), there is nothing in *IS-LM* to suggest that lowering *LM* would not suffice to restore full employment whatever the level of investment. In other words, either an expansionary monetary policy or a reduction in the level of money wages—if pushed far enough—would suffice to offset the effect of any decline in aggregate investment on the level of output and employment. But such a result was not what Keynes wanted: his objective was to show that the functioning of a laissez-faire economy might—under certain highly relevant circumstances—lead to underemployment of resources from which it could be rescued only by direct action of the government (public investment).

That is, Keynes argued that the state of animal spirits might sink so low that there was no positive rate of interest that would induce enough aggregate (private) investment to reach full employment; reducing the interest rate could not accomplish this objective by itself. In such situations—which (it was contended) were exemplified by conditions in the United States and the United Kingdom of the 1930s—full employment could be attained (with a given consumption function) only through in-

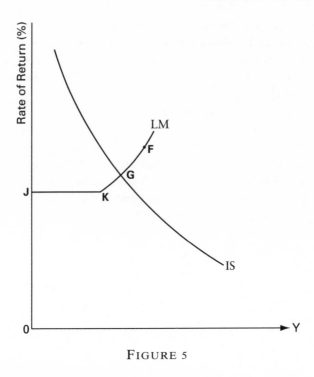

FIGURE 5

creased public investment or subsidies (e.g., tax concessions) to private investors. And these were the policies that Keynes proposed, especially public investment.

So far as the general public was concerned, *The General Theory* was a rationalization of the need for public investment to increase employment, and for eschewing wage cuts as a route to that objective. But while not ignoring these implications, the analytical interest of the economics community was even more piqued by the implied behavior of the interest rate in the presence of an alleged shortage of aggregate investment opportunities (excess of *desired* aggregate saving over *desired* aggregate investment) at full employment. However low the rate of interest might be, it remained above zero: why didn't competition drive it still lower?

The answer suggested by KP was the *liquidity trap*. This phenomenon is portrayed in figure 5 by the flat section of *LM* (between *J* and *K*) which indicates that the community is holding more cash than it needs comfortably to support the transactions required by the current level of output. From this it can easily be shown that the community would not allow a larger quantity of cash to drive the rate of interest below its existing level. In such a situation action by the monetary authority to increase investment through expansion of the money supply would have no effect upon the level of output.

Keynes's rationalization of the liquidity trap was that at sufficiently low rates of interest the prospect of a guaranteed interest payment became insufficient to induce savers to risk capital loss from unexpected increases in the interest rate. The disputed validity of this argument soon became lost in the discussion of the Pigou effect (see below), but in any case its salience for KP was always much exaggerated.

The exaggerated importance of the liquidity trap for KP was an artifact of the construction of the mec schedule. As set forth in The General Theory, a saver is faced with the option of investing (i.e., taking a share of an investment opportunity) or lending his resources without risk of default at the gilt-edge rate of interest. By excluding securities attended with some default risk, the whole range of (more or less) risky bonds, promissory notes, and so on was swept into the category of investment, and variations in the credit worthiness of potential borrowers were subsumed under the category of determinants of the locus of the investment function.

Thus a low state of animal spirits might reflect the dim view taken by savers of the credit worthiness of prospective borrowers (i.e., the high premium they demanded to offset perceived default risk) as well as an adverse perception of profit opportunities by investors. Savers demanding only gilt-edge securities in exchange for their cash might indeed be unable to find borrowers at any positive rate of interest while would-be borrowers of uncertain credit status were unable to obtain loans even at very high rates of interest. A "sufficiently complete" set of securities markets would provide intermediate assets that would enable risk averse savers indirectly to bankroll risky investors, with the issuers of the intermediate securities earning a middleman's profit for risk bearing. But, unfortunately, the conceptual organization of KP provides no way of discussing the role of financial intermediation in a capitalist economy, and the consequences of its intermittent breakdowns.[20]

Before leaving this brief review of KP I feel it necessary to warn the reader that the *IS-LM* synthesis of RAP and KP associated with figure 5 is but one of a number of attempts to interrelate the two sets of ideas. Although the most widely known and (probably) the easiest to present,

20. For a good discussion of this subject see J. G. Gurley and E. S. Shaw (1960).

there is no consensus that *IS-LM* is the best—or even a satisfactory—
method of analyzing this interrelation. Among the alternatives that the
reader might consult are Lange (1944), Patinkin (1965), Clower (1965)
and Leijonhufvud (1968). However, all of these and others are highly technical and frequently mathematical.

To establish a grand synthesis of RAP and KP is a continuing challenge
to economic theorists that elicits their ingenuity and technical skill. But
for less specialized purposes, one would not go far astray if she considered
the two paradigms as alternative and disparate ways of viewing an economy, KP requiring a variable to represent some measure of "degree of
resource utilization" and RAP allowing no place for such a variable. Ability to distinguish the times and circumstances where one paradigm should
be applied from those requiring the other is no small part of the economist's expertise.

THE CONSUMPTION FUNCTION AND MONETARISM

Despite the deficiencies of KP in accommodating financial intermediation, this was not an important cause of neoclassical objection to the notion of a liquidity trap. That objection arose from consideration of the
effect of an increased stock of money balances (at a given rate of interest
and given price level) upon consumption expenditure. Such an increase
would be tantamount to an increase in real wealth which, in RAP, would
lead to an increase in consumption. Thus, regardless of the effect on investment, an increase in the stock of money (or its equivalent, a reduction
in the level of money wages and product prices) would have the effect of
increasing the levels of output and employment and thereby maintain the
disputed claim that a capitalist economy working solely through the operation of free markets would—eventually—restore full employment. The
practical importance of this effect—called the Pigou effect after its putative discoverer—was much disputed.[21] But no matter: it provided a handle
for attacking the Keynesian Paradigm.

In the structure of KP, consumption is assigned a passive role. Via the
multiplier, it serves as an instrument to transform a given amount of aggregate investment to an equilibrium level of aggregate income. But in
order for it to do this, it is necessary to portray the rate of current aggre-

---

21. A. C. Pigou (1947). Pigou did not consider the point of much importance as a guide
to policy: his concern was to maintain the integrity of RAP. For a recent discussion of the
issue see James Tobin (1993).

gate consumption as being dominated by the level of current income, as in The General Theory.[22]

The validity of this portrayal has been the subject of much dispute, both on theoretical and empirical grounds. But it is unnecessary for us to consider this extensive and convoluted literature. In the mid-1990s the discussion of saving behavior has progressed far beyond its state in the 1930s, and is dominated by an RAP view characterized by the assumption that saving decisions are best portrayed as resulting from attempts to maximize utility over time: there is no longer a distinctly Keynesian view of saving. An important reason for the demise of the Keynesian consumption function is general agreement that the dichotomization of aggregate expenditure into saving and consumption is inappropriate for analyzing changes in the level of economic activity. Expenditure on consumer durables, residential housing, and education all function as outlets for saving even though they are governed by household rather than business decisions, and would therefore have been considered as consumption in The General Theory.

But however saving and investment are defined, there is a persisting Keynesian view that (1) a substantial component of aggregate expenditure is sensitive to the state of animal spirits, and therefore given to marked fluctuations regardless of movements of relative prices or interest rates while (2) a substantial part of household income is committed to certain types of saving (e.g., debt repayment, contractually mandated saving plans) that cannot readily be invested in highly risky ventures. As the aggregate amount of "committed saving" is insensitive to variations in animal spirits, such variations produce marked fluctuations in the difference between (1) and (2) and lead to similarly directed variations in aggregate expenditure that cannot be readily offset by movements of interest rates and/or relative prices.

This view is counter to the RAP contention that in the absence of inappropriate fluctuations in the stock of real cash balances, movements of interest rates and relative prices will prevent long run variations in the level of aggregate expenditure and output.[23] In effect it is argued that,

22. To be sure, in *The General Theory* the consumption function included the rate of interest as an argument—i.e., $C = C(Y, r)$—and also, though as an obiter dictum, the level of wealth. However, the role assigned to these variables as determinants of the rate of aggregate saving at a given level of aggregate income was distinctly secondary.

23. The distinction between real and nominal (or money) values is critical to appreciation of RAP arguments about aggregates. Real values refer to aggregates whose elements

regardless of low animal spirits, if the stock of real money is maintained intact, the chain of intermediate financial markets will so adjust risk premiums that savings will either find investment outlets or be consumed without reducing aggregate output.

This RAP contention is part of what is popularly known as *monetarism*. This doctrine stems directly from the RAP adjunct that explains the relation between the nominal stock of money and the general price level. The idea is that $MV = Y$ where Y is aggregate expenditure as defined in KP; M is the community's stock of (nominal) money and V is the (average) velocity of circulation of money in the time interval to which Y refers. It is assumed that V changes only very slowly and is insensitive to the state of animal spirits so that Y varies (approximately) with M, with relative prices and interest rates (including risk premiums) adjusting as needed. Obviously, an economy that behaves in this manner will be one in which the Pigou effect operates to increase aggregate output in response to increases in the real stock of money.

Monetarists do not claim that relative prices and interest rates function so as to keep the economy continuously at full employment. They recognize that sluggish adjustments of wages and product prices may and have led to short-run variations in output and employment.[24] The issue between them and Keynesians is whether there are substantial intervals during which the ongoing but sluggish adjustment processes may be ignored, with output and employment treated as variables subject to purposive manipulation by monetary-fiscal authorities.

KP, UNEMPLOYMENT, AND MICROFOUNDATIONS

The neoclassical response to the assertion that there might be involuntary unemployment in a "free market economy" was not to deny the possibility of such a fact, but to reject the idea that such a state of affairs might represent an equilibrium. That is, the neoclassicals of the 1940s and 50s envisaged the possibility of substantial time periods during which the

---

are valued at constant prices; i.e., are deflated. Money or nominal values are undeflated. RAP holds that economic laws will hold only when expressed in real terms. While I shall not elaborate, it is appropriate to note that the analytical basis for the distinction between real and money values applies literally only to equilibrium prices: making and applying the proper distinction when one price or more is not an equilibrium price requires case by case analysis.

24. See, for example, the discussion of Milton Friedman and Anna J. Schwartz (1982), pp. 41–58.

economy was out of equilibrium and the behavior of prices and quantities failed to conform to the implications of RAP. However, this concept of equilibrium was applied only to aggregate variables, that is, to aggregate quantities of an industry or an entire economy, but not to individual decision makers who were assumed always to be in equilibrium (optimizing). This disparity of treatment was inconsistent with a literal interpretation of RAP, a fact that disturbed a growing number of RAP adherents.

Beginning in the late 1960s, these adherents increasingly insisted that equilibrium required that every decision be an optimization, and that lagging adjustments of prices and quantities be explained as the result of explicitly specified intertemporal optimization plans, and not attributed to the working of vaguely described "frictions." To make clear the implications of this view for labor market behavior, let us contrast it with that of KP.

Though not always made explicit, the KP view of the typical labor market participant is that in each period she stands ready to supply a unit (say a standard work week) of "her kind" of labor at an existing money wage, sometimes finding an employer and sometimes not, but without interrelation between her labor supply in one period and in the next.

By contrast, modern RAP adherents—sometimes called New Classicals[25]—consider the typical worker to have an intertemporal labor supply plan which relates her reservation wage and desired hours of work in any given period to (1) her experience in previous periods, (2) her expectations of wage rates and probability of finding employment in future periods, and (3) a long-term (e.g., lifetime) plan for maximizing utility which determines, inter alia, her planned long-term labor supply.[26] This plan is based on the assumption that the employment outcome in each period is the realization of a stochastic process in which, given the reservation

25. K. D. Hoover (1988) provides an excellent statement and critique of the views of this group of economists. The leading figures in this group are Robert Lucas, Thomas Sargent, Neil Wallace, and Edward Prescott. The identification of RAP with New Classical views requires some explanation. Many RAP adherents are unfamiliar with the details of New Classical arguments, while others would accept them only in part. However, the New Classicals are the only group that has systematically required that all explanations of behavior be consistent with the RAP requirement that such behavior be the outcome of expected utility maximization by every resource owner. This methodological purism is at the root both of the appeal of the New Classicals to the larger body of RAP adherents, and to the resistance of some of the "more practically minded" among them.

26. The reservation wage is the lowest wage that would be accepted rather than rejecting a job offer.

wage- and job-search procedure embodied in the plan, some probability exists that she will be unemployed. While such an outcome may be unsatisfactory, it need not be "involuntary" because a rational job-seeker might choose to repeat her behavior if she were again confronted with the identical circumstances prevailing at the outset of the period in which she failed to find a job.

For the New Classical, unemployment in a given period is one possible outcome of a stochastic process: it reflects a situation in which a worker failed to obtain a job that she would have accepted. But it does not necessarily represent a waste of time: it may present an opportunity for activities like returning to school, or traveling, which are parts of a lifetime labor-supply plan. Because of having so used "unemployed" time, a worker may accept employment at a later date that she would otherwise have declined; or she may acquiesce in present unemployment because of having "overworked" previously. Thus, in any given period, unemployment may reflect intertemporal substitution of labor supply rather than a permanent loss of desired employment and potential output. The extent to which unemployment in a given period causes subsequent increases in labor supply, or reflects previous "deposits" of work made in anticipation of later withdrawals from the labor force, cannot be determined from data referring only to the current period.

From the viewpoint of KP, given-year unemployment and the corresponding fall of actual below-potential output, reflect permanent loss of production whose magnitude can be measured from current year statistics without need to examine linkages with events in preceding or future years. New Classicals stress the importance of such possible linkages: for them the economic significance of unemployment in a given year can only be appraised (if at all) by comparing actual and potential output over a long period of time.

The possibility of intertemporal substitution of labor supply leads to a non-Keynesian interpretation of unemployment. Though many of the currently unemployed would accept employment if offered, few are "driven to desperation" by a perceived lack of present work opportunities. This accounts for their unwillingness to "take any job" and thereby drive wages into the free fall which a one-period model might lead one to expect; this leaves the scarce job opportunities for the more desperate among the unemployed and relaxes the downward pressure on the money wage rate.

To be sure, a period of high unemployment—or better, of low employment—is a time of low household income and resulting dissatisfaction. This dissatisfaction is greatly intensified by uncertainty about when the bad times will end: it is uncertainty as to its duration, as much as the fact of current unemployment, that is responsible for the audible distress of many of the unemployed. But to account for this distress does not require abandonment of RAP: it requires only recognition of the importance of intertemporal linkages of labor supply, a matter to which older RAP adherents had paid insufficient attention.

As might be surmised, the New Classicals do not have much use for the unemployment concept, and prefer to operate with the dichotomy of gainful employment (or some synonym) and time used within the household. To implement the notion of unemployment, which reflects the difference between labor force membership and employment, it is necessary that those not gainfully employed report whether they are (or are not) in the labor force—roughly, available for employment. Typically, such reports turn on statements of intention by putative job seekers as these appear in answers to a questionnaire.

While not essential to the paradigm, RAP adherents (including the New Classicals) have a strong affinity for propositions expressing relations among behavioral variables, especially about price-quantity behavior, and a corresponding aversion to propositions that cannot be so characterized. Accordingly, they prefer to avoid propositions in any way dependent upon reports of frustrated intentions, of which arguments about unemployment, and a fortiori involuntary unemployment, are prime examples. To the New Classical, any valid statement about the quantity of labor service performed can be made in terms of observed prices and quantities without reference to reports of frustrated job searches.

KP AND THE PRICE LEVEL: THE UNEMPLOYMENT-INFLATION TRADEOFF

The effect of the New Classicals' argument is to make the *IS-LM* diagram of figure 5 conceptually inapplicable to an RAP-compatible analysis. But, the validity of its argument notwithstanding, this diagram is a very convenient point of departure for a discussion of KP at full employment.

In KP, movements of aggregate output along *LM* to the left of *F* (due to shifts of *IS*) have been assumed not to affect either the wage rate or of the general price level of products which it determines. At *F*, shifts of *LM* cannot affect aggregate output, but only the level of product prices. This would suffice for the purposes of expositing KP. If Keynes had been un-concerned with professional opinion, or less of a neoclassical economist himself, he might have put the argument in some such oversimplified form. Whatever the reason, Keynes chose to relate the price level to the level of output for points to the left of F. This was not only an obeisance to the RAP view that, with a fixed capital stock and a given wage rate, marginal cost (and product price) must increase with output,[27] but also (and more important) recognition that as the economy moved closer to full employment, w would tend to rise.

The effect of this was to shift focus from an economy in which—at less than full employment—the rate of investment and the consumption function determined the level of aggregate output at a fixed level of product prices, to one in which monetary authorities must choose from a menu of levels of aggregate output and product prices, with greater output and employment obtainable only at the cost of higher product prices. While this construction helped to reconcile KP with RAP, it had the distinct drawback of blurring KP's exemplar. No longer could increased aggregate output be "purchased for free," but only in exchange for higher product prices; most Keynesians did not believe this tradeoff was required—at least at high levels of unemployment.

Admitting that w would tend to rise with the level of aggregate output (i.e., with proximity to full employment) removed w from the list of vari-ables at the disposal of policy makers. In economists' jargon, it made the money wage rate endogenous. The question then arose as to how w be-haves. The commonsense view that money wages rise more slowly as the level of unemployment increases found empirical support in a paper of A. W. Phillips (1958). While hardly qualifying as news, and despite a lack of immediate theoretical support, the argument of Phillips's article at-tracted wide professional interest; soon calculations of employment-inflation tradeoffs filled technical journals and, with but a short lag, gov-ernment documents and the media as well.[28]

27. This proposition was resisted by many (most?) Keynesians almost from the begin-ning. By 1990, the appeal of KP to its adherents seemed to derive as much from its desire to avoid the assumption of competitive product markets as from desire to allow for depar-tures from full employment. For examples, see R. J. Gordon (1990) and N. G. Mankiw (1989).

28. Although Phillips's article related unemployment to the level of money wages rather than to product prices, it was generally accepted that movements of the former would cause

Thus, as of the early 1960s, the Keynesian position on monetary-fiscal policy became one of stressing the existence of a tradeoff between higher levels of output and higher rates of inflation (the unemployment-inflation tradeoff), and its adherents were usually found among those urging the authorities to bear the inflationary cost of such measures as were needed to increase employment.[29] The opposing view was (and is) that public perception that macroeconomic policy was directed toward accepting a rate of inflation higher than what is current, would cause an increase in the supply prices of inputs, especially of wage rates.[30] This, in turn, would reduce the effect on output and employment of any given stimulus to effective demand, thereby increasing the amount of stimulus required to reach an initial employment target. But such an increase in stimulus would give an additional fillip to input prices, further increasing the magnitude of the required stimulus, and so on. It is easy to show that the end result of this process would be to drive the effect of monetary-fiscal policy on output and employment to zero; which means that monetary-fiscal policy would not be able to affect aggregate output and employment, but only the rate of inflation.

In essence this argument is an adjunct to RAP to cover situations where there is unemployment. The idea is that one consequence of the presence of transaction costs in labor markets is that normally some workers will be temporarily without engagements (i.e., unemployed). The expected number of these at any time is the equilibrium, or "natural" rate of unemployment.[31] Regardless of whether the natural rate of unemployment is equal to what would exist in full employment—a matter of consid-

---

movements of the latter, so that the two were conflated in calculations of unemployment-inflation tradeoffs.

29. The reader will note a shift of perspective from that of the 1930s when Keynesians (like others) analyzed the relations of wage and price *levels*, to that of post–World War II (up to the present) when economists speak of the relation between rates of change of these variables. The presumption is that some inflation is to be expected; the policy question becomes, "how much?"

30. Obviously, such an argument implies that the supply of labor depends at least partially upon the real wage rate.

31. The expression "natural rate of unemployment" was introduced by Milton Friedman, and is used in a manner analogous to Knut Wicksell's "natural rate of interest," which was its probable source of inspiration. As the term "natural rate" came to acquire some negative resonance, it has fallen into desuetude and been replaced by the acronym NAIRU (Non Accelerating Inflation Rate of Unemployment).

erable dispute—attempts to reduce unemployment below this level through monetary policy can have only temporary success.[32] That is, the equilibrium rate of unemployment, like that of other quantity variables in RAP models, is independent of monetary policy.

The considerable appeal of this theoretical argument was greatly reinforced by the appearance of stagflation in the 1970s.[33] Exogenous increases in raw material prices at levels of aggregate output well below full employment, and a responding increase in labor supply prices—especially of unionized labor—markedly reduced the salience of the unemployment-inflation tradeoff as a determinant of macroeconomic policy. Although the high unemployment levels of the 1980s (persisting in Europe into the 1990s) have kept the possibility of exploiting an unemployment-inflation tradeoff on the agenda of economic policy makers, the memory of stagflation has prevented any return to the confident pre-1970 presumption that some tradeoff will always exist.

Nevertheless, contemporary Keynesians continue to view the possible exploitation of an unemployment-inflation tradeoff as a live option for macroeconomic policy. The flavor of their thinking is well presented in Alan Blinder (1992).[34] The essence of the argument is that the social cost of inflation is exaggerated and, hyperinflation aside, is in any case less than that of unemployment, whose cost falls largely on the poor.

To the argument that an apparent unemployment-inflation tradeoff would disappear as soon as it was generally perceived that the government was attempting to exploit it, the Keynesian answer is some amalgam of the following: (1) both the fact and the perception of a systematic government policy arise so slowly that there is ample time for monetary-fiscal stimulus to work on the level of output before being countered by increasing supply prices of inputs; (2) once "inflationary psychology" takes hold, or even before, the stimulus can be turned off so that inflation will not accelerate; (3) noise in the mechanism that generates macroeconomic policy is such that there is little danger that a succession of "go and then stop" bursts of

32. This implies that the equilibrium unemployment percentage can be reduced only by "structural" changes; i.e., changes in the process by which job seekers are matched with prospective employers.

33. Though this theoretical argument is much in the spirit of the New Classicals, it stems from papers by Friedman (1968) and Phelps (1967), neither of whom would be identified as a New Classical.

34. Also see, "Symposium on The Natural Rate of Unemployment," in the *Journal of Economic Perspectives* 11, no. 1 (Winter 1997): 3–108.

monetary-fiscal stimulus will have a cumulative inflationary effect;[35] and (4) uncertainty accumulates so rapidly with length of the planning horizon that the possibility of adverse inflationary consequences in the distant future should not inhibit attempts to capture short-term gains in output and employment: in other words, "in the long run we are all dead." As we shall see later on, it is very hard to appraise the merits of this Keynesian rebuttal relative to those of the RAP-inspired argument that prompts it. But in any case, it is not part of our present task to attempt such an appraisal.

SUMMARY

While it is obvious that a major objective of KP is to provide a theoretical basis for using macroeconomic policy to increase the extent of resource use, the place of the paradigm in an economist's tool bag should not turn on its role in policy making. Rather it should depend on the extent to which the degree or extent of resource use—especially employment of labor—properly can be used as a factor in differentiating among periods of economic history, and whether its exogenous variables can serve as a major explanatory factor of such differences. Although it would be easier to apply KP if the behavior of product prices did not depend upon the degree of resource use, the absence of such independence is not essential for such application.

The point is that use of "degree of resource employment" in the explanation of the behavior of any economic variable is not compatible with RAP. Variations in the level of aggregate output, even over substantial periods of time, are explained by RAP as temporary realizations of an ongoing process that is not comprehensible when truncated from its intertemporal moorings. KP regards such variations—at least in some cases—as indicative of different states of the world characterized by different states of animal spirits and disconnected from one another. Though desire for a change in policy recommendations motivated invention of KP, and no doubt has contributed greatly to its appeal, it is the change of analytical framework that KP introduced that has been crucial to its influence on the culture of economics.

35. Or, as Joseph Stiglitz (1997, p. 10) put it, "although no one knows exactly where the NAIRU is, . . . in testing the waters, we do not risk drowning. If need be, we can always reverse course."

F I V E

OF DEBT AND TAXES: KP VERSUS RAP

Interpreting the economic significance of public debt provides a striking illustration of the differing implications of KP and RAP. In a capsule, RAP asserts that "there is no free lunch": to this KP adds "but, under the right circumstances, it is possible to snitch a sandwich." That *The General Theory* says nothing explicit about public debt is not surprising: in intention and effect it marginalizes debt as a determinant of output and employment, allowing it to enter only indirectly through its impact on the determinants of *IS* and *LM* (in figure 5).

However, the Keynesian attitude toward public debt as an instrument of monetary-fiscal policy was strikingly expressed in Keynes (1940).[1] The view of debt and taxes taken there, involving compulsory saving with repayment at the discretion of the monetary-fiscal authorities, was in sharp contrast with the RAP-associated view of public debt as a contractual obligation that acts as a binding constraint upon the decisions open to taxpayers and to the state.[2]

The contrast between the KP and RAP views of public finance has a diachronic as well as a conceptual aspect. In the mid-1960s, to the applause of most Keynesians, the U.S. government made an effort to fine tune the economy through a general tax cut; the possible effect of this action on the national debt received scant consideration. Three decades later, with the support of many RAP adherents, that government is attempting highly divisive reductions in aggregate expenditure including curtailment of entitlements to health care and (possibly) to old-age pensions in order to balance the federal budget and prevent further accumulation of debt to be "paid by our grandchildren."[3] The objective of this chap-

1. *How to Pay for the War* (New York: Harcourt, Brace).
2. Since RAP proper has no place for a state, any discussion of an RAP view of public debt, or of public finance generally, requires creation of a suitable adjunct, as will be discussed below.
3. The issues involved are, of course, more complex than this remark would suggest. However, the contrast of paradigms and related metaphors used in discussions of economic policy in the two periods is striking.

ter is not to account for this change in the climate of opinion, but to exploit it as a means of contrasting the very different conceptual organizations operative in these two historical episodes.

FUNCTIONAL FINANCE

The most lucid statement of KP as it applies to Public Finance is A. P. Lerner's "Functional Finance."[4] Lerner considered the problems of fiscal policy in a static, short-run context consonant with KP: the avowed objective of policy was to achieve full employment without inflation. Taxation was thought to be simply an instrument for shifting the consumption function in the following manner.[5] If output should fall below the full employment level, reduce taxes to increase the amount of income retained by households, thereby increasing aggregate expenditure and output. This is to be repeated as needed until the economy reaches full employment.

Conversely, if for any reason aggregate expenditure were to become "excessive" at full employment, resulting in inflation, increase taxes relative to government expenditure until reduced aggregate consumption eliminates the excess demand for output. For Lerner, the function of taxes was simply to raise, or lower, aggregate consumption. If necessary to drive the economy to full employment, taxes could be made negative; that is, be replaced by subsidies to households.

But government payments to the private sector need not be financed by taxes: printing money is easier, and more appropriate, when the sole objective of expenditure is to increase aggregate demand and output. The same line of reasoning raises the question of why the government should borrow and pay interest when it can obtain control over the same quantity of resources by printing an equivalent quantity of money. The answer is that (at given prices and interest rates) the public might prefer to hold some part of the claims on wealth thus created in the form of (government) bonds rather than as cash, and their attempts to implement such preferences would raise interest rates, thereby reducing private investment.

Should the government desire to shield the economy from this potentially adverse effect of its fiscal operations, it could do so by issuing bonds (instead of printing money) in the quantity required to keep the interest rate at its preexisting level, or at whatever level was desired. In other

4. See Lerner (1943) and (1944), chap. 24.

5. In this context, Lerner took the rate of private investment as a datum and proposed to control aggregate expenditure solely by adjustment of aggregate consumption.

words, variation in the size of the public debt (defined as equal to the value of outstanding government bonds) would be a simple reflex of the government's efforts to maintain full employment while keeping the rate of interest and investment at desired levels.[6]

If, for any reason, the public should decide it wanted to cash in their bonds, the government could accommodate it by creating sufficient money to make the required bond purchases. If the resulting increase in individuals' cash holdings led to an increased rate of consumption greater than what would be compatible with an acceptable rate of inflation at full employment, the government would raise taxes enough to reduce after-tax income sufficiently to hold inflation to an acceptable rate.[7]

In short, so long as it is willingly held, the magnitude of the public debt need be of no concern to economic policy makers. While desired changes in this magnitude might require action by the monetary-fiscal authorities, the actions required would be straightforward: a combination of changes in the money stock and taxes on wealth such as to make the public satisfied to hold the outstanding stock of government bonds.

As stated, this argument applies only to a closed economy: this is the context in which KP is most easily presented. But this limitation is not of great importance for the present purpose.[8] More important are the static assumptions implicit in the argument. No consideration is given to the lag between economic events and recognition of them by policy makers, or to the further lag between recognition and the taking of corrective action, or the still further lag of public response to the corrective action, and so on. The effect of these lags, aggravated both by the attempts of rational decision makers to anticipate the behavior of other decision makers, and by unanticipated exogenously caused changes of behavior, is to raise serious questions as to how well the actual effects of the actions taken by monetary-fiscal authorities would correspond to what was intended.

A second difficulty arises from the uncertain relation of unemployment to inflation. As we have seen, the conceptual framework of KP is most clear when, at output levels below full employment, the effect of an

6. Subject to the overriding commitment to maintain full employment, the government's choice of the mix of bonds, money creation, and taxation would be determined by the desired levels of private investment, public expenditure, and income distribution. However, for the purpose of this discussion it is not necessary to explore such details.

7. To fix ideas, the reader may think of the "acceptable" rate of inflation as zero. However, Lerner's argument neither made nor required this assumption.

8. We will discuss the implications of foreign-held national debt below.

increase in aggregate expenditure is to increase aggregate output (and employment) with wages and product prices unchanged and, at full employment, to increase prices while leaving aggregate output unchanged. In such a world, the monetary-fiscal authorities can determine whether to apply the brake of taxation or the accelerator of expenditure simply by determining the level of current resource use relative to capacity. Where the relation of output and prices is more complicated, the authorities must consider, inter alia, the unemployment-inflation tradeoff, thus blurring the sharp distinction between states of full employment and of underemployment.

THE STATE IN KP AND IN RAP

These difficulties, and others, kept Keynes and most Keynesians from becoming unqualified supporters of functional finance.[9] But that is beside the point: more clearly than elsewhere, "Functional Finance" presents the framework in which it can be perceived how monetary-fiscal policy might make it possible to "snitch a sandwich" without making anyone poorer. Implicit in this framework is the assumption that, aside from her capacity to work, an individual's property is at the disposal of the state. The extent of an individual's saving or consumption is determined by what the government leaves her, and under functional finance that is determined by a (governmental) decision based on anticipation of the state of the economy (i.e., whether or not it will be in full employment) and a judgment about how after-tax income should be distributed.

In this context public debt, like money, is simply a claim against the state. Its magnitude is of no greater (or lesser) concern than the magnitude of the money stock. Attempts by the public to reduce holdings of either asset in order to finance increased expenditure might generate inflationary pressure. Whether it actually did so would depend upon the reaction of the state, that is, on whether the state could and would raise taxes sufficiently to offset the inflationary pressure.

The ability and willingness of the state to raise taxes to fight inflation depends upon its characteristics: these are specified neither in KP nor in RAP. By implication, KP (especially functional finance) is an appeal for giving the state whatever powers are required to achieve noninflationary

---

9. David Colander (1984) contains an excellent discussion of Keynes' reaction to functional finance. In fairness to Lerner, it should be noted that in later work (e.g., *Flation* [1973]) he amplified functional finance to take account of the complications arising from the possibility of inflation at less than full employment.

full employment.[10] To introduce the state to RAP would require construction of a paradigm adjunct, the characteristics of which are a matter of continuing controversy (see chapter 10).

In order to be compatible with the conceptual organization of RAP, the characteristics of the state must satisfy two conditions: (1) its role in economic activity must be sufficiently small as not to require abandonment of the proposition that the alternative cost of production of any commodity can be measured by its market price[11] and (2) its powers of direct and indirect taxation must be so limited as not to vitiate the assumption that every decision maker has a well-defined resource constraint. However imprecisely, these restrictions have the effect of limiting the capacity of the state to borrow and spend, and recognition of this limit is an important determinant of the actions it may contemplate.

Satisfaction of these two conditions implies that the state cannot create (much) *real* money. Any attempt to utilize its power to create legal tender (beyond a low limit) would cause a corresponding depreciation of the currency's value such as would leave the real value of the money stock virtually unchanged. Thus, under RAP, monetary and fiscal policy are disjointed: decisions about borrowing and taxation are entirely independent of those about the money supply.[12] But under functional finance, monetary and fiscal actions are inseparable: tax payments reduce the public's stock of cash while public expenditure increases it.[13] Put differently, under functional finance no individual's wealth is fixed, but is conditional upon the exactions of the state acting under its goal of full employment without inflation. The post-tax distribution of wealth is determined (somehow) by the state as a policy decision.

This implies a very different model of the world from that envisaged in any RAP discussion of monetary policy. It might be remarked that the effect of such uncertainty about one's wealth—tantamount to uncertainty

10. Together with an implied claim that the grant of such powers would not have otherwise undesirable effects.

11. The similarity of the restriction on the importance of monopolies and of the state—as a condition for the viability of RAP—should be apparent.

12. The proclivity of RAP adherents for explaining macroeconomic phenomena—and discussing policy about them—in terms of the actions of monetary authorities, and not of monetary-fiscal authorities, is not incidental.

13. This feature of functional finance is not essential to its argument, although it serves to simplify it. Functional finance would be compatible with money creation by private parties as well as by the Treasury. However, privately created money would be alien to the spirit of functional finance.

about property rights—on incentives to work and save is not given explicit consideration in functional finance.

Nothing that has been said so far about the behavior of the state implies that it would behave rationally. Indeed, until its characteristics are specified more fully, it is impossible to know what it would mean for a state to behave rationally—or otherwise. However, the spirit of RAP requires that the state conduct itself so as not to permit the existence of an (uneaten) free lunch, and its adherents have always accepted this requirement. But the existence of such lunches is precisely what The General Theory alleges, accompanied by suggestions as to how they might be consumed.[14] Thus, if an additional dollar of public debt could go unrepaid, failure to borrow it would be tantamount to passing up a bite of free lunch. To justify rejection of such a borrowing opportunity, an RAP adherent must deny the possibility that the entailed debt could go unrepaid; for her, the only question concerns the date of the inevitable repayment.

REPAYMENT OF PUBLIC DEBT

From the RAP viewpoint, in a certain world the existence of public debt would create no analytical problems beyond those that would arise from the existence of private debt. An issue of government bonds would be (in effect) accompanied by an issue of tax bills specifying the amounts due at various dates in the future (up to and including the date of redemption) on account of the indebtedness incurred. Under RAP, taxpayers would treat these accrued tax liabilities as though they were private debt. The only possible reason for an individual to prefer that the state borrow, instead of paying as it goes, would be expectation of a favorable shift in the tax structure between the moment of borrowing and the date of repayment. As this possibility is irrelevant to the present discussion, we shall ignore it.

Under RAP, in the real (i.e., uncertain) world the only proper rationalizations for a preference for public borrowing over current taxation are some combination of (1) tax optimism and (2) capital market "imperfections." (1) To understate the matter considerably, it is very difficult for any individual to impute the increment to his tax liabilities implied by a proposed increment to the public debt. Therefore, depending upon pre-

14. For example, "If the Treasury were to fill old bottles with banknotes, [and] bury them at suitable depths in disused coal mines . . . there need be no more unemployment and, with the help of the repercussions, the real income of the community, and its capital wealth also, would probably become a good deal greater than it actually is." Keynes (1936), p. 129.

vailing attitudes, the public might entertain a generally more optimistic outlook than would exist in a certain world.[15] Such optimism could not help but increase if there were some chance that the date of redemption could be deferred indefinitely. (2) The interest rates paid by the government are lower than those paid by individuals.[16] Hence, deferring one's tax obligations and using the retained funds to make payments which one would otherwise finance by individual borrowing might generate a net gain.[17]

Obviously, proposals for public expenditures—especially large ones—that must be financed by current taxation can be highly divisive. Thus, used as a substitute for current taxation, public borrowing can serve as a political emollient. But, under RAP, this merely defers the distributional conflict to the time of debt redemption. That is, public borrowing has the effect of transferring to our heirs political struggle rather than net financial obligation.

The effect on attitudes toward public debt of shifting from the frame of RAP to that of KP is to reduce concern over possible future taxes. KP holds out the distinct hope that the debt might not have to be repaid at all, and that, in any case, the date of repayment would be indefinite. Obviously this serves to encourage both substitution of borrowing for current taxation and increase of public expenditure overall; RAP adherents must (and do) oppose resort to either of these expedients.

If the date of debt redemption is perceived as indefinite, RAP is at a great disadvantage in popular debate, though not necessarily in professional discussion. In the court of public opinion, such arguments as "something may turn up," and "in the long run we are all dead," are effective counters to RAP arguments that current increases in output and employment should be foregone in order to avoid the greater decreases they would cause at some time in the indefinite future. The RAP argument must be—and is—that anticipations of the future affect behavior in the present, with the result that the present gains promised by functional finance–style policies are illusory. At best they would be ephemeral, and, if the policies were to be followed for any substantial period, gains would be more than offset by losses of real output associated with the rapid inflation that would ensue.

---

15. Of course, the reverse might also be the case.

16. Whether the existence of such a differential would be compatible with RAP raises difficult questions that are irrelevant to the present discussion.

17. I eschew the question of whether such opportunities for substituting public for private borrowing are adequately—or excessively—exploited.

Clearly this argument is reminiscent of that presented in the previous chapter as an RAP objection to using monetary policy to reduce unemployment below its natural rate. Although expansion of the money supply to increase employment might cause an initial increase in aggregate output, people would soon learn to anticipate the inflationary consequences of such action, which would lead to a worsening of the unemployment-inflation tradeoff, and so on, with the result that sooner or later the possibility of effecting any increase in output through monetary-fiscal policy would vanish, and attempts to effect it would lead to hyperinflation.[18]

Now let us apply this argument to public debt. While there are many ways of linking growth of the public debt to the generation of inflationary expectations, the simplest is through the incentive that growth in the debt gives policy makers to promote inflation in order to reduce its burden. At a given rate of interest, any increase in the ratio of the public debt to the national income increases the share of the latter that must be taken in taxes in order to service the debt without making the ratio of debt to income rise still further.[19] An increase in the share of national income taken as taxes reduces the incentive to productive activity of all kinds.

Moreover, such increase would increase the difficulty encountered by incumbent politicians in finding a distribution of the tax burden that would be acceptable to a majority of the electorate. This would increase the likelihood that, in order to avoid responsibility for imposing a tax burden that most citizens would find objectionable, politicians would contrive to have money created in lieu of increased taxes, in the hope that

18. In terms of either figure 4 or 5, this argument amounts to saying that the location of F becomes highly sensitive to the price expectations generated by perception of the monetary-fiscal policy being followed. This is one member of a family of arguments (developed by the New Classicals) designed to show the ineffectiveness of monetary policy in accomplishing a sustained alteration of real magnitudes. The most famous of these arguments is the Lucas Critique. For a survey of such arguments see Hoover (1988), chapters 4–7.

19. The reader may well ask why interest on the debt must be financed by taxation. Why not borrow still more to finance part or all of the interest due on the existing Debt? To answer that this type of chain letter or Ponzi financing must eventually break down, and that the public would surely refuse to hold government bonds as soon as the existence of such a policy was detected, is a valid but incomplete reply. What is missing is recognition that there is no specifiable relation of the ratio of public debt to community income, or of the rate of growth of this ratio, and willingness of the public to hold public debt. (It may be noted that while KP is not incompatible with the possibility of a sustainable Ponzi scheme, no Keynesian has ever suggested that public policy should exploit such a possibility.)

they could more easily escape blame for the resulting inflation than for the increased tax bill that would otherwise be required.

Despite the force of this argument, and a half century of intermittent searching, economists have not discovered any generally accepted theory of the relation of public debt to national income, or even of a conceptual upper limit to the ratio of the former to the latter. Keynesians note that while this ratio increased sharply during World War II, leading to considerable inflation during the war years and the immediate postwar period, the inflation did not go to the extreme of hyperinflation, and was accompanied by a very large increase in real output. If in war, why not in peace?

The RAP answer is that willingness of the public to hold government bonds at any (nominal) rate of interest depends upon the purpose for which the borrowing is made. During a war or other perceived national emergency, both feelings of public spirit—which could not properly be invoked by RAP adherents—and confidence that the borrowing did not indicate governmental unwillingness to pay its normal bills without inflating the currency, would lead to a much greater willingness to hold public debt than would otherwise exist. But if it were believed that debt was being incurred because the government was politically incapable of raising sufficient tax revenue to match the expenditures it felt compelled to make, bond holders might well feel that each new increment to the public debt was fresh evidence of the government's incapacity to raise taxes to fight off an inflation—should one commence—and thus provide fresh reason for demanding a higher reward for bearing the risk associated with trading present for future dollars. But beyond this adjuration to caution, RAP has little to say about the relation of public debt to national income.

The Two Price Regimes

As we have seen, KP envisages the existence of two distinct regimes for the setting of wage rates and product prices. One of these, which we may term the noninflationary regime, obtains when aggregate output is below the economy's capability. The other, the inflationary regime, obtains when the economy is operating at capacity (full employment).

In the noninflationary regime, prices are governed primarily by historical costs of production, to which they are related by a variety of institutionally established formulas. But in the inflationary regime producers are concerned with the future cost—which they expect to be higher than historical cost—of replacing inventories and, in the case of labor, future costs of living. Thus the inflationary regime reveals markedly higher sensitivity to indicators of future price movements—what is usually termed inflationary psychology—then the non-inflationary.

RAP adherents would contend that the noninflationary regime could exist for only a short period of time, and solely in the absence of a systematic policy to exploit it by use of monetary policy to increase output. In addition, they would insist that the current level of output and employment provides an inadequate basis for judging whether or not the economy is in a noninflationary regime. Whether it is in such a regime depends upon the state of public confidence in the future course of prices which is influenced by much more than the current presence—or absence—of excess productive capacity of plant and machinery and unemployment of labor. That is, in the imagery of figure 5, a series of upward shifts of *LM* may drive product prices upward even though the economy is operating well below capacity and with substantial unemployment.

Once the economy is settled into an inflationary regime, it is very difficult to shift it to the other regime. This fact makes those responsible for avoiding inflation extremely apprehensive of public-sector behavior that might arouse inflationary expectations. This apprehensiveness often causes central bankers and other spokespersons for the financial community to talk nervously, albeit vaguely, of the dangers of inflation while there is no observable sign either of unusual price increases, or of shortages of any kind of input.

RESPECTIVE ATTITUDES TOWARD INFLATION

Despite exceptions, KP adherents can usually be distinguished from RAP supporters by their greater willingness to brave the hazards of inflation. This willingness stems partly from their belief in the possibility of a net gain in output and employment over time from a policy of keeping aggregate demand high—a possibility that RAP adherents deny. This belief is reinforced by preference for the (alleged) distributive effects of a policy aimed at accepting some risk of inflation as tradeoff for staying closer to full employment; such a preference—and belief in the efficacy of the tradeoff to promote employment—is much more common among Keynesians than among RAP adherents.[20]

20. The main distributive effect is an increase in the relative incomes of low-paid workers who allegedly gain most from increased working hours per year that result from fuller employment. While not formally entailed by their paradigm, KP adherents tend to attach greater weight to this effect than to such redistribution as might arise from the price changes associated with inflation.

Though muted in recent years, another factor underlying the somewhat more relaxed attitude of KP adherents toward inflation is their willingness to accept temporary price controls and other abridgments of property rights (e.g., curbs on international capital movements) in order to brake unacceptable outbursts of inflation. RAP opposition to this attitude stems partly from belief that such controls cannot be effective for very long, but also from objection to the intervention of the state into the resource allocation process on grounds both of efficiency and equity.

REPAYING PUBLIC DEBT

One of the most striking consequences of admitting the possibility of increasing aggregate output and employment through monetary-fiscal action is a change in perspective toward public debt. In KP the primary criterion for appraising a monetary-fiscal act is its affect upon aggregate output and employment. Any accompanying change in the level of public debt is considered to be incidental and, in any case, capable of being offset by appropriate application of the canons of Functional Finance whenever desired.

By contrast, as a corollary to the no free lunch principle, RAP implies that any increment in public debt must entail a projected stream of tax-financed repayments of equal present value. This implies that the proceeds of the borrowing must be invested so as to increase future real output or that the debt increment will entail a transfer of real aggregate income from the future to the present. The possibility of increasing real wealth by increasing aggregate expenditure, however accomplished, is precluded.

Another perspective on the contrast between the KP and RAP views of public debt is provided by considering the question of what it would mean to pay off the national debt. To avoid irrelevant complications, let us abstract from the (important and difficult) question of how the implied tax burden would be distributed; let us assume that a consensus on this matter is somehow reached. Under KP, the effect of paying off the debt would be a decline in consumption as a result of reducing household wealth by wiping out holdings of government bonds.[21]

21. In most expositions of The General Theory, household consumption is made to depend upon current income rather than wealth. But, aside from its unrealism, this assumption is not essential to KP and, in addition, would be very inconvenient for the argument of the next few paragraphs. Accordingly, it is abandoned.

Under RAP, there would be no such effect. The reduction in public debt would be exactly offset by the reduction in the present value of tax obligations to provide for its servicing with no effect on the wealth of the typical household. That is, under KP government bonds would be treated by the public as real wealth, but under RAP they would not. From the standpoint of RAP, acceptance of the idea that an increment of government bonds would have the same effect upon aggregate consumption as an equal increment in the (dollar value) of any other asset is to assert the existence of a government bond illusion analogous to the theoretically proscribed money illusion. KP entails no such proscription.

KP AND FOREIGN-HELD DEBT

The argument of the previous sections proceeded on the assumption that all public debt was held by nationals of the indebted country. In such case, it might truly be said of the public debt that, collectively, "we owe it to ourselves." But if part or all of the debt is owed to foreigners, a possible need to repay it might create problems that require explicit consideration. The argument of this section refers only to situations where the debt is denominated in the currency of the borrowing country, for example, where the United States government promises repayment of principal and interest in dollars.

All of these problems relate in one way or another to the effect of large-scale capital movements on the rate of exchange between the currencies of the debtor and creditor countries. Consider the case where, for whatever reason, foreign creditors decide that they wish to terminate or reduce substantially their holdings of the debt of a particular country. Unless offset by an enhanced demand for the debtor country's exports or privately issued securities, the effect would be to increase the relative supply of the debtor country's currency, thereby driving down its exchange rate. How far this decline would go depends upon the reciprocal elasticities of demand for goods and private securities, but in principle the decline could be very large and its effects highly adverse to the debtor country. But, for several reasons, such an outcome would be very unlikely to occur.

1. Especially if the debtor country provided a large market for the creditor's exports, the creditor government(s) would not sit idly by and allow a deterioration of their export markets through appreciation of their currencies. Instead, they would—however reluctantly—buy the bonds their nationals were selling in order to prevent this appreciation from hap-

pening. In effect there would be a substitution of foreign public credit for foreign private credit: often such substitution has been accompanied by renegotiation of the terms of indebtedness in favor of the debtor.

2. Failing (1), the debtor country—often with the tacit approval of creditor governments—will impose restraints on the repatriation of principal and interest by foreign creditors. This amounts to discriminatory expropriation of the property of foreign lenders, a fact that does not reduce the appeal of such measures to nationals of the debtor countries.

3. Failing ability to restrict capital movements, a debtor government may default outright. This is almost always considered an option inferior to (2), and is rarely utilized because creditor governments prefer the greater leverage available to them under an agreement to restrict capital movements. After all, there is not much one government can do to collect from another government that is reluctant to pay: overt use of force is a very costly expedient.

To an RAP adherent, default—open or disguised—would not seem an efficient course of action. Under RAP, such behavior would surely ruin a country's credit, and could be committed only once. But, following many real-world clues, KP accepts that capital markets are forgiving, at least to some extent.[22] Thus, for KP adherents, the complications of international borrowing do not preclude increasing the public debt as a way of snitching a sandwich.

As written, neither KP nor its functional finance variant explicitly addresses the matter of defaulting on obligations. However, the spirit of KP is much informed by recognition of this possibility, and the opportunities it presents for stretching resource constraints. Keynes's *How to Pay for the War* is a series of suggestions for manipulating debt as a technique for giving the state discretionary control over resources without resort to overt taxation. And Keynes's rhetoric—for example, "if a man owes you a thousand he is your debtor; if he owes you a million, he is your partner"—is laced with references to the permeability of the membrane between debt and equity.

The spirit of *The General Theory* argues that claims to property can sometimes be impediments to the economic welfare of the community

---

22. It could be argued plausibly that a rational expectations–RAP view of international public lending would cause international lenders to allow for a nonnegligible probability that the terms of a loan, as written, will not be honored. While analyzing the implications of such a state of affairs for the behavior of a rational borrower would be very interesting, it would not be relevant to the present discussion.

and that, when they are, adroit manipulation by the state can circumvent the wishes of their owners to the owners' own (ultimate) benefit. As Keynes and many Keynesians saw (and still see) it, an essential ingredient of successful manipulation is practical wisdom in the timing of actions and the communication of confidence-building messages. But such wisdom is not reducible to formula, and therefore not readily expressed in a form congenial to those looking for scientific guidance.

PUBLIC DEBT IN RAP

Since RAP contains no explicit place for a state, the title of this section may appear oxymoronic. However, despite the problems created by recognition of its existence, RAP adherents must—and do—analyze the consequences of state actions: specifically, public expenditure, borrowing, and taxation. To reconcile such analyses with RAP it is necessary to restrict the effects that government actions are permitted to have upon prices and quantities. In particular, RAP precludes any behavior that would imply either money illusion or violation of the no free lunch restriction.[23] Let us first consider the implications of no free lunch under the assumptions of a closed economy.

Taken literally, RAP implies no restriction upon the amount of public debt an economy might have previously incurred. This is because all transactors would be assumed to have already adjusted to such debt as had been previously undertaken, with prices and quantities adjusting accordingly. But prospective changes in the debt—up or down—are another matter. No increase in the debt that permitted a Pareto improvement would be considered possible because such an increase would imply a free lunch. Hence the idea of borrowing in period n and then reborrowing in period $n + 1$ to repay both principal and interest, and so on ad infinitum, is ruled out.[24]

This means that any increase in the public debt must be repaid at some time in the future, and rational expectations implies that everyone acts as

23. It should be noted that the existence of money illusion may imply the possibility of a free lunch. If there is money illusion and the state has the power to create legal tender money, then exercise of this power may create a Pareto improvement. Whether this constituted a free lunch would depend upon the resource cost of creating money.

24. N.B., RAP would rule out this possibility even if everyone thought that refinancing could be successfully conducted into the indefinite future! This is because acceptance of such a possibility would be inconsistent with a limited (i.e., finite) stock of resources. While not germane to the present discussion, it is worth noting that such a restriction applies to individual borrowers as well.

though he were aware of this fact. Hence a government deficit entails creation of debt that must some day be paid back, and concern about the day of reckoning is proper.

On this view, any increase in government expenditure must be offset by an increase in taxes, now or later. If the state chooses to pay by borrowing instead of taxing, this will reduce each individual's current tax bill, but impose on her a liability for an equal amount of future taxes (plus interest) for which—assuming rationality—she must make provision. Thus, providing that certain further conditions are met,[25] an increment in public debt will affect an individual's behavior in exactly the same way as an (equal) increment in her personal debt. In particular, whether the state borrows or taxes an individual an additional dollar, the effect on her consumption and saving will be the same. Put differently, an individual's current saving is affected only by the amount of change in the state's expenditure and not by the method used to finance it.

Under these conditions, price-quantity behavior will be invariant to the method by which the state finances its expenditure, that is, invariant to the ratio of current borrowing to current tax receipts. An economy satisfying these conditions is said to exhibit Ricardian equivalence.[26] While RAP does not imply Ricardian equivalence, they are very much in the same spirit and many RAP adherents consider Ricardian equivalence to have merit as a first approximation to the implications of an empirically valid model. The reader will note that Ricardian equivalence is yet another case where RAP suggests a model in which, despite superficial appearances, manipulation of financial variables—especially by the state— proves ineffective as a means of influencing real variables. (Other prominent examples are associated with the Phillips curve and the natural rate of unemployment [see above, chapter 4), and the alleged inability of corporate dividend policy to influence stock prices associated with the Modigliani-Miller theorem discussed in chapter 8.)

Nevertheless, many economists who do not wish to depart from RAP

25. The most important of these conditions are: (1) no individual is optimizing at a "corner" as opposed to an internal maximum; (2) no individual is either myopic or hyperopic with respect to the valuation of present or future satisfactions; (3) each individual either expects an infinite life or values the utility of his heirs exactly as he values his own; and (4) rational expectations apply not only to individual wealth and prices, but also to future tax burdens.

26. John J. Seater (1993) provides a detailed survey of this topic and an extensive bibliography.

refuse to accept Ricardian equivalence on the ground that the special assumptions it requires are unacceptable. But while the resulting debate has been prominent in professional journals and touches on matters of practical importance, it is not germane to our concerns, and we shall not pursue the issues it raises.[27]

RAP vs. KP: A Summary

In this chapter and its predecessor, I have attempted to describe the principal features of KP and to contrast them with those of RAP. The reason for so much attention to this particular paradigm is its widespread influence within the economics community, an influence which persists two-thirds of a century after its classic presentation in *The General Theory*. Unlike the situation of the mid-1950s, when it was said "we are all Keynesians now," few economists of the 1990s are altogether Keynesian. Yet many of them will, in some circumstances and on some issues, attempt to apply Keynesian ideas. At bottom, all such attempts may be placed under the rubric of attempts to snitch a sandwich. RAP adherents deplore such attempts, their arguments varying between outright denial of the existence of the sandwich and concern that attempts to eat it will prove counterproductive.

27. Those interested in the discussion can get a good start by reading the symposium, "Budget Deficit," in the *Journal of Economic Perspectives* (Spring 1989).

SIX

SOME OTHER PARADIGMS

Although the existence of both RAP and KP would suffice to justify the statement that Economics contains a plurality of paradigms, describing a few others enriches the argument. The paradigms selected for description do not exhaust the list of candidates, and I do not suggest that those included are more important than others which have been omitted. The basis of selection was usefulness in advancing the argument of the book.[1]

No other paradigm has been developed in detail comparable to RAP, nor does any pretend to a comparable breadth of application. In many cases the impact of a paradigm upon the corpus of economics arises solely from its confrontation with one or another implication of RAP. This fact both reflects and reinforces the "dominance" of the latter. However, paradigms are formed for a variety of reasons, not all of them related to research, so that the long shadow of RAP does not hover over all of them.

STABLE AGGREGATES

Among the ways in which KP is distinguished from RAP is that it involves a stable relation between aggregate income and aggregate consumption expenditure; the *consumption function*. Such a relation could be compatible with RAP only if it were derived from the condition that every consumer was maximizing utility subject to the usual resource constraints. While not explicitly precluding this possibility, The General Theory made no attempt at such a derivation, and was manifestly unconcerned with whether or not it could be done.

To find any stable aggregate relation that is not derivable from an RAP

---

1. Some readers might ask why I have failed to include so important an idea as Game Theory in the discussion. The reason is that Game Theory is a technique applicable to paradigms, rather than a paradigm itself. The characteristics of Game Theory are discussed, though briefly, in Chapter 11.

compatible model is to confront RAP with an anomaly.[2] However, economists have proposed a number of such (allegedly) stable aggregate relations other than the consumption function: a good collection of these is
offered by Lawrence Klein (1983).[3] Klein terms these relations "Great
Ratios," remarking that "Economists often analyze the economic situation
as though some or all of these parameters were stable (constants)."[4] The
list of Great Ratios consists of the savings ratio,[5] the capital-output ratio,
the wage share (of national income), the velocity ratio, and the labor force
participation ratio. After elimination of secular trends, Klein and Kosobud find each of these ratios to be a parametric constant and, in particular,
to be independent of relative prices and income. Generally, to make quantities independent of prices and/or income is anomalous to RAP and creates an opportunity for advancing an alternative paradigm.[6] However, neither Klein nor—so far as I am aware—other devotees of Great Ratios
have availed themselves of such opportunities beyond what is implied by
adhering to the Keynesian paradigm and making one price or another
exogenous, that is, non-market clearing.

   Although not included in Klein's list of Great Ratios, there is an aggregate expenditure relation (incompatible with RAP) that has played an
important role in the conceptual organization associated with the Keynesian paradigm. This relation arises from the (disputed) tendency for the

   2. In this context, it is essential to distinguish between aggregate relations that are alleged to hold between aggregations of equilibrium quantities at equilibrium prices from
other aggregate relations. Only the latter create anomalies for RAP. For example: a stable
demand function for money, à la Milton Friedman, is part of an RAP-compatible quantity
theory of money. But a statistically constant V in $MV = PT$, unrelated to prices and income,
would constitute an anomaly for RAP.
   3. See also L. R. Klein and R. F. Kosobud (1961). Although Klein is careful to distinguish Great Ratios from "economic laws" (and to note departures from constancy) this
distinction is of no significance for our argument: any use of a relation not derivable from
RAP constitutes an anomaly for RAP.
   4. Klein (1983), p. 13.
   5. The savings ratio (the percentage of aggregate income saved) is a transform of one
possible form of the consumption function.
   6. Any "economic law" purporting to interrelate aggregate quantities is subject to the
same comment. For example, the comment would apply to Pareto's "law of income distribution" (discussed in Klein (1983), pp. 115–16). However, the comment would not apply to
Engel's law (relating the fraction of a household's income spent on food to the level of its
income), as this law involves no non-RAP relationship, but merely restricts the characteristics of admissible utility functions.

share of a recipient's income that is saved to increase with the level of her income. Aggregating across recipients, this tendency implies that increasing the inequality with which a given income is distributed will increase the percentage that is saved and, more generally, that a consumption function will shift down (or up) as the inequality with which income is distributed increases or decreases.[7] Thus, given the rate of aggregate investment and the propensity to consume of individual recipients, aggregate income and employment will vary inversely with distributional inequality.

If we substitute the fraction of national income received by labor for the measure of distributional inequality used in the preceding paragraph, an aggregate relation emerges between labor's share and the level of national income. Under full employment this becomes a relation between labor's share and the rate of investment. The rationale for this relationship is the allegedly lower propensity to consume from wages than from other types of income. This relationship is usually identified with the writings of the late Lord (Nicholas) Kaldor and played an important role in his various papers on economic growth.[8]

Yet a further example of a relation among aggregate variables is that alleged to hold between (aggregate) saving and investment *within individual countries* stemming from an (alleged) lack of integration of world capital markets.[9] While not essential to our argument, it is worth noting that this contention is an important prop for the argument that economic growth in the United States is being restrained by an insufficient saving ratio (i.e., by an excessive propensity to consume).

In a nutshell, adherence to RAP requires a skeptical view of alleged economic laws based solely on observed empirical regularities. Unless they can be rationalized by construction of a paradigm adjunct, such regularities must be regarded as anomalous to RAP.

THE CLASSICAL DISTRIBUTION PARADIGM

Because RAP does not provide for pejorative evaluation of choice patterns so long as they are rational, it allows no pattern to claim special merit. In particular, it offers no support for claims of preference for pat-

---

7. As used in this section, "inequality" is (roughly) what is measured by the conventional Gini coefficient.

8. I have discussed this relationship, and its implications for RAP, in M. W. Reder (1959).

9. The existence of this (disputed) relation is associated with the work of Martin Feldstein. See M. Feldstein and C. Horioka (1980) and M. Feldstein and P. Bacchetta (1990).

terns held to be conducive to saving or to economic growth. This is not the case for (some) other paradigms, in which capital accumulation and economic growth are given an honorific niche. Prominent among these is what I term the *classical distribution paradigm.*

Roughly, this paradigm is the theory of distribution presented in Adam Smith's *The Wealth of Nations* (Book 1, chapters 8–10) as modified in Ricardo's principles and polished by John Stuart Mill and other classical economists. Since discussion of this paradigm is a staple of the history of economic thought, and plays only a limited role in the subject's contemporary culture, I shall not discuss its details but merely contrast its main features with those of RAP.[10]

RAP is concerned with resource owners, each associated with a convex utility function and a bundle of resources, but otherwise undescribed. In particular, the nutritional requirements of these resource owners are not specified. By contrast, in the classical distribution paradigm the actors are humans as we know them, requiring food for survival. Obtaining food sufficient for survival and reproduction was the primary objective of every economic agent, with other desiderata secondary. Based on historical and contemporary observation, the overwhelming part of the labor force was assumed to consist of laborers whose productivity in terms of food was sufficiently low that most of their real income was used to pay for the means of subsistence (including reproduction), with only a negligible fraction available for other purposes. Accordingly, there was little opportunity for employment in producing non-food items, and the overwhelming part of the labor force was compelled to engage in food production.

Agricultural workers were assumed to be employed by farmers who owned the crop and compensated the workers by wages paid in foodstuffs. The (employing) farmer's share of the crop covered his own consumption needs and left a surplus, part of which was saved to provide food for workers during the growing period of the next crop, and part to pay rent to the owners of the land. The stock of food used to maintain workers during the growing period (the wages fund) constituted the major part of the farmer's capital, which provided the effective demand for labor.

The greater the stock of capital, the greater the demand for labor and, given the size of the labor force, the higher the level of wages. Consequently, with a given labor force, the wage level increased with the pro-

---

10. For details of this paradigm, the interested reader may consult Blaug (1997), chapter 3.

pensity to save. But in addition to the demand for labor to grow food, labor was demanded by landlords and farmers (primarily the former), to provide direct services. (Provision of such services constituted "unproductive labor," as we will see below).

In the short run, the supply of labor was assumed proportional to the fixed population.[11] In the long run, labor supply was assumed to vary as births responded (positively) to the level of wages. It was assumed that, as of any given time, there was a subsistence minimum corresponding to a particular wage level at which the population would remain stationary. At a wage above this level, the relatively abundant food supply would lead to more (surviving) children and a larger work force, and conversely, for a wage below the subsistence minimum.

Similarly, it was assumed that there was a minimum rate of return below which the capital stock would not be maintained. The purpose of this assumption was to assure a positive return to capital in equilibrium. Rent, the payment to the owner of the land, was defined as the residual of the sale value of the product, after subtracting wages and payments to the suppliers of capital. It was assumed that rent could not be negative, and that the owner of a particular plot of land would receive the difference between the value of output on that plot and the value of what could be produced on a plot that would yield no rent.

In this paradigm, landlords were assumed either to "waste" their incomes in consumption of services provided by "unproductive" laborers, or to lend their savings to farmers who would use it to hire workers and thereby increase productive employment. Similarly, savings by farmers would augment the demand for labor. Hence an increase in the propensity to save tended both to increase real wages and the volume of aggregate output, temporarily. But so long as the subsistence minimum remained unchanged, an increase in wages could not be permanent. A temporary increase in wages would lead to an increase in population (and labor force) thereby driving wages down toward the subsistence minimum. This effect could be avoided only by workers raising the "supply price of reproduction," that is, by changing their attitudes toward the relation between reproduction and income in a manner tantamount to a collective refusal

11. In discussing the theory of distribution, classical economists generally assumed that the supply of labor services varied in proportion to the population. Possible variations in length of the work week, gainful employment of women and children, etc., were confined to ad hoc discussions of public policy, and not integrated with the theory.

to maintain the current population except at wage levels above the initial subsistence minimum.

Except for one complication, the classical distribution paradigm could be viewed as one in which economic progress (measured by per capita real income) was the resultant of a race between the forces making for a positive secular trend in the savings ratio and those making for a similar trend in the net reproduction rate (of the population) at a given level of wages. The complication is fixity of the supply of land. This fixity implied that an increase in the quantity of labor-capital units[12] would compel their owners to compete for employment by accepting reduced wages and profits, thereby permitting higher rents to be earned on given plots of land but discouraging both population growth and saving. Development of this argument leads to the conclusion that in a stationary state the real income of the labor force would be set by the cultural and biological factors that determined the wage at which the population would become stationary.[13]

After correcting the ambiguities and shortcomings in the argument concerning the relation among the savings ratio, the rate of population growth, and the level of real wages, the implications of the surviving propositions are not very strong as applied to nonstationary states. It is only when the stationary state is alleged to be close at hand, that the (alleged) relation between real wages and population growth becomes a salient factor in denying the possibility of raising living standards except by changing reproductive behavior.

It was belief in the immediacy of the stationary state that underlay the great contemporary influence of Malthus's thesis on population, and the "iron law of wages" that it inspired. And when events in the second half of the nineteenth century made such belief less credible, this influence attenuated, and the practical relevance of the classical distribution paradigm diminished along with it.

In its original form, the idea that economic progress (i.e., growth of real per capita income) is severely limited by a fixed supply of land is now considered to be irrelevant to all but the most primitive communities, if

12. Classical economists did not usually explore the possibility of varying the ratio of labor to capital.

13. The essence of this argument is contained in Adam Smith's *The Wealth of Nations* (1776, Book 1, chapter 8). However, the implications of a fixed stock of land were not generally appreciated until the publication of Thomas Robert Malthus's *An Essay on Principles of Population* (1798).

even there. However, in an altered form, in the last quarter-century there has been a resurrection of the idea that the planet is endowed with a fixed stock of natural materials—animal, vegetable, and mineral—which it is technically impossible to enhance or even to maintain if it is being "used up" faster than what is consistent with some tight upper bound.

Whether classified as investment or consumption, productive activity by humans involving physical transformation of materials has the effect of using up this endowment. Since higher real income, either for an individual or for the community as a whole, involves a greater amount of such activity, there is tension between population size and per capita income if the stock of endowed resources is not to be trenched upon. Such trenching is commonly described as damaging the environment.

Varying with the particular environmental defender, it is held that we are at or near the upper limit to the rate of aggregate worldwide production that can occur without reducing the planet's stock of endowed resources. Accordingly, it is necessary either that we halt the growth of worldwide population, reduce the level of per capita income, or accept some combination of the two, if we are not to trench upon the stock of endowed resources that are alleged to be irreplaceable.

While its critical variable has changed from a limited supply of foodstuffs (mainly grain) in the early nineteenth century, to a more diffuse set of irreplaceable and/or irreparable environmental characteristics in the late twentieth, the structure of the argument is the same: neither technological advance nor accumulation of capital, nor greater or more diligent human effort, can do much to increase real output per capita, without reducing an endowed stock of resources.[14] Now, as almost two centuries ago, this paradigm is a staple of arguments aimed at persuading the public of an alleged need to restrict population growth in order to maintain living standards in the face of a natural resources constraint. Now, as in the early nineteenth century, the suggestion that population size might be deliberately manipulated raises theological and moral concerns: what is different in the late twentieth century is the extension of these concerns to innovations designed to loosen the technological constraint (e.g., genetic engineering). Until very recently, such innovations were not conceived to be feasible.

14. In the original Malthusian context, the possibility of increasing output by wearing out the land was not explicitly considered. However, the spirit of the argument would in no way have been altered if this possibility had been allowed.

To summarize, the exemplar of the classical distribution paradigm was the tension among the forces making for population growth, capital accumulation, a fixed supply of land, and a fixed technology. This exemplar was applied not only to Great Britain, but also to other countries to explain differences in wealth, living standards, and other gross socioeconomic characteristics. In making this application the classical economists abstracted from problems relating to the optimal mix of final outputs in order to focus upon the forces determining the distribution of income among three factors of production, each of which was identified with a particular social class. Their concern was with the relation of this distribution to the process of capital accumulation and the characteristics of a stationary state. Despite prescient departures from the simple scheme of the exemplar, proponents of the paradigm generally argued as though the standard of living (real income) of laborers depended solely upon the quantity of food they consumed.

The proper mix of consumption items—the central focus of RAP—was considered to be of concern only to the small fraction of the population receiving nonwage income: landlords and other suppliers of capital. But consumption by these groups was considered "unproductive" in that it contributed nothing to further production. In this, the classical economists expressed a valuation of the choices of resource owners that was contrary to a market valuation. This is in conflict both with RAP and much late-twentieth-century common sense. Though, as we shall see in chapter 12, contemporary economics is not free of second guessing of market valuations, the discussion of this topic had best be deferred.

Re: Marx

Regardless of his wishes, an author wishing to consider the role of ideology in economic thinking must pay some attention to Marx. More than any other figure in the history of economic thought, Marx contended that an economic theory is an expression of the ideology of a particular class of participants in the productive process. For Marx, a class of participants was defined by the characteristics of its role in the productive process: the most important characteristics being its property rights—or lack of them—in the means of production and the activities required (if any) to fulfill its role. Hence the feudal land owners, the bourgeoisie (capitalists), and the wage-earning proletariat.

For Marx, the function of an economic theory was to provide the members of a class with a picture of the economic process suitable for assisting them in daily activities, especially collective action to advance their eco nomic interests. A proper economic theory reflects the experienc and expresses the aspirations of the class which is its advocate: it serves both as a means of educating—heightening the self-awareness of—members of the class, and as an instrument of political propaganda. In a nutshell, the primary purpose of an economic theory was promotion of an ideology.

Because Marx's influence on the economics culture has been marginal, and is probably diminishing, I shall eschew detailed consideration of the Marxian paradigms, of which there are at least two. One of these, which I term the *exploitation paradigm,* takes the classical distribution theory as a point of departure to develop a theory of distribution whose most salient implication is that property income (profits and interest) derives from surplus value which results from the underpayment of labor. This theory is used to develop a theory of "capitalist crises" characterized by unemployment and depression.

For almost a century and a half this theory, and its proper interpretation, has been the subject of scholarly and nonscholarly debate. At its best, these debates involve issues of great technical interest to economists and have been published in leading professional journals. Ironically, in recent years as the intellectual salience of Marxism has declined with the defeat of Socialism in Eastern Europe, the quality of the discussion of the technical side of its economics has sharply improved. However, the details of this literature are not germane to our concerns.[15]

While the exploitation paradigm is the aspect of Marx's work that is of most interest to economists, it is probably not the most influential of the paradigms suggested by his writings. I would assign that place to the theory of history as the record of class struggles, with classes defined by the position of their members in the process of production, especially their status as producers or as recipients of surplus. In this paradigm, the driving force of history is change in the technique of production: such change makes appropriate alterations of existing institutions governing property relationships highly beneficial to the process of economic development.[16] Put in Marxian language, changes in the technique or mode

15. John E. Roemer (1986) contains a good list of references to recent Marxian economics.

16. In this sentence, Marxists would say "essential" rather than "highly beneficial."

of production create a contradiction between the forces of production (technology) and the relations of production (property relations), whose resolution can be effected only by the struggle of the class benefiting from the new mode of production against the class standing to lose by its implementation.

This paradigm is essentially what Marxists call Historical Materialism, and its most famous and influential statement is to be found in *The Communist Manifesto*. Historical materialism can be hitched to the exploitation paradigm, and Marx and most Marxian economists have attempted to make the hitch. However, the linkage between the two is problematic: there have been many, and often inconsistent, harnesses proposed, and historical-materialist arguments are often advanced without reference to the exploitation paradigm. Conversely, the exploitation paradigm is presented either as a piece of religious dogma, or as a highly technical argument—often quite mathematical—of concern only to aficionados of economic theory, and only problematically supportive of Marx's contentions.

I am not at all certain that historical materialism should be presented as an economic paradigm of the same sort as the others discussed here. However, I shall spare the reader an ambivalent taxonomic argument and simply point out that historical materialism provides a conceptual organization that has had, for almost a century and a half, a continuing influence on all of the social sciences as well as on political discourse. The vicissitudes of the historical predictions associated with this paradigm are so well known as to obviate recapitulation. Alienation is yet another theme in Marxist literature that might be considered to have generated a paradigm of some interest, but I shall not pursue the matter.

BEYOND RATIONALITY: CONTRA RAP

In this section we consider some "negative paradigms." These are paradigms whose exemplars consist of denials of one or another proposition of RAP. While the effect of such denials is to open the possibility of considering relationships precluded by RAP, usually they are not associated with much guidance as to how to replace the disputed proposition. Despite this limitation, each of the negative paradigms presented has served as a focal point for a literature stressing the need for such a replacement.

As was set forth in chapter 3, a cornerstone of RAP is the assumption that a resource owner behaves as if he allocated his resources so as to maximize his utility. Such behavior is defined as *rational*. In order for rational behavior to generate the well-behaved demand functions required for RAP, a utility function must be assumed to possess certain general characteristics described in chapter 3. Although the propriety of such an assumption has been disputed, RAP adherents customarily treat these characteristics as being properties of a normal utility function.

Thus, in analyzing the market behavior of prices and quantities, the characteristics ascribed to utility functions are treated as maintained hypotheses. That is, subject to the restrictions of the paradigm, RAP adherents generally ascribe to utility functions whatever properties are necessary to reconcile observed price-quantity behavior with the maintained hypothesis that all actors are behaving rationally. However, this RAP research strategy is unsatisfactory to many psychologists and decision theorists, as well as to (some) economists, who wish to make statements about the rationality of individual decision makers subject to direct test.

Generally, the making of such tests requires the study of individual, as distinguished from market, behavior. To move from the study of price-quantity behavior of entire markets to the analysis of the choice behavior of the individuals who transact in them is to move from the mainstream of general economics to several distinct areas of specialized research. One of these is concerned with analyzing the choices made by individual households when confronted by alternative combinations of resource constraints (e.g., prices and income levels). Usually the data for such analyses are generated by household surveys of one kind or another.

The collection and analysis of survey data is an important application of econometric technique and is generally considered to be one of the more successful fields of such application. As there is an excellent and fairly recent survey of theory, techniques, results, and problems within this field (Deaton and Muellbauer 1980) I shall venture only two remarks: (1) In virtually all of this literature, rationality is a maintained hypothesis: the research problem is to find the utility function (or distribution of functions over the population) that reconciles the market behavior observed with this maintained hypothesis. (2) The literature is characterized by adherence to the "principle of parsimony": that is, the researchers seek to find a single or, at worst, a family of temporally invariant utility functions that performs the reconciliation specified in (1). In the event that a plurality of utility functions is admitted, the assignment of a given household to one function or another is determined by the value(s) of a (very) limited number of parameters that serve to characterize the household. Otherwise, the exercise of reconciling observed behavior with the maintained hypothesis would be too easy, and the resulting estimates of the parameters of household demand functions too imprecise, to be of much scientific value.[17]

The second area of research on individual behavior is of more immediate concern to the present discussion than the first. While this area has been cultivated more intensively by psychologists than by economists, it is attracting a growing number of the latter as well.[18] This research area is generally described as *choice theory* or *decision theory,* and focuses on the generation and analysis of experimental data in settings where the hypothesis of rationality is left open to refutation.

As the devotees of this subfield are concerned only indirectly, if at all, with explaining "ordinary" market behavior, the choice objects studied are quite varied and not at all focused upon those confronting a conventional household in its daily routine. Indeed, the major class of choice objects studied are "gambles" of various kinds, with behavioral conformity of choice makers to the axioms of the Von Neumann-Morgenstern schema used as test(s) of the rationality hypothesis.[19]

Interpretation and appraisal of the outcome of such tests has spawned a substantial literature spanning journals in economics and psychology. While this literature is filled with ongoing debate, it is clear that a significant group of students believes that, at least in some instances, the data reject the rationality hypothesis.[20]

---

17. While utility functions are permitted to vary over time, they are allowed to do so only in a manner sufficiently well-specified that it is possible to distinguish (at least approximately) the effect of price changes on quantities taken with the utility function unchanged, from the effect due to shifts of the function itself. Otherwise, knowledge of the characteristics of the utility function would be of no value in predicting the effect of a change in price on the quantity taken by the market.

18. The relevant literature is discussed in Bruno S. Frey and Reiner E. Eichenberger (1991). Further discussion (and references) may be found in the various essays in R. Hogarth and M. W. Reder (1987). Also see Mark J. Machina (1987, 1989, 1990) and Peter C. Fishburn (1987).

19. The von Neumann-Morgenstern utility function was first presented in their famous book, *The Theory of Games and Economic Behavior* (1953). Also see the presentation by Machina (1987). It should be noted that acceptance of expected utility maximization as a criterion of rationality implies that any departure from risk neutrality is irrational. Yet, in many contexts RAP adherents posit both risk aversion and rationality. Thus the von Neumann-Morgenstern criterion of rationality differs from what is often applied by mainstream RAP economists.

20. See Frey and Eichenberger (1991).

Framing Effects

In particular, it is contended that preferences and choices over a set of alternatives may vary with the context in which the alternatives are presented. The context of presentation is frequently described as a "frame," and the anomalies (to the rationality hypothesis) caused by changing the frame while leaving the choice objects and resource constraints fixed, are called framing effects.[21]

Thus it is reported that experimental subjects prefer gamble A to gamble B, or B to A, depending upon which gamble is presented as implying an expected loss (and which an expected gain) despite the fact that the expected payoffs of the two gambles are equal.[22] That is, in addition to expected payoffs, the choice between gambles is affected by the frame in which they are presented: subjects seem to prefer a frame in which an expected payoff is presented as a "gain" to one in which an identical payoff is presented as a "loss."[23] The literature contains numerous other examples having the (same) effect of undermining one or another axiom of the Von Neumann-Morgenstern utility schema. Much, though not all, of this literature is concerned with experimental results. (For example, Frey and Eichenberger (1991) refer to a number of nonexperimental phenomena which various authors have interpreted as inconsistent with the rationality hypothesis.)

However, although empirical researchers on individual-choice behavior have developed a lively community with its own vocabulary, research programs, classic articles, outstanding anomalies, and other characteristics of a Kuhnian subculture, their paradigm has had but little impact upon the main corpus of economics. This is because this research community has not as yet developed any generally accepted theory of choice-making

21. For an introduction to the notion of framing effects, see Tversky and Kahnemann (1987) and the subsequent discussion in Hogarth and Reder (1987). One important consequence of framing effects is the class of phenomena known as "preference reversals," discussed in Tversky's and Kahnemann's essay. I am inclined to consider Bruno Frey's (1992, chap. 12) ipsative theory of human behavior as a particular and interesting example of a framing effect. In effect, the ipsative theory proposes that factual judgments referring to oneself are systematically different from analogous judgments referring to others.

22. See Tversky and Kahnemann (1987).

23. The reader is warned that distinguishing frame from choice objects may create serious problems, the resolution of which is critical to deciding whether or not to abandon the rationality hypothesis in a specific context. This is to say that the introduction of framing effects to the study of choice behavior is attended with difficulties. Fortunately, the argument of this book does not require that we pursue the matter.

behavior alternative to RAP, but has found its unifying principle in adherence to a common methodology.

The outstanding features of this methodology are: (1) inferring individual preferences from choice-making behavior in experimental settings; (2) treating the rationality hypothesis as open to rejection rather than as maintained, and (3) emphasizing the contextual characteristics of the experimental situation as a means of explaining perceived departures from rationality.

Perhaps because this research community is at least as strongly oriented toward psychology as toward economics, its empirical findings have been analyzed and discussed piecemeal without concern for their impact upon an overarching paradigm. To be sure, though general theories are sought, concern with the paradigmatic implications of particular findings is far less than what is typical in economics.[24] In particular, there is little tendency to scrutinize empirical findings through the lens of a relatively tight prior generated by the implications of a paradigm.[25]

As a result of this "one finding at a time" approach, the research mores of this community appear closer in spirit to those of laboratory sciences than to those of economics. This difference of approach is primarily responsible for the relatively small impact of their research upon the main corpus of economics. Choice (decision) theorists make few assertions about the breadth of application of their findings: they emphasize the sensitivity of their results to details of experimental context, and devote little effort to developing the implications of their findings for nonexperimental (i.e., "real world") situations. Consequently, economists have felt free to use or neglect these findings—on grounds of real-world relevance—as their paradigmatically oriented inclinations have led them.

Economists wishing to attack RAP have often cited anomalies generated by experimental research as evidence for the particular point they are seeking to make. Some researchers of empirical choice behavior (notably Tversky and Kahnemann 1987) have explicitly attacked "economists" (RAP devotees) for continuing their adherence to the rationality hypothesis in the face of experimental evidence to the contrary, but their challenge has been methodological rather than substantive. They have invited econ-

24. For example, Tversky and Kahnemann's prospect theory.

25. Thus Machina (1989) says "Whereas experimental psychologists can be satisfied as long as their models of individual behavior perform properly in the laboratory, *economists are responsible for the logical implications of their behavioral models when embedded in social settings* (italics in original).

omists to abandon the hypothesis of rationality—at least in some contexts—but have not specified the alterations in economic theory that they would propose to effect. As a result their work has thus far had only limited impact upon *positive* economics.[26]

However, an important target of opponents of the rationality hypothesis has not been the positive aspect of RAP, but its normative associations. That is, much of the criticism directed at this hypothesis is directed at analyses of the effects of public policies—implemented or proposed—that require the rational behavior of all participants as a maintained hypothesis. Put differently, a major concern of economists in maintaining (or rejecting) the rationality hypothesis arises from its role in welfare economics, as we shall see.[27]

Bounded Rationality

I shall not attempt to review the growing literature on reconsideration of rationality beyond commenting on a few ideas that have at least the potential of becoming roots of paradigms. One of these is the concept of *bounded rationality,* identified with Herbert A. Simon.[28] Here, the basic idea is to describe decision making as an attempt to solve problems in specific settings rather than as an attempt at (constrained) optimization of some objective function.

Whether the outcome of a particular resource allocation decision should be considered as a solution to a problem depends upon the situation and purposes of the decision maker. In the event that a "solution" is found, the decision maker does not ask whether it might be possible to do still better (i.e., to optimize), but goes on to another problem. Thus the decision maker is said to "satisfice," or to seek a result satisfactory for the problem at hand, rather than to optimize.[29]

26. An exception to this statement is the work of R. J. Herrnstein with various co-authors in which they propose a theory of choice making in which individuals (sometimes) "meliorate" rather than maximize utility. See R. J. Herrnstein and Drazen Prelec (1991).

27. The special place of welfare economics in the culture of the discipline is discussed in chapter 9. Accordingly, to avoid repetition, I shall defer discussion of the matter to that chapter.

28. In his autobiography (1991, p. 165) Simon remarks that his 1957 paper, "A Behavioral Model of Rational Choice," is the one most frequently chosen for citation by economists wishing to refer to bounded rationality and satisficing.

29. It has been suggested (by Jacob Marschak) that satisficing becomes identical with optimizing when the cost of ascertaining and calculating the consequences of each of the possible alternatives is taken into account. That is, the outcome of satisficing reflects not

It is no part of our task to evaluate bounded rationality as a framework for decision theory alternative to (unbounded) rationality. It suffices to note that it has been seriously proposed as such an alternative.[30] However, it is not inappropriate to remark that its impact upon positive economics has thus far been relatively limited. The main reason for this is that the implications of bounded rationality for market behavior are difficult to distinguish from those of transaction costs. Consequently, in order to preserve the paradigm, RAP adherents prefer to interpret behavior such as that of price makers and price takers (described in chapter 3) as conventional profit maximization in the presence of transaction costs rather than as manifestations of a departure from rationality.[31]

If asked "how would positive economics be altered if utility maximization were replaced by satisficing as the characteristic goal of economic activity?," an economist would be obliged to respond somewhat as follows: (1) by introducing the notion of "aspiration level," and (2) by greatly broadening the types of behavior considered to be compatible with economic theory.

1. The idea that the behavior of a choice or decision maker is influenced by his aspiration level is embedded in a great deal of experimental research, both in psychology and (to a lesser extent) in economics. This means that an individual's behavior depends not only upon his resources and preference function, but also upon what he believes to be attainable in a given situation. Thus, to the extent that aspiration level is a salient variable for explaining choice behavior, RAP is inadequate.

2. Suppose, for the sake of argument, we accepted Simon's contention that all purposive behavior is problem solving, and powerfully influenced by the setting of the problem. Such acceptance would imply abandonment of virtually all implications of RAP concerning the relation of changes in quantity to changes in price and the consequent evisceration of that paradigm. But what would be put in its place? Bounded rationality can be made compatible with almost any story of the process of setting prices: it can accommodate a wide variety of stories of oligopolistic price setting, especially those that portray the (price setting) process as using rules of thumb to promote efficiency in signaling the strategic intentions of the

only the scarcity of (other) resources, but also the scarcity of information about the consequences of choosing from among the feasible alternatives.

30. For an extensive discussion of this proposal see John Conlisk (1996). This reference contains an extensive bibliography.

31. For further illustrations of this point, see ibid., pp. 675–82.

price setters. Bounded rationality is also consistent with accounts of be-havior that emphasize the following of conventions (e.g., collective bar-gaining patterns) as techniques for minimizing transaction costs, minimi-zation of interpersonal and intergroup friction, and so on.

Thus, as compared with RAP, bounded rationality greatly expands the types of price-quantity relations that may be considered as theoretically acceptable. However, it offers no guidance in constructing theories of such relations beyond the (good) advice to consider the cost of reaching deci-sions as important. In short, as thus far developed, bounded rationality serves as a portmanteau rationale for a very wide range of behaviors, in-cluding some that may be interpreted as inconsistent with RAP, without hazard to its own credibility.

Misperceptions of Utility

In *The Joyless Economy,* Tibor Scitovsky attacks RAP and its implications more directly than any of the other alternative paradigms discussed in this section.[32] Rather than leave the resource owner's preference function as a black box whose characteristics must be inferred from choice behavior, Scitovsky presents (in chapters 2–4) a specific model of the production of satisfaction based on the physiology of the central nervous system. As the details of the model do not directly concern us, the reader can best obtain them by reading the original.

The principal implication of the model is the division of satisfactions into those of comfort and those of pleasure: roughly, "feelings of comfort and discomfort have to do with the level of arousal . . . whereas feelings of pleasure are created by changes in the arousal level" (p. 61). The point of the argument is that we (especially Americans) overemphasize the im-portance of comfort to the neglect of stimulation, and are bored and un-happy as a result.

Scitovsky contrasts European behavior and mores with American: the former allegedly giving greater weight to the pleasure derived from stimu-lation, and the latter emphasizing material comfort and the counterpro-ductive saving of time. To Americans, the implicit advice is to become more like Europeans are—or were:[33] to Europeans the advice is, beware

32. Tibor Scitovsky (1976). Also see *Critical Review* 10, no. 4 (Fall 1996), which is de-voted to a discussion of *The Joyless Economy.*

33. In the 1992 revised edition of *The Joyless Economy,* Scitovsky recognizes that the contrast between European and American folkways and behavior patterns has been consid-erably reduced during the past 15 to 20 years.

of Americanization. Generically, we are all advised to beware of prepackaging and mass-produced items.

While recognizing the benefits of scale economies associated with standardization and mass production, Scitovsky argues that capture of these benefits often entails monotony and reduced sensitivity to the pleasures derived from stimulation: if pushed too far, the sacrifice of stimulation may outweigh the benefits of greater comfort. By contrast, RAP implies that rationality generates a tropism for optimum balance, a view that Scitovsky rejects. Arguing from a wide variety of evidence, he concludes that in developed economies—especially the United States—many (most?) individuals, in reaching for greater comfort, sacrifice so much stimulation that they fail to achieve the maximum attainable level of well-being (utility).

The evidence adduced consists of answers to questionnaires, quasi-anthropological judgments by students of comparative culture, and research results of psychologists. To accept such evidence would require abandonment of rationality as a maintained hypothesis which, of itself, would be unacceptable to RAP adherents. Even to economists who have reservations about the universal applicability of rationality, this evidence has not been persuasive. As Scitovsky relates in the preface to the second edition (p. xi) "Economists are deeply divided into the Establishment and its radical left-critics, but they were like a harmonious and happy family in their unanimous hostility to my ideas."

One important reason for this hostility is the kind of evidence he asks them to accept. As already noted, most (though not all) RAP adherents believe that what can be known about utility functions must be inferable solely from price-quantity behavior. However, even among those economists who are willing to grant legitimacy to information (about utility functions) obtained from other sources, only a small group would be willing to use such information as a basis for conclusions that are inconsistent with rationality.[34] Yet, at many points, Scitovsky's argument uses nonprice-quantity information for precisely this purpose.

Even among the minority of economists who are explicitly hostile to rationality, there is wide disagreement as to what behavioral assumptions—if any—should replace it. For example, Herbert Simon denies that

34. That is, some economists accept evidence other than inferences from price-quantity behavior provided it does not entail rejection of rationality, but not otherwise: In other words, the presumed validity of the rationality hypothesis affects the criteria for admissibility of certain kinds of evidence (see below).

psychological phenomena must be explained neurologically, "not because of in principle opposition to reductionism but because complex behavior can be reduced to neural processes only in successive steps, not in a single leap . . . for psychology, a theory at the level of symbols, located midway between complex thought processes and neurons, is essential."[35] Another example to the same point is Robert Frank's argument, which we shall consider next.

The small degree of support offered to rationality opponents from within the profession reflects the predisposition among economists to minimize the psychological commitments entailed by economic theory. This predisposition has been strongly reinforced by the failure of psychologists to approach a consensus on the relevant issues, or even to agree on their relative saliency.[36] Thus it is likely that economists will avoid commitment to Scitovsky's quite specific model of the "neurological basis of utility production"[37] until—at a minimum—it obtains some currency among psychologists.[38]

Emotion and Rationality

Robert H. Frank's *Passions within Reason* (1988) offers a challenge to the rationality hypothesis different from that of *The Joyless Economy*. Despite many points of similarity between the two books, I shall focus on the differences. Both books stress that "hard wiring" within the human organism imposes constraints on the characteristics of utility functions that are far more restrictive than those specified in RAP.[39] But while offering a considerable list of citations to both physiological and psychological literature on the specifics of hard wiring, Frank's argument does not entail

35. Simon (1991), pp. 191–92.

36. This predisposition is reinforced by the history of unsuccessful attempts to incorporate psychological theories (e.g., the Weber-Fechner law) into the corpus of economics.

37. Or any other theory of comparable specificity and detail.

38. It might be noted that other attempts to specify tastes beyond what is required for RAP have failed to find favor within economics. For example, the attempt of even so famous an economist as Sir R. G. Hawtrey (1925) to whom Scitovsky acknowledges great indebtedness, has received very little attention.

39. As Frank remarks (1988, pp. 85, 146), the notion of hard-wired—i.e., organically rooted—behavior patterns is very similar to eighteenth- and nineteenth-century explanations of both moral sentiments and seemingly irrational types of behavior as due to biologically rooted "instincts."

acceptance of any particular model of the human organism:[40] it suffices that organisms be so constructed that emotions sometimes override the dictates of rationality in determining the conduct of appreciable numbers of individuals.

Frank's argument is sharply focused on the (alleged) failure of individuals consistently to exploit opportunities for personal gain. In particular, (he claims that) they often fail to exploit opportunities to gain advantage at the expense of persons with whom they sympathize, or in violation of accepted conventions. While there are a number of possible rationalizations of such behavior, what Frank emphasizes—and what is most subversive of RAP—is that (because of hard wiring) individuals derive personal satisfaction from behaving in a socially approved manner, *even when such behavior cannot be observed by others.*

In addition to citing a considerable volume of evidence from experiments,[41] Frank supports his contention that individuals often fail to behave opportunistically by observing the prevalence of such behavior as giving strangers information as to the time of day, street directions, and so forth. He also notes that contributions to charities, churches, and the like occur in appreciable quantity even under circumstances where failure to contribute could not be detected, and that people take the time and trouble to vote even when the probability that their vote will affect the outcome is negligible.

It is not necessary to counter Frank's argument in detail but merely to remark that a standard RAP counterargument is that while the assumption that the behavior of all economic agents always conforms to every implication of the hypothesis of rationality often falls short of descriptive accuracy, nevertheless it has great heuristic value in formulating valid generalizations. For example, although it sometimes happens that individuals make voluntary and anonymous contributions to support collective institutions, it would not be seriously proposed that voluntary contributions

---

40. Although Frank offers some detailed psychological argument (especially in chapter eight), his basic argument does not depend upon acceptance of any particular model of the neuropsychology of the human organism. It should be noted that Frank's references to psychological literature have very little overlap with Scitovsky's.

41. Probably the most important of these references is Robert Axelrod (1984). Axelrod reports that in two-person game situations, experimental subjects exhibit a tropism for strategies of tit-for-tat, reciprocating manifestations of cooperation, and eschewing opportunities for greater advantage at the expense of another party who had been cooperative.

be substituted for taxes as a method of financing governments. Put more strongly, it would not be seriously suggested that tax laws be written, or revenue estimates made, on any assumption other than that each individual taxpayer seeks to minimize his payments.

But without necessarily denying that there are circumstances where the metaphor of rationality is suggestive of sound institutional arrangements, Frank would argue that there are other circumstances where the reverse is the case. For example, because individuals are sometimes less opportunistic than rationality would suggest, long-term contracts involve smaller expected losses to the exposed party and are therefore of more frequent occurrence than one would expect in an RAP world.

The quantitative importance of such examples for *positive* economics is unclear because of the extremely sketchy specification of the relevant cost functions, both within RAP and in Frank's book. Nevertheless, Frank's argument will be hotly contested because of its implication for *welfare* economics. This implication arises from Frank's argument that it may be *individually,* as well as socially, advantageous for an individual to be so constituted as to shun opportunities to gain through opportunistic behavior.

Consider: there would be a social gain from the saving on costs of negotiating, administering, and adjudicating long-term contracts that would appear if potential contracting parties felt they could trust one another to adhere to the spirit of agreements despite the absence of cost-effective means of compelling such adherence. Similarly, social gains would arise from the augmented set of agreements that would become mutually advantageous to the contracting parties in the presence of greater trust. These gains would accrue disproportionately to those individuals who were perceived as relatively more trustworthy than most other potential partners in a contemplated (joint) undertaking.

Imaginably, it might be even more advantageous for an individual to be so constituted as to be capable of dissembling as trustworthy while retaining the capacity to behave opportunistically when a suitable occasion arose. It is here that predispositions enter the argument: if faking attitudes were "costless," it would be individually advantageous to feign trustworthiness while, in fact, being opportunistic. But—Frank argues—the human constitution is such that it is so difficult for (most of) us to project a consistently false impression of our character that the most effective (only possible?) way for most people to appear trustworthy is in fact to be trustworthy.

Such trustworthiness is facilitated by appropriate social conditioning (e.g., proper upbringing) and a psycho-physiological makeup such as to cause pangs of guilt were an individual to violate the dictates of his moral upbringing by behaving opportunistically.[42] Therefore parents who seek to foster character traits conducive to success will encourage their children to acquire traits associated with trustworthiness.[43]

Acquisition of such traits is facilitated by genetically influenced neurological characteristics that generate sympathy for persons with whom we have continuing relationships. Accordingly, sociobiological processes may have operated to make the human species resistant to the temptations of opportunism, and therefore to promote social efficiency despite the failure of individuals consistently to pursue their own advantage.[44]

The effect of this is to open wide the door to explanations of individual behavior—even narrowly economic behavior—that are inconsistent with RAP, as well as to the possibility that proposals of collective actions that seem futile because of the opportunistic behavior ascribed to individuals (e.g., free riding, tax avoiding) may sometimes be feasible.

What unifies the various "antirationalists" is opposition to RAP as an exclusive source of explanation for human behavior and as a guide to its improvement, rather than adherence to any particular alternative theory or support for any particular empirical finding. Although the various antirationalist authors have not thus far embarked on a common scientific research program, there are signs that a scientific subculture is beginning to form around the idea that the process of choice making contains systematic departures from rationality. This subculture includes psychologists like Tversky, Kahnemann, and Herrnstein; economists like Thaler, Frank, and Scitovsky; and philosophers, political scientists, and sociologists, as well (see below, chapter 14). One manifestation of this subculture is cross-disciplinary collaboration between economists and psychologists.[45]

42. It could be contended that seemingly irrational behavior by guilt-feeling and/or sympathetic individuals is utility maximizing, given the "peculiarities" of those individuals' utility functions. However, such an argument would make it impossible ever to recognize nonmaximizing behavior, and thereby render the rationality hypothesis void of content.

43. Yet another reason for parents to avoid encouraging their children to be opportunistic is the fear that they themselves might be among their children's victims.

44. This line of argument by Frank and others often involves sociobiological processes that promote the survival chances of individuals who possess a tropism for socially beneficial behavior. This is discussed below in chapter 14.

45. As examples of such collaboration I cite Amos Tversky and Richard H. Thaler (1990); Daniel Kahnemann, Jack L. Knetsch, and Richard H. Thaler (1986); and Robert H. Frank, Thomas Gilovich, and Dennis T. Regan (1993).

Another manifestation is the publication by psychologists in professional journals of economics and, perhaps, some exportation by economists to the literature of psychology.[46] While such interdisciplinary collaboration is in its infancy, its occurrence lends support to the idea that a new paradigm, not yet well defined, may be emerging.

Although a primary focus of this paradigm would be denial of the descriptive accuracy of the rationality hypothesis, and insistence upon the importance of (claimed) violations thereof, its prospective adherents would probably be as much concerned with welfare economics as with positive aspects of the subject. Such interest is manifested overtly in an interesting paper of Akerlof and Dickens[47] who argue, inter alia, that the effects of "cognitive dissonance" may serve to rationalize (1) legislation requiring use of safety equipment; (2) governmental provision of old age insurance (financed by tax payments), and (3) imposition of lower penalties for criminal acts than those suggested by models of behavior that embody the assumption of "ordinary rationality."[48]

Although it does not affect the implications of their argument for welfare and public policy, it is important to note that—unlike other antirationalist arguments—Akerlof and Dickens's discussion does not involve failure to maximize utility. Instead, Akerlof and Dickens interpret cognitive dissonance as implying introduction of beliefs about the state of the world into the choice maker's decision procedure. That is, an individual's choices are made to depend, not only upon the utility that the choice objects yield, but also upon his beliefs about (say) the merits of his selections relative

46. On issues associated with rationality, it is psychologists who have been concerned with changing the views of economists rather than the reverse. This might explain why the flow of papers from psychologists to journals of economics has been greater than the reverse flow.

It is interesting to note that in the paper of Frank et al. cited in note 45, and in several other publications there cited, experimental evidence was found indicating that economists are more prone than others to engage in rational, as distinguished from conventional and/ or "fair," behavior when presented with an opportunity to choose among alternative courses of action. These findings were challenged by Anthony M. Yezer, Robert S. Goldfarb, and Paul J. Poppen (1996) and defended by Frank et al. (1996).

47. George A. Akerlof and William T. Dickens (1982).

48. As Akerlof and Dickens put it (1982, p. 307, n. 1), "The approach of this paper to what economists might call the economics of 'irrational' behavior differs from that of Gary Becker (who) views irrational behavior as random deviations from economic rationality. We use the findings of psychologists who view irrational behavior as predictable, and therefore not totally random. Welfare implications seem to follow from the predictability of such behavior."

to those of unchosen alternatives. Choices are made so as to maximize an augmented utility function: that is, an objective function the arguments of which include not only the quantities of conventional choice objects but also the psychic comfort derived from having made "correct" choices.

In their "fundamental" model, Akerlof and Dickens make an individual believe (incorrectly) that his job is safe only if he has previously worked on it; other individuals are assumed to recognize that the job is unsafe. The effect of previous employment in inducing an incorrect belief about a job's safety is taken to exemplify the working of cognitive dissonance—the tendency of individuals to adopt beliefs that make actions already taken (or under commitment) appear to have been more appropriate than they would have appeared under the beliefs that would have been adopted had their actions been different.

In other words, an individual's utility level is affected by (some of) his beliefs, but these beliefs are selected so as to rationalize his previous actions. Thus his actions have both a direct effect upon his utility, and an indirect one via their impact upon his beliefs. From this, under the assumption that all individuals act rationally, Akerlof and Dickens show that requiring workers to take costly safety measures (that they would not take voluntarily) may make consumers of the product better off (because of lower prices) without reducing the utility of (any) coerced worker: this is tantamount to a Pareto improvement.

The validity of the Akerlof and Dickens argument is crucially dependent upon the psychological evidence for the occurrence of cognitive dissonance effects, and the range of phenomena affected by dissonance. I shall not attempt to appraise the evidence from experimental psychology that Akerlof and Dickens offer, and limit my comments upon it to the remark that the evidence is completely disjoint with that presented by other proponents of an antirationality position. Indeed, despite their own claims to the contrary, it is not clear that Akerlof and Dickens are properly interpreted as "antirationalists": their argument can be construed as compatible with RAP, but with utility functions augmented by (unfamiliar) variables reflecting beliefs of the choice maker.

To relate framing effects to those of cognitive dissonance and divide responsibility for the production of RAP-anomalous phenomena between the two would seem an important task for economists seeking to establish an anti-RAP paradigm. That they have not yet begun to undertake such a task reflects their preoccupation with attacking RAP and delegitimizing its associated welfare economics, to the exclusion of developing a positive theory of human behavior that would encompass nonrationality. In effect, the antirationalists seem to be content with arguing that, because human behavior often contradicts the implications of rationality, economists should be more cautious in drawing inferences and recommending policies based on the assumption of its validity.

But aside from feeling more humble, it is not clear what economists are being advised to do. While some antirationalists might suggest abandoning all of conventional economic theory, not all or even most of them would do so. Recommendations for specific modifications of economic theory are scant and almost always take the form of prescribing alterations that would *permit* some particular types of phenomena, but fail to specify the circumstances under which such phenomena might be expected to occur.[49] In effect, it is demanded that economic theory (i.e., RAP) be altered so as to permit consideration of a wider set of behaviors, but without suggestion as to how to offset the loss of explanatory power that such an alteration would entail.

STRONG HISTORY AND NETWORK EXTERNALITIES

As I indicated in chapter 3, the paradigm proper of RAP is ahistoric; indeed, it is literally static. None of the relationships that it encompasses may include lags. History, dynamics, disequilibrium, and so on enter RAP only by way of various paradigm adjuncts. However, all temporal behavior patterns reconcilable with RAP must be ergodic and, in particular, must involve ultimate convergence to a repetitive pattern determined solely by the tastes, techniques, and resources of the economic agents. While overly restrictive, the essential character of RAP-compatible temporal patterns is conveyed by the statement that they must converge eventually—in the "long run"—to a repetitively stationary state whose characteristics are determined by (unchanging) tastes, techniques, and resources.[50]

It is the contention of an emerging group of economists that to demand RAP compatibility of price-quantity data precludes consideration of valid

49. For example, it is demanded that the theory of rational expectations be altered (or abandoned) so as to allow for the possibility of "speculative bubbles" (see below, chapter 8). But nothing is said as to the circumstances under which such bubbles might arise, or of their characteristics, other than that they would be incompatible with the (related) hypotheses of rational expectations and efficient markets.

50. RAP does not require the existence of a repetitive stationary state: it is logically compatible with repeated cycles or other temporal variations of state so long as (given sufficient time) the model returns to the state specified in the paradigm proper, which is assumed to be its starting point. However, the literature has not been much concerned with this detail.

and important explanatory hypotheses. In effect, RAP requires either (a) that a given piece of price-quantity behavior be explicable by an RAP compatible hypothesis or (b) that the reported behavior be rejected as the result of observational error, sample bias, or the outcome of (RAP compatible) forces not properly taken into account. The "strong history" advocates reject this disjunction, arguing that there are important phenomena whose correct explanation is not RAP-compatible.

One such phenomenon results from increasing returns (internal to the firm) that cannot be realized unless there are associated network(s) of a size adequate for the support of a sufficiently high level of output. The need for such a network may arise from any of a number of considerations: (1) if the product is durable and likely to require future repair, the difficulty (cost) of obtaining repair service will vary with the number of qualified suppliers. This number will in turn vary directly with the volume of output.[51] Hence the desirability of a firm's product, and its demand price to a given customer, will vary with what that customer believes the volume of the firm's output will be.

A widespread perception that the level of output will be insufficient to evoke an "adequate" number of service providers will depress the demand for the firm's output and (because of increasing returns) increase its unit cost and the selling price needed to cover it. Desire to own products (or brands) that are widely accepted will have analogous effects on demand, unit costs, and cost-covering selling prices of products that are perceived as unlikely to obtain such acceptance.

Still further: products whose use is dependent upon availability of complementary inputs will suffer loss of use value to prospective purchasers if such complements are unavailable, or available only at much greater cost than analogous complements to rival products. Therefore, in the presence of increasing returns, failure to obtain a sufficient network of suppliers of complementary inputs will depress demand and output, and raise unit cost and (zero-profit) selling price.[52]

That a technology characterized by increasing returns will be inhospi-

51. The relevant measure of volume of output must be inferred from context: in some cases the term will refer to cumulative output as of a given date; in others, to a rate of output as of a particular moment of time, etc.

52. The details of the argument may be found in M. L. Katz and Carl Shapiro (1985). Further discussion (including some dissent as to the empirical importance of the phenomena) may be found in a symposium, "Network Externalities," in the *Journal of Economic Perspectives* 8, no. 2 (Spring 1994): 93–158.

table to firms unable to achieve them will hardly come as news to RAP adherents. What is new is the jointure (by the strong history advocates) of increasing returns with *endogenous* technology in an anti-RAP argument to the effect that rational private profit seeking may lead to the adoption of technologies less efficient than the best available.[53]

The essence of the argument is as follows: consider a set of entrepreneurs faced with choosing among several alternative technologies, all subject to increasing returns to scale at initial rates of output, but with unknown relative efficiencies when used at optimum scale.[54] Adoption of a specific technology is assumed to entail commitment to subsequent purchases of ancillary equipment compatible with that technology, but with no other. The information available at the moment of technology choice is the cumulative number of adoptions to that moment, and the current prices of equipment associated with that technology: current prices are assumed proportional to current unit production costs.

If, for any reason, a particular technology should secure a transient advantage in number of adoptions it would gain further competitive advantages through the relative reduction of unit costs and selling prices and the effect of widespread adoption that is indicative of access to greater network advantages. Thus a head start or an initial spurt might yield cumulative advantage—through exploitation of scale economies—that could never be overcome by a latecomer, even if the latecomer were more efficient at full-scale operation.

This conclusion, which is antithetic to RAP, depends critically upon the postulated lack of information about unit costs of the competing technologies at full-scale operation. Existence of such information is (implicitly) assumed in the paradigm proper of RAP, and it is both plausible and customary also to assume that entrepreneurs possessing such information would, under competitive conditions, adopt the technology having the lowest unit cost at full capacity.[55] Since in the real world such information is never available, the validity of RAP will turn on what information is available to entrepreneurs at critical moments of technology choice and

---

53. See W. Brian Arthur (1989); Paul A. David (1992).

54. In the present context, "efficiency" is defined as the inverse of unit cost.

55. It is important to emphasize that the efficiency-tropism of RAP models is dependent on the presence of competition and that, even under competition, its salience may vary depending upon dynamic considerations. For example, if technology is subject to rapid and unpredictable change, concern with cost savings attainable only after long time intervals will be attenuated, and the salience of such savings will become sensitive to long-term interest rates.

the extent to which such (imperfectly informed) choices influence subsequent adoptions.

In this context it is not difficult either to produce models that support RAP, or alternatives that lead to the opposite conclusion; the question is which model is appropriate to the problem at hand. Given the wide acceptance of RAP, the question facing the strong history supporters is, Can you produce concrete examples where an inefficient technology has survived despite the availability of one that was demonstrably superior?

An answer is the now famous case of QWERTY. QWERTY refers to the arrangement of the standard typewriter (and computer) keyboard which, it is claimed, is inferior in terms of use facility (as reflected in operator speed) to known alternatives of no greater production cost. Yet, despite several attempts, none of these alternatives has thus far succeeded in displacing QWERTY because of the difficulty of inducing users to incur the entailed cost (especially time and trouble) of retraining operators and replacing established training curricula.[56]

In a nutshell, QWERTY's early advantage appears to have had a lasting effect in that more efficient alternatives have thus far been unable to overcome it. However, as so often happens in economics, this account of a specific historical sequence has not gone unchallenged.[57] Moreover, whatever the facts of the QWERTY story, until compelled by a number of other examples to the same effect, RAP defenders will not abandon the presumption that (under competitive conditions) more efficient techniques tend to drive out less efficient.

Such examples have not yet been produced. While there is no lack of illustrations of path dependence in economics, especially in the history of technology,[58] aside from QWERTY there have been no proffers of "smoking guns" where dynamic considerations have locked resource users into demonstrably inefficient choices of technology.

This is not to dispute the occurrence of lock-in effects, hysteresis and other features of nonergodic processes that cannot be readily incorporated in RAP models. But it *is* to question their importance. Specifically, it remains to be shown that the effects of nonergodic phenomena are of such salience as to preclude their being encapsulated within the disturbance terms of RAP models.

However, for the sake of argument, suppose that certain important

---

56. The details of QWERTY are set forth in P. A. David (1985).
57. See S. J. Liebowitz and Stephen Margolis (1990).
58. See David (1992); also P. A. David and Shane Greenstein (1990).

nonergodic phenomena cannot be accommodated within an RAP framework. To account for such phenomena RAP would have to be amended. But in what ways? Thus far the strong history advocates have given no clue as to how to proceed beyond the general admonition to be sensitive to the possible influence of nonergodic processes, and avoid the casual assumption that whatever is observed is the outcome of a process that is efficient in the long run.

If strong history is to be considered a paradigm, then in its present state it is a negative one: it tells us what to avoid and, in so doing, limits the scope of RAP—perhaps seriously. But it does not suggest what to put in its place. Failing such a directive, strong history implies weak(er) economics, but nothing more.

The effects of strong history upon RAP could arise from endogeneity of tastes as well as from endogeneity of technology. But whether stemming from endogenous tastes, endogenous technology, or endogenous information (e.g., learning by doing), strong history is associated with a conceptual organization in which lessons for the future are strongly conditioned by the (interpreted) record of the past, with correlatively less emphasis upon the "structure of the world." Conversely, RAP is associated with a conceptual organization in which guides to future conduct are based primarily on a set of interrelated hypotheses about the structure of the world and a deemphasis upon the influence of history.

AN AUSTRIAN PARADIGM?

Whether the long tradition of Austrian economics is associated with a paradigm is a difficult question. The diversity of views among the economists, of various nationalities, who identify themselves as "Austrian" does not make it easier either to find an answer, or to avoid misrepresenting the views of some claimants to the label. The following remarks are intended to apply to certain stereotypical views, frequently termed Austrian, but not to be identified as those of any particular "Austrian."[59]

It is convenient to begin by asserting that Austrian economics is a variant of RAP, and then to specify its differentiating characteristics. The identification with RAP stems from the common assumption that control

---

59. I have found Karen I. Vaughn (1994) highly informative on the diverse threads in the Austrian tapestry. I have also learned much from Israel Kirzner's (1987) article in *The New Palgrave Dictionary* as well as from G. P. O'Driscoll and M. J. Rizzo (1985); from Bruce Caldwell (1982), pp. 119–24; and from Kevin Hoover (1988), chapter 10. I had not encountered Peter J. Boettke (1994) until after this section had been written. A quick look suggests that many of the essays included therein will repay careful study.

of economic resources is vested in individual decision makers, each of whom allocates them among alternative uses so as to maximize his own utility. In mainstream RAP the individual's resource constraints include both wealth and market prices of potential objects of expenditure: these prices are assumed to be equilibrium prices. Austrians reject this latter assumption, arguing that markets do not clear continuously and that it is the action of individuals in achieving the potential gains from arbitrage that exist in disequilibrium that is important.[60] Thus the real world contains, not equilibrium prices, but a multidimensional manifold of offers to buy and sell within which rational individuals are continuously seeking opportunities for utility gains through arbitrage and otherwise.[61]

If continued indefinitely under stationary conditions, this process would (or might) lead to an equilibrium in which the "law of one price" held, but such continuation does not occur. The process is constantly interrupted by shocks so that market disequilibrium is perpetual. Austrians reject the RAP notion that the concept of an equilibrium may serve as a simplifying approximation to the process of price-quantity adjustments in favor of the greater realism provided by explicit analysis of the process in detail.

But only rarely has this pursuit of realism led to empirical studies of specific economic phenomena. Instead, Austrians have focused upon improving and extending the framework of their theory for the purpose of better conceptualization. However, identifying its use with the oversimplifications of equilibrium, they have studiously avoided mathematics, which has further alienated their work from mainstream theory during the past half century. Thus Austrian economics has become an esoteric branch of economic theory distinguished largely by its critical attitude toward the techniques and assumptions of those in the mainstream.

The negative posture of the Austrians is rooted in their view of economics as a science. They deny that prediction of human behavior is pos-

---

60. When every individual maximizes subject to the constraints of equilibrium prices, rational behavior becomes tantamount to equilibrium. But when the resource constraints are not equilibrium prices, as in Austrian analyses, individual maximization becomes "subjective," i.e., each individual maximizes subject to the limits of the constraints as he *perceives* them. Thus, outside an Arrow-Debreu world, universal rationality (utility maximization) among individuals may coexist with disequilibrium in some (or all) markets.

61. It is important to note that in disequilibrium there is dispersion not only among prices of specific commodities, but also among the characteristics of what is being sought and offered. The seeking of utility gains involves not only searching for the best price but also for the optimal bundle of characteristics.

sible.[62] Hence there is no point in constructing simplifying (e.g., equilibrium) models in order to facilitate prediction. The purpose of studying economics, and other social sciences, is only to facilitate understanding (see below, chapter 7). Therefore, with the parlous exception of mobilizing resistance to government intervention in economic activity, economics can have no proper function in the making of public policy.

This leaves little room for welfare economics.[63] Indeed, the idea of comparing the efficiency of one allocation of resources with that of another through procedures that involve use of market prices as representative of equilibrium prices runs afoul of the Austrian objection to such representation. Hence Austrians cannot argue for a particular government action, or refusal to act, on the ground that it would lead to a better allocation of resources, except in the fluke case where literally everyone would be better off under one resource allocation than under any of the relevant alternatives. Attempts to create such cases synthetically, by compensating the losers from an action from the proceeds of a tax on the gainers (see chapter 9), are precluded by the unavailability of equilibrium prices as instruments for measuring the requisite compensation quantities.

Thus, if there *were* an Austrian paradigm, it would be a negative one based on denial of the legitimacy of considering prediction and, a fortiori, control as proper objectives of economics. This denial is intimately related to the denial of the propriety of using concepts or procedures involving the notion of equilibrium. The insistence on making the striving for gains in utility—rather than the equilibrium to which such striving might lead under idealized conditions—the focus of analysis leads to an emphasis upon entrepreneurial (e.g., arbitrage seeking) activity. This focus is the link to the great value placed by Austrians upon freedom of individual action without explicit reference to the efficiency of the equilibrium resource allocation to which such action might lead if it were allowed to persist.

---

62. That is, they argue that to predict a person's behavior would imply knowing a behavioral function governing that behavior. But such knowledge would imply that the person was not free to make choices, in which case rationality would have no meaning. Since Austrians assume rationality, this option is ruled out, thereby precluding their recognition of the possibility of prediction in this domain. Put differently, to predict the behavior of a rational individual would require knowledge, not only of his utility function, but also of his information set; such knowledge (at least of others) is assumed to be unobtainable.

63. One of the very few discussions of welfare economics from an avowedly Austrian viewpoint is Roy E. Cordato (1992).

FEMINIST ECONOMICS: A FUTURE PARADIGM?

To attempt to predict the content of an as yet uninvented paradigm would be more than a little silly. However, it is not difficult to perceive demand for a paradigm that others are actively attempting to create. Feminist economics is an outstanding example of such a paradigm.

The growth of female participation in the labor force and the concomitant change in the structure of the family have created a demand for reconsideration of women's place in the household and in the economy. From the viewpoint of RAP this demand could be met by an elaboration of the analytical structure of the model of the household without greatly altering the underlying paradigm.

Such an elaboration would involve expanding the household decision function to allow for its choices to result from the interaction of two or more (rational) individuals. The expanded function would deal explicitly with the property arrangements among the household members, the intrahousehold trading of time for other goods and services, the allocation of the burden of providing collective goods for the household, the bargaining procedures for determining the terms of trade among the household members, and so on.

To the enrichment of RAP, such an expansion of household economics is already well under way. In addition to the augmentation of the household decision function to incorporate a plurality of individuals, the utility function of each individual has been enhanced to allow choice behavior to reflect sentiments of altruism and hostility toward other household members, as well as the traditional self-focused sources of satisfaction.[64] But, although enriched, the household decision function remains embedded within RAP in that it assumes the value of each resource unit to be both market determined and independent of the identity of its owner. Although acceptable to many female economists, I suspect that the adverse bearing of such assumptions on claims of feminine exploitation will make them unacceptable to some feminists and lead them to seek an alternative paradigm.

There is already a considerable feminist (and non-RAP) literature designed to elucidate the structure and behavioral characteristics of house-

---

64. The RAP literature on the choice behavior of the household and/or the family is already large and growing. A good starting place is Gary S. Becker (1981). A very interesting formal extension of the traditional single-person choice function is Marjorie B. McElroy and Mary Jean Horney (1981).

holds in the context of (claimed) gender domination.[65] However, the analyses are decidedly and intentionally interdisciplinary, and not aimed at creating an economic paradigm. They can be construed as an attempt to create or (better) demand a new conceptual organization, but exhibit little concern for establishing the potential of such an organization for improving the analysis of observed phenomena.[66]

One element of such a conceptual organization is the notion of power, and sensitivity to the perceived lack of same. Throughout feminist literature there are descriptions of powerlessness, demands for empowerment, and the like. Similar themes are prominent in the literatures of disadvantaged ethnic groups, regional separatists, and some variants of Marxism. A related concept, which is also prominent in this literature, is exploitation. Neither of these concepts is present in RAP nor can be easily assimilated to that paradigm: in particular, neither is translatable to the possession— or lack of—property rights. While it is no part of my task to create a conceptual organization incorporating either notion, in chapter 12 I will discuss some of the problems involved in doing so.

The need for a non-RAP paradigm (say) to rationalize the demand for legislation to impose Comparative Worth criteria in wage setting should be apparent to anyone interested in promoting the standing of Feminist arguments in the economics culture. But to establish such a paradigm it would be essential to show how (some of) its implications contradicted those of RAP while providing better explanations of the empirical phenomena alleged to show violation of comparative worth criteria. In any case, whatever the reason, a paradigm capable of this task has yet to appear.

CONCLUSION

The purpose of chapters 3 through 6 of this book has been to give content to the notion of a paradigm in economics. Chapters 4 through 6 have described several paradigms other than RAP, so that the reader may better comprehend the roots of the methodologically tinged debates that keep

65. A good introduction to this literature is M. A. Ferber and J. A. Nelson (1993). Also see Samuel Bowles and Herbert Gintis (1986), chap. 8.

66. The economic focus of feminist writing on the economic status of women is on their relative compensation, job status, and occupational distribution. Without attempting to evaluate this work, it can be remarked that it does not attempt to show how such conceptual differences as it has with RAP are reflected in differing interpretations of empirical phenomena.

recurring among economists. These debates, whose issues evade resolution by the approved procedures of science, cast doubt on the scientific status of the subject of economics and undermine the claims to expertise of its practitioners. Now we turn to consideration of the extent to which this state of affairs can be improved and how the limits to such improvement affect the functioning of the economics community.

THE CRITERIA OF VALIDITY
IN ECONOMICS

In chapter 2 I described some generic criteria used in all scientific disciplines to determine the validity of propositions; among these, consonance with a paradigm was given prominence. Let us now see how economists choose among the various criteria of validity available to them.

PREDICTION AND CONTROL

While capability to predict and/or control phenomena is not a sine qua non of a successful science, possession of this capability is a major source of prestige and, typically, a successful science possesses it. Indeed, the justification of public support for scientific research usually runs in terms of its potential contribution to economic welfare and national defence via improvements in technology. Judged by this standard, economics has not been highly successful, and the culture of economics has been greatly influenced by the diverse internal reactions to this recognized infirmity of the discipline.

One reaction has been to accept that prediction and control are criteria of successful sciences, and to curtail the domain of the discipline accordingly, carefully limiting both subject matter and the conditions under which claims are made either of prediction or control. This reaction usually accompanies exhortations to improve requisite techniques.

A second reaction is to deny that prediction and control are proper objectives of economics, and to claim that advancement of "understanding" is the appropriate criterion for judging the quality of a piece of economic research.[1] (Some of the ideas associated with the concept of understanding are discussed later in this chapter.) Although there are economists who, out of deference to the criterion of understanding, would ignore the demand for prediction and control, they are distinctly in the

---

1. R. H. Coase (1994, chap. 2) argues this position quite strongly, explicitly attacking Milton Friedman's position to the contrary. My own view is somewhere between these two positions, but to present the case for it would convert this book into a methodological tract.

minority. At the end of the twentieth century, in all sciences and among the educated public, success in prediction and/or control is usually considered to be the most powerful evidence that can be adduced to support a theory or the discipline in which it is produced. And failure to contribute to such success is generally considered good reason for denying a theory or discipline approbation and support.

Understanding (*verstehen,* after Max Weber) is not despised among the practitioners of any science, but when it conflicts with evidence associated with successful prediction and control it is generally agreed among "educated people" that what had been previously "understood" must be amended. That is, it is generally agreed that the deliverances of understanding must be made to conform with the implications of the conceptual framework associated with successful prediction and control, whenever a consensus is reached on those implications.

The willingness of (many) economists to uphold "contribution to understanding," as distinguished from "facilitation of prediction and control," as a criterion for judging economic research is not indicative of an antiscientific attitude, but of the weakness of most economic research when judged by the latter criterion. That is, if economics provided more frequent and more salient examples of successful prediction and control, there would be much less effort spent in attempting to defend theories as contributions to understanding when they fail empirical tests, or are without practically testable implications.

There are two major reasons for the failure of economics to satisfy the criterion of facilitating prediction and/or control: (1) The inability of economists thus far to test hypotheses by procedures commonly used in the natural sciences, and (2) the intractability of its subject matter.

In general, methods prevalent in the natural sciences involve specifying a set of conditions (the 'if') under which a specified movement of particular variable(s) will lead to a specified movement of some other variable(s) (the 'then'). Included in the 'if' is a stipulation that all other relevant phenomena are unchanged (or constrained to change in some particular way); for example, the assumption of ceteris paribus.

To satisfy the if, natural scientists customarily resort to laboratory experiments in which variables assumed constant (or changed in a specified manner) are controlled to within prescribed tolerances. The if is thus known to be satisfied—up to specified limits—and the behavior of the then is used as evidence for the truth or falsity of the hypothesis. But in economics, laboratory procedures have not commonly been used to test hypotheses, and therefore it is only rarely known how well the if has been satisfied. Hence, implications for the hypothesis of the behavior of the then are problematic: even if the behavior fails to conform to the prediction of the hypothesis it may be argued (validly) that the hypothesis is true, nevertheless, and that its seeming invalidation results solely from the failure of the if.[2] An analogous argument can be devised for disregarding evidence for a then that appears to support a hypothesis if it can be shown that the if had been violated in such a way as to bias the then in favor of the hypothesis.[3]

Natural scientists overcome such difficulties through laboratory experiments whose raison d'être is control of the if. But thus far most economists have failed to follow their example. Although now (in the mid 1990s) active research groups are attempting to develop an experimental economics, it will be argued below that this effort is not likely to free the subject from difficulty with "violated ifs." Moreover, whatever the success of these undertakings, transforming economics to a predominantly experimental science would entail a radical change in its culture.

The second reason for the poor performance of economics in facilitating prediction and control of relevant phenomena is related to the subject matter itself. Even "behavioral generalizations" of economics that appear to have held in particular times and places, subsequently have been prone to fail in unpredictable ways when applied to new situations. Such failures are usually attributed to previously unsuspected "structural changes," that is, to changes in tastes, techniques, resources, and/or information.

While such changes are also possible within the domain of any natural science—the problem of induction is ubiquitous—unsuspected changes of structure simply do not have the salience in the natural sciences that they possess in the social sciences.[4] Moreover, economists are bothered,

2. Of course, an allegation that a valid hypothesis has failed a test because of a violation of its 'if' is subject to challenge. Much debate about the bearing of historical evidence upon the validity of one hypothesis or another consists of argument about whether the nature and extent of the violation of an 'if' is sufficient to warrant disregard of the failure of the correlative 'then' in considering a hypothesis to have been rejected.

3. The problem of testing a hypothesis when it is not certain that the 'if' has been satisfied is similar to the Quine-Duhem problem discussed in D. M. Hausman (1992), pp. 306–7.

4. It would be possible to argue that the laws of natural and social sciences are both subject to failure in application because of unsuspected structural changes, but that the laws of the natural sciences hold over sufficiently well specified domains for such long periods that unsuspected structural changes are of very much less practical importance.

not only by a generalized fear that (what they consider) the underlying determinants of behavior may change without warning, but also by an additional concern that is peculiar to social scientists, which is that the subjects of behavioral laws may be led to alter their behavior by learning the 'laws' that are believed to be governing that behavior. This concern is exemplified in the hypothesis of rational expectations, and is especially manifested in the Lucas critique, which derives from it (see above, chapter 4).

A major reason for the preoccupation of economists with the stability of the behavioral relations they claim to have found is the uncertainty of the foundations of such relations. This uncertainty stems from the ever-present possibility that the implied 'ifs' are imperfectly satisfied. That is, the difficulty of deciding whether a hypothesized relationship among variables actually holds in any particular geographic area at any particular time,[5] is exacerbated by the possibility that, while such a relationship might have held at some other time and place, in "transportation" it had been subjected to an unpredictable structural change such as would invalidate the 'if'.[6]

Unfortunately, few, if any, economic relationships exist whose temporal stability would not be subject to serious doubt if proposed as an instrument either of prediction or control. This is not to say that such relationships are without proper use, but it does imply that we must specify what that use is to be. This can best be done as part of a more general discussion of how economists appraise the relative merits of different examples (or programs) of economic research.[7]

---

5. In conflating relationships over time with those across space, I am assuming implicitly that economic laws are independent of geography; i.e., they are the same in all countries, states, etc. This assumption is not accepted consistently: most economists would gladly accept laws that were country specific, if only they were stable over time. However, they would also regard laws that varied from one country to another as a challenge (anomaly?) to find additional economically meaningful variables that could account for the cross-country differences.

6. When I speak of unpredictable changes in a relationship, I refer (for example) to a shift of a regression function considered to be "true" for the period prior to the shift. *Predictable* changes over time (i.e., trends, cycles, seasonals, etc.) can be incorporated as variables in an invariant relationship.

7. Much of the argument of this chapter could be described as a discussion of the criteria for theory choice. Among the various treatments of this subject that I have read I found Bruce Caldwell (1982) especially helpful.

PREDICTION AND OTHER CRITERIA OF
SUCCESS IN ECONOMIC RESEARCH

It would surely be incorrect to suppose that the practitioners of any recognized science were indifferent as to whether their students or the general
public understood their subject. But there is no consensus as to what constitutes understanding, and the central tendency of opinion probably varies from one discipline to another. In the natural sciences, to understand
an observed behavior is to be aware of (1) some body of theoretical propositions that would imply its occurrence under specifiable circumstances
and (2) the basis for believing the underlying theory. A case where two
(or more) theories both implied occurrence of a particular behavior are
rare, and would constitute a revolutionary situation in the sense of Kuhn
(1970). Such a situation would lead to strenuous efforts either to demonstrate that despite appearances the theories were really identical, or to
find a basis for preferring one of them. The basis for such a preference
would be ability to "account for" the behavior in question, and other behaviors as well, in the sense of being able to predict its occurrence (and
non-occurrence) under specified conditions. But such preference would
not depend upon the relative congeniality of the contending theories to
the intuitions or preconceptions of the scientists involved.

However, it is different in the social sciences generally, and in economics particularly. Here, the difficulties of deciding whether the 'if' of a theory (or hypothesis) has been satisfied well enough to warrant acceptance
of a specified set of behaviors as evidence for its validity often leaves
practitioners who wish to make conditional predictions without adequate
means for appraising competing theories on the basis of their performance. As a result, adherents of competing theories are left to debate the
salience of various bits of observed behavior for testing the theories, and
to squabble interminably over the interpretation of events purporting to
bear on the satisfaction of the various ifs.[8]

The inconclusiveness of these debates, reflected in the persistence of
competing paradigms, leads economists to seek other criteria for preferring one theory to another. Thus, when some "facts" (e.g., signs of regression coefficients) appear to favor one theory, while other facts seem to

---

8. For example, econometricians evince a good deal of concern as to whether a time
series regression covers a homogeneous period in which the structural relations remain unchanged, or whether it covers a period during which one or more regime changes have
occurred. Often it is very difficult to decide whether seemingly anomalous observations indicate a change of regime, with the theory unrefuted, or a disconfirmation of the theory.

favor an alternative, an economist is free—or even compelled—to rely upon his pre-investigative hunches in making a choice. It is at this point, that "understanding" properly enters the story of theory choice.

INTELLECTUAL CONGENIALITY AS A CRITERION OF THEORY SELECTION

The idea that the objective of social science is to enhance the understanding of phenomena is usually identified with Max Weber.[9] While I believe that in the following paragraphs I interpret understanding *(verstehen)* in the Weberian spirit, I make no strong claims on this point. As I use the term, to 'understand' the working of an economy is both to empathize with the motivations of its individual members, and to comprehend how their behavior led to observed social phenomena. In other words, a theory that contributes to our understanding of an economy is one that facilitates both empathy with its constituent members, and inference of the consequences of their behavior.

Where the deduced implications of a theory can be compared with observed behavior, conflicts may arise between the deliverances of experience and those of understanding. In such cases, theory appraisal becomes critically dependent upon the relative weight attached to each of these two bases of judgment.

In the natural sciences, the history of successful replication of experiments and the general consistency of accepted theories with what is observed causes the preponderance of weight to be placed upon evidence derived from comparisons of prediction with observation. Thus the "hunches" of natural scientists are said to be checked against empirical observations, with the latter providing the ultimate touchstone of validity. However, in economics the failures of attempts at prediction and control have so undermined confidence in controlled observation as a criterion of validity that, varying with person and problem, economists have come to place substantial weight upon a theory's conformity with understanding.

For example, it has been said that the Austrians and (at least) some of the New Classicals have come to believe "that social science has no choice but to attempt to *understand* the actions of individuals through a sort of imaginative leap—to see the world as they (the actors) themselves see it."[10] Thus, if it is thought that individuals are rational in some specific sense, then conformity with the implications of rationality becomes a cri-

9. See, e.g., Weber (1949), pp. 40–47.
10. Hoover (1988) p. 234.

terion of theory validity. As a result, for some RAP adherents, the problematic outcome of (much) empirical research is not a cause for paradigm doubt; it is rather an occasion for remarking on the deficiencies of empirical research techniques (especially quantitative ones) used in the social sciences.

However, it is not only among RAP adherents that one finds reliance upon contribution to understanding used as a criterion of theory validity. Whether all aspects of intellectual congeniality can be reduced to understanding is neither obvious nor important for this argument.[11] For our purpose, it does not matter whether an economist prefers Theory A to Theory B because he empathizes with the motives ascribed to individuals by A, or because A satisfies some a priori ideas he entertains about (say) behavior conforming to social norms, or some third criterion other than facilitation of accurate prediction. What does matter is that none of these criteria of theory preference involves appeal to prediction and control.

Let us consider an illustration of how intellectual congeniality, or lack of it, has caused economists to prefer one theory to another without reference to its capability of generating correct predictions.

INVOLUNTARY UNEMPLOYMENT: A CASE IN POINT

Arguments about whether there is or can be involuntary unemployment in a competitive economy are very apt to reveal strong prejudices as to the proper criteria for choosing a theory or paradigm. The argument for the possibility of involuntary unemployment has already been discussed (in chapter 4) in connection with the Keynesian paradigm. The opposing RAP adjunct is commonly associated with the Lucas-Rapping labor-supply function.[12]

In essence, this supply function is constructed on the maintained hypothesis that all individuals (successfully) maximize utility at all times. In the Lucas-Rapping framework, the appearance of unemployment reflects a transitory reduction in quantity of labor supplied in response to a temporarily low real wage rate that results from a temporarily low level of aggregate product demand. That is, a low level of labor performed is due to workers withdrawing from the labor force in response to a low level of the (market clearing) real wage rate and not—as Keynesians would have

---

11. I have emphasized understanding to the neglect of other aspects of intellectual congeniality because of its prominence in discussions of methodology in economics.

12. This is detailed in Robert E. Lucas, Jr., and Leonard A. Rapping (1969). For a good critical discussion of this paper, see Hoover (1988), chapter 2.

it—from a low level of job offers by employers at a given nominal wage rate.[13] The reduction of labor supply is interpreted as resulting from adherence to an intertemporal optimization plan in which less labor is supplied when the real wage rate is below normal, and more when it is above, leading to an interpretation of unemployment as the reflection of intertemporal substitution of labor supply.[14]

It is not to the present point to argue for or against the Lucas-Rapping supply function, or some updated variant, but to point out that it has met with bitter resistance on the ground that it is counterintuitive to interpret unemployment, especially during a major depression, as resulting from voluntary reduction of labor supply. Suggestions that there are, or would be, unfilled jobs "out there" if only workers would accept the wages that such jobs afforded, are simply rejected out of hand on the basis of the empathetic intuition that "those people need jobs and would (if necessary) accept less than the going wage in order to get them." This intuition is reinforced by reports of responses to questions in labor force surveys where (in effect) people are asked if they desire employment but are unable to obtain it.

Without attempting to resolve a much-disputed issue, let me remark that if one were restricted to variables reflecting behavior only (i.e., wage rates, employment quantities, product prices, worker incomes, etc.) the explanation of unemployment implied by the Lucas-Rapping supply function would be indistinguishable from the one implied by the Keynesian theory of employment. The perceived difference between the two arises from the differing interpretations placed upon nonbehavioral variables reflecting the frustration of expressed or empathetically inferred intentions of job seekers.

13. Thus the Lucas-Rapping labor supply function serves as a paradigm adjunct that preserves RAP in the face of the seeming anomaly of involuntary unemployment. It might be remarked that this confrontation of the Keynesian paradigm with RAP provides an excellent illustration of how paradigms influence conceptual organization: the Keynesian paradigm portrays unemployed workers as victims of labor-market failure while RAP portrays them as successful maximizers of lifetime utility who substitute greater labor supply in high wage periods of prosperity for less work in low wage periods of depression. The counterintuitive nature of the Lucas-Rapping argument is apparent, but this does not (and should not) settle the issue.

14. Lucas-Rapping does not directly address the question of why, in depressions, it appears that some workers retain jobs at wages equal to and possibly above those that unemployed workers (of apparently equal quality) would accept. This and related matters are discussed below, in chapter 8.

At bottom, the Lucas-Rapping/RAP rejection of the possibility of involuntary unemployment stems from insistence that acceptable models involve quantitative responses (e.g., employment) to prices and wealth-income variables, with behavioral intentions entering only as analytical constructions to rationalize observed behavior.[15] The Keynesian (man-in-the-street) contrary view stems from aversion to models that require rejection of the testimony of persons whose behavior is being explained, especially when such testimony is consonant with the intuition of the *educated* layman.

Analogous conflicts of interpretation between adherents of the two paradigms arise in discussions about the alleged occurrence of credit rationing and, indeed, in any discussion where market failure is alleged. The point is that in such disputes disagreements about the behavior of prices and quantities are incidental: at stake is the paradigm to be applied to the explanation of the behavior.

REALISM OF ASSUMPTIONS

Very frequently, in the course of explaining one phenomenon or another, an economist will argue that his explanation has the advantage of being based on "realistic" assumptions. In my view, such an argument is at bottom an appeal to intellectual congeniality. Examples of this type of argument appear when it is claimed that a particular model has merit because it does not assume perfect competition, which is (held to be) unrealistic; or that a model is (or is not) acceptable because it embodies rational expectations (which is held to be unrealistic); or when a model is unacceptable because it does or does not assume clearing of certain markets.

It has been argued strongly by Friedman (1953), and vehemently disputed by others, that realism of assumptions is not indicative of the scientific merit of a theory. The essence of Friedman's argument is as follows. Literal realism is impossible of attainment because, as with any theoretical construct, the concepts of RAP are idealizations (akin to Euclidean points and lines) that cannot correspond exactly to their real world counterparts. Moreover, there is no canonical metric by which one could measure the degree of approximation of theoretically assumed conditions to those ac-

---

15. That is, behavioral intentions are permitted to enter the model only as analytical constructions to permit statements to the effect that people were trying to accomplish what in fact they had been observed to accomplish. Thus, the possibility of deviation of realized (i.e., observed) quantities from desired quantities is precluded.

tually found in the phenomena being studied, even if one should desire to do so.

The futile quest for such a metric can be avoided by making the performance of a model in facilitating prediction the criterion for judging the appropriateness of the assumptions made in its construction. That is, as is the case in natural sciences, the standards for judging the assumptions used in a model should be the accuracy and importance of the conditional predictions they generate, and the salience of the model to their generation.[16] Other criteria, such as realism of assumptions, should be considered irrelevant and, in any case, are impossible of consistent application.

This line of argument is generally acceptable to those satisfied with reliance on behavioristic criteria in theory appraisal. Economists of this description are generally sympathetic to models embodying perfect competition, rational expectations, and market clearing: in short, they are RAP adherents. Although, as was already noted, there are RAP adherents who are not strict epistemological behaviorists,[17] the main body of opposition to methodological behaviorism comes from those who find the assumptions of perfect competition, universal market clearing, and rational expectations intellectually uncongenial: unrealism of assumptions is just one of their complaints.

RETRODICTION; OR, PREDICTION OF THE PAST

Judging from my concern with the performance of economics as an instrument of prediction, the reader might suppose that forecasting has been the primary objective of empirical research in economics. But surely this would be incorrect: in economics, most empirical research has been directed at providing explanations of the past. That is, the objective of such research has been to test the implications of theories (or the conjectures of theorists) by showing that an econometrically acceptable model would

16. The salience of a model or theory to a predicted result is of very great importance in establishing confidence in its validity. That the occurrence of nuclear fission was predicted by physical theory is, by itself, not so impressive; what establishes confidence in the theory is the combination of successful prediction with the absence of any proposed alternative explanation of the phenomenon. That is, what establishes confidence in a theory is showing that it is highly salient—essential—to the explanation of relevant phenomena. It will be argued in this chapter and the next that economic theories do poorly on the salience criterion.

17. E.g., the Austrians (see above, chap. 6) and Coase (1994).

fit historical data, meaning data reflecting events occurring before the start of the investigation.[18]

While such tests are less severe than conditional predictions of the future—the conventional if-then statements—they are not easy tests if the econometric model is made to satisfy the constraints implied by a "good" theory.[19] But more often than not such constraints are fudged in one way or another in order to get "satisfactory" results.[20] Sometimes more than one model is found to give a reasonably good fit to the data, so that further tests are required in order to determine which of the contending theories is best. Obviously, conditional prediction—of the future—should be a primary method of hypothesis testing, but its employment in economics has thus far been very limited. There are several reasons for this.

1. Often the frame of reference of a study is explicitly historical, that is, it refers to a specific time period and makes no pretence of seeking a 'law' that could be used for if-then prediction.

2. It is difficult to interpret the relation of what has been observed to what had been predicted. In other words, because tastes, technology, legal structure, and so on are known to change over time, it often happens that observed phenomena that seem anomalous to a theory can be explained away as resulting from failure of the 'if', rather than considered as evidence of the invalidity of the if-then relation.[21]

3. By far the most important reason for not appraising economic hypotheses by their implied predictions is that the economics profession does not require that such a standard be met as a condition of scientific recognition. Relations among observable economic variables that are both theoretically interesting and of sufficient stability across time and space as to support conditional predictions are hard to find. And because some parts of economics that are most deficient in this respect are also of

18. As will become obvious, the following discussion is focused primarily on explicit econometric models, but with inessential modification, it would apply as well to nonquantitative empirical research.

19. In this context a good theory is one that implies many restrictions—the more the better—on the signs and values that regression coefficients may assume, so that there are many opportunities for the data to reject it. I do not suggest that theories which are good in this sense are limited to those compatible with RAP.

20. Roughly, results are considered to be satisfactory if the regression equations give a "good fit" to the data, and their estimated coefficients have the signs and magnitudes implied by the theory being tested, in addition to having high *t values*.

21. Here again, we have the Quine-Duhem problem, previously mentioned.

the greatest public interest (e.g., macroeconomics), the profession has come to consider the best results obtainable "in the present state of the art" as the criterion of validity rather than insisting upon the preferred criterion of successful out-of-sample forecasting. As a result, successful retrodiction is accepted as adequate support of a theory for purposes of establishing the professional reputation of its author, if not as a basis for committing resources.

This is not to suggest that economists cannot make successful empirical tests of the more-or-less stable relations implied by economic theory, such as the relation between the limits of geographical differences in the prices of a given commodity and the cost of transportation, or between local wage rates and the prices of nonimportable goods and services. However, although they may serve to substantiate valid implications of economic theory, establishment of such relationships does not attract wide interest, either within the profession or without. The relationships that typically are of greatest interest are of uncertain stability and related to salient issues of public policy.

Indeed, what very often makes a relationship interesting is the idea that it can be exploited to predict the consequences of a proposed change in public policy. That is, the relationship is interesting because it is considered to be a means of predicting the consequences of exercising control. But, unfortunately, such use is likely to make a relationship change (exhibit instability). This is because the change in policy (or law) is likely to affect not only the behavior explicitly commanded or interdicted, but also to induce expectations of further governmental action such as would cause changes in the underlying behavior patterns that determine the relationship on which the prediction was based.

This uncertain stability of behavioral relationships tends to heighten the salience of intellectual congeniality in the process of theory appraisal. However, in a society where the procedures of natural science have the prestige that they have in ours, the probative value of "mere" intellectual congeniality is very limited. Both economists and the general public demand that a theory be "empirically tested" in some manner as a condition of acceptance.

To some degree, successful retrodiction would meet this demand if stability over time of the functional form and parameters of the model could be assumed. But since such stability is highly problematic, successful retrodiction is considerably discounted when offered as the sole basis for acceptance of a proposed economic law. Nevertheless, inability to perform adequately in retrodiction is a heavy mark against a theory, and normally outweighs considerations of intellectual congeniality in determining its status within the economics culture.

As I noted in chapter 2, successful retrodiction has played an honorable role in establishing the credibility of physical theories. The greater weight attached to successful retrodiction in physics (than in economics) in establishing the credibility of a hypothesis is due primarily to the greater credence accorded (in physics) to the implied assumption of intertemporal stability of structural relations. Also note that in physics acceptance of a hypothesis based solely on retrodictive evidence is usually tentative pending confirmation through successful prediction.[22]

In short, recognizing the inability of economic theory to generate reliable if-then predictions, economists offer retrodictions as a substitute basis for preferring one theory to another: that is, they test theories empirically by fitting regressions to historical data. The success of a theory in meeting such tests depends not only upon the inherent validity of the theory, but also upon the stringency of both the theoretical and the statistical standards that the tests impose.

If, as often happens, the process of selecting empirical counterparts to the variables of a theory gives considerable latitude to the investigator, it becomes relatively easy to find some set of proxies[23] for one or more theoretical variables that will provide a satisfactory fit to the data and imply "success" for the theory. But the price of such success is that it is often possible to find an alternative theory which explains equally well the behavior either of a given set of proxies or of some modified set that is not a demonstrably inferior representation of the theoretical concepts.

Because economic theories specify quantitative relationships only very loosely, typically specifying only the signs of partial derivatives but not their magnitudes, and/or the presence but not the duration of time lags, it is often possible to generate a number of empirical variants—equally

22. If, despite success in conditional prediction, a theory performed badly in retrodiction, such failure surely would be construed as an anomaly requiring the reconciliation of theory with evidence. However, this is not to suggest that the economics culture (or that of physics) treats failures of prediction and retrodiction as of equal probative weight.

23. Any empirical representation of a variable will differ from its theoretical counterpart because of errors of measurement. In addition, usually because the data desired are unavailable, economists use proxy variables as substitutes. The practice of making do with the best proxies available—rather than stating that a theory is untestable on currently available data—is a source of much discontent with empirical work in economics.

consonant with a given theory—by altering time lags and/or specific functional forms. This makes it difficult either to apply or to test a theory by confronting its implications with observed events. It is in this context that the contrast of economic theories with those in successful natural sciences is especially marked.

This contrast has prompted a good deal of complaint about the low standards of hypothesis testing tolerated in empirical economic research.[24] Prominent among the proposed remedies is addition of "robustness" as a criterion of appraisal both of economic theory and of econometric testing procedures. That is, it is proposed that preference be given to theories and testing procedures the results of which do not depend upon (are insensitive to) the choice of proxies to be used, or upon the lags or functional forms chosen, except where the lag or form is dictated by the theory.[25]

Despite its methodological validity, strict adherence to such a criterion of theory choice would have the effect of drastically reducing the number of theories considered capable of accounting for empirical phenomena, even in retrospect. For this reason, economists have been happy to proclaim the robustness of their models whenever they can, but are reluctant to relinquish them merely because they cannot. Here is where intellectual congeniality enters as a criterion of theory appraisal.

Prediction and Technical Façade

In a society that places great store on natural science as a source of practical wisdom, the appearance of conformity with its procedures gives an important cachet to a discipline that purports to offer guidance to conduct, especially of public authorities. Hence, in view of its limited ability to display examples of practical success in the making of if-then predictions, it is very important for economics to display such conformity. One of the easiest ways of doing this has been to imitate the styles of theoretical formulation, exposition, and social organization used in the natural sciences. Thus increasingly during the past half century economic theory has come to be expressed in mathematical terms. Its validation has become a

24. A prominent example of such criticism is E. E. Leamer (1978). Also see Leamer (1983).

25. In the rare case that a theory is sufficiently rich as to imply specific functional forms and/or lagged relations, only observation of those specific relations or lags can be considered as lending it support. In such cases, observations comporting better with alternative functional forms or lags would constitute rejection of the theory by the data.

matter of formulating and testing statistical hypotheses purportedly derived from mathematically expressed theories whose preferred form of exposition is in an article in a professional journal comprehensible only to fellow specialists.

In a natural science, such developments would be rationalized by a record of successful prediction and control to which elegant mathematical formulations and ingenious applications of statistical techniques could be presented as ancillary. As such a rationalization is only rarely available to practitioners of the social sciences, an alternative justification is needed. I believe the following justification is close to what would be offered by most economists.

Until recently, a major blemish to the scientific facade of economics was the failure of its mathematical and statistical techniques to measure up to the standards of those employed in the natural sciences. During the past 25 to 50 years economics has made great progress in removing these technical deficiencies so that now it is able to function as a quantitative science, with its research output judged by the same criteria as those applied in the natural sciences.

That economics still falls short of the natural sciences in respect of prediction and control is due mainly to the greater complexity of its subject matter, but this deficiency is, at least in part, only temporary. Economics is still an "infant science" and, given time and resources, application of its current methodology will eventually yield practical results (i.e., if-then predictions) that, subject to the limits imposed by its subject matter, will approach those achieved in the natural sciences.

The degree to which such faith is shared among economists is uncertain. Varying with time and problem, most of us share it to some extent, with "degree of faith" best represented as a spectrum. At one end of the spectrum are those, like the Austrians, who would reject outright the idea that economics could—or should aspire to—be an if-then science. But, whatever its validity, this is a minority view. Most economists feel the need to reconcile the theories that they advocate, and/or believe to be implied by research findings that they accept, with newly discovered facts and relevant current events. That is, they believe that their work says something about the real world, and is therefore capable of being refuted, or at least embarrassed, by empirical phenomena.

In general, for reasons that we have seen, economists recognize that the clean refutations and striking confirmations that occur frequently in natural science are, for the foreseeable future, beyond their grasp.[26] However they also recognize that an interesting theory generates expectations about future events, the disappointment of which requires, at the very least, an explanation.[27] While such explanations are usually possible, they often involve resort to ad hocery whose utilization tends to discredit the theory being defended.[28] Because of this, adherents of a theory will sometimes allow it to be rejected by "facts" even though a rationalization of the anomaly is available. However this does not prevent seemingly refuted theories from rising again, slightly modified and with new advocates.

26. In speaking of confirmation, I do not intend to dispute Popper's denial of the possibility of confirming a theory. All that I mean by saying that a theory has been "confirmed" is that it has successfully withstood a sufficient number of serious attempts at disconfirmation as to lead knowledgeable people to bet on the failure of further attempts at disconfirmation.

27. An economic theory generates expectations concerning (future) events when it is associated with the occurrence of a particular sequence of events. Typically, such association arises from particular events that inspired its proposal and have been prominently cited as illustrative of its operation. Thus, Keynes's General Theory is associated with a situation of marked underemployment of resources combined with low interest rates and downward stickiness of prices. In such circumstances, the theory suggests that an increase in aggregate (nominal) investment will lead to an increase in real aggregate output and employment. Formally stated, the theory contains the standard ceteris paribus conditions: e.g., the consumption and liquidity preference functions are given and unchanging. However, as generally understood, the theory is taken to imply that these conditions are in fact satisfied well enough so that the variables that drive events are monetary policy and aggregate investment. Therefore, if an exogenous increase in aggregate investment failed to lead to an increase in aggregate real output, failure of the theory would be alleged. To refute such allegation would require showing that some ceteris paribus condition had failed to hold, e.g., that the consumption function shifted. The acceptability of such an argument would depend upon the details of the case, such as whether the alleged failure of ceteris paribus was confirmed by the behavior of observable phenomena.

28. In this context, I term an argument in support of a theory to be ad hoc if it is (a) first offered as a defense against empirical observations that appear to reject the theory and (b) not implied by the theory. An ad hoc argument gains credibility if it can be supported by observable phenomena, and might even qualify as a reformulation of the theory if it entails previously unrecognized implications (of the theory) for observable behavior. Resort to an ad hoc argument tends to discredit the theory it seeks to support by suggesting weakness in the theory's foundations. I wish to emphasize that the definition of ad hoc in this note is proposed only for the present context and is not offered as a generic definition. For other concepts of ad hoc and ad hocery, see Hausman (1992).

CONGENIALITY AND BIAS

Traditional descriptions of scientific method tend to emphasize the importance of impersonality and/or impartiality. The validity of the results of a scientific investigation are considered to be conditioned upon their independence of the identity or volition of the participants. It is usually understood that such descriptions are really prescriptions: an ideal investigation is one where such independence is achieved, and investigators are admonished to spare no effort in getting as close to the ideal as possible.

Taken literally, this conception of scientific procedure implies that, when properly done, the outcome of a scientific investigation will be independent of the ambient culture in which it is performed. Never universally accepted, this view was much more widespread before 1960 than since; Kuhn's 1962 essay, "The Structure of Scientific Revolutions," will serve as a convenient demarcator of the change of attitude. In spite of this wobbling of the philosophical underpinning, the procedures of practicing scientists have not greatly changed, though it is possible that the resonance of methodological tumult has been greater in economics than in the natural sciences.

It has often been remarked in oral discussion, and occasionally in print, that in economics the publication process is biased in favor of (publishing) certain types of results.[29] In particular, editors like articles that contain "news": such articles attract the interest of readers and lead to increased readership and professional approval of the publishing journal. Thus papers of given quality that report confirmation of a result that is already generally accepted, or rejection of a novel theory, are less likely to be published than papers of equal quality reporting the reverse conclusion.

But although editors seek papers that contain news, they desire only certain kinds of news. Thus if an accepted theory implies that a particular regression coefficient has a positive sign (with a significant t statistic), a new application of that theory will meet with a more favorable editorial reception if it incorporates a positively signed coefficient. Should an investigator obtain such a regression coefficient, she will be prone to incorporate it into a submitted article. However, should a trial regression yield a negatively signed coefficient, she will try a different procedure: a new proxy for the relevant variable will be sought, a new data set will be inves-

29. A good collection of references making this point is to be found in Robert S. Goldfarb (1995).

tigated, or some new control variables will be introduced and the regression run again. This process is likely to continue until an acceptable regression coefficient is obtained, or the project is abandoned.

Such research procedures are termed *data mining* and are generally frowned upon. Yet they are commonly practiced and, given the state of the art, it is hard to avoid them altogether. But their utilization has the following undesirable consequence: consider a set of equally competent investigators working more or less independently on a common problem. On the basis of variations in the data sets employed, and/or in the details of the models and statistical procedures utilized, some researchers will obtain regressions with characteristics favorable to publication, but others will not. The favored results will get published while the others are either redone until they "give the right answer," or are abandoned unpublished. Thus the consensus of *published* results will conform to what is editorially favored, but published results will be a biased sample of all results generated by the entire set of investigators. Allegedly, and I think correctly, this publication bias is apt to distort the "expert" opinion of economists as to whether there is a consensus of research findings on a particular issue and, if so, on its characteristics.[30]

Though there is no reason for supposing that journal editors in economics and in the natural sciences attach different importance to conformity with established findings as a criterion for publication, the application of this criterion leads to very different publication filters in the two domains. The difference is well illustrated by the oft-recurring situation where the regression coefficient of a variable required (by the theory proposed) to be interpreted as an indicator of the slope of a demand curve exhibits the "wrong" sign. If submitted to a journal, this anomalous sign would constitute a focal point for referee criticism and editorial concern that would at least delay publication and, most likely, cause rejection. But the same theoretical preconceptions that inhibit referees and editors are no less internalized by researchers who view a positively inclined demand curve, not as a novel discovery, but as the result of some combination of a badly selected proxy, poor data, inappropriate statistical technique, and incorrect theorizing. Hence the paper with the anomalous result would not be submitted or, indeed, even written. Instead, proxies, data, theory, and econometric procedures would be reconsidered, repeatedly if neces-

---

30. See, for example, Goldfarb (1995).

sary, until the anomaly was resolved or the project abandoned. The possibility of treating a positively inclined demand curve as a novelty is not given serious consideration.

The situation is different in the natural sciences. There, once established, an anomalous empirical finding is treated as publishable news, and the affected theoretical propositions put into the class of those requiring amendment or abandonment. The reason for the difference of treatment is not that natural scientists are less confident of their theories than economists, or that they are more receptive to empirical evidence, but that they are far better able to reach a consensus on the status of an empirical finding. Typically they can replicate the circumstances from which the finding emerged with sufficient fidelity as to satisfy the relevant scientific community, and usually they can do it quite promptly, with the result that accepted theories—and their proponents—are disciplined by accepted facts.

Notoriously, this is not the case in economics. There the attempt to gain acceptance of an anomalous finding regularly meets with opposition on the grounds that the result is conditional on peculiarities of time, place, or other special characteristics of the data analyzed, or on idiosyncrasies of the research procedures used. The nature of the phenomena studied— that is, their variability over time, space, and across individuals relative to the strength of the relationships of interest, together with the imprecision of feasible measurements—is such that it is only rarely that a strong consensus can be mustered in support of the validity of any empirical finding that is anomalous to an accepted theoretical proposition.

As a result, challenges to widely and strongly held theoretical propositions that are based solely on anomalous empirical findings rarely have sufficient empirical support to make adherents of the theory (journal editors, in particular) take them seriously. As Paul Samuelson has said, It takes a theory to kill a theory. Facts alone—i.e. the facts (empirical evidence) available to economists—will never do it. Against an entrenched theory, facts come into play only as they support (or undermine) an alternative theory that has exhibited an appeal to some part of the profession.[31] It is otherwise in the natural sciences where the facts that it is feasible to obtain are far more persuasive, relative to theoretical arguments,

---

31. The history of The General Theory provides a number of examples of facts entering into the process of theory appraisal.

than those available to economists.[32] The main reason for this difference is the very limited use of experimental procedures that has thus far been made by economists.

Before concluding this section, a clarifying remark is in order. As used here, the term "facts" or, alternatively, "empirical evidence" has referred primarily to recorded price-quantity data. But restricting the data considered relevant for appraisal of a theoretical proposition to price-quantity records reduces the stock of available evidence, and is the subject of considerable controversy. As Paul Romer puts it in connection with research in growth theory,

> Economists often complain that we do not have enough data to differentiate between the available theories, but what constitutes relevant data is itself endogenous. If we set our standards for what constitutes relevant evidence too high and pose our tests too narrowly, we will indeed end up with too little data. We can thereby enshrine economic orthodoxy and make it invulnerable to challenge. If we do not have any models that can fit the data, the temptation will be to set very high standards for admissible evidence, because we would prefer not to reject the only models that we have.[33]

SOME QUALIFYING REMARKS[34]

The argument of the preceding section has stressed the importance of institutional factors in generating the consensus among economists that demand curves are negatively inclined. Some readers have complained that the argument went so far as to suggest that the consensual belief was unfounded and simply a cultural artifact. Since I do not intend the argument to be read in this way, let me amplify it.

The short-run price-quantity behavior of commodities sold on an organized exchange, or of those standardized sufficiently well as closely to approximate such behavior—such as fruit and vegetable produce—generally exhibits the inverse response of price to change in quantity that is the

32. I continue to hold this opinion despite occasional discouraging news from observers of the natural sciences. For a recent example of the latter, see a report of a recent review of a conference on biomedical peer review in the *Economist,* 27 September–5 October 1997, pp. 89–90.

33. Romer (1994), p. 20.

34. The argument of this section has benefited greatly from the critical remarks of Robert Flanagan.

basis of the strong intuitive feeling of economists that demand curves are negatively inclined. That is, like the housewife at the grocery, the economist "knows" that by damaging crops, bad weather will drive up prices of fresh produce. The direction of this effect is invariant through time and, in some cases, so is the elasticity of demand. Thus there are genuine "laws of demand."

To be applied, such laws do not require invocation of a complicated 'if' that can be established only with considerable uncertainty and much difficulty, i.e., by invoking ceteris paribus. All that such laws require is determination of the direction of movement of the relevant quantity. But these laws hold only when nature, or the deliberate action of humans, has achieved virtual standardization of the quantity units (see above, chap. 3, pp. 61–63); failing this, the applicability of the law becomes problematic. Do increases in quantity tend to be associated with improvement or worsening of average quality? Are there institutional rules or contracts relating prices to unit costs or requiring quantity rationing among potential customers? Clearly, the answers to these and similar questions will bear on the direction of the price change that results from a change in quantity.

Moreover, even on organized exchanges, the assumption that an increase in quantity supplied will lower price will not always hold. Whether it does hold in any given case depends critically upon whether, and to what extent, the quantity increase had been anticipated and the price bid up prior to the occurrence of the increase in quantity. To be sure it is true that, ceteris paribus, the specified relation between prices and quantities will always hold. But this is an implication of RAP, not an empirical proposition. The empirical question is whether, in any given case, "ceteris is paribus."

EXPERIMENTAL ECONOMICS: A DIGRESSION

At several points I have asserted without attempt at argument that economics is a science that has been unable to utilize laboratory experiments to test its hypotheses. As such statements are inconsistent with a large and growing literature reporting such experiments, I must attempt to defend my neglect of this body of research.[35]

At the outset let me stipulate that this body of work is generally characterized by careful attention to details of laboratory procedure and the

---

35. For an introduction to this literature see Vernon L. Smith (1994) or Charles R. Plott (1982). John H. Kagel and Alvin E. Roth (1995) presents an up-to-date survey of the subject. These references contain extensive bibliographies.

theoretical interpretation of experimental results. Whatever the complaints of technical shortcomings that might be offered, they play no role in the argument of this section.

It will not be denied that most economists are reluctant to give full weight to the outcomes of laboratory experiments as sources of data for testing economic theories. Where the results of laboratory experiments support a hypothesis, its advocates may cite them as collateral evidence, but will be reluctant to let them bear a major part of the load of an argument.[36] And those with adverse priors will be far less concerned with rebutting the implications of laboratory findings than those obtained from "natural experiments."

Charles Plott objects to such rhetorical practices, properly insisting that laboratory results are facts requiring explanation by a relevant theory quite as much as nonlaboratory phenomena.[37] Failure to perform well in the laboratory context should be regarded as presenting as much of a challenge to a theory as failure to perform in the "real world." And, indeed, in laboratory sciences experimental results generate the major part of the phenomena to be explained, and are given full weight in the process of appraising a theory. But in economics, if a theory were to perform well in the real world, failures in the laboratory would be treated as a minor curiosity, with a distinct tendency to treat the resulting anomalies as artifacts of laboratory procedure.

This cross-disciplinary difference in attitude toward laboratory results stems from the unwillingness of economists to accept an assumption analogous to (what Vernon Smith terms) "parallelism": an assumption customarily accepted in the physical sciences.[38] The inability of economists to accept parallelism, "the maintained hypothesis that the same physical laws hold everywhere," has a number of roots of which I shall mention three: (1) institutions (which vary with time and place) matter, (2) the failure of economic theory to provide any guidance as to how an individual's behavior in a given situation will vary with the fraction of her total resources that are placed at risk, and (3) the difficulty of designing experiments that

36. For example, Robert Lucas (1986) cites the results of laboratory experiments with pigeons as subjects as evidence in support of the "weak axiom of revealed preference" as a step in an argument on behalf of the quantity theory of money. But it is hard to imagine that Lucas would have considered failure of the pigeons to behave appropriately as constituting a serious anomaly for either the weak axiom or the quantity theory.

37. Plott (1982), pp. 1486 and 1519 ff.

38. Vernon L. Smith (1987).

permit choices to affect utility over long periods of time. Let me comment briefly on each of these.

1. That institutions matter is a point made by Vernon Smith in a recent overview of the state of laboratory economics.[39] He argues that the "institutions" of a laboratory experiment are the rules of the laboratory game that determine "the information states and individual incentives in the trading game; institutions matter because incentives and information matter."

But this implies that necessarily any laboratory situation is significantly different from any nonlaboratory situation because, unavoidably, participants in a laboratory experiment are aware of where they are. While it is possible that this will not matter, so far as I am aware there is no theoretical basis for such an assumption, or for the reverse: we simply don't know. In particular, in most experimental market games, the objects of purchase or sale are unambiguously defined as they would be on an organized exchange. The complications introduced by the possibility of variations of quality or collateral contract terms, and the possible interactions of such variations with variations in measured prices, are not permitted to arise. The sensitivity of laboratory results to these and other simplifications of nonlaboratory environments (such as the absence of intermittent arrival of new information) might well be considerable.

2. The potential compensation for participating in an experiment is rarely sufficient to make an appreciable difference to the lifestyle of a subject. Waiving many other questions about the effect of incentives on the performance of experimental subjects, there is the potential for serious qualitative differences of behavior as between situations where the results matter a great deal to the subject and where they do not. Neither economics nor psychology as yet offers a handle on how to measure or allow for such differences in applying experimental results to nonexperimental situations. The obvious remedy for this difficulty—raising the stakes for the laboratory subjects—encounters the equally obvious obstacle: cost.[40]

3. The design of laboratory experiments is such that performance in experiments has no long-term effect on the postexperimental prospects

39. Vernon L. Smith (1994), pp. 116–17.

40. For example, to study experimentally the effect on behavior of varying the payoff matrices in a bargaining game where the variations were of a magnitude such as would alter substantially a subject's real income over a period of several years would require, inter alia, a payment of many thousands of dollars to each subject.

(either of utility or wealth) of the subjects. Nor is it feasible to train and/ or acculturate subjects for long periods of time prior to commencing an experiment. Again, the obstacle is cost: to induce subjects to devote (say) several years of their lives—full time—to an experiment would be prohibitively expensive, to say nothing of the potential sample bias that would be generated by the process of finding subjects who were both willing to participate and otherwise suitable. As a result of these resource constraints, some important determinants of nonexperimental behavior are effectively excluded from the purview of experimental research.

To such reservations about the applicability of their findings, experimentalists reply with a variant of the "infant science" argument; in other words, the objections offered, like many others that might be offered, pertain only to what experimental work has been able to accomplish thus far. With patience and adequate funding, experiments can be made more elaborate and able to take into account factors that so far have been omitted.[41] While such an argument is impossible to refute, I empathize with Robert Solow's (1986) remark: "I am all for trying (such experiments) but I am allowed to be skeptical."

To avoid misunderstanding, let me emphasize that my reservations about experimental economics are not based on distrust of experimental methods per se, nor on the belief that their valid application is necessarily restricted to unimportant phenomena. Rather they result from the combination of high cost, paucity of theoretical tools for guiding the construction of experiments pertinent to decisions affecting large fractions of an individual's lifetime resources, and the practical problems of organizing complicated experiments.

Finally, and most important, if explanation of the outcomes of laboratory experiments were ever to become a major objective of economic theory, it would cause a drastic change in the culture of the subject to accommodate the greatly enhanced role for laboratory skill. For good or ill, such a change would involve a fundamental overhaul of the training process of economists and, incidentally, render irrelevant much of the argument of this book.

Although I do not believe that such a drastic change in the culture of the subject is likely to occur in the foreseeable future, I expect that, within a limited domain, experimental results will grow in importance as a source

41. I regard Plott's excellent discussion in section V, "Defense of Experiments" (1982, pp. 1519–23), as an offer of such an argument.

of empirical information. While I shall not attempt to demarcate this domain, it includes markets where prices are set by auction, as distinguished from those where prices are posted by one or another of the transacting parties.

Experimental work has already had successful application in designing rules governing the conduct of auctions to achieve specified results.[42] As this work is properly considered part of applied welfare economics, discussion will be deferred to chapter 9, and to chapter 12.

SCIENCE, VALIDITY, AND CONCEPTUAL ORGANIZATION

Given its deficiencies as an instrument of prediction and control, it is not surprising that the public should be skeptical of the claims of economics to scientific status. Indeed, what requires explanation is the considerable respect that such claims are accorded. The explanation that I shall offer runs in terms of the need for conceptualizing the organizational problems of a society characterized by division of labor and the consequent need for exchange. It will facilitate exposition to begin with the requirements of public policy formulation, though, as we shall see, the need for conceptualization derives from other problems as well.

In judging how prosperous a country is, how rapidly it is accumulating wealth, how its output is divided among claimants and related questions, it is necessary somehow to reduce magnitudes of heterogeneous goods and services to a common unit for purposes of measurement and comparison. Such measurements are used in attempts to allocate the burden of taxes both within nations and, increasingly, internationally.

In principle, such measurements could be made in any of a large number of ways: the common unit could be chosen arbitrarily.[43] However, at least among nonsocialist countries, the constructors of the national (and international) income and product accounts adopt the convention that units of output are to be valued at their market prices. This convention could be rationalized either on the ground that such accounts should facilitate application of RAP, or on the less controversial ground that records of market values are relatively easy to collect (and hence to compare), and that market prices serve no worse than some arbitrarily selected basis

42. See Smith (1994), pp. 115–16, and below in chapter 12.

43. E.g., the common unit of output could be made some function of the number of hours of "common" labor required to produce it, or of the number of units of some other required input. The history of economic thought is filled with suggestions to this effect.

of valuation. For the present, let us accept the latter rationalization and proceed.

To measure either an individual's or a community's (net) production in a given period requires measuring the value that has been added during that period. This requires subtraction of the (market) value of inputs from that of outputs and making allowance for changes in inventories, depreciation of capital goods, and so on. All of these measurements are supposed to reflect transaction prices but, notoriously, many of the prices must be imputed. However accomplished, such imputations must reflect conventions governing the relation of prices not directly observed to prices reported in market transactions.[44] Hence, even for the purposes of private business, the construction of accounts requires recognition of conventions regarding the interrelation of different ways of measuring price. As these conventions have pecuniary consequences (e.g., in deciding how much of a firm's net receipts is eligible for distribution as dividends) they must be defensible, which means they require a rationale that typically is provided by (some kind of) economic theory.

However, the role of economic theory in social accounting is far greater than in private. As this is discussed at length in chapter 9 (in connection with welfare economics and cost-benefit analysis), we shall not elaborate here. For the moment it will suffice to remark on the need to employ concepts of economic theory in any determination of whether a particular payment reflects a use of resources or a transfer of wealth without the occurrence of production. Or whether a particular payment reflects productive activity or rent seeking. Or in determining the cost associated with depletion of a natural resource attributable to the production of a given period when the effect of the depletion is spread over many periods of time.

Further to illustrate the role of economic theory in framing the concepts used to describe the operation of an exchange economy, consider how to formulate the rationale for charging compound (as opposed to simple) interest without resorting to concepts of economic theory. For yet another example, try to explain the interrelation of the items in a balance of payments to one another, and to the exchange value of a currency, without making resort to economic theory.

44. In many cases, information on market prices does not come from direct observation, but is inferred from reports of dollar values of transactions.

My point is that economic theory has the social function of providing a set of interrelated concepts that enable one to describe and/or comprehend the functioning of an economy in which specialization, division of labor, and exchange predominate.[45] Fulfillment of this task does not require any capability of prediction or control: it is necessary only to provide the understanding requisite for engaging in discourse about the subject. As Joseph Stiglitz puts it (in discussing the natural rate of unemployment), "the natural rate provides a useful framework for thinking about policy questions even if there is considerable uncertainty about its exact magnitude."[46]

There is, of course, more than one set of concepts that might be used to describe the operation of an exchange economy. Without attempting to make it an identifying characteristic, a difference of descriptive concepts is likely to be indicative of a difference of paradigms. Thus, an RAP description would not include the concept of unutilized productive capacity, while a Keynesian description would.

Though a list of all crucial concepts and a sketch of the relations among them would be an important part of the conceptual organization associated with a paradigm, it would not be the whole of it. There also are theories about the empirical relations obtaining among the variables used in the paradigm. Thus in RAP there is the idea that individuals are always maximizing their utility, and a variety of theorems concerning the relations among observable variables that follow from it, for example, the equality of marginal cost and price, the equality of returns to units of (comparable) resources in alternative uses, the relation of present values of assets to the streams of receipts with which they are associated, the tendency of shortages and/or surpluses to disappear in free markets, and the absence of opportunities for arbitrage gains.

Taken together, these various theorems or propositions constitute an instrument for assimilating new information and deducing its implications for the future behavior of various components of the economy.

If such theorems enabled one to use new information to make successful predictions, that would greatly reinforce the belief placed in the associ-

---

45. That is, an economic paradigm in effect suggests a flow diagram of an economy, and instructions for its use. While use of a particular diagram does not entail acceptance of an associated paradigm, typically such diagrams are useful in exposition of one particular paradigm and irrelevant to others.

46. Stiglitz (1997), p. 10. At the time of writing, Stiglitz was chairman of the (U.S.) President's Council of Economic Advisors.

ated paradigm. While such reinforcement has been scarce this has not prevented economists from adhering to paradigms on grounds of intellectual congeniality whenever their performance on empirical tests was "not too much worse" than that of competing alternatives.

Failure to predict the future, or even to rationalize the past, does not necessarily cause abandonment of a theory, provided that the theory performs other useful functions. In particular, a paradigm that facilitates participation in discourse about the economy in a manner satisfactory to the participants may retain its adherents despite its shortcomings as an instrument of prediction and control.[47]

Thus, regardless of its performance as a source of successful prediction, the Keynesian paradigm has retained a corps of adherents who find it congenial to think of macroeconomic phenomena in terms of an aggregate investment schedule that may (or may not) be interest elastic, interest rates that may (or may not) be responsive to central bank policy, and a consumption function that may (or may not) be sensitive to changes in income distribution and tax policy. Conversely, RAP adherents prefer to think about such phenomena in terms of movements in the quantity of money, relative prices, and real versus nominal quantities.

But this is not to say that paradigm adherents are impervious to empirical evidence and cling to a paradigm "no matter what the numbers show." For example, the empirical findings on the difference in the relation of savings to income when estimated from cross-sectional data and when estimated from time series of national aggregates caused a considerable rethinking of the Keynesian paradigm in the late 1950s and early 1960s.[48] Empirical findings about the consumption function also prompted much debate about the previously accepted belief in the efficacy of income redistribution as a means of altering the level of aggregate consumption expenditure.

The point in citing these examples of theoretical concern with the out-

---

47. Put differently, prediction and control aside, paradigm acceptance depends largely on intellectual congeniality, possibly defined as minimization of cognitive dissonance; see above, pp. 38–39.

48. The key piece in the relevant literature is Friedman (1957). The effect of Friedman's argument was to force economists (including Keynesians) to specify the consumption function in far greater detail than previously. The resulting debate, still unresolved, between Keynesians and RAP supporters developed into a dispute about whether changes in aggregate investment are a better predictor of changes in aggregate real output than changes in the quantity of money.

comes of empirical research is not to suggest that it is typical for "facts" to change minds despite analytical preconceptions, but to note that attention has been paid to facts and that sometimes theories have been adjusted (refined) as a result. The tendency to cling to theories despite facts that appear to reject them, does not reflect willful disregard of evidence so much as the absence of an alternative theory that better accommodates the recalcitrant facts and, even more, the parlous nature of the facts on which a choice among theories must be based.

As Thomas Kuhn put it, in the context of physics,

> Anomalous observations ... cannot tempt (a scientist) to abandon his theory until another one is suggested to replace it. ... In scientific practice the real confirmation questions always involve the comparison of two theories with each other and with the world, not the comparison of a single theory with the world. In these three-way comparisons, measurement has a particular advantage.[49]

What I have tried to do here is explain the very limited extent to which this also applies in economics.

To summarize: an exchange economy is a complicated and abstract idea whose manifestations are fraught with highly important consequences both for individual behavior and for social policy. According to their own lights, some people function adequately in their daily lives without reference to any explicit set of ideas as to how an exchange economy operates. Others, including most readers of this book, cannot or refuse to do so, and require a conceptual organization—a set of interrelated concepts and propositions—that enables them to comprehend it.

An economic paradigm is designed to satisfy this need: it does so by emphasizing some aspects of the economy to the neglect of others. Hence a given conceptual organization will vary in intellectual congeniality to different individuals in accordance with their roles in society. In our society, comparative success in facilitating prediction and control confers a great advantage upon any paradigm in competing for adherents; such success tends to make a set of ideas acceptable regardless of its other characteristics.

In appraising the validity of a set of ideas, great weight is attached to its capability of facilitating prediction and/or control, even when the "prediction" is limited to retrodiction of past events. This concern with capability of prediction derives from the great prestige of the natural sci-

49. T. S. Kuhn (1977), p. 211.

ences which rests on such capability. But because (in economics) differences among paradigms in comparative capability to predict are so uncertain, or can be explained away so easily, that choice among them rests heavily upon the intellectual congeniality of the conceptual organizations with which they are associated.

The reader will observe that the argument of this section, and especially of the last few paragraphs, is largely a reformulation and elaboration of the jigsaw puzzle metaphor of chapter 2. The purpose of the repetition is simply to make clear the relevance of that argument to economics.

PARADIGM, CONCEPTUAL ORGANIZATION, AND IDEOLOGY

Where adherence to a paradigm depends heavily upon the congeniality of its associated conceptual organization (CO), the possible influence of ideology upon theory appraisal becomes a matter for concern. Since the relation of ideology to paradigm goes through CO, it is desirable to describe the relations among these concepts as they are used here. A CO is a set of related concepts, and propositions making use of them, that presents a description of some particular aspect of the world. (As used here, any given science is associated with a specific aspect of the world.) While the relationship need not be one-to-one, any given paradigm will be associated with at least one distinct CO, and COs related to different paradigms are very likely to differ in at least one important characteristic.

Thus RAP is associated with a CO involving commodities, markets, prices, utility, and production functions, etc., and propositions about them. The Keynesian paradigm, on the other hand, is associated with a CO embodying aggregate relationships such as an (aggregate) consumption function, an investment schedule, a quantity of unemployed labor, etc., and propositions involving them.

An *ideology* includes a CO that may derive from a science, but may spring from other source(s) as well, for example, a religion. To partake of an ideology, a CO must allow room for the purposive action of an individual (and/or a group) to contribute to the achievement of some specified social objective(s). Thus, one Marxian ideology derives from the version of a Marxian CO that incorporates a notion of history as being driven by a struggle between social classes, and allows a role for individuals to participate as "instruments of a class."[50]

---

50. The problem of explaining the motivation of individual actors in the historical process (especially bourgeois intellectuals) has been well recognized in Marxian literature.

So defined, an ideology may also function as a guide to individual behavior in some specified context(s). While the most important of these contexts is political advocacy and action, ideologies may and have prescribed behavior in private business dealings, treatment of the environment, behavior towards individuals of specified characteristics (e.g., women, people with physical disabilities, members of specific racial or ethnic groups), and so forth. To perform such a role, an ideology must contain a view of how the world can possibly function, how it does function in fact, how it ought to function, and how individual action can contribute to improving its functioning.[51]

A CO associated with a science can provide an approach to appraising the consequences of individual or group action, but the value judgment—the 'ought'—must be exogenous (see below, pp. 257–59). Thus the Keynesian paradigm may suggest how full employment might be achieved, but it offers no argument on behalf of such an objective. The (exogenous) value judgment provides the link between the scientific aspect of an argument and its perceived implications for purposive behavior. Necessarily, the value judgment must be one that is congenial to the audience to whom the argument and associated behavioral recommendations are addressed.[52]

In addition to a CO and one or more value judgements, an ideology will usually contain some beliefs about how the world functions in its non-economic aspects; such beliefs may include elements of COs from other sciences. For an ideology to be coherent, all of these disparate elements must somehow be reconciled. Such reconciliation is notoriously difficult and subject to frequent attempts at revision. For many "practically oriented" people, coherence of an ideology, especially in matters of detail, is not a matter of primary importance. But for those who are professionally concerned with ideas, incoherence is extremely uncongenial. Accordingly,

51. To say the same thing in a somewhat different way, an ideology is almost always associated with promotion of an overall social goal or objective whose attainment provides a rationale for actions—both of individuals and arms of government—aimed at promoting that attainment.

52. I take it as self-evident that the value judgments implicit in an ideology must be congenial to those who hold the ideology. Thus, those advancing an ideological argument must in effect select value judgments believed to be congenial to the intended audience. For example, the audience for a Keynesian proposal to reduce unemployment is understood to consist of individuals who would benefit from, or would otherwise favor, such reduction. Similarly, a physician who prescribes fever-reducing medicine assumes that the patient shares his view that an absence of fever is desirable.

the construction of a CO must be compatible with the other elements of any ideology of which it partakes.

A CO becomes more acceptable if it helps to rationalize (other) ideas and behavior patterns that have already been adopted. Conversely, the fact of entertaining a particular CO may exert a powerful influence upon the behavior and other ideas (the ideology) of an individual.

While the channels of influence between a CO and the other elements of an ideology accommodate flows from both directions, the relative strength of these flows differs from one person to another.[53] Yet every individual is assumed to be strongly motivated to keep her ideology in harmony with her CO. While there may be other ways of rationalizing this assumption, I shall mention only one: minimization of cognitive dissonance.[54]

An individual is perceived as being made uncomfortable by self-perceived inconsistency among his various beliefs about how the world functions, or between any of these beliefs and the actions he undertakes. Normally, such discomfort is reduced by some combination of adjustments in ideas and behavior. For simplicity, and without argument, I shall assume that the adjustment made is always that which is most convenient (i.e., which entails lowest psychic cost).

For example, if an individual's ideology tells him that saving should be encouraged, he will be uncomfortable if told to believe that, under relevant circumstances, an increase in the propensity to save will tend to cause unemployment. This discomfort will lead him either to reject the Keynesian paradigm, modify his ideology in some manner, or both. It is, of course, possible for individuals to ignore conflict among their beliefs and proceed with their daily activities and even (some might say especially) their political activities; many do so. However, there are others—hopefully most readers of this book—who would regard such intellectual in-

---

53. While it is an interesting topic for speculation, the argument of this book does not require that we pursue the question of the relative impacts of CO and value judgments upon one another. However, it is worth remarking that among professional economists the tendency for choice of ideology to be dominated by one's CO is unusually strong.

54. See Festinger (1957). As used here, cognitive dissonance is an inverse of intellectual congeniality. Note also that cognitive dissonance is related to the notion of framing effects discussed above, in chap. 6. The relation follows from the idea that an individual "chooses" his beliefs so as to minimize cognitive dissonance. To approach a choice situation without a frame or, even worse, with an incoherent frame, would be so uncomfortable as to make its occurrence very infrequent.

sensitivity with disdain, and struggle to maintain (what they regard as) consistency both among their various beliefs, and between their beliefs generally, and their behavior. Those who compel their behavior to conform to their beliefs, and/or force all of their "other" beliefs to conform to a small set of interrelated beliefs—the dominant belief set—are described as "principled" by those who approve of the dominant belief set, and as "rigid," "dogmatic," or "ideological" by those otherwise disposed.

Prominent among individuals with a dominant belief set are those with strong ideologies. Among economists, the term "ideological" is often used to convey opprobrium, especially when it is suggested that the behavior so designated includes appraisal or presentation of empirical evidence in a manner calculated to promote a conclusion favorable to a particular theory or paradigm. Although there are many examples of such ideological behavior, it would serve no purpose to dwell on the matter. Rather let me assert that the economists who command wide respect within the profession typically give great weight to empirical evidence in appraising the validity of propositions whenever such evidence is generally perceived to be relevant and unambiguous.

However, in economics, the salience of empirical evidence in determining the validity of propositions is greatly reduced by the inconclusiveness of so much of its empirical research. This inconclusiveness permits intellectual congeniality to assume a prominence in the appraisal of theories and paradigms that is far greater than what is accorded in natural sciences. It is this characteristic of economics that makes it the locus of an interface between ideology and science.

EIGHT

"SUCCESSES" OF POSITIVE ECONOMICS: TWO EXAMPLES

A major contention of this book is that some of the principal characteristics of the subculture of Economics result from its relative lack of success at the tasks of prediction and control. Thus far no argument has been offered in support of this alleged lack of success: this chapter attempts to remedy that deficiency.

Because of the broad and steadily increasing scope of economics, it is impossible to offer a survey of its achievements and failures that would be both comprehensive and reasonably detailed. The best I can do is to select examples that are important, illustrative of the point, and representative of the best work that the culture has produced. While it is possible that there are examples to the contrary, I do not believe that to be the case.

To fit the material of this chapter into the overall argument of the book, I offer the following brief reprise. In economics, as in other sciences, the preferred criteria for validation of a hypothesis or theory are based on successful prediction and control. But failure to satisfy these criteria has encouraged consideration of others, and the need for defending such consideration has been a source of continuing methodological dispute and collective self-doubt within the economics community.

It is my contention that, so long as economists attempt to judge their performance(s) *solely* by criteria dependent upon prediction and control, this self-doubt is likely to persist. Because of the status of science, and the dependence of that status on successful prediction and control, it is unlikely that economics will ever be able to free itself entirely from the incubus of these criteria of validation. But, as I argued in chapter 7, economics can and has made use of other criteria of validation in addition to those of prediction and control. The relation of these other criteria to prediction and control will never be clear until the reasons for limiting the role of the latter are appreciated.

As practiced, at least for the past half century, positive economics has been an exercise in prediction—more precisely retrodiction—with an eye to control (i.e., policy making). Two of the subfields of greatest progress (as judged by volume of research papers, deployment of the most sophisti-

175

cated and up-to-date techniques of economic theory and econometrics, quantification of results, and inspiration for new developments of economic theory and econometrics) have been *labor economics* and *finance.* Achievements in these fields are among the great success stories of economics in the past 50 years. If positive economics hasn't made it in these subfields, it hasn't made it anywhere.

But an account of achievements in these two subfields is not a story of successful retrodictions: what has been achieved must—and can—be appreciated in other terms. However, since the research results are presented as empirical hypotheses and tests thereof, it is necessary to show why, in terms of their own preferred criteria, the "success" of these subfields has been, at best, highly problematic, leaving both opportunity and need for application of other criteria of appraisal.

To avoid misunderstanding, let me be explicit on the following point: I make no claim that there is anything inherent in its objectives or subject matter that dooms economics to failure at the game of prediction and control. My contention is simply that it has not yet been successful at this game and, for a variety of reasons, is not likely to be so in the foreseeable future.

Labor Economics
Marginal Productivity and Human Capital

For the purposes of this section I shall consider labor economics to be restricted to the study of the compensation and employment of labor. This restriction is solely for the purpose of focusing the argument: there is no intention of depreciating other parts of this broad subject. For convenience, I shall identify as central the proposition that the compensation (wage) for a unit of labor service—usually an hour—is equal to the value of the marginal product of that service.

This proposition is a cornerstone of RAP and is a maintained hypothesis in most attempts to explain wage and/or employment behavior. That is, such studies are so framed that to find that the data rejected the hypothesis proposed would create an anomaly for RAP. That the hypothesis is maintained rather than directly tested is a consequence of the very loose specification of production processes with which economics customarily operates. A direct test would require explicit measurement of the marginal product of the workers under study; such measurement is difficult and only rarely attempted.

In its early period, roughly 1930 to 1960, the empirical study of labor markets focused on explaining the average wage of large aggregates of labor such as "all workers in the manufacturing industries of the United States," or the differences in average wages of workers in different industries. These studies were often associated with attempts to fit empirical production functions.[1]

Prior to 1960, dissent from the labor market implications of RAP—and there was much of it—was expressed through objections to the assumption of competition in product markets (monopoly) and/or in labor markets (monopsony). While such dissent continues in the late 1990s, it has to a considerable extent lost salience in the study of labor markets because of developments in RAP that greatly extended the capability of that paradigm to accommodate seemingly anomalous price-quantity (wage-employment) phenomena. These developments began with the theory of human capital.[2]

While anticipations of this theory can be found in Marshall, and even in Adam Smith, its full development and exploitation dates from the publication of Gary Becker's (1964) *Human Capital*. This theory is an extension—an adjunct—of RAP to account for the fact that very often neither the product of an hour of labor service nor its compensation accrue simultaneously, but accrue over time. As the time shapes of the accrual patterns are rarely similar, a theory of the wage paid (for an hour of labor service) must take account of the implicit interest owed by one party of an employment relation to the other. Moreover, once the role of time is recognized, it becomes necessary also to recognize that an hour of labor service is not rendered from an endowed stock of productive capacity, but by a "productive instrument" itself produced by (previous) nurturing and training. The spirit of RAP requires that such nurturing and training be considered as investment in a human instrument with its quantity and return explained in a manner consonant with the theory of (nonhuman) capital.

To do this, it has been necessary to analyze the compensation and supply of labor as part of a general theory embracing the behavior of (1) the creating and nurturing entity, e.g., the family; (2) the educational process; and (3) the intertemporal allocation of time, effort, and compensation within the employing entity. Creation of such a theory has been a major preoccupation of RAP-adhering labor economists for the past quarter

---

1. See for example P. H. Douglas (1934, 1948). A more recent survey of the relevant literature is Paul A. Samuelson (1979).

2. In the pre-1960 period, there were also numerous studies of differences in average wage rates of workers across occupations, industries, and locations. Typically, these studies were not explicitly related to economic theory and I shall not discuss them.

century. For our purposes, it is sufficient to discuss (2) and (3): the household has special problems of its own, and its analysis would only reinforce the thrust of our argument.

Schooling and Earnings

Human capital may be formed either by schooling or by work experience: most individuals embody some of both. Let us start with the case of schooling. The proposition that an individual's rate of earnings increases with years of schooling has been confirmed empirically in such a variety of circumstances of time and place that exceptions are considered to be quite extraordinary. Similarly, the proposition that the rate of earnings increases with years of work experience up to a point in the life cycle and thereafter declines, is also an established empirical generalization.[3]

Following Becker and Mincer,[4] RAP adherents have interpreted the combination of these two propositions as an implication of the theory of human capital, and hence of RAP. While deferred compensation (discussed below) might provide an alternative explanation of this phenomenon, for the moment I shall ignore this possibility to focus on the issue of whether time spent either in school or in the labor force is a reliable indicator of investment in human capital.

Because time can always be spent more or less efficiently, there can be no mechanical relation between time spent in schooling and the resulting formation of human capital. While analogous difficulties arise in using dollars invested as a proxy for the quantity of nonhuman capital formed, it is not necessary to explore this issue.[5]

---

3. These two propositions are combined in the Mincer earnings equation which relates (annual) earnings of an individual in any given year to years of schooling competed and years of work experience according to the equation,

$$\log y = \log y_0 + rS + b_1X - b_2X^2$$

where y is annual income, S is years of schooling and X is years of work experience. For the wide applicability of this equation, in different countries and in different time periods, see Sherwin Rosen (1992).

4. Becker (1964) and Jacob Mincer (1974).

5. In discussing investment in nonhuman capital, it is customary to speak as though the physical characteristics of the outcome, (say) a machine, were predetermined and the effect of incorrect anticipations reflected solely in cost overruns in the production process. For human capital, the obverse convention is usually adopted: i.e., the input (years of training) is assumed fixed and variations of efficiency in the investment process reflected solely in the quality of the result (earning power). Nevertheless, the conceptual framework is the same in both cases.

As envisaged in RAP, human capital is produced either by spending time in school or in acquiring work experience. In both cases, it is assumed that production is efficient: human capital is produced in accordance with a publicly known "technology" so as to minimize its cost of production. But specification of this technology is a major source of trouble.

In the case of schooling, a year of completed schooling (the commonly used measure of input) may incorporate more or fewer days of instruction of a greater or smaller number of hours. After standardizing for number of hours per annum, there remains the problem of correcting for differences in the quality of instruction. Economic theory and common sense unite in contending that the effect of an hour of instruction on learning is likely to vary with the "quality" of the instruction: plausibly, quality of instruction may be assumed to vary with the quality of the instructor and with the quantity of nonhuman resources used in the instructional process.[6] Thus it is not surprising that dollars spent per student per year of schooling (standardized for number of hours of instruction) is often used as an indicator of school quality. However, the effect of unions on teacher salaries introduces considerable noise into estimated relationships between expenditure per student and per student quantity of resources applied to teaching.

Still further complications, related to "student quality," attend the estimation of this relation. Obviously, the amount of learning that can result from a given teacher working with a given quantity of resources will vary with the ability and effort of the student(s). Characterizing student "ability," and measuring "effort to learn," present unsolved problems that are central to educational psychology. Moreover, differences in student effort and ability are often confounded with differences in parental resources devoted to education outside of school. As it is difficult directly to measure either student ability or parental inputs, often they are proxied jointly by measures of parental wealth, education, or other indicators of social status. Such proxies understandably improve the fit of educational production functions, but including them as arguments greatly increases the difficulty of interpreting such functions as technological-pedagogical relationships.

A yet further problem plagues builders of "supply functions of human capital." The production of human capital is not a matter of causing the occurrence of learning of *some* kind, but of causing learning that enhances earning power. Notoriously, there is great disagreement among partici-

---

6. Typically, measures of teacher compensation are used as proxies for teacher quality.

pants in the educational process as to the proper allocation of resources among activities designed to promote enhancement of earning power as opposed to other educational objectives like cultural attainment, social adjustment, good citizenship, or physical fitness. Obviously, shifts in the relative emphasis placed upon these various objectives would be likely to cause shifts in the relation of resource input to enhanced earning power, even if there were a fixed relation between resource inputs and "generalized" learning. Thus, variations—across countries and across communities within a given country—in the burdens of socialization they impose upon schools may cause parallel differences in the resource quantities required for production of a given quantity of human capital.

To summarize, there is widespread agreement as to the functional form and other general characteristics (i.e., signs of the parameters) of the statistical relation between (an individual's) annual earnings and (years of schooling completed plus years of work experience).[7] Moreover, a relationship so characterized has been found to apply in many places and in many time periods.[8] But it does not follow that there is anything approaching this degree of consensus as to the validity of possible if-then applications of this generalization.

Thus, in summarizing the outcome of a recent conference, "The Effect of School Resources on Student Achievement and Adult Success," the editor of the volume concludes

> Increased spending on school inputs has not been shown to be an effective way to improve student achievement in most instances where this strategy has been attempted. Individual studies show that in some cases additional school resources have been effectively used to improve student test scores, but this experience is not the dominant one in recent experience. Most studies show, however, that in the past additional school resources tended to improve the earnings capacity of students. This summary of past studies is reflected in both of the surveys included in this volume. . . . However, Betts's survey and the new statistical analyses of Heckman, Layne-Farrar and Todd suggest that this conclusion may be fragile.
>
> Statistical evidence and recent historical experience suggest

7. See Rosen (1992). For a recent new wrinkle on this relationship that enriches but ultimately supports the "general human capital" model, see Daniel Neumark and Paul Taubman, (1995).

8. See Rosen (1992), pp. 162–63.

to me that school performance is unlikely to be improved by investing extra money in the nation's schools. Increased spending on school inputs without any change in the current arrangements for managing schools offers little promise of improving either student performance or adult earnings.[9]

Though interesting, the pessimistic tone of Burtless's final remarks are not to our point, which concerns the insecurity of the empirical foundation of the human-capital model as applied to schooling. As reflected in the studies in that volume, and in the editor's able summary, the empirical support for the presumed direction of the effects of resource inputs upon either student performance or adult earnings is subject to serious professional doubt. That the relation of schooling to earnings appears much firmer than that of schooling to measures of student learning is interesting and deserving of the attention it is receiving. But it does nothing to inspire confidence in the grasp that the human-capital model affords of the relation between inputs of resources to schooling and the resulting outputs.

In short, labor economists are simply unable to assert with any confidence what effect an *exogenously caused* increase in years of schooling completed would have on the earnings of (say) a typical member of the labor force. As Rosen puts it, in describing the scientific contribution of Jacob Mincer,

> [Mincer's] work does not follow the deep structural econometric approach that has been pursued so vigorously in the past two decades. Rather, it is a less formal blend of theory and data; less demanding on the precise information contained in a specific data source than the structural approach requires, but more demanding in searching for different manifestations of the same idea in various contexts.[10]

The distinction between "the search for different manifestations of the same idea in different contexts" and a "deep structural econometric approach" is precisely the difference between a historical generalization of the sort found by Mincer, and structural relations of the sort required for the if-then relations that are the hallmark of a technologically applicable science.

---

9. Gary Burtless (1996). The authors of the chapters in this conference volume include many of the leading researchers in the economics of education and labor economics.

10. Rosen (1992), p. 158.

Productivity, Effort, Timing, and Method of Compensation

Serious as the problems attending the relation between schooling and earnings may be, they pale by comparison with those attending the immensely complicated relation between work experience and subsequent earnings. I shall describe the several facets of this relationship in a series and integrate the various results at the end.

1. In RAP proper, no distinction is made between the characteristics of human productive productive agents (i.e., labor), and those of other agents. To account for the manifest differences in methods of compensation (e.g., between wages and interest) it is necessary to construct paradigm adjuncts that reflect the special features of the agents. What most distinguishes labor from other productive services is the worker's ability to vary productivity by altering effort. In the conventional production function, there is no place for the concept of effort: it is assumed that a worker's level of effort is uniquely specified by the production function independent of incentive to perform, so that it is impossible for the method of payment to affect either marginal productivity or the level of compensation.

Although occasionally recognized, this deficiency of conventional wage theory did not greatly disturb economists until the 1970s, when the problem of agency came to the fore. This shift in the focus of attention was prompted by recognition of the extent to which transactions were delegated to agents by owners of resources.[11] From the perspective of agency theory, an employer is conceived not as a recipe-constrained chef selecting ingredients, but as a master contractor minimizing cost through the selection and control (through manipulation of pecuniary incentives) of a group of subcontractors.

While agency theory is entirely in keeping with RAP in that every decision maker is assumed to be maximizing his own utility, it pushes implications of the technological aspects of cost minimization into the background in order to concentrate on the characteristics of the set of contracts selected. The selection criterion is *efficiency:* to be efficient, a contract must be, inter alia, "incentive compatible."[12]

---

11. The details of this development need not detain us. However, important landmarks are Gary S. Becker and George J. Stigler (1974) and Steven N. S. Cheung (1969).

12. Incentive compatibility refers to the self-seeking behavior in which a rational individual will engage under a contract that relates compensation to one or another aspect of performance. Optimization by the employer implies offering only such contracts as minimize the cost of inducing a given level of performance (e.g., output) by a (rational) employed

The relevance of subcontracting to wage theory becomes apparent as soon as it is recognized that any worker may be considered to be a subcontractor. (In the production function view of the firm, the employer considers workers as hired automatons incapable of intentionally varying any aspect of an hour of hired service.)[13] Viewed as a master contractor, the employer is faced with the problem of inducing performance by his hired work force, with the structure of the employment contract a major element of the induction process. While performance has many dimensions, a major focus of the literature has been upon one, *employment duration:* in particular, the possibility of quitting at a time inconvenient to the employer.

2. Consider an employer faced with the problem of whether to provide an employee with on-the-job training. Suppose that the effect of such training is to increase the productivity of the worker substantially more than it costs to provide it, but that the enhanced productivity is as valuable to some other employer(s) as to the present one. In such case, on completion of the training a rational worker would insist on a wage increase equal to the value of the enhancement of his productivity, because he could obtain such an increase elsewhere. This would leave the employer with no return from his investment in the worker's training.

Foreseeing (or soon learning of) this consequence, a rational employer would cease to pay for workers' training and hire workers already trained (at their own expense or that of some other employer) at no greater wage

---

agent. In keeping with RAP it is assumed that employers as well as agents are rational, and that each is aware of the rationality of the other. Therefore every agent calculates his expected utility under a proposed contract on the assumption that the behavior of the prospective employer reflects his (the employer's) efforts to maximize his own expected utility. Similarly, the employer calculates his expected payoff on the assumption that the actions of the agent are such as to maximize his (the agent's) expected utility.

A contract is *incentive compatible* when it is consistent with the optimizing proclivities of both the employer and the agent. If the parties behave rationally, a contract that is not incentive compatible will "unravel"; i.e., the anticipation of self-seeking behavior by the other party will be such as to cause one or both parties to refuse the contract. The tools of game theory are especially useful in investigating the incentive compatibility of proposed contracts.

13. At the extreme, a worker becomes analytically indistinguishable from an automaton where her compensation is on a piece rate basis with no guarantee of minimum payment and if the unprocessed raw material is valueless and there is no risk of damage to tools or machinery. One of the very rare instances where these stringent conditions were satisfied occurred in California fruit harvesting prior to unionization. An excellent discussion of this case is L. H. Fisher (1953).

than would be required to retain a worker whose training he had financed. If this were all that was involved, it would follow that (in such case) no employer would ever contribute to the training of his workforce and that all employee training would be self-financed.[14]

However, often it is possible for an employer to offset the cost of a worker's training by paying her less than the value of her current marginal product, in effect making an implicit exchange of training for acceptance of a wage below the market clearing level. After completing the training, the worker recoups the implicit investment by obtaining higher earnings, whether paid by the training period employer or by another.[15]

As some of this training will be applicable only within the firm, there will be appreciable periods of time during which a worker will have a higher marginal product to the present employer than to any other. This raises the possibility that during such periods an employer might be able to set a worker's current wage below her current marginal product (to the firm) without fear of her quitting. But there is a countervailing consideration: a worker who feels underpaid or otherwise mistreated might—consciously or otherwise—work at less than full efficiency, though not so poorly as to provoke dismissal. Recognizing this, a rational employer would balance the temptation to reduce outlay on labor per hour against the desire to induce greater employee effort. Conversely, a rational worker would balance the enticement of "greater leisure on the job" against the desire for higher compensation and/or reduction of the risk of dismissal.

3. The complexity of this two-person game should already be obvious, but it becomes even more complex once explicit consideration is taken of

14. In the example presented in the text, human capital theory implies that the cost of training would be borne entirely by the worker. Training that is applicable in a number of firms is termed *general training* and the associated earning power, general human capital. Training that is usable only within one firm is called *specific training* and its earning power, specific human capital. RAP implies that the cost of general training will be born entirely by the worker, but that of specific training will be (somehow) shared between the employer and the worker. The allocation of the cost of specific training is complicated and its details need not concern us. (The distinction between general and specific human capital was introduced by Becker (1964)). Except when it is employer financed, schooling is considered to be general training; except when employee financed, on-the-job training is assumed to be specific. Though not important in the present context, it may be remarked that most on-the-job training is a mixture of general and specific training.

15. Of course, this implicit exchange (of lower wages for training) will not usually be perceived as such by either the worker or the employer.

the implications of various limitations upon the information receiving and processing capabilities of the players.[16] The effect is to create the possibility of a wide variety of relationships between the marginal product of an hour of labor and its contemporaneous compensation depending upon factors not readily encompassed within RAP.

The most widely used models envisage an employment relation lasting for a substantial period of time and including an initial period during which an employee is paid less than his current marginal product followed by a later period when the reverse relation obtains. During the initial period the employer stands to gain more from continuing the relation than the worker, so that he finds it necessary to offer the carrot of future pay increases and promotions to retain the worker and keep him motivated to perform satisfactorily.

This is accomplished by in effect withholding part of the worker's marginal product during the first period and paying it out during the second period. One by-product of this is creation of a stake owned by the worker but held by the employer which the worker can redeem only through satisfactory performance over some period of time; this gives the employer some assurance that workers whose training he has financed will not quit prematurely. The worker accepts this state of affairs in the belief that during the second period she will receive sufficiently more than her current marginal product as to compensate for the earlier deferral of earnings.

Of course, during the second period the employer might be tempted to break the implicit contract by finding some pretext to dismiss the worker prematurely. Rational employers would be motivated to eschew such "opportunistic" behavior (or at least carefully to weigh possible costs against perceived benefits) only by fear of losing the reputation for fair treatment of employees. It is only through possession of such a reputation for honorable dealing that an employer could induce a rational worker to accept two period contracts such as that described above, and loss of it would greatly impair an employer's ability to hire and retain a trained labor force.

Evidence for the concern of large firms with their reputation as fair

---

16. Despite an older, more-or-less descriptive literature about the "effort bargain" in books and journals in the field of industrial relations, the attention of general economists to this problem began with the influential paper of A. A. Alchian and H. Demsetz (1972), which gave a central place in the theory of the firm to the problems created by the possibility of "shirking." More recently, discussions of effort have been conflated (in the literature on optimal contracting) with the problem of designing contracts so as to insure incentive compatibility.

employers is provided by the widespread practice of making substantial payments to workers in exchange for acceptance of early retirement. Often these payments are required neither by statute nor by contract, but simply reflect concern to maintain a reputation as a good employer.[17]

In effect, during the latter part of a worker's career her employer would gain if she (say) won a lottery and (voluntarily) decided to retire prematurely. During this latter period, part of a worker's pay is akin to a pension with the moment of retirement determining when it becomes a pension in its entirety. The fact that most pension plans require that the worker retire at some specified age as a condition of eligibility suggests strongly that the employer values the option of an "opprobrium free"[18] termination of the worker's service, and therefore is willing to pay something in exchange for it.

To summarize, as enhanced by efforts to accommodate real world complications, RAP does not imply any specific relation between compensation paid and the value of *contemporaneous* services rendered to the productive process. Generalized by a human-capital extension, RAP implies only a complicated intertemporal relationship between imputed marginal contributions to a productive process and receipt of compensation for them. Empirical study of such relationships is in its infancy, and the interpretations of possible results are highly various, as will be seen in the following section.

RAP and Other Theories of Compensation: An Overview

Since 1950, recognition of the function of human capital in the production process, combined with a still-growing appreciation of the importance of the effort-incentive nexus in generating the productivity of human agents, has led economists to recognize that equality of a worker's current rate of compensation with his contemporaneous marginal product is not implied by RAP. In particular, on-the-job training and deferred compensation have driven a wedge between a worker's marginal product and his con-

17. The interpretation of the various forms of severance pay or pay for early retirement given here is based on the assumption that employers are rational in the strict RAP sense. Of course, among noneconomists, other interpretations are more customary. It may be remarked that, like other manifestations of alleged employer generosity, the magnitude of employer largesse to terminated workers is strongly affected by their financial condition.

18. That is, "termination" of a worker in accordance with a preannounced retirement plan carries no suggestion of employer bad faith. On this issue, see Edward Lazear (1979).

temporaneous rate of compensation. Adherence to RAP requires that one believe that the expected present value of the contribution of current labor service is equal to the expected present value of the accrued obligations to pay compensation, but since neither present value is observable—at least in practice—satisfaction of this equality cannot serve as an empirical test of the theory.

Unobservability of these present values makes it possible for both adherents and opponents of RAP to use the same phenomena as support for different and even incompatible stories of labor-market behavior. For example, the idea that employers pay workers less than their marginal product before some climacteric, and more than their marginal product thereafter until retirement, can be rationalized in at least two ways: (1) as a consequence of the maximization of the present value of an intertemporal plan by a rational employer as described above or (2) as a kind of potlatch, or gift exchange in which payment for services is determined by social norms which require that payment vary with the characteristics of the person rendering the service (e.g., age, sex, length of employment, or race) and characteristics of the employer (e.g., size and wealth of the firm, or identification as local or "foreign").[19]

Advocates of the gift exchange story contend that, because of social norms, the excess of marginal product over compensation in early career might occur regardless of whether there was an accompanying enhancement of the subsequent productivity of employees through training and/or experience. RAP adherents argue that, in the absence of a link between early "overpayment" and subsequent productivity enhancement combined with an absence of opportunistic quitting, the early overpayment would not occur. However, very often neither alleged training nor employer concern for reputation as a "good" employer is directly observable, so that the extent, or even the occurrence, of employer investment in specific human capital is problematic. As a result, normally it is not feasible to bring empirical evidence to bear upon a choice between the two explanations. Further to complicate the matter, it is entirely possible that in

19. Employer violations of social norms will (allegedly) be punished by poor morale and reduced output among current employees and by difficulty in attracting recruits. Typically, the characteristics of these norms are not specified carefully, but this is unimportant. What is important is that workers have a common reaction to given employer actions, which the employer can anticipate and thereby avoid by eschewing acts that are likely to give offence. For an excellent example of an argument in this vein see G. A. Akerlof (1984).

many (most?) cases, both explanations are applicable; the implications of social norms for wage structure may be identical with those of simultaneous optimization by employers and workers.

The difficulty of distinguishing between these seemingly alternative stories is reflected in the considerable popularity of the "efficiency wage" theory in recent years.[20] In a nutshell this theory argues that it is efficient—profit maximizing—for an employer to pay a worker more than the minimum necessary to induce her to accept (or not quit) the job, in order to induce her maximum effort. Though only loosely specified, the extra amount is alleged to depend upon what the worker believes would be fair, which, in turn, reflects community norms. In practice, adoption of such policies will, it is contended, induce a positive association of wages for given jobs across firms in accordance with indicators of ability to pay, such as size, past profitability, etc. and also with such personal characteristics as might affect the worker's notions of what is fair.

Thus, a wage structure embodying efficiency wages might also be compatible with RAP in a world where the relation of employee effort to compensation was dependent upon the characteristics of workers, jobs, and employers that served as determinants of the fairness of wages. But while such a rationalization of wage structure might be compatible with the letter of RAP, it is far removed from its spirit, which requires that explanations run in terms of relations of prices and quantities. Indeed, unless a theory specifying the functional relation of an efficient wage to a set of characteristics of employers, workers, and jobs is proposed, an efficient wage theory is without testable implications. To the present, such specifications have been both ad hoc and not easily recognized as implications of RAP.[21]

The discussion of the preceding few paragraphs by no means exhausts the channels through which limitations of information affect the relation between the marginal product of a unit of labor service and its compensation. However, they suffice to indicate the reason for considering RAP to be a very uncertain guide to this relationship.

20. In the last decade, there has been a large number of papers dealing with efficiency wages. For a recent bibliography, see James B. Rebitzer and Lowell J. Taylor (1995).

21. Akerlof (1984) offers an explicitly non-RAP—what he terms a sociological—explanation of the wage structure of a particular group of workers. Clearly, his intention is to dispute the applicability of neoclassical theory (i.e., RAP) to this body of data. However, without much difficulty one could convert his "sociological" explanation into an efficiency story which, though vacuous, *would* be compatible with RAP.

Executive Compensation

The previous few sections have indicated the difficulties of using RAP as a guide to explaining differences in the compensation paid to workers of differing characteristics. In this section I present a particular case to highlight those difficulties. At a sufficient level of abstraction, explaining the compensation of executives should present problems no different from those of explaining the compensation of any other group of employees. However, as a practical matter this is not the case. Because compensation of the highest ranking executives in an organization is so great relative to that of his or her immediate subordinates, and because the pay of executives generally is so much greater than that of the average employee, the subject of executive compensation has attracted envious attention. Often the spur of envy is implemented by the availability of an arguable metric for judging executive performance: company profits.

This metric is most directly applicable to the chief executive officer (CEO) of profit-seeking companies, but the effect of competition for executive talent tends to spread its applicability to the entire corps of executives. An RAP explanation would imply that executives were compensated in accordance with their putative contribution to the value of the company. For a variety of reasons this contribution cannot be gauged from current accounting profits but, at least in the case of publicly traded companies, the change in market evaluation of a firm's equity plus dividends paid during an accounting period provides an estimate of the firm's financial gain during the period that is relevant to the compensation of its CEO.

The relevance of this criterion of company performance to the determination of CEO compensation is indicated by the frequency with which employment contracts of executives contain incentives (e.g., stock options) based on the performance of the common stock. It is not my purpose to argue either the adequacy of any particular empirical formulation as an expression of RAP or its efficacy as an explanation of executive compensation. My point is that, regardless of how they appraise currently available empirical studies, RAP adherents insist that a satisfactory explanation of executive compensation must be compatible with the paradigm. But among those who are willing to depart from RAP, some insist that high-level executives are overpaid by RAP standards.

A leading example of this genre is Derek Bok (1993). His argument is that RAP does not apply, because neither the boards of directors who hire CEOs, nor the executives themselves, have sufficient information about the effect of executive performance on company profits or of the capabilities of available alternative executives to engender the results of a competitive market. As he puts it,

> In the perfectly competitive world so dear to classical economists, all chief executives would receive amounts approximating what they added to the net profits of their company. . . .
>
> In the real world, matters do not work out quite so felicitously. . . . Because of imperfect knowledge, there will normally be a substantial gap between the lowest pay that a CEO would accept and the best offer that directors could bring themselves to approve. . . .
>
> The process of fixing executive compensation, then, is unusual because of the vast range of possible outcomes. In the face of such uncertainty, most top executives are in an unusually strong position to strike a favorable bargain, because they exert such influence over the process. CEOs almost always serve as chairmen of the board. They typically have a good deal to say about the choice of new board members. They are the key people who decide on the fees paid to directors. . . . They often choose the consultant who presents recommendations on their next pay increase to the board. . . . In this environment, the task of fixing the compensation of top executives is hardly an arms length transaction comparable to setting the salaries of middle managers and other kinds of employees. . . .
>
> It is impossible to calculate how much CEOs have contributed to their own firm's bottom line. . . . The entire process of fixing compensation is shrouded in uncertainty, and the CEO typically exerts more influence than any individual over the final outcome. This procedure differs so much from any market for services that Adam Smith ever imagined that it cannot conceivably sanctify the amounts currently earned by corporate leaders.[22]

An RAP adherent might well reply that this line of argument does not properly take into account the constraints on compensation imposed by competition in the market for "executive labor." To be sure, once a CEO aspirant is well launched on a career in a given firm, he may be locked in by his specific human capital so that his compensation contains a good deal of quasi-rent and is therefore apparently subject to the discretion of the employer. But to attract new recruits to the process, the expected

---

22. Bok (1993), pp. 96–100. (Bok is a former president of Harvard University.)

present value of the prospective career reward (as valued at the outset) must not be less than that available to them in alternative career opportunities. The need to remain competitive with alternative opportunities sets a lower constraint upon the career compensation an employer can offer a prospective recruit.

This constraint might be quite loose[23] and, had he wished, Bok could readily have accommodated an RAP account of executive compensation (properly) noting that such an account could be compatible with almost any observed pattern of career earnings for a series of cohorts of executive candidates. But, significantly, he refused to do so. Instead he chose to attack RAP.

Although his opening is a bit snide—

> As Groucho Marx once said, "If you don't like my principles, ... I have others." In much the same way, those who defend the earnings of top executives conjure up other arguments to calm the skeptics who remain unmoved by appeals to market principles. With such large sums at stake, it is hardly surprising that so much ingenuity has been expended on the search for justifications.[24]

—the attack is straightforward. Let me quote further:

> Economists have contributed one of the most intriguing reasons for encouraging huge earnings in corporations and other hierarchical institutions. Reaching the highest rank in such organizations, it is said, can be likened to a tournament. By giving very attractive prizes to the winner—i.e., the CEO—a company can induce would-be successors at lower levels in the hierarchy to work even harder. With commendable imagination, economists have turned to sport to test their theory by observing the effects of large prizes on the play of professional golfers. . . .
>
> Despite the inventiveness of this theory, it may not provide an accurate account of why large companies pay such high salaries and bonuses. . . . As yet, however, those who have compared the practices of varying kinds of corporations have

23. For example, the same present value of a multiyear income stream might arise from a wide variety of time shapes. In particular they may be compatible with either relatively low payments in the late (CEO) years offset by relatively high payments in the early years, or the reverse.

24. Bok (1993), p. 100.

found no evidence that boards of directors act in this way in setting the CEO's compensation.

The study that Bok cites as evidence against the rank-order tournament theory is not particularly persuasive, but that is beside the point. It is clear that Bok's opposition to the theory is based, not on empirical evidence, but upon his perception of the process by which executive compensation is set.[25] He correctly perceives that the rank-order tournament theory is a proposed amplification of the RAP conceptual organization that he wants rejected in toto. His desire to have it rejected can hardly be based upon the theory's predictive failures—the theory implies hardly any refutable predictions[26]—but rests upon its incompatibility with his observations of the process of setting executive compensation.

Beyond his intellectual discomfort with a theory that he believes to be descriptively inaccurate, Bok wants to discredit a theory that he believes will be used to justify a system of compensation that he regards as socially deleterious. Bok's concern with its ideological implications is a (very important) part of his objection to the conceptual organization projected by the rank-order tournament theory.

Despite its intrinsic interest, my concern with the explanation of Executive Compensation derives mainly from what it reveals about the impotence of RAP. Despite Bok's open rejection of RAP (e.g., "ignorance, influence from chief executives, and other distortions cause the 'market' for CEOs to stray much too far from the competitive ideal to vindicate the paychecks that result when rivals vie for an executive's services," p. 106), its adherents are unable to generate empirical findings that could provide the basis for a convincing rebuttal. The best they can do is to offer an interesting story (i.e., the rank-order tournament theory) that might be compatible with RAP. But Bok can offer an alternative explanation that is not compatible with RAP. Thus, when remarking that "there have been only two periods of unusually rapid increases in top executive salaries during the past seventy five years—the 1920s and the 1980s," Bok asserts that "the reasons have more to do with the prevailing ideology of these decades than with the competition for chief executives" (p. 106n). Though the support that he offers for this assertion is meager in the extreme, barring a belief in RAP, it is not too much weaker than what can be mobilized for its refutation.

25. See ibid., chapter 5.
26. The remark in n. 23 suggests why this is the case.

Unionism and Relative Wages

To appreciate both the achievements and the limitations of modern labor economics, one can hardly do better than to consider the late H. G. Lewis's (1963, 1986) studies of the effect of labor unions on (relative) wage rates. These are not original studies, but extremely meticulous critical surveys of the entire literature on the effect of unionism on relative wage rates in the United States.[27] Lewis not only appraised the various studies, but where possible replicated them, making adjustments to the data and improving the statistical procedures as needed.

A primary objective of each study was to produce an estimate of the union/nonunion wage gap in the United States. In the earlier survey, Lewis estimated that in 1957–58, the gap was between 10 and 15 percent. In the later survey, he presents estimates for each year between 1967 and 1979: these range from 12 percent to 20 percent, with a mean value of 15 percent, and show an upward trend.[28] Lewis believed that these estimates set "upper bounds" on the mean wage gap because "in general such estimates suffer from upward bias resulting from the omission of control variables correlated with the union status variable."[29]

The derivation of these estimates from the underlying studies was *judgmental,* that is, the process by which the estimates were derived involved decisions that had no explicit rationale. That the estimates are widely accepted as the "best available" testifies to the standards of evidence operative in the field and the correlative importance of expert judgment. Lewis' estimates are widely credited because of his long and careful study of the relevant phenomena and the lack of a generally accepted procedure that does not require resort to expert judgment. It is worth noting that Lewis' status as an expert derives in good part because his surveys (and other work) reveal a high level of command, not only of the subject matter, but also of the relevant tools of economic theory and econometrics.

But appeal to authority (expertise) as warrant for findings of fact (i.e., estimates of the union/nonunion wage gap) is a relatively small complaint when compared with those arising from the process of estimating "union

27. To avoid understating Lewis's contribution to this body of research, let me note that a substantial number of the early studies (covered in the earlier volume) were doctoral dissertations done under Lewis's very active direction.

28. Lewis (1986), p. 9.

29. Ibid.

effects." If union affiliation were stochastically independent of other factors affecting wage rates, estimating the effect of unionism on wage rates
would be relatively simple:[30] one would compare the wage rates of unionized workers with those of otherwise comparable nonunion workers. But
notoriously, and for a variety of reasons, unionism is positively correlated
with other variables which are themselves associated with higher wage
rates. To overcome the difficulty introduced by this correlation one must
disentangle the estimated effect upon wage rates of unionism and of all
other relevant variables from a set of interrelated regression equations.

Unfortunately, despite many proposals, there is no generally accepted
method for making such estimates, and "the practical value of the(se)
alternative estimators for this problem is in dispute at the present moment
and will probably remain so until there is a better understanding of the
determinants of U_i."[31] (U_i is union status of the ith individual.) It is the
inadequate understanding of the determinants of union status (i.e., union
affiliation), especially of the determinants that are associated with wage
rates regardless of unionism, that is primarily responsible for the failure
to obtain reliable estimates of the effect of unionism on wage rates.
Whether this failure is due to inability to find a theoretically acceptable
union affiliation equation or to temporal instability of its parameters, or
both, is an open question. In either case, a satisfactory union affiliation
equation has not yet been discovered.

This renders problematic the validity of any statement about the effect
of unionism on wage rates—or on any other variable.[32] This is because
one cannot know what changes in other wage-influencing variables are
entailed by the emergence (or increase in the extent) of unionism until
the union affiliation equation, inter alia, is specified and estimated. But
this is only one of many obstacles to a satisfactory assessment of the effects of unionism. As Pencavel puts it:

> For the particular goal of providing more relevant information
> for economic policy, what is required is not simply more empir-

30. What is said here about the effect of unionism upon wage rates applies equally well
to its effect upon any other variable of interest.

31. John Pencavel (1991), pp. 15–16. Pencavel points out (p. 16n) that some writers (e.g.,
Lewis) are skeptical of the ability of simultaneous equation techniques to produce satisfactory estimates of union effects, while others are more optimistic. It should be remarked that
Pencavel's book is an excellent survey of the union wage effects literature that is considerably more up-to-date than Lewis's. In addition, Pencavel offers a detailed critique of both
the economic theory and the econometric procedures used in obtaining these results.

32. The assertion of this sentence applies on any reasonable definition of unionism.

ical work. The computation of more and more correlations will not resolve some of the modelling questions raised. . . . Simply knowing that wages are higher in unionized establishments than in comparable nonunion establishments does not necessarily imply that resource allocation has been affected in a particular way; higher wages may imply no more than a redistribution of rents in the economy. The relevant policy would seem to depend on how unions behave and how the allocation of resources is affected. These issues have only started being resolved.[33]

I would go beyond Pencavel only in asking how likely it is that "these issues" will be resolved before the further evolution of unionism replaces them with different ones.

Minimum Wages

From the late nineteenth century to the present, it has been a staple proposition of RAP that whatever increases the marginal cost of employing labor will reduce the quantity that is employed. This proposition has been used regularly as an argument against trade union demands that would raise the hourly cost of employing labor, and against government regulations having the same effect. Prominent among such regulations are minimum wage laws: laws prescribing statutory minimum rates of pay for a specific class of jobs, and/or a specific class of individuals.

Not surprisingly, the interest groups who support minimum wage legislation, and the economists who agree with their policy objectives, dispute the applicability of RAP to this situation even when they do not dispute the validity of the paradigm itself. The most influential of their arguments, and the one that is most relevant here, is that the alleged negative relation between quantity of employment and the minimum hourly wage rate is not found empirically.

The most recent, and by far the most extensive, effort in support of this position is a study by David E. Card and Alan B. Krueger (1995). Analyzing data generated by the "natural experiments" performed by various state governments and the federal government through the enactment of minimum wage laws, they find that

the bulk of the empirical evidence on the employment effects of the minimum wage suggests that increases in the minimum wage have had, if anything, a small positive effect on employ-

33. Pencavel (1992), p. 194.

ment, rather than an adverse effect. In our opinion, the conventional [read RAP] view that increases in the minimum wage necessarily have an adverse effect on employment has very weak empirical foundations. (p. 236)

To an RAP adherent—and even to those whose adherence is hedged with reservations—this conclusion is rather startling. Consequently, it occasions no surprise that the work has been severely criticized on both technical and substantive grounds.[34] It is not necessary for us to take sides in this debate to note that, stripped of controversial wrapping, the main finding of Card and Krueger is not really disputed: that is, that the noise generated by "other forces" bearing on the wage-employment relation is so loud that it drowns out whatever message the labor demand function is sending.

As Kennan puts it,

Myth and Measurement's lasting contribution may well be to show that we just don't know how many jobs would be lost if the minimum wage were increased to $5.15, and that we are unlikely to find out by using more sophisticated methods of inference on the existing body of data. What is needed is more sophisticated data. (1995, p. 1964)

After concurring heartily in this conclusion, one should add: but, even then, there is no strong presumption that the strength of the relation between wages and the quantity of employment relative to the accompanying noise will be sufficient to generate useable estimates of the effect upon the latter of changes in the former.

I fear that the overall tone of the discussion in this first part of the chapter may seem to deprecate the achievements of labor economics during the past 50 years. But such is not my intention: to the contrary, I believe that, during this period, labor economics has made great strides in theoretical sophistication, in the quality of the empirical material it utilizes, and in the quality of the econometric techniques it brings to bear in implementing theoretical hypotheses. However, my enthusiasm is curbed when I consider the progress toward if-then predictions that these achievements represent or promise in the foreseeable future. While it is possible that such progress may yet occur, it is also possible that the signal-to-noise ratio inherent in the subject matter is too low for any fea-

---

34. For a detailed review, see John Kennan (1995).

sible development of technique to extract a usable basis for making conditional predictions. This does not imply that labor economics is without practical value; only that its value lies elsewhere (see chapter 12).

FINANCE: THE BEHAVIOR OF SECURITY PRICES

It would be an exaggeration to say that prior to the 1950s economists did not believe that the behavior of security prices was a matter for their concern. However, it is true that prior to the "rational expectations revolution" they did not feel that failure to explain the behavior of security prices constituted a serious challenge to the standing of RAP.[35]

Finding a formula to predict future security prices shares the fascination of alchemy, and attracts—even now—a large group of seekers after quick wealth. In a simple sense, the ultimate challenge for any student of economics is to provide a satisfactory answer to the derisive question, "If you're so smart, why ain't you rich?" Since professions of disinterest in the objective have never been convincing, provision of a satisfactory answer should always have been high on the profession's agenda. That it wasn't may tell us something about the research priorities of economists.

Although most economists were willing to cede intellectual jurisdiction of stock market phenomena to others, at least since the turn of the twentieth century there has been recurring, albeit scattered, professional interest in the subject.[36] In the late 1950s and early 60s, this interest interacted with developments in the (RAP) theory of portfolio selection to generate the random walk theory of security prices.[37] The critical links of the random walk theory to the theory of portfolio selection are the two following propositions: (1) in equilibrium all opportunities for (profitable) arbitrage are fully exploited, and (2) any systematic (i.e., nonrandom)

35. Keynes's remark in *The General Theory* (1936, p. 158) about stock prices reflecting "what average opinion expects the average opinion to be" is suggestive of the conventional wisdom of the profession until about 1960.

36. For the history of early research into the history of stock market behavior, especially its random character, see Paul Cootner (1964).

37. The idea that the market price of any security follows a random walk has been around since the turn of the twentieth century. *Random walk* is a concept of the theory of stochastic processes where it refers to a time series in which the first differences of the observations are serially uncorrelated and their distributions are identical and mutually independent. Hence, if the price of a security follows a random walk, it will be impossible to use its history to predict its future. This negative proposition is the main point of the random walk hypothesis (or theory) of security prices.

component of the time series of recorded prices of a security is a source of information about its future prices. As (1) follows immediately from the definition of equilibrium in an RAP model, let us focus on (2).

Suppose that through an innovation of statistical technique an individual was enabled to discern in the recorded price data of a particular security a rough approximation to a cycle (of specific frequency and amplitude) that had been undiscerned previously. Utilizing knowledge of this cycle, he could forecast future movements in the price of this security and, by appropriately timed trades, make arbitrage profits. If this forecasting innovation could be kept secret, these profits would continue indefinitely.[38] But among adherents of this theory, it is generally believed that such innovations occur only very infrequently, are always quickly discovered, and are therefore evanescent.[39]

As a result, the theory is taken to imply that the presence of any detectable systematic (i.e., nonrandom) component in the price series of a security would cause all traders to alter their temporal patterns of buying and selling in order to garner arbitrage profits. Therefore, in equilibrium no arbitrage profits will be available to any trader. Moreover, an equilibrium will be characterized by the absence of any temporal pattern in the price series of any security (or other tradable asset) such as would permit any individual to obtain arbitrage profits by rearranging the temporal pattern of her purchases and sales. Markets in which the behavior of security prices closely approximates the behavior that would obtain in such an equilibrium are said to be 'efficient'. (Hereafter, I shall follow the convention of referring to the theory that markets are efficient as the efficient market hypothesis, or EMH.)

If markets were efficient, no one could earn arbitrage profits by acting on inferences from the history of security prices. This implies that the very considerable body of investment advice based on the characteristics of charts of (past) security prices is misguided, to say the least. Thus the theory of efficient markets implies that any investment strategy based on the characteristics of recorded security prices (such strategies are commonly called "Chartist") would be inferior to a "buy and hold" strategy,

38. Situations where knowledge of an innovation can be limited to the innovator are referred to as (cases where there is) "private information," and are explicitly excluded from the purview of (some variants of) the efficient market hypothesis.

39. However, in the nature of the case, the occurrence of a situation in which private information existed could never be known (publicly) until after the fact.

since the latter would have the virtue of minimizing transaction costs without sacrificing yield at any given level of risk.[40]

It is not to the present point to review the continuing debate between Chartists of various kinds and adherents of the efficient market theory.[41] Suffice it to say that starting from a very low base around 1970, investment in Index Funds[42]—a favorite method of following a buy and hold strategy—has since grown relative to all investment in listed equities; however, Chartism is by no means dead.

That holding Index Funds is a preferred means of implementing a buy and hold investment strategy reflects the fact that in equilibrium it is possible to obtain a higher expected yield only by bearing additional risk. To see why this should be so, note that in EMH the concepts of risk and yield refer to an investor's total portfolio rather than to any of its separate components. In the simplified version of this theory that is commonly used in applied work, it is assumed that a portfolio is associated with a stream of anticipated stochastic returns whose distribution is fully characterized by two parameters, *mean* and *variance*.[43] The first of these parameters is treated as the expected return, and the second as the risk, of the entire portfolio.

To identify risk, a property of an individual's utility function, with the variance of the distribution of returns of his portfolio requires a rather elaborate argument that involves some fairly drastic simplifications. For our purpose, the details may be omitted: given its assumptions, it is generally accepted that the argument is valid.[44] The important point is that, if markets are efficient, any portfolio with a higher expected return than some other portfolio must be attended with a higher degree of risk. In effect, a set of efficient markets imposes a tradeoff between risk and ex-

40. Transaction costs include, inter alia, brokerage commissions and taxes on transactions.

41. The interested reader should consult Helen Allen and Mark P. Taylor (1992).

42. An index fund is a mutual fund whose portfolio of securities is weighted so as to make movements of its unit price vary proportionately to movements of an index of stocks (such as the S&P index) representing a broad section of the entire stock market.

43. This simplified model is generally termed the Capital Asset Pricing model, or CAPM. Barring some arbitrary and highly improbable conjuncture of disturbances, the assumptions of CAPM imply that the probability distribution of a portfolio's returns is normal and unchanging through time.

44. The details of this argument are presented in any good textbook on the theory of finance. Though very condensed, a good short reference is Stephen A. Ross (1987).

pected return that is analogous to the rate of exchange represented by the slope of AB in figure 2 of chapter 3.

Derivatives and the Law of One Price

The alleged relation of risk and expected returns provides a testable implication of RAP that has been utilized literally hundreds of times during the past quarter century.[45] On the whole, and despite exceptions, the outcome of these tests has been judged as having "not rejected" the theory of efficient markets.[46] As a result, since the early 1970s there has been growing acceptance of EMH both among analysts (i.e., economists) and participants (investors, investment advisors, brokers, and accountants) in financial markets. This trend in acceptance has been reflected in the growing number of financial economists graduated from business schools, in their relative salaries, and in the prestige of finance specialists within the economics profession.[47]

Perhaps the most important indicator of the practical acceptance of the theory of efficient markets is its use in the creation of "derivative securities," or "derivatives" for short. In essence, derivatives are claims whose value depends upon the value of one or more underlying securities. A prime example of a derivative security is an option to buy or sell a specific security at a specified price prior to some particular date.

If the relevant markets are efficient, the price of a derivative security will be determined by a stochastic function of the price of the underlying security, the (risk free) rate of interest, and the time interval till expiration of the option represented by the derivative: this function is given by the Black-Scholes formula for the price of an option to buy or sell a security.[48] Given market efficiency, the relative prices of derivatives and underlying securities will be kept (very) close to their Black-Scholes values by the activity of arbitrageurs.

During the past twenty years, the price behavior of derivatives has been generally supportive of both EMH and Black-Scholes.[49] Further sup-

45. For a sample of these references see Malkiel (1987) and/or Ross (1987).

46. Typically, the tests have involved determining whether or not what is measured as expected return is positively associated with what is measured as risk.

47. One indication of the prestige of financial economics is the 1990 award of the Nobel Prize in Economics to three of the major contributors to this specialty and the 1997 award to two others. (See chapter 13.)

48. The Black-Scholes formula, cited in the award of the 1997 Nobel prize, was first presented in Fischer Black and Myron S. Scholes (1973).

49. See Malkiel (1987) or Ross (1987).

port is provided by the tremendous growth in the use of derivative securities as vehicles for speculation and risk hedging, and in the construction of very complicated contracts for such purposes.[50]

In principle, the price movements of derivatives should follow those of the underlying securities. However, due to the increased popularity of derivatives, movements of their prices have occasionally affected those of the underlying securities—especially around settlement dates for option contracts—with the result that the derivative markets have been blamed for causing turbulence in the markets for (underlying) securities, leading to calls for their regulation, or even their abolition.[51] The validity of such complaints does not concern us: it is the fact of "real world" impact of the theory of efficient markets to which attention is drawn.

In its contribution to the growth of Index Funds and markets for derivatives generally; and to the growth of institutions to facilitate the trading of such assets, EMH has had an impact on everyday behavior similar in kind to that made by a technologically relevant discovery in a successful natural science. This impact is neither to be denied nor belittled. However, in order to appreciate this impact properly, it is necessary to understand its relation to the law of one price and its consequent limitations.

Despite many subtleties of interpretation and allowance for minor qualifications, EMH is a direct implication of the proposition that arbitrage profits are *evanescent;* envisaged profits vanish so rapidly under the rush of traders' efforts to obtain them that no one can devise a rational investment strategy based on their successful capture.[52]

Denial of the possibility of arbitrage profits is but an extension of "the law of one price" (i.e., the 'law' that a given commodity cannot be sold at two different prices at a given time), and is subject to the same qualifications. One of these is connected with transaction costs. If there are costs of transacting, especially of changing trading partners, different prices may be charged for the same good provided that the difference between the price charged by any given transactor and the lowest price paid by anyone in the market does not exceed the cost of switching to the lowest price seller from an alternative supplier.

---

50. As the Nobel prize committee wrote, "Nowadays, thousands of traders and investors use the (Black-Scholes) formula every day" (*New York Times,* 15 October 1997, p. C-1). According to the *Economist* (18–24 October 1997, p. 75), the value of outstanding derivatives in 1995/96 exceeded $30 trillion.

51. See Merton H. Miller (1994).

52. Stated alternatively, capture of arbitrage profit is entirely a matter of luck.

Thus it is generally conceded by RAP adherents that movements in the price of gold between the "gold points," which are determined by transaction costs, are not to be explained by the RAP theory of exchange rates. However, in the context of this concession it is typically assumed that the distance between the gold points is very small relative to the range of potentially observable gold prices.[53] Similarly, in most cases where the possibility of successful arbitrage among securities has been found, it has also been found that the profits from such arbitrage would have been insufficient to cover the transaction costs involved. As Malkiel puts it:

> departures from randomness are generally remarkably small and an investor who pays transaction costs cannot choose a profitable investment strategy on the basis of these anomalies. Thus, while the random-walk hypothesis is not strictly upheld, the departures from randomness that do exist are not large enough to leave unexploited investment opportunities. Consequently, the empirical evidence presents strong evidence in favour of EMH. The history of stock price movements does not offer investors any information that permits them to outperform a simple buy-and-hold investment strategy.[54]

Briefly, EMH has survived one type of test quite well: tests for the non-existence of unexploited opportunities for arbitrage profits. But, like the phenomenon of arbitrage itself, the feasibility of making such tests is restricted to organized exchanges where the law of one price holds at least approximately.[55]

While this might be said to be tantamount to the establishment of a scientific 'law', I would suggest that it would be better to call it a principle to which any proposed law of price-quantity behavior must conform. This principle, the impossibility of finding a trading strategy that would yield

53. For example, Kenneth Rogoff (1996, p. 650) finds that "For some highly traded commodities, the law of one price holds very well, as Table 2 illustrates for the case of gold." However, he goes on to remark that "As we shall see later, however, commodities where the deviations from the law of one price damp out very quickly are the exception rather than the rule." It should be noted that the exceptions are traded on organized exchanges.

54. Malkiel (1987), p. 121.

55. Even on organized exchanges, market failure is possible, but is sufficiently infrequent as to be neglected in most contexts. When one focuses on sufficiently small price movements of sufficiently short duration, anomalies to EMH appear even on organized exchanges with the usual difficulties—and controversies—of interpretation. For recent examples see the *Economist*, 17 January 1998, p. 71, and Christie and Schultz (1994).

positive arbitrage profits, constitutes an empirically well-supported generalization to which any proposed law must either conform or confront: in the latter case, the burden of proof would be upon the proponents of the proposed law. While this characteristic is shared by most scientific laws, such laws have the further property of entailing one or more additional if-then statements that can be tested. It is because the principle of efficient markets does not have this property that I prefer not to term it a law.

Nevertheless, law or not, the principle of efficient markets is a substantive contribution to empirical knowledge and an important illustration of "what economics is good for" (see chapter 11)—so long as its limitations are explicitly recognized. Its proper application is limited to prices set on organized exchanges, because only on such exchanges is the homogeneity of units of a traded asset sufficiently well assured as to make it feasible to trade without examination of the specific units traded.[56] This is not to assert that apart from an organized exchange the principle of efficient markets does not hold, but only that it loses power: i.e. outside the context of an organized exchange transaction costs are so high and so variable that a very large part of all price movements are placed beyond the purview of the forces reflected in the law of one price.[57]

Private Information and the Testing of EMH

A second limitation upon EMH refers to a proviso not previously mentioned: a successful strategy for capturing arbitrage profits is impossible *only in the absence of private information.* That is, the efficiency of markets imposes no obstacle to the arbitrage profits of an individual who has somehow obtained access to knowledge of price-relevant future events that is denied to all—or almost all—others. As can be seen readily, the explanatory power of EMH varies inversely with the extent to which price movements reflect private information.[58]

Since by its definition the presence of private information is not di-

56. It will be obvious to even the most casual observer of the activity on an organized exchange that the trading proceeds at a pace that is utterly incompatible with examination of the characteristics of each unit bought or sold. In a nutshell, trading on organized exchanges is driven by hope of favorable price movements and not by hope of getting superior specimens of whatever is bought.

57. In effect, outside of organized exchanges, the "gold points" for particular commodities become so wide as to make conventional explanations of exchange rate movements irrelevant to most observed behavior.

58. Generally, a model that satisfies EMH will also satisfy RAP, and I shall treat the former as implying the latter.

rectly observable, the testability of EMH requires that the absence of private information be a maintained hypothesis. That is, whenever EMH appears to be rejected by the data, the presence of private information is always a possible explanation of the failure. Given its very limited observability, it is very unsatisfactory to invoke the presence of private information as a means of "saving" EMH when it seems to be rejected by the data. Accordingly, only rarely has it been invoked, and then with detailed justification for doing so. The success of EMH reflects the fact that (inter alia) it has been unnecessary to resort to such hypothesis-saving stratagems.

Stated differently, the nonrejection of EMH implies acceptance of the non-existence and/or negligibility of private information. This raises a fundamental question about the function of private information in the operation of an (organized) exchange: if arbitrage profits require private information, do professional traders believe that normally they have such information, or are they bearing risk without compensation?

While this is not the place for detailed argument, let me suggest one possible answer to this question. Traders seek and regularly acquire price-relevant information in advance of the general public. But this information is derived from a variety of "communications," differing across recipients in detail and moment of receipt, which are also received by a number of similar but noncolluding traders. Each of these traders attempts to transact as soon as she deciphers the "message" in the communications. It is these transactions that drive the moment-to-moment price movements on an exchange, and the relative success of a trader in capturing arbitrage profits depends upon her speed in gathering and acting (transacting) on such messages.

It is at least possible that some traders are possessed of sufficient skill (and energy) at this process as to earn positive arbitrage profits on average. But this does not imply a contradiction of EMH because the differential information that such profits would reflect might be (I suspect are) dissipated so rapidly (in fractions of a trading day) that it is not reflected in the ordinary records of transaction prices which provide the empirical material for testing EMH. The data needed to detect the presence of evanescent private information would be very difficult to obtain and, so far as I am aware, have never been gathered.

As described above, trading in derivative securities might seem to be a zero-sum game of gambling for high stakes that yields no net social product. While widely held, this perception is incorrect. Derivative securities (e.g., put and call options), perform the function of enabling individuals who are risk averse, and/or for whom the cost of gathering information is relatively expensive, to transfer the risk to professional trader-speculators who have these disadvantages in lesser degree and can thus supply risk-bearing at lesser cost. For such traders, the gathering of information relevant to future price movements is ancillary both to specialized risk hedging and the seeking of arbitrage profits which are, for this reason, joint products.

In other words, arbitraging should not be considered as a distinct activity, but rather as a by-product of risk hedging for nontraders. The expected profits for facilitating such risk hedging are payment for bearing the risk and offsetting the cost of acquiring specialized knowledge ancillary to the activity. Hence rational arbitrageurs need not expect positive expected profits directly related to this activity; arbitraging is simply another name for striving for maximum profit in the process of providing risk hedges.

The above discussion of EMH is brief and necessarily superficial, but not (I hope) misleading. Nuances have been overlooked, and seeming anomalies—and their proposed reconciliations with EMH—bypassed. The ongoing debates about whether one or another anomaly can be reconciled with EMH turn largely upon (1) whether or not arbitrage profits that might appear to have been obtainable would have been offset by transaction costs, and/or (2) whether the expected gains allegedly obtainable would have been offset by the incremental risk attendant upon implementation of the implied strategy.[59]

Without attempting to judge the state of the debate between adherents of EMH and its critics, for the purpose of this argument I shall argue as though EMH has thus far survived challenges to its validity. I do this because, by a wide margin, EMH is the most successful predictive hypothesis that economics has yet offered.[60] If, despite its achievements to date, EMH should eventually be found wanting, the essentially negative argument of this chapter would hold a fortiori.

My reservations about EMH are due to its limited and essentially negative empirical implications: EMH is a denial of the possibility of profit-

---

59. It may be noted that often measurement of incremental risk is difficult and attended with great controversy.

60. Both the law of one price and Gresham's law are variants of this hypothesis.

able arbitrage. When EMH is interpreted as implying more than this, empirical tests of it have had the indecisive outcomes characteristic of hypothesis testing in other branches of economics.

Consider, for example, the controversy over "excess volatility" of stock prices. It is generally agreed that, if EMH is valid, the price of a share of stock should be equal to the expected present value of its future dividends, and that therefore temporal variations in recorded stock prices should be smaller than variations in actual dividends.[61] It has been argued strongly by a number of economists, notably Robert J. Shiller (1981), that the reverse has been the case (i.e., that stock prices have varied more than dividends), implying a rejection of EMH by the data. Shiller goes on to contend that the "excess volatility" of stock prices is due to the operation of fashions or fads on at least part of the investing public.

This contention is incompatible with RAP generally, and Rational Expectations in particular. Accordingly, it has been vigorously attacked by RAP/EMH adherents who dispute both the empirical results and Shiller's theoretical interpretation of them.[62] Whether stock prices fluctuate more (or less) than the flow of dividend payments turns out to depend upon the assumptions made about how information on the prospect for future dividends is reflected in the record of current and past dividend payments. The debate has turned upon arcane technical issues, and no consensus among the participants is in prospect. As we have seen, this is not unlike the state of affairs in other branches of economics.

SUMMARY

In this long chapter, I have tried to illustrate the limitations of economics as a predictive science. I have done this by selecting two fields where great strides have been made during the past half century, and showing how little this has meant in terms of generating successful if-then predictions. I assert, though for reasons of space have not argued, that the situation is no better—and usually worse—in other branches of the subject. This is not to denigrate either the analytical achievements of these fields or their practical utility, matters that will be addressed in chapter 11.

61. This is because (say) quarter-to-quarter variations in dividends are likely to reflect transitory variations in earnings to which the stock price would respond sluggishly, if at all, because rational investors would not expect unusually high or low dividends to persist.

62. For an exchange that is especially well focused on the issues of concern to our argument see the chapters by Merton H. Miller, Allen W. Kleidon, and Robert J. Shiller in Hogarth and Reder (1987).

But it *is* to say that, save for the limited exception in the case of Finance, economics has not yet generated successful if-then propositions; nor is it likely to do so in the foreseeable future. The exception for finance is limited to certain implications of EMH which are negative in character and amount to a denial of the possibility of devising a successful strategy for earning expected arbitrage profits (net of transaction cost). The main applicability of these propositions is to organized exchanges where arbitrage is feasible. Outside this particular domain, EMH is either vacuous or unsusceptible of confirmation by empirical testing.

A final caveat: in discussing achievements in the field of Finance, I have deliberately downplayed the reservations to EMH that continue to be expressed by some economists.[63] This is because such reservations, if found valid, would serve only to strengthen the negative argument of this book concerning the capability of economics to generate valid if-then propositions. While I lean toward acceptance of EMH, I feel obliged to warn the reader of the existence of (some) dissent within the profession.

63. See Allen and Taylor (1992); J. B. De Long, A. Shleifer, L. H. Summers and R. J. Waldmann (1991).

PART THREE

WELFARE ECONOMICS
AND IDEOLOGY

WELFARE ECONOMICS

An account of the culture of economics must include a discussion of the branch known as welfare economics. Not only does this branch cover vital parts of what economics has to say about public policy, but it encompasses some of the subject's most cherished technical achievements. Moreover, its intimate connection with the concept of efficiency makes it integral to the conceptual organization of RAP. Nevertheless, this chapter and its successor interrupt the flow of the argument, for which I apologize to the reader: my only excuse is inability to find a better place for this essential material.

The purpose of welfare economics is to design and apply criteria of desirability to possible alternative states of an economy. The idea of using the findings of science to select the state of an economy has an intuitive appeal to anyone who believes that the purposive use of scientific knowledge is the crowning achievement of western civilization. In this spirit strong demands are made upon economists to help policy makers improve the "health" of the economy. As can be readily imagined, considerable disagreement exists both as to the capability of policy makers to serve as healers of an infirm economy and as to the propriety of their attempting to do so.

Nevertheless, a very substantial part—I would judge a majority—of the economics profession accepts that there are some circumstances in which policy makers can improve the functioning of an economy by indicating which among alternative courses of action is best, and that it is proper that they should offer advice with this objective in mind. Granted this objective, the economics community is virtually unanimous as to the relevance of its expertise. If the policy maker is to play doctor to the economy, economics is the science—or at least one of the highly relevant sciences—that must be utilized.

As applied to the economy, the doctor-patient metaphor has a difficulty. On her home turf, the objective of the medical doctor is implicit but unambiguous: for practical purposes, specifying what constitutes healthy functioning of an organism, or an improvement thereof, presents no conceptual problem. For an economy, it is otherwise.

Design and application of measures of performance, for an economy or a segment thereof, provide primary illustrations of the economist's expertise and its social function; this branch of the subject is welfare economics. Welfare economics has no good counterpart in other sciences, and its role in economics is a salient characteristic of the disciplinary culture. But although highly technical and constituting a major field for the display of professional skill, welfare economics does not involve the proposing or testing of empirical hypotheses.

WELFARE ECONOMICS AND SOCIAL CHOICE

A discussion of welfare economics begins conveniently with a characterization of the manner in which selections among alternative economic states is to be made, and the criteria to be used in appraising the quality of the resulting choices. A simple characterization is to describe the choice maker as an individual exercising preferences described by a utility function defined over possible alternative states of the economy. Such a function might be represented by figure 1 in chapter 3, interpreting each point in the X,Y plane as a different state of the economy. However, in making such a representation, it would be important to bear in mind that although the interpretation of the shapes of the indifference curves and the budget line used in the context of individual choice among commodity bundles could also apply to situations where the choice objects were alternative states of the economy, this is not necessarily the case.

Because the information required for choosing among states of the economy is always grossly inadequate, such a characterization of economic policy making is generally recognized as inherently defective. But this difficulty is often overlooked, because of the fascination of economists (and others) with the conceptual problems associated with the notion of "social choice."

In the simplest example of social choice making, all choice makers (e.g., individuals) have identical indifference maps over states of the economy (in the sense of figure 1). In this case, a social choice is identical with the choice of every single chooser, and choice can be identified as a consensus. But, for many reasons, there are always differences among individuals in preferences over states of the economy so that, if a social choice is somehow to be related to the preferences of more than one individual, the characteristics of the relationship between the social choice making procedure and the preferences of the various individuals must be specified.[1]

Thus appraisal of the quality of a social choice will depend upon how the appraising economist believes the outcomes of the social choice making procedure should be related to individual preferences. As can readily be perceived, the specification of such a relationship is not part of economics as the subject is normally defined, and has implications going far beyond its purview. It also is clear that some relationships might be more satisfactory than others.

The analysis of social choice is widely considered to be a distinct field, overlapping part of economics, but going well beyond it to include parts of political science and philosophy. However, economists have made major contributions to the field and have set the tone of its discourse, which is sharply focused on the formal characteristics of voting rules[2] and greatly concerned with logical rigor.

Although greatly esteemed within the profession,[3] the literature on social choice is almost disjoint from the main body of economic research. That is, this literature is not concerned with how the economy functions, but with the rules for relating social choices to individual preferences.[4] At least thus far, social choice theorists have not attempted to explain the choices made among alternative voting rules or the economic consequences of adopting one rule rather than another, but have focused upon the logical implications of alternative voting rules for the relating of social choices to individual preferences. This focus has highlighted a (negative) result of Arrow (1951, 1987): the famous Impossibility Theorem.

In essence, this theorem states that, except for the case where all individuals have identical preferences, if individual preferences satisfy certain generally accepted and seemingly innocuous conditions whose main effect

1. While there are, of course, many reasons why preferences over states of the economy should vary among individuals, a primary reason is that each distribution of wealth implies (by definition) a different state of the economy, so that given individuals will generally prefer states where their own wealth is greater to states where it is less.

2. For a good summary of the relevant literature together with an extensive bibliography see Amartya Sen (1987).

3. One indication of this esteem is that at least two Nobel prizes, Arrow's in 1971 and Buchanan's in 1986, and arguably others, have rested heavily upon contributions to this field.

4. Concern with the characteristics of rules for social choice spills over into many problems of characterizing and explaining individual choices. Thus, within economics and at its interface with psychology, contributors to social choice theory often participate in research on utility theory and the theory of individual choice, as well.

is to assure logical consistency among the choices of a single individual, it will be impossible to construct a voting rule that would prevent outcomes (social choices) that are generally considered unacceptable. The most important of such unacceptable outcomes are violations of Pareto optimality (see below), and intransitivity among social choices when individual preferences are transitive.[5]

Much effort has been devoted to finding a way to relax one or another of Arrow's conditions so as to obtain a voting rule that is intuitively acceptable, but also precludes unacceptable social choices. To the present such efforts have been largely unsuccessful and, in any case, are not very relevant to our main theme. More to the point, is the effect of the impossibility theorem on such notions as The General Welfare, The Interest of Society or The Common Good.

So long as it is maintained that the good of society must be related to the levels of (individual) utility attained by its members, the difficulty posed by Arrow's theorem will remain a major obstacle for anyone seeking to formulate or exploit a concept of the good of the whole society. Philosophy has been concerned with these issues for several millennia, but the heavy influence of welfare economics on the subject is of relatively recent origin. Welfare economics' ticket of admission to this debate has been its highly sophisticated analysis of the relation of individual utility to the good of society; hence the importance of the impossibility theorem.

However, not all recent discussion of these topics has defined social welfare as an aggregate function of the welfare of its individual members. For example, Rawls's (1971) *A Theory of Justice,* and much of the large literature it has inspired, assumes the welfare of society to depend (inter alia) upon the distribution of wealth among its members.[6] It will occasion no surprise that those who believe that the general welfare must vary inversely with the degree to which some criterion of distributional justice is violated, should clash with those who believe that any acceptable criterion of social welfare must satisfy Pareto optimality.

Nowadays, the historical link of economics with moral philosophy is maintained largely through the channel of welfare economics. A large part of the reciprocal influence of economics and other intellectual disciplines

5. Intransitivity among social choices is exemplified by $A > B$ and $B > C$, but $C > A$, where $>$ indicates "is preferred to."

6. It is easy to show that where the social welfare depends upon the distribution of wealth (as well as upon its aggregate magnitude), circumstances where Pareto optimality is inconsistent with the good of society are likely to arise.

upon one another flows through this channel, and many leading economists, past and present, have swum in it. But this is only one of the channels through which welfare economics has influenced the general current
of ideas and, indirectly, public policy.

While policy formulation involves notions of the general welfare, its
implementation also requires judgments of fact; especially judgments
about the consequences of specific actions of government. In making such
judgments, a policy maker must use both positive economics to predict
and/or retrodict, as well as possible, the results of contemplated government actions, and welfare economics to appraise the predicted result in
terms of some criterion of social benefit.

The predictions made, and the criteria used to appraise them, are
strongly influenced by an underlying paradigm. Many paradigms are associated with distinct though not always explicit forms of welfare economics.
Differences among the forms of welfare economics are most clearly revealed in the criteria used in judging economic actions of the state, and
these will be discussed later.

Although there is a variety of forms of welfare economics, each associated with a particular paradigm, only one has thus far been developed in
any detail: this form is associated with RAP, and occasionally—for emphasis—I shall refer to it as RAP-welfare economics. But in so doing I
shall be violating common usage, because most economists identify (all)
welfare economics with this particular variant, and are scarcely aware of
other variants even when they make use of them. Consequently, when I
speak of welfare economics without a modifier, I shall be referring to the
RAP variant.

RAP–Welfare Economics and Pareto Optimality

The desideratum of RAP welfare economics is that the state of the economy should be such that it would be impossible to reallocate resources so
that any one individual could gain (utility) without some other individu-
al(s) losing. States satisfying this condition are called Pareto optimal, and
may be represented, for a two-person economy, by any point on the contract curve, WW', of figure 2, in chapter 3. Such points reflect situations
where all possible trades that could benefit both parties have been made.
For any point off of WW', F, it is always possible to find one or more points
on WW', J, such that a movement from F to J (reflecting an exchange of
commodities) will increase the utility levels of both individuals. The point
of Pareto optimality is that all such opportunities for mutually beneficial

exchange should be exploited.[7] The multiplicity of points on WW' reflects the fact that (normally) a Pareto optimum is not unique, so that an economy with identical resources and producing identical outputs may have many such points, each corresponding to a particular distribution of wealth (resources) among its individual members.

Put differently, the RAP view of welfare implies that an economy, A, in which every individual has more of every item that is considered good (and no more of any that is considered bad) than in some other economy, B, is superior to B: that is, A is Pareto superior to B. So defined, a Pareto-superior economy would be generally accepted as unambiguously better than its alternative, but the conclusion would be vacuous. Real-world situations always involve more of some goods and less of others, so that calculation of trade-offs between less of some items and more of others is essential for judgments of Pareto superiority. This is where RAP comes in.

RAP approaches such calculations in the following way: imagine a hypothetical "government" to be considering whether or not to take a potentially beneficial action (e.g., to provide the economy with more of good X), but to finance the provision with revenue collected from a hypothetical lump-sum tax. Suppose the government has adopted Pareto optimality as its choice (decision) criterion: i.e., only those actions that result in Pareto improvements (move the economy to a Pareto-superior position) are to be undertaken. Then the decision to provide X and collect the hypothetical tax becomes a problem in applied welfare economics.

The government's problem is to calculate the value of the benefit or loss to each individual as the net result of the action and the tax combined, and then to sum these amounts over all individuals. The value of the benefit to any given individual would be equal to the amount (positive or negative) of a hypothetical lump-sum tax that would leave each individual on the same indifference curve as he would have been on had the government not bestowed the benefit.[8] The difference of this hypothetical tax

7. The reader is reminded that, in the absence of transaction costs, RAP implies that production and exchange are indistinguishable. For readers interested in pursuing the development of transaction cost economics, the collection of essays in Oliver E. Williamson and Scott E. Masten (1995) is an excellent starting place.

8. Note that in a careful development of this argument, "government" is an (improper) synonym for a deus ex machina acting upon a society of individuals in an Arrow-Debreu world. In such a world, governments do not exist. Despite this, economists frequently discuss potential Pareto-improving actions as being taken by a government as though the government were an infinitely powerful deus ex machina whose use entailed no cost. This unfortu-

from the increment to the individual's actual tax payments required to defray the cost of providing more of X is defined as the individual's net gain (or loss) from the combined effect of the action and the tax.[9]

Such gains, summed over all individuals, are defined as the gain to the community. The significance of such hypothetical taxes in measuring (changes in) economic welfare may be seen from the following consideration: if the sum (over all individuals) of all the above gains and losses were positive, then it would be possible for the government to levy the hypothetical taxes on those who were net gainers and use the proceeds fully to compensate those who were net losers, and have a residual surplus available for distribution. That is, prior to distribution of the surplus, losers would be fully compensated and gainers left no worse off as the combined result of the action and the tax. But, by distributing the surplus so that every individual got some (positive) share, everyone could be placed on a higher indifference curve—made better off—thereby accomplishing a Pareto improvement.[10] Put differently, wherever it is possible for the gainers from an action to finance the compensation (or, for short, compensate) the losers while retaining some portion of their gains, a Pareto improvement will be possible of attainment. Hence the term "compensation principle" is used as a designation for the criterion for selecting actions that can be judged Pareto improving, provided losers are compensated.

Although not implied by RAP, making Pareto improvements whenever possible is a criterion for public policy that has wide appeal, both to economists and others. However, virtually no action of a government would benefit everyone, so that this criterion would hardly ever apply unless compensation were actually paid to losers from revenue collected from gainers.

For fairly obvious reasons, this is hardly ever done: (1) the information necessary to measure the appropriate taxes and benefits is unobtainable, and (2) while the idea of making Pareto improvements wherever possible has wide appeal, there is no agreement that the existing distribution of wealth is satisfactory, so that a suggestion that (say) wealthy losers should

---

nate practice is responsible for a good deal of confusion, as will be described in chapter 10.

9. The reason for requiring that the tax be lump sum is to make its dollar amount independent of how the individual uses his resources. Otherwise, the required amount of the tax would vary with the elasticity of demand for whatever commodity was being taxed.

10. The reverse of all this would apply where the sum of the differences (over all individuals) was negative.

be compensated from taxes imposed on impecunious gainers would meet with great resistance and has, in fact, rarely been made.[11]

Consequently, taken literally, the Pareto improvement criterion does not function as a guide to policy making. However, in modified form, it is very influential. The relevant modification involves comparing the magnitudes of the lump-sum taxes with the payments required to determine whether a proposed action would constitute a Pareto improvement, but not actually collecting and paying them. If the sum of these hypothetical quantities should be positive, the action is judged a Pareto improvement; conversely, if the sum should be negative, it is not. In effect this makes the criterion for good economic policy the increase of "total community welfare," regardless of its distribution. Although some economists might accept such a criterion, many others—including some RAP-adherents—would insist that distribution should matter.

At this point, the reader might well ask for an operational definition of the entity the distribution of which does—or does not—matter. An easy answer would be national income as conventionally measured, but this would be misleading because of the importance of leisure time and working conditions in determining the level of utility attained by an individual or a household. For most economists a satisfactory indicator of individual welfare would be one which increased with pecuniary income (after taxes) and decreased both with working hours per week and the physical hazards and general unpleasantness of the job(s) held.

Bearing in mind the qualifications sometimes required to take account of changes in hours and working conditions, and the state of the environment, most economists would agree that an individual's welfare increases or decreases with his pecuniary income in dollars of constant purchasing power or, alternatively, real income.[12] Accordingly, they judge a govern-

11. Where the total amount available to compensate losers is large relative to the community's income, the effect of actually taxing gainers and compensating losers could materially alter the "preaction" distribution of wealth. Although this possibility can create difficult conceptual problems, fortunately, they are not relevant to the present discussion.

The reader will note that, in emphasizing Pareto optimality as the criterion of welfare, RAP makes resource allocation the salient desideratum to the neglect of distribution. As exemplified in figure 2, the judgment is made that to be on the contract curve is better than to be off, but nothing is (or can be) said about the desirability of one point on the curve as compared with another.

12. For brevity, I shall refer hereafter to the effects of actions or policies on command of goods and services as "pecuniary effects," and to effects on hours and conditions of work, the environment, etc., as "nonpecuniary effects."

ment action or policy to have increased the general welfare if it increases
per capita real income without having "undesirable" effects on its distribution, or adversely affecting hours or conditions of work, or the environment. While evaluations of the effect of distributive changes (in national
income) on the general welfare vary among economists, the typical procedure is to ignore such changes unless they are thought to be correlated
with the level of individual wealth or with personal characteristics thought
to be politically sensitive.

In short, acceptance of the criterion of Pareto improvement as a basis
for appraising governmental actions and policies is qualified by reservations about their nonpecuniary effects, and their effects on the distribution of wealth and income. Thus, as a first approximation, general welfare
is assumed to vary in the same direction as real per capita national income. Varying both with the action analyzed, and the analyst, this approximation is sometimes improved upon to correct for nonpecuniary effects
and/or for pecuniary effects that are correlated with income. However,
such corrections are usually considered to be secondary to the main effect
on per capita real income.[13]

EXTERNALITIES AND COST-BENEFIT ANALYSIS

All of the allegedly beneficial effects of free exchange among individuals
presume that an act of exchange influences the utility of no one except
the parties directly involved. Otherwise, rationality of trading individuals
would not suffice to lead them to Pareto-optimal quantities, as in figure 2,
in chapter 3. In the real world, exchange and production frequently affect
individuals other than those directly involved.[14]

The paradigmatic example is the case of a factory emitting smoke that
soils the possessions of people in the neighborhood and possibly endan-
gers their health. As the smoke is assumed to have no effect on the utility
of the (presumably absent) factory owner, she is therefore unmotivated
to abate the nuisance by limiting output or otherwise. This provides an
opportunity for the government to take a Pareto-improving action by reducing smoke emission (through taxation or otherwise), combined with

13. Usually, such corrections are neither quantified nor otherwise made commensurate
with the effects on per capita real income. Rather they are listed as separate matters, for
readers to consider as best they can. Atypically, an author will sometimes venture a judgment
as to the relative importance of the various effects, and their salience to the welfare judgment offered.

14. Remember that, in the absence of transaction costs, in an RAP world there is no
distinction between production and exchange.

compensation to the factory owners—and possibly their suppliers—who would lose real income because of the reduction of output and/or the change in productive methods entailed by the abatement of smoke production.

In attempting to effect a Pareto improvement, the government's first step should be to calculate and compare the sums of the costs and benefits associated with each of the various alternative programs under consideration.[15] It should then choose the program that generates the greatest excess of benefits over costs. During the last half century, the making of such calculations has become an important application of economics and provides an illustration of how economics provides expertise for the solution of social problems.

The most common name for such applications of economics is cost-benefit analysis. There are numerous studies where this conceptual framework has been applied, especially in appraising the effects of proposed actions on the environment and the desirability of proposed public investment projects.[16] This framework has also been used to study, retrospectively, the costs and benefits of projects long completed.[17]

The concepts used in such studies are essentially those requisite to calculating whether a proposed action is Pareto improving. However, the procedures used in making the actual calculations are quite varied. The part of the cost that reflects use of resources that are or could be purchased on the market can be valued at market prices: despite many vexing problems of obtaining data on prices and quantities, this part of the problem is relatively easy. It is the calculation of benefits (and costs) that have no market counterparts that presents serious difficulties.[18] These difficulties must be surmounted ad hoc, and knowledge of the procedures that may or may not be used for this purpose is a substantial part of the applied economist's stock in trade.

15. Including abstention from action as one possible program.

16. For a brief introduction to the subject, see S. Chakravarty (1987). The practice of cost-benefit analysis has a lengthy history, stretching back to the middle of the nineteenth century, both in France and in the United States. For an interesting and thoughtful account of this history, see Porter (1995).

17. For a leading example, see Robert W. Fogel (1964).

18. Despite the convenience of doing so, often it is not appropriate to base cost-benefit calculations on available market prices. The most common occurrence of such situations is where departures from conditions of competitive equilibrium are marked. Often in such cases theoretically constructed prices, called "shadow prices," are substituted for market prices. The use of shadow prices is always problematic, and their calculation an esoteric exercise in economic theory. For a brief discussion of the topic see R. Kanbur (1987).

The preferred procedures are those that draw inferences from behavioral relations among observed prices and quantities,[19] or from quantitative relations derived from the laws of one or another hard science:[20] however, such relations are not usually available. In their absence, answers to questionnaires may be substituted as evidence of subjective valuations of the effects of proposed actions, but these are usually considered to be an inferior source of evidence which is subject to distrust.[21]

For our purpose, the salient point to be made about the empirical procedures of cost-benefit analysis is that appraisal of their results does not usually involve the testing of predictions. Though the results may be used to support the choice of one project over another, and sometimes to guide the execution of projects already adopted, the validity of cost-benefit analyses is hardly ever tested by using them as a basis for the making of predictions and comparing such predictions with realizations.

How, then, is the validity of a cost-benefit analysis tested, if at all? And if it is not tested, how are good studies to be distinguished from bad? Let us consider the second question first. One attribute of a good study is the high quality of the conceptual structure used to direct the calculation of costs and benefits. The quality of a conceptual structure is reflected both in its mathematical elegance and in the appropriateness of the decisions it embodies as to which (possible) effects are to be calculated and which are to be ignored. A second characteristic is the quality of the empirical evidence used to measure costs and benefits: this refers both to the appropriateness of the proxies for conceptual magnitudes and to the quality of the data used, and of the statistical techniques employed.

Finally, the results of a good study must be compatible with those of other studies and with dominant professional opinion concerning the characteristics of the behavioral relations assumed to be valid. A study whose results were strikingly at odds with those of other studies, or which were incompatible with RAP, likely would be judged to be of low quality.

---

19. For example, inferences from (properly estimated) supply and/or demand functions.

20. For example, estimates of production cost based on engineering relations or on the biochemical relations governing the production of organic substances.

21. See below (pp. 294–96) for remarks on the general cultural prejudice against data not derived from observed behavior, especially data from questionnaires. However, questionnaire data is not totally rejected as a source of empirical evidence: for example, recently a committee of the National Academy of Sciences recommended use of questionnaire data to obtain individual valuations of the gain or loss resulting from various environmental changes. See the symposium, "Contingent Valuation," in the *Journal of Economic Perspectives* 8, no. 4 (Fall 1994): 3–64.

From such a judgment there is no practicable appeal to a test of experience. That is, there is no accepted way of measuring the benefits and costs that are realized from a governmental action and comparing them with what had been projected in the calculations. One reason for this incapability is that much of both the costs and the benefits of a project cannot be inferred from observations of prices and quantities, but must be estimated from subjective reports (via questionnaires and interviews) about the costs incurred and/or the benefits derived. We have already remarked on the skepticism with which the results of such reports are received.

A second reason is that, if a set of cost and benefit estimates were treated as projections of what would happen were a particular course of action to be undertaken, then it would be essential to "allow for" (a) differences in the course of action actually undertaken from those on which the cost-benefit estimates were based and (b) the effect of unanticipated changes in economic conditions that impinge upon the magnitudes of either the costs or benefits derived. The entailed calculations would involve, in exaggerated form, all the difficulties that attend the testing of if-then propositions in positive economics that we have already discussed.

In any case, it has never been suggested that cost-benefit studies be evaluated by attempting to compare the costs and benefits realized with those that had been projected. However, the evaluation of cost-benefit studies provides an outstanding illustration of how economics appraises contributions by a combination of consilience with a conceptual organization, typically RAP; with previously accepted empirical findings; with conformity to technical criteria of excellence; and (occasionally) by suggestions of innovative procedures (like making pollution permits marketable) that can be considered to promote Pareto improvements.

It is worth noting that the evaluation of cost-benefit studies is very sensitive to paradigm shifts. For example, a committed Keynesian would probably reject as invalid a study that did not account for an increase in employment opportunities as a benefit, while an RAP adherent would insist on counting the cost of any increase in employment in terms of forgone leisure and household production. In short, the esteem in which a given study is held is likely to be sensitive to changes in the style or procedures used in similar studies, independent of what transpires in its subject matter.

THE COASE THEOREM AND THE ROLE OF THE STATE

The Coase theorem challenges the adequacy of the factory smoke exemplar by raising the question of whether it is better to compel the smoke producers to desist and accept compensation for their added costs, or to induce (compel) the victims to move away from the source of pollution and compensate them for the resulting cost and inconvenience. While addressing many of the same problems, the Coase theorem takes a different perspective from that of conventional welfare economics.[22]

Conventional welfare economics assumes that the abatement of an undesired externality requires action by the state; for Coase, the situation calls for a transaction between the injured and injuring parties. The utility gains and losses are the same in both perspectives but, in welfare economics, compensation of the injured is assumed to come from government payments financed by taxes on the polluters. For Coase, the polluters must purchase the consent of the polluted, as would be done in a negotiated settlement of a potential law suit.

In the Coase framework, the potential damage should be averted only if the benefit of halting it exceeds the cost of doing so. Whether the smoke emission is halted, or the damage that it causes is eliminated by movement of those polluted will depend upon the cost of preventing the smoke emission relative to the cost of moving those who would be damaged by it.

Assuming rationality and the absence of transaction costs, the least-cost method of terminating the smoke damage will be adopted, if the damage is in fact terminated. If the cost of terminating the damage by the cheapest method available exceeds the cost of moving the victims and compensating them for the inconvenience, it will be Pareto superior to permit the smoke to continue and move the victims.

Crucial to the Coasean analysis is the role of *transaction cost,* a concept not explicitly discussed in welfare economics. Loosely, transaction cost reflects the value of the resources used to obtain and enforce agreement on contract terms between two (or more) legally distinct entities. By definition, transaction cost cannot arise from cooperative activities within a single legal entity, such as a firm. Thus a merger between two firms would eliminate any transaction cost associated with compensation payments from one to the other on account of an externality. While such elimination

---

22. The theorem defies concise statement. The original presentation is Coase (1960); for a brief overview, see Robert D. Cooter (1987). For the purposes of this book the remarks in the text will suffice to identify the concept.

would be a factor favorable to a potential merger of the two firms, it is also the case that a merger might generate a need for greater administrative activity to coordinate production and delivery between the erstwhile independent sections of the new firm: administrative activity (e.g., making decisions, issuing explanations and instructions) also entails costs. Comparison of the increase in administrative cost against the reduction in transaction cost determines the efficiency of the firms if merged relative to what it would have been had they remained distinct.[23]

In the case of smoke pollution, transaction costs consist of the costs of identifying the smoke victims, measuring their losses, negotiating, and perhaps litigating their compensation. If these are negligible, the choice between smoke abatement and victim withdrawal (removal) will depend upon whether the cost of abatement is greater or less than the cost of withdrawal, and the efficient result will be attained through private negotiation.

If the cost of abatement is less than that of withdrawal, the polluters will compensate the polluted for the trouble of removing themselves; in the reverse case, the polluters will be compensated (by the polluted) for the cost of abating the smoke. The choice will be that which minimizes production costs. But this choice will be reversed in the event that the difference in transaction costs is greater and in the opposite direction from that in production costs.[24]

Though the assertion is counterintuitive, the above argument is independent of the location of property rights. The efficient choice between smoke abatement and victim removal is the same regardless of whether the polluter has the right to pollute and/or the victims the right to remain free of pollution.[25] This does not imply that the choice of production method is independent of the relative wealth of the holders of the various property rights: it is very likely that the transaction cost of altering the behavior of a rich person will be greater than what would be required to alter the behavior of a poor one. Thus, if polluters tended to be rich, and

---

23. Of course, there are factors other than coping with technical externalities that bear upon the relative efficiency of merger versus use of the market. Comparison of the relative costs of coordinating production through administration and the market is the driving force in Coase's theory of the firm. For an extended discussion of transaction costs see Williamson and Masten (1995).

24. The distinction between production and transaction cost will be discussed below.

25. It is assumed implicitly that the assignment of property rights to the parties is consistent and complete, i.e., that the behavior one individual may successfully demand of another is completely determined in any state of the world.

victims to be poor, it would tend to be cheaper (under otherwise identical circumstances) to let pollution continue; if the rich were the victims and the poor the polluters the opposite would be true.[26]

The contrast between the Coasean view of externalities and that of conventional—i.e., Pigovian[27]—welfare economics stems from their divergent views of property rights and transaction costs. Coase argues as if the property rights of all community members in every possible state of the world were completely defined and mutually consistent, so that either a factory owner would have the right to emit smoke or the neighboring householders would have the right to be smoke free, but not both. Therefore, the party dissatisfied with the assignment of rights could either bribe the offender to cease exercising her rights or accept the situation.

From the Pigovian viewpoint it might appear that, if transaction costs prevented a buyout of assigned rights that would otherwise be Pareto improving, the state could increase welfare by intervening with taxes and subsidies to effect the blocked improvement. In effect the state would use its resources to overcome the impeding transaction costs. To such a suggestion the Coasean would reply that such intervention would entail transaction costs of its own, and that there is no presumption that these costs would be less than those of the private parties.[28]

To speak of the transaction costs associated with state intervention raises questions as to the nature of the state's activities. Since both the Coasean and Pigovian approaches to externalities purport to operate within the RAP framework, such questions are awkward: RAP proper has no place for a state. To permit discussion of its activities it is necessary to create a paradigm adjunct. The adjuncts implicit in the Pigovian and Coasean approaches differ, although neither is very satisfactory.

The Pigovian adjunct makes the state a deus ex machina characterized only by unlimited power to tax and bestow benefits, and the objective of promoting the "general welfare." (A major determinant of the general welfare is per capita real income supplemented by distributional considerations, as discussed above.) In the context of the smoke pollution problem, the resources required for effecting a Pareto-improving intervention are assumed (implicitly) to be paid out of general tax funds, although the matter is not discussed explicitly. Why the state should choose to rectify

26. This is to say that the relative marginal utility of nonpecuniary benefits is usually greater to the rich than to the poor.

27. After A. C. Pigou, its most famous expositor.

28. Indeed, he might well remark that a major objection to the Pigovian tradition is its neglect of the costs of state action.

the ill effects of one particular externality rather than those of some other one is not considered. The spirit of the adjunct would suggest that the state should act to rectify all such situations, the scope of its interventions being set so that the net benefits conferred by a "marginal intervention" would be zero. That such a policy might lead to a major role for state intervention in the economy is not precluded. In a nutshell, this is a framework that allows for the existence of a welfare state, although it does not mandate it.

It is otherwise with the Coasean approach. Here the state is considered to be the agent of its citizens. As more is said about this relationship in chapter 10, for the moment I shall limit my remarks to its bearing on the treatment of externalities. What a Pigovian perceives as an externality is, to a Coasean, an innovative and/or unanticipated exercise of a property right. If that right were unambiguous, but efficiency required that it should not be exercised, then, in the absence of transaction costs, the Coasean would expect the affected parties to prevent its exercise through negotiation.[29] The Coasean would interpret state intervention to prevent the exercise of a property right as a disguised expropriation of its holder and thus, in effect, a redistribution of wealth.

Often where a Pigovian would perceive an externality as an opportunity for the state to take a Pareto-improving action that transaction costs prevented the affected parties from taking on their own, a Coasean would perceive only an assignment of property rights that some people disliked. Adopting the view that property is "a bundle of rights," Coaseans believe that many (most?) Pigovian externalities result from attempts by one party or another to innovate (i.e., exercise previously unexercised) rights associated with particular instances of property. They would hold that the resulting disputes should be settled through negotiation or, where necessary, by the courts, but without resort to direct legislative intervention.

In short, where Pigovians see externalities, Coaseans see disputes over property rights.[30] This leaves the Coasean state a much smaller field for action to increase the general welfare than it does the Pigovian state. The Coasean state is not precluded from transferring property rights from one

29. As used in this sentence and elsewhere, unless defined otherwise, "efficiency" is synonymous with Pareto improvement or Pareto optimality.

30. Taking the Coasean view of property rights as a point of departure, Richard Epstein (1985) has developed the argument that government regulations curbing previously established property rights are de facto expropriations of property which, as such, require compensation.

party to another by legislative fiat, but its supporting theory does not suggest or facilitate comparison of the various potential transfers in terms of their effects on the general welfare. What the Pigovian sees as Pareto-improving interventions, the Coasean sees as redistributions of property rights whose net effect is incommensurable with any proper measure of general welfare, but which serve to expand the scope of the state's activities and the quantity of resources that it uses.

While it does not deny that there may be activities that can be best performed by the state, the Coasean view is not associated with any attempt to identify them, or with insuring that sufficient resources are devoted to their performance. Rather it emphasizes the cost of the resources that the state uses, and its (alleged) tendency to misuse them. In contrast with the Pigovian view of the state as a potentially beneficent deus ex machina, the Coasean "laissez-faire" view considers the state as a (highly imperfect) agent of its property owning citizens.[31] Its deficiencies as an agent stem from a tendency to develop an agenda of its own (or of its senior employees) which causes it both to misuse such resources as are entrusted to its care and to seek stewardship of more resources than a fully informed citizenry would grant.

As elaborated in chapter 10, the Coasean perspective of the state is negative. It sees the state as tending to grasp functions that can be performed better by others, to create functions for itself that would be better left unperformed, and generally to use too large a share of the community's resources.[32]

WELFARE ECONOMICS AND PARETO OPTIMALITY

In discussing the performance of economic organizations and/or institutions, a recurrent theme is their efficiency, or lack of it. While other criteria of efficiency are sometimes proposed on an ad hoc basis, the dominant one is Pareto Optimality (PO): departures from PO are indicative of inefficiency. Externalities are one cause of such departures, but there are others. Any discrepancy between price and marginal cost, or difference in prices paid for similar items that cannot be accounted for by differences in cost, is an opportunity for making a Pareto improvement. But how to achieve such improvements is a matter of dispute.

31. Note the affiliation of what I term the "Coasean" view with a laissez-faire view. The reason for this affiliation will be described below in chapter 10.

32. Those wishing amplification of Coase's views should see Coase (1988), chapters 1, 5, and 6 and Medema (1994), especially chapter 5.

Economists in the Pigovian tradition tend to rest content with showing that a situation is such that a set of hypothetical taxes and subsidies could effect a Pareto improvement. Others, in what I call the Coasean tradition, object, arguing that the costs associated with measures the state must take to eliminate the alleged inefficiency must be considered before making a welfare judgment.[33]

Detecting and demonstrating the existence of a departure from PO is part and parcel of the economist's expertise. In a situation where the effect on the general welfare indicated by an alleged relation of marginal cost to price is in dispute, the noneconomist is likely to attend only to the consequences for the distribution of income as between buyers and sellers; but the economist will also see—often focus upon—the induced inefficiency caused by misallocation of resources. Sensitivity to the existence of such inefficiencies is an important aspect of the economist's expertise.

But this expertise does not carry over to calculation of the costs of whatever measures are needed to eliminate the inefficiencies. Here, the economist must borrow estimates for estimating procedures from other disciplines or accept the judgment of outside experts. Typically, the Coaseans who urge consideration of such costs do not have the requisite calculations to offer. However, their primary objective is to point to the existence of such costs and to protest the practice of inferring the propriety of governmental corrective action solely from a demonstration of the appearance of a resource misallocation.

MEASUREMENT OF OUTPUT AND APPLIED WELFARE ECONOMICS

In both the conception and the numerical calculation of the magnitude of welfare loss associated with a given instance of inefficiency, the economist has the opportunity to display professional expertise of the highest order. However, in no way do such calculations lead to if-then statements. There is no sequence of events occurring subsequent to calculation of a welfare gain (or loss) that can affect its credibility. The validity of such calculations may be tested by their conformity with accepted procedures, by the accuracy of the data they utilize, and by their consonance with other calculations deemed to be relevant, but not by their success in facilitating prediction.

---

33. For reasons of convenience I have identified this tradition with Ronald Coase. However, it might equally well—or better—be identified with George Stigler (see chapter 10).

Although not always so recognized, the measurement of output—especially aggregate national production—constitutes an important application of welfare economics. Whenever possible, the quantities of physical outputs and associated inputs are inferred from the volume of transactions in which the elements of physical input and output are valued at recorded prices. In the absence of market transactions, attempts are made to approximate what market prices would have been had such transactions occurred.

While such measurements do not require that the economy conform to the specifications of RAP, their construction and interpretation is much easier if it is assumed that it does. Accordingly, unless there is compelling need to do otherwise, this assumption is made though usually without much supporting argument. It is not my purpose to offer a general critique of this branch of economic statistics, but rather to point out its interrelation with welfare economics.

Let us begin with the concept of production or, synonymously, output. Somewhere in every beginning course in economics an attempt is made to define aggregate net output, and to distinguish transactions which it includes from those it does not. RAP does not offer any basis for making such distinctions and, de facto, it assumes that whatever induces a rational consumer to part with resources must bring him as much utility as any other possible transaction, and that whatever generates that utility constitutes production.

The great bulk of the items entering into measurements of aggregate output are compatible with this agnostic view of production. However, there are some exceptions. For example, solely on the basis of common sense, the constructors of social accounts exclude transactions that reflect gifts or transfers as distinguished from those that reflect acts of production.[34] Another exception arises where payment for productive services reflect rent seeking rather than productive activity.[35]

Rent seeking arises where each of several individuals uses resources in a quest for property rights in a preexisting source of income, such as a

---

34. In this context, "common sense" involves consideration of evidence other than what is normally considered acceptable in appraising economic hypotheses. For example, evidence used to decide whether a payment is a transfer may include statements made by the payer and/or empathetic inferences by the economic analyst of payer intent.

35. Theoretical cognizance of the phenomenon of rent seeking is a recent innovation generally credited to Gordon Tullock (1967) and Anne O. Kreuger (1974). A good brief summary of the central ideas is Gordon Tullock (1987).

monopoly or a sinecure. Since capture of a rent source does not involve production, payments for use of resources employed in rent seeking should not be incorporated in estimates of aggregate production.

But often such payments *are* so incorporated. In many cases, it is practically difficult to distinguish payments made in the course of rent seeking from other payments, and often there are conceptual problems as well.[36] As a result the various elements of a measure of aggregate production differ in conceptual appropriateness as well as in empirical accuracy. The practical importance of these flaws varies with the problem to which the measurements are applied.

Despite these and other complications, the process of measuring aggregate production has been driven by concern to make its results congenial to the spirit of RAP. This has resulted in a concept of aggregate production and welfare that is broadly inclusive of all goods or services that are voluntarily paid for, or of whatever can be considered as a close substitute for what is voluntarily paid for. This concept of aggregate production is more inclusive than others, associated with different paradigms, that distinguish "productive" from "unproductive" uses of resources and exclude the latter. Let us examine, briefly, a few of the alternative conceptions of welfare associated with economic paradigms other than RAP.[37]

OTHER TYPES OF WELFARE ECONOMICS

To avoid confusion, let me reiterate that, as commonly used, "welfare economics" refers exclusively to RAP-welfare economics, and that I have no quarrel with this identification. Non-RAP-welfare economics is far less developed than that of RAP, and my sole reason for attempting to stretch the reference of the term is to indicate the impact of other paradigms on the culture of the subject.

Keynesian Welfare Economics

To describe maximization of employment as the primary objective of macroeconomic policy would be a caricature of the argument of *The General*

36. Many of the conceptual problems arise from the fact that the objects of rent seeking may arise in the private sector as well as in the public. For example, the efforts to obtain a patent, especially when there are many seekers, will involve substantial elements of rent seeking. More generally, the activity involved in establishing any claim to property rights, however costly, cannot be considered as contributing to output.

37. I do not assert that every paradigm is associated with a particular brand of welfare economics: such a statement may or may not be true. However, several paradigms are associated with a variant of welfare economics that is distinctive in one way or another.

Theory. Yet, it is precisely the insistence on taking into account the effects of economic events, especially government actions, on the quantity of employment (number of jobs) available that distinguishes Keynesian views on policy proposals from those implied by RAP. From the RAP perspective, a decrease in employment with output unchanged represents an increase in efficiency and, subject to qualifications already discussed, in welfare. But from the Keynesian perspective this may or may not be true, depending upon whether or not effective demand is maintained at a full-employment level. Under conditions of full employment, the two perspectives converge, and their welfare implications become similar.[38]

But when the economy is at less than full employment, the Keynesian paradigm envisages labor economizing measures as a cause of reduced employment opportunities, and therefore of reduced welfare.[39] Accordingly, in a depressed economy, Keynes could argue for protection of domestic markets to preserve jobs, for make-work schemes that were admittedly unproductive, for intentional budget deficits, and so on in defiance of RAP and the conventional wisdom with which it is associated.[40]

To contend that *The General Theory* was written simply to rationalize policy recommendations such as the above would go too far. But it will not be denied that provision of a theoretical basis for advocating such policies was a major reason both for the creation of the Keynesian paradigm and for the speed with which it gained acceptance.

In comparison with RAP, the welfare economics of the Keynesian par-

38. The precise definition of full employment—a concept alien to RAP—need not detain us: it has been discussed in chapters 4 and 5. In this context, it is sufficient to think of full employment as a state of the economy in which it is assumed that economizing on the employment of labor promotes the general welfare.

39. The possibility of an optimal tradeoff between efficiency and employment under conditions of less than full employment is obvious but difficult to formulate explicitly within either the Keynesian paradigm or RAP. So far as I am aware, no one has attempted to develop such a concept.

40. Perhaps the most striking illustration of this aspect of Keynes's thinking is the following: "If the Treasury were to fill old bottles with banknotes, bury them at suitable depths in disused coal mines which are then filled up to the surface with town rubbish, and leave it to private enterprise on well-tried principles of *laissez-faire* to dig the notes up again (the right to do so being obtained, of course, by tendering for leases of the note-bearing territory), there need be no more underemployment and, with the help of the repercussions, the real income of the community, and its capital wealth also, would probably become a good deal greater than it actually is. It would, indeed, be more sensible to build houses and the like; but if there are political and practical difficulties in the way of this, the above would be better than nothing" Keynes (1936), p. 129.

adigm is extremely thin, being limited to the simple proposition that, in the absence of full employment, utilizing employment opportunities is to be counted as a benefit. But as the history of the last three quarters of the twentieth century testify, this proposition has the power to motivate policy proposals that are at once paradoxical and highly persuasive.

Mercantilist Welfare Economics

Though it bears some similarity to Keynesian ideas, it is best to neglect the resemblance and treat mercantilism as a paradigm sui generis. The basic feature of the mercantilist conceptual organization is that an economy is akin to a profit-maximizing enterprise whose objective is capital accumulation. Beyond the minimum necessary for maintenance of the work force, consumption is considered wasteful, so increasing per capita real income would not promote the community welfare.[41]

Thus, the proper objective of economic activity, welfare, is to add to the stock of real domestic capital and/or to increase net exports. An increase in net exports would be reflected either in the economy's (country's) gold stock or in net claims on foreigners, which were considered as equivalent to gold.[42]

The welfare implications of such a CO are simple and fairly obvious: (1) promote exports and discourage imports; (2) limit consumption to what is necessary to achieve maximum capital accumulation, which implies holding wages down to the minimum necessary to maintain the productive efficiency of the labor force; and (3) discourage consumption either out of profits or by the sovereign (e.g., the royal court).[43]

The affinity of such ideas about economic policy to Calvinist doctrines of thrift and self-denial is obvious. But while mercantilism was an ideological ally of capitalism, it was no friend to laissez-faire. Rather, it encouraged government action to help those who brought in gold or engaged in building up the domestic capital stock. Insofar as pro-accumulation policies increase employment, mercantilist and Keynesian welfare economics

41. Complications could arise if one introduced the possibility of expanding the population in order to increase the size of the labor force and thereby increase output and capital accumulation. However, consideration of such a possibility would obscure the point being made without contributing to the argument.

42. When such claims were considered at all.

43. The goal of mercantilist policy invites a distinction between productive and unproductive consumption, i.e., between consumption that increases the productivity of the labor force and that which does not serve this purpose. Though such a distinction was often made, it was not developed systematically, and it does not serve our purpose to pursue it.

move together. They diverge where Keynesianism rationalizes measures that increase consumption and discourage thrift.

Though mercantilism is properly identified as a seventeenth- and early eighteenth-century doctrine, the reader will readily perceive that some of its embers continue to glow brightly at the approach of the twenty-first century. In most developed countries, and especially in the United States, there is great concern among economists and others about an alleged deficiency of savings and a consequent need for corrective action by the government.

The rationale for judging the performance of an economy to be unsatisfactory is different in the 1990s from what it was four centuries earlier. Clearly, need to enhance the "power of the state" or the "glory of the sovereign" will no longer serve to elicit personal sacrifice. In place of such concepts, contemporary purveyors of collective thrift variously cite need to avoid difficulties with the balance of payments and consequent depreciation of the currency, or to avoid deterioration of public credit and/or higher taxes in the future, as reasons for reducing current consumption.

Though the verbiage may differ, the goal remains the same: reducing aggregate current consumption to promote the aggregate accumulation of claims against foreigners (including gold) and/or to reduce the accumulation of aggregate claims by foreigners against "us." By implication, Pareto optimality is rejected as a criterion of sound policy. It is held that the amount of savings generated by the choices of individuals is insufficient for some collective objective and that somehow the resulting deficiency must be made good. Whether the shortfall of saving is due to a failure of individuals to recognize how much saving is in their individual interest, or whether there is a collective interest that outweighs that of individuals, is not clear. In either case, the recommended policy response would be the same.

It would be possible to develop the welfare economics implicit in each of the paradigms discussed in chapter 6. But while these have intrinsic interest, their discussion would constitute a diversion from our main theme. Accordingly, I shall remark briefly on only one further conception of welfare economics, but one that is radically different from that of RAP.

Nonutilitarian Welfare Economics

Thus far, I have not considered the possibility that, while the objective of a society might be the well-being of its individual members, that well-being might not be indicated by their attained levels of utility. However, there is a substantial anti-utilitarian literature at the interface of economics and philosophy which I have ignored, despite its subtlety and intrinsic interest to anyone concerned with the relation of social welfare to social organization.

A leading contributor to this literature is Amartya Sen (1984) who has suggested enhancement of the "capabilities" of a community's members as a possible welfare objective alternative to maximization of some function of their utilities. Without judging the validity of this or other possible criteria of good social organization and/or policy, I eschew discussion of the matter because it is irrelevant to the argument of this book: for good or ill, the culture of economics is rooted in a utilitarian conception of welfare. Although in the past half century economists have tried to limit their dependence on utilitarian concepts (e.g., revealed preference, or avoidance of interpersonal comparisons of utility), reliance on market-generated phenomena as their primary source of empirical material has so far made it impossible to avoid interpreting Pareto improvement in terms of (or translatable into) increments of market valued real net output. Talk though some have of "empowerment" and the like as alternative indicators (to utility) of individual well-being, in applied work these potential indicators have not—at least as yet—been implemented.[44]

SUMMARY

Welfare economics seeks to guide policy making by providing one or more criteria to serve as standards of appraisal of economic performance. Provision of such criteria is a major function of an economic paradigm and, as we shall see, the criteria offered serve not only as a guide to policy making but also as a component of ideology. While in principle any paradigm could generate a distinct type of welfare economics, not all of them have done so; among those that have, only RAP has developed its welfare aspect in any detail. As a result, the term "welfare economics" is usually applied only to the RAP variety.

While application of (RAP) welfare economics is a very important

44. Since this chapter was written, I have become acquainted with Partha Dasgupta's (1993) massive book, which also views an individual's well being in terms of her capability of functioning, and considers command over commodities as one input to such capability. Substantive discussion of the issues raised by Sen and Dasgupta is beyond the scope of this book, and in any case, is clearly outside the culture of economics as here conceived. Nevertheless, the books provide, inter alia, an interesting extended comment on certain characteristics of the culture of economics.

channel for the deployment of economic expertise, it does not involve the generation of testable predictions (or retrodictions). The quality of a piece of applied welfare economics is judged by the technique displayed in its generation, and by the consonance of its results both with those of positive economics and other applications of welfare economics.

Because welfare economics is intimately concerned with the possibility of economic action by the state, its application is greatly affected by the (implicit) conception of the state that is presumed to do the acting. As RAP proper has no place for a state, application of welfare economics requires construction of a paradigm adjunct to remedy the deficiency. The details of this construction are a focal point of debate about economic policy and constitute a major topic of chapter 10.

TEN

RAP AND THE IDEOLOGY
OF LAISSEZ-FAIRE

R AP itself is not an ideology, but its links with the ideology of
laissez-faire are so numerous and so strong that many laymen
suppose that accepting one is tantamount to embracing the other.
This supposition can and has caused great misunderstanding both of the
paradigm and of the ideology.

Grasp of the essentials of RAP is a sine qua non for membership in
the economics community. And comprehension of RAP tends to generate
appreciation of the merits of laissez-faire even when that appreciation
does not extend to acceptance. Nevertheless, the distinction between the
paradigm and the ideology is sharp and very important. In the paradigm
proper there is no place for the state; the state does not exist. In the ideology of laissez-faire, the state is an entity that, although variously defined,
is always characterized as having a strong tropism for improper behavior.
Whatever theory of the state they may entertain, it is always a bête noire
for laissez-faire advocates.

Generically, a paradigm is a research tool. Its acceptance does not entail embracement of any particular ideology, and many RAP adherents
are free, or nearly so, of ideological commitments. To adhere to an ideology is to accept certain value judgments as to the desirability of a particular set of social/political/economic arrangements and a commitment to
promote their realization. Manifestly, such adherence can neither entail
nor be entailed by acceptance of a research paradigm.

Nevertheless, the association of adherence to RAP and commitment
to laissez-faire is obvious and not hard to explain. In a nutshell, to believe
that the economy would function well (optimally?) if only the state did
not exist, is highly conducive to believing that the general welfare would
be promoted by limiting the role of the state in economic life as much
as possible.

RAP and laissez-faire is not the only paradigm-ideology couple in the
culture of economics. Class struggle and one or another variant of Marxian economic theory constitutes another such couple and, arguably, the
Keynesian paradigm and the welfare state a third. However, the salience

of the RAP–laissez-faire pairing in the literature of economics is so marked that I shall concentrate upon the specifics of this case, and leave it to the reader to extend the argument to others.

But before turning to the specifics of RAP–laissez-faire, let me offer a brief remark on the general relation of paradigms and ideologies. The thought processes of members of a scientific community are greatly concerned with the consonance (or dissonance) of particular ideas or propositions with one or another paradigm: relation of ideas to ideology is secondary, if even relevant. But for those not encumbered by membership in such a community, there is often a reverse emphasis: here, the relation of ideas to ideology dominates.

Put differently, members of scientific subcultures choose among alternative sets of beliefs so as to minimize intellectual discomfort, with the relation of the selected set to possible commitments to extrascientific action a matter of secondary concern. This distinguishes them from (most) other individuals who, in trying to minimize the dissonance of their beliefs with felt commitments to action, give a subordinate role to internal consistency among their various ideas.[1]

In the following discussion of laissez-faire, I shall ignore as much as possible differences of view among its adherents. Such differences have always existed as of any given time, and the central tendency of opinion has changed over time since Adam Smith. Nevertheless, the current adherents of laissez-faire have been eager to acknowledge indebtedness to their predecessors, and to emphasize the continuity of the laissez-faire tradition. Though what I shall refer to as the laissez-faire ideology cannot be identified with the views of any one writer, it is well approximated by the views of Milton Friedman.[2]

PROPERTY RIGHTS AND THE STATE

In a world conforming to RAP proper, all transactions would be voluntary and free of (transaction) costs. By implication, property rights in any item capable of rendering utility to anyone are completely assigned to a specific individual, and are costlessly enforced. The possibility that property rights could be contested is precluded by assumption, so that the state has no role either in their establishment or their maintenance.

1. It might be noted that, for anyone, adherence to an ideology is reinforced if the goals of the ideology appear to promote personal (e.g., career) interests. The discussion of the next several paragraphs is supplementary to what was said in chapter 7, pp. 171–74.

2. Especially as expressed in *Capitalism and Freedom* (1962).

Although it is not usually stressed, no laissez-faire adherent would deny that establishment and enforcement of property rights is a very important function of the state. Nor would it be denied that the performance of this function requires the use of scarce resources, from which follows the need for taxation. In principle, description of the process (technology) by which resources are obtained and used to establish and maintain property rights should imply at least the rudiments of a theory of the state. However, and despite numerous though uncoordinated attempts, RAP has never been associated with a generally accepted theory of the state: in particular, it has never had one focused on the process of establishing and administering property rights.

RAP neither needs nor offers an account of how property rights get established, but it assumes that, once established, property rights cannot be alienated except voluntarily or through "lawful" taxation. Disputes over assignment of property rights are assumed to be settled by a legal process governed by the courts. While the legal process and the courts are created by the state, it is assumed that once created they function independently of the state, and follow rules internal to the legal system. That is, the administration of the law is conceived to be governed by experts (judges) in accordance with the rules of a specialized subculture.[3]

The security of property rights rests on the assumption that even when one of the parties is the state, disputed claims will be settled solely in accordance with the dictates of the legal subculture and independently of the wishes or interests of the state. While strict separation of the state from the legal system is obviously impossible, both because of the power of the state to legislate on the organization and powers of the courts and because of its role in the selection of members of the judiciary, nevertheless there are societies where property rights are reasonably secure. Advocates of laissez-faire generally consider the common characteristics of such societies to be essential to a good society.

While a useful theory of the state might offer some clue as to how to establish such a society, neither RAP nor any other paradigm of which I am aware offers any. In general, achievement of such a society is promoted by a state that refrains from acts that curtail property rights that had been recognized previously, by courts whose rulings are predictable from previous decisions and are independent of the identities of the par-

3. Although it is much more highly developed and widely recognized than the subculture of economics, the structural parallelism of the subculture of law with that of economics should be obvious.

ties involved,[4] and by governments that eschew arbitrary increases in taxation. However these desiderata are but exhortations to the state and, indirectly, to participants in the political process. They do not offer guidance on how to make states improve their behavior, or insight as to why some of them behave as well as they do.

The negative view of the state that is characteristic of laissez-faire advocates has many and diverse roots. Undoubtedly, bitter experience with overactive governments has been a major source of a generalized desire to limit the functions and powers of the state as much as possible. But there are also theoretical reasons for this predilection. As I do not know of any one statement that suitably expresses these reasons, I offer the following characterization which I believe captures their major thrust.

THE LAISSEZ-FAIRE VIEW OF THE STATE: A SKETCH

1. The state is the collective agent of its principals (citizens) and exists to serve their interests (utility functions). It would function best if the interests of its (numerous) principals were identical though, even if they were, there would remain a principal-agent (conflict of interest) problem similar to that arising in ordinary private relationships. But there is a diversity of interests among the principals which would greatly complicate the state-agent's task of determining a proper course of action even in the absence of a principal-agent problem.[5]

2. The intentions of a government can be effected only through the actions of individuals empowered to act on its behalf. That is, a government can act only through its agents, each of whom considers (in varying degree) his own interests as well as those of the government-employer. Hence, in giving effect to its intentions, government is faced with a standard principal-agent problem analogous to those faced in the private sector.[6] While shortcomings of the monitoring process, reflected in graft and corruption, occur in the private as well as in the public sector, their extent is assumed to be much greater in the latter.

The main reason why efficiency losses are greater from public-sector activity is the absence of competition. In the private sector, failure to monitor agents, or to curb efficiency losses from other causes, results in higher

4. The metaphor of Justice as blindfolded is apt.

5. See the discussion of social choice and the Arrow impossibility theorem in chapter 9. A classic and very influential discussion of the problems alluded to in the text is Buchanan and Tullock (1962).

6. This problem is distinct from the problem of the citizen in trying to control the actions of "the government" mentioned under (1).

prices or lesser quality of service than those obtainable from alternative suppliers who are more efficient. As customer, the buyer can limit his losses by switching suppliers; as taxpayer, he must bear them.

Recognition of their monopoly position enables high-ranking government officials to set prices and quantities so as to generate rent for themselves, while also allowing some to trickle down to subordinate agents. Conversely, private producers under competitive pressure to limit costs and prices must exert themselves to minimize losses from agent malfeasance, and are compelled to limit their own rent-taking to what is permitted by the actions of their competitors. Thus, where the public sector can be identified with monopoly, and the private sector with competition, the case for preferring private enterprise is clear. But where this identification breaks down, further consideration is necessary, as we shall see.

3. Wastage of resources aside, government activity of any kind entails a cost that would not arise from comparable private activity. This cost arises from the fact that employment of resources, especially personnel, creates a demand for continuation of the activity. That is, the employees associated with a particular public sector activity often earn rent (as a share of monopoly revenue and/or tax proceeds) and are therefore motivated to demand its continuation.[7] This impedes termination of projects that have outlived their usefulness and motivates demands for creation of new projects regardless of (lack of) demand from consumers.

4. The argument advanced under (3) is essentially an argument against the state doing anything, that is, an argument for anarchy. However, laissez-faire supporters are not anarchists, and never have been. In addition to the role they concede to the state in law enforcement, since Adam Smith they have accepted that "defense is better than opulence," and conceded to the state a monopoly in its provision.

Defense and law enforcement are the two exceptions to the general rule (accepted by laissez-faire supporters) that production should be left to private initiative. Other than these, there is no "social objective" considered to be of sufficient importance as to warrant government action in its pursuit. This position places laissez-faire supporters in opposition to a panoply of measures to promote social improvement by governmental action. This opposition to schemes to have the government "do good" is,

7. This general line of argument against public sector activity has been stressed by Mancur Olson (1982).

in the public mind, the most salient characteristic of the laissez-faire ideology.

5. Adherence to laissez-faire does not imply any particular view as to the proper distribution of wealth or income beyond a bias for the status quo. A society is conceived (see (1) above in this section) as a voluntary association of individuals (or households) who bring to it preexisting assets and join conditional upon observance of certain rules binding upon all members and their agents, and especially upon the government. The right to tax is conceded only for certain purposes and is subject to specific restraints; the right to redistribute assets for the purpose of achieving a desired pattern of wealth distribution usually is not considered to have been granted to the state. While this does not preclude the possibility that an otherwise desirable action of the state might have the incidental effect of redistributing wealth or income, it does militate against considering such an effect as justification for such action.

There is an interesting exception to the general aversion of laissez-faire advocates to using the power of the state to redistribute wealth. Henry C. Simons (a staunch advocate of laissez-faire) was strongly in favor of using progressive taxation to achieve greater equality in the distribution of income for reasons that he considered "aesthetic."[8] This view has been largely rejected by later laissez-faire adherents, who prefer to avoid commitment to Simons's value judgment, and emphasize the (adverse) incentive effects of progressive taxation. But, whatever their preferences on the matter, laissez-faire supporters usually do not consider the "proper" distribution of income or wealth to be a major issue of economic policy.

VOTING RIGHTS

Any reasonably complete theory of the state must include some account of how lawmakers are selected. Yet on this topic, laissez-faire writers vary from silent to ambivalent. Animated as it is by belief in individual rationality, one would expect that laissez-faire doctrine would posit voters who voted their pocket-books, entailing the consequence that the distribution of wealth would be unstable under a suffrage that made voting power disproportionate to wealth. Surely this possibility was feared by nineteenth-century defenders of laissez-faire who were, as a result, far from advocating equality of voting power.

In the twentieth century, and especially since World War II, equal vo-

8. See Simons (1938).

ting rights for all has been so taken for granted that laissez-faire supporters have generally been silent on the matter lest they prejudice their audience against their other contentions. What I take to be a typical attitude is expressed by Milton Friedman who quotes A. V. Dicey (approvingly) as follows: "Surely a sensible and a benevolent man may well ask himself whether England as a whole will gain by enacting that the receipt of poor relief, in the shape of a pension, shall be consistent with the pensioner's retaining the right to join in the election of a Member of Parliament."[9] But despite expressed misgivings, Friedman concludes, "I see no solution to this problem except to rely on the self-restraint and good will of the electorate."[10]

The compatibility of an egalitarian suffrage with an unequal distribution of wealth would be extremely parlous if voters exercised the franchise as an economic asset. However, the multiplicity of voter concerns and the complexity of the political process have combined to reduce the perils of an egalitarian suffrage to the security of large fortunes. This has led, in the 1980s and 90s, to a reversal of the redistributive proclivity exhibited by voters in the earlier part of the century throughout Europe and the United States. As a result, the earlier fears of laissez-faire supporters have dulled and become obscured by a sophisticated appreciation of how wealth can be a source of political advantage as well as a cause of envy.

Regulatory Capture

Recognition that wealth can be a source of political advantage has been associated with a renewed interest of RAP adherents in political economy. This interest is intimately related to laissez-faire doctrines both through the ideological commitment of some leading RAP adherents and because of their concern to create a theory of the state capable of filling a perceived deficiency of RAP. Fulfilling the latter task will, it is implicitly believed, reveal the ineffectiveness of the state as an instrument for accomplishing the proper objectives of a capitalist society whose members are politically free.

The analysis in this section takes as its point of departure the behavior of the state as a regulator of private economic behavior. Until the last quarter century, laissez-faire supporters had stressed the harm done to resource allocation by ill-advised interventions of the state in economic

9. Friedman (1962), p. 194.
10. Ibid.

activity. Since about 1970, following George Stigler, they have argued increasingly that such intervention has been ineffective in achieving its desired objective: protection of buyers from monopoly exactions.[11] Using the regulation of public utilities as an exemplar, Stigler showed that the price-quantity behavior of regulated firms was not appreciably different from that of comparable unregulated firms. That is, regulatory bodies created for the purpose of limiting the prices charged and profits earned by private monopolies failed to achieve either objective because of the political obstacles erected by the regulated firms. In effect, the regulatory bodies were "captured" by the regulated firms.

The theory of regulatory capture has generated a substantial empirical literature comparing the behavior of regulated and unregulated private firms, and of private and publicly owned monopolies, the result of which has been generally supportive of Stigler's contention.[12] But the implications of the argument go far beyond the issue of whether to regulate monopolies. Stigler's argument is relevant to any attempt of the state to regulate the (otherwise lawful) behavior of private firms.

In effect, the generalized theory of regulatory capture gives laissez-faire a two-pronged argument against government intervention in the operation of the private economy. (1) Where producer interests are politically dominant, a regulatory agency will be captured and the intended effects of the regulations thwarted. The main effect of the unsuccessful attempts at regulation will be wastage of resources in political struggle. (2) Where producer interests are not strong enough to capture a regulatory agency, and the regulations are therefore at least partially effective, there will be losses of efficiency on account of resource misallocation.[13] These are additional to the cost of political struggle. Either way, attempts to intervene in the workings of a market cause a waste of resources.

Whether a particular intervention will be nullified by the political clout of the regulated parties or survive to cause resource misallocation depends upon the relative political strength of the intended beneficiaries (of the regulation) and of those regulated. Assessment of the relative strength of such contending factions must be done case by case, with judgmental

11. The leading reference is George J. Stigler (1971).

12. A summary of the relevant literature is Roger G. Noll (1989), vol. 2, chap. 22.

13. The putative benefits from income redistribution sought by interventionists are largely ignored by laissez-faire supporters because, even if it could be achieved, redistribution is rejected as a proper objective of government policy.

factors being very important. However, in the assessment process the theory of the free rider has been very prominent.[14] This theory asserts that (rational) individuals will refrain from contributing financial support for any collective project, regardless of the benefit they might derive, if they believe that sufficient support will be provided by others. (That is, people will take a "free ride" whenever they can.)

The bearing of this proposition on the effectiveness of government regulation depends upon the characteristics of those regulated and of the intended beneficiaries of the regulation. Most often regulations are directed at producers and intended to benefit consumers (households). But typically the number of producers affected by a regulation is small, and the ease of communication among them is adequate to facilitate formation of a pressure group capable of overcoming the free-rider problem, while the reverse is typical of consumers.[15]

One impediment to organization of the purchasers of any particular product is that often a buyer will derive only a negligible fraction of her utility from consumption of that product, and is therefore unwilling to take time or trouble to improve the arrangements for its supply. A second obstacle is that frequently purchasers are widely dispersed, or otherwise unrelated to one another, so that it is costly to communicate with any appreciable number of them. Where these difficulties of organization are abated, as in the case of rent controls in a specific urban area, the political influence of regulated suppliers may be counterbalanced, more or less, by that of benefited demanders, with prices and quantities being determined as the outcome of political struggle. The adverse effect of such partially effective regulation on the quantity and quality of rental housing is frequently offered as illustration of the adverse effects of government interference with the operation of a free market.

In brief, the message of laissez-faire is as follows. Whether emasculated by political efforts of the regulated, or left potent to cripple the Invisible Hand, regulatory interference with the operation of *competitive* markets cannot benefit society. But what about monopoly?

14. The idea of free riding has a long history in the theory of public finance (the need of the state to rely on taxation rather than voluntary contributions) and in trade union literature on the need for compulsory dues payments. However, the general importance of the idea was not properly appreciated before the exposition of Mancur Olson (1965).

15. That is, producers typically participate in a number of networks with other producers and are thus "endowed" with communication links, while the reverse is true of consumers. Networks are discussed below in chapter 14.

MONOPOLY

As we have seen, adherence to RAP implies belief in the limited importance of monopoly. This is an important point of coincidence between RAP and laissez-faire. However, some RAP adherents would permit the state to exploit or even to create monopoly situations to achieve social goals of one kind or another, while laissez-faire supporters would not. In other words, RAP adherents may or may not be laissez-faire supporters, but laissez-faire supporters must be RAP adherents.[16]

The RAP denial of the salience of monopoly runs directly counter to the thrust of the theoretical revolution of the early 1930s, which argued that "Monopolistic Competition" was widespread, and very important. It was no accident that RAP adherents who were also laissez-faire advocates, notably Milton Friedman and George Stigler, took the lead in disputing the importance of the phenomena stressed by this theoretical innovation. While the theoretical focus of the debate has shifted somewhat since the 1950s, disagreement about the importance of departures from competitive equilibrium remains a major line of demarcation between RAP adherents and others.

To argue the limited importance of monopoly is the laissez-faire supporters' first line of defense against the contention that the presence of monopoly justifies government intervention in the private economy. Their argument is that, as of any given time, monopolies use only a small fraction of aggregate resources, so their operation does not have an appreciable effect on factor prices. Moreover, such monopolies as do exist at any moment tend to be eroded with the passage of time, due to changes in tastes and technology, so that whatever harm they might do would be largely evanescent. Thus, for example, monopolies created by the granting of patents to inventors last for only a limited number of years, and then disappear.

Indeed, the patent system is an illustration of how monopoly is created by government action. Arguably, in this case, the creation of monopolies can be justified by the need to establish property rights for inventors in order to provide adequate incentives for inventive activity. In cases such as occupational licensing, no such justification can apply and, laissez-faire advocates argue, a proper laissez-faire regime would engender less monopoly than now exists.

16. This is deliberately overstated, though only slightly. A libertarian might support laissez-faire on moral grounds regardless of economic consequences, but not many econo-

But regardless of how private monopolies originate, laissez-faire supporters have felt obliged to recognize that they exist and to take a position on how the state should deal with them. Obviously the government should not create monopolies except (possibly) where they are essential to the protection of property rights, as in the case of patents. As for monopolies not created by action of the state, that is, "natural monopolies," three positions are possible: (1) public ownership and operation; (2) private ownership subject to regulation, and (3) private ownership without regulation. While Henry Simons (1934) favored (1), this position has been largely abandoned by contemporary laissez-faire supporters. While avoiding blanket endorsement of (3), current supporters of laissez-faire generally tend toward it,[17] rejecting the possibility of successful regulation because of the danger of regulatory takeover, and rejecting public ownership because of aversion to state activity. Without going into detail, it is appropriate to remark that the argument against use of regulation to curb use of monopoly power also applies to use of the antitrust laws or other legislation to promote competition.

To summarize: an important—arguably necessary—condition for adherence to laissez-faire is belief that in a capitalist economy monopoly has, at most, a minor effect on the allocation of resources and the distribution of income.[18] A necessary condition for acceptance of the proposition that the market price of any commodity is a close approximation to its (alternative) cost of production—a major implication of RAP—is that the effect of monopoly on that price, or on the price of any inputs to the production process, is negligible. The coincidence of these conditions is a major cause of the conceptual symbiosis of RAP and laissez-faire.

MARKETS, PRICES, AND LAISSEZ-FAIRE

Like other adherents of RAP, laissez-faire supporters strongly prefer to use prices as instruments of resource allocation whenever possible. But, unlike other RAP adherents, their preference for the price instrument is secondary to their desire to minimize the role of the state in economic

---

mists would take this position. Arguably, the exceptions would include many "Austrians" (see above, chapter 6).

17. See, for example, Friedman (1962), p. 128.

18. As used here, "minor" means that the total impact of monopoly on factor prices (see above, chapter 3) is small. A famous attempt to measure the effect of monopoly is A. C. Harburger (1964).

life. While they accept novel schemes for government use of prices in resource allocation, like market-based charges for permits to emit pollutants or differential charges for road use varying with the state of demand, the approbation of laissez-faire adherents for such exercises of the economist's art tends to be limited.

Since they are usually adherents of RAP, it is likely that laissez-faire supporters will prefer to allocate resources by prices rather than by other means,[19] but their enthusiasm is reserved for proposals that exclude government participation altogether. They are especially prone to rejoice about discoveries of previously unnoticed examples where the working of a private-sector market had solved an allocation problem for which it had been argued that public-sector action was required.[20]

In effect, laissez-faire advocates take the position that, with very infrequent exceptions, production by private profit seekers is always more efficient than production by the state.[21] While use of markets is regarded only as an instrument necessary to the operation of a private economy, no serious consideration is given to the possibility of private methods of production that do not involve the use of markets. Thus, in laissez-faire thinking, production for profit and use of markets for exchange are conflated.

Consequently, ingenious social devices that exploit the technical skill of economists to allocate resources, but serve to facilitate the operation of governments, have no special appeal to laissez-faire supporters. Devices, such as those used in the auctioning of communication spectra (discussed in chapter 11), that serve to get the government out of direct management of resources, tend to meet with approval, but use of multipart prices to increase the efficiency of public producers receives a mixed reception. More efficiency is better, but if efficiency serves mainly to help the working of (public) institutions that would better have been privatized, it is regarded as a mixed blessing at best.

While laissez-faire advocates are eager to claim the virtues of efficiency for private production (it *is* a good debating point), their ideology

19. For example, Milton Friedman's concern with the efficient marketing of government securities, noted in chapter 12, below.

20. See for example, Coase (1988), chapter 7, on lighthouses.

21. Following Adam Smith, it is assumed that production by private, not-for-profit entities will be less efficient than by profit seekers because of the insufficiency of altruism to motivate producers.

does not require that they do so. Ultimately, the underlying value to which they appeal is the nonviolability of property rights: however desirable, efficiency is secondary.

As I understand it, the laissez-faire case for private production cum market transactions may be stated roughly as follows. By definition, market transactions are voluntary. Hence production processes that involve only market transactions require no involuntary transfer of property rights. Conversely, production or any other activity by government that entails taxation involves an involuntary transfer and is to that extent to be deplored. Showing that avoidance of involuntary transfers serves to enhance efficiency strengthens the case for laissez-faire, but efficiency is not its ultimate rationale.

In the language of welfare economics, laissez-faire supporters posit a social-welfare function in which the welfare of society depends only upon the welfare (utility) of its individual members, each of whom is a constrained maximizer of a conventional RAP utility function. In general, there will be a different Pareto optimum for each initial allocation of resources, and no comparison of the desirability of the different optima is possible. This implies that it is impossible to increase community welfare by any governmental action that does not make everyone better off. (N.B., The political transaction cost of compensating losers by taxing gainers must be counted in determining whether a government action would be Pareto superior). Further, it is assumed that any possible cooperative action that would be Pareto superior will be learned about and acted upon more readily by those who benefit directly than by a government. Hence, save for exceptions already noted, the government is without function in promoting the social welfare.

THE STATE AND TAXATION

In sum, the laissez-faire ideology is directed at finding fault with government intervention in productive processes, and suggests no redeeming virtues that government might possess. Despite this, few laissez-faire advocates are anarchists. Concurring in the Smithian dictum that "defense is better than opulence," they accept that there is a need for national defense as well as for law enforcement, and concede that the government must provide for it. Further, and largely because of the need to overcome free riding, they concede that financing such activities requires taxation.

To rationalize the collection of taxes it is necessary to posit some rudimentary characteristics of the state as tax collector. Without attributing the following sketch of a "contract theory of the state" to contemporary adherents of laissez-faire, I suggest that it offers a convenient rationale for their arguments about taxation. They consider the state to be the collective agent of individuals (households) who delegate it power to act in behalf of their common interest for specified objectives, and to tax them in accordance with an agreed (or at least well-understood) formula for that purpose. Use of tax proceeds to pursue other objectives is to act ultra vires and constitutes an (indirect) seizure of property.

In accepting the authority of the state to pursue specific objectives the citizen-taxpayer considers that he has agreed to bear taxation only to a limited and well-understood fraction of his resources. However, because the resource use implied by the objectives accepted (e.g., defense) is indefinite, the notion of agency cannot be applied literally, with the result that unforeseen exigencies of battle and military technology may entail a tax burden far beyond what the citizen had expected to bear. But as the nature of citizenship implies acceptance of this risk, its potential consequences are not normally considered to be confiscation by laissez-faire supporters.[22]

It is otherwise with unanticipated changes of purpose by the state, especially accretions of function. Here laissez-faire draws a line, and denies the propriety of using the power to tax for obtention of resources to be used for purposes not envisaged in the founding of the state. Resistance to such accretions of function by the state is the primary characteristic by which laissez-faire is identified by the general public.

SOCIAL OBJECTIVES AND LAISSEZ-FAIRE

The spirit of laissez-faire militates against recognizing that the state has any concern with achieving social or collective objectives. However, as we have seen, virtually all of its adherents accept that there are exceptions (e.g., defense and the maintenance of laws) that require action by the state. Let us now consider some other cases where the propriety of a passive state is problematic.

The Social Minimum

The social minimum (e.g., of per capita real income) has always had a problematic role in positive economics. This role is not unrelated to the

---

22. As a historical account of the origin of states this is absurd, as sophisticated supporters of laissez-faire are well aware. Nevertheless, at times they argue "as if" such an account were descriptively accurate.

ideology of laissez-faire. In the context of RAP, to guarantee a minimum income to anyone regardless of her productive contribution is subversive of efficiency, and nothing that a rational citizen would urge the state to do. Since the early nineteenth century, laissez-faire writing has been replete with complaints about the adverse effect of indiscriminate charity on effort and on the birth rate. As Simon Newcomb put it, "the offer of alms increases the supply of beggars."

Despite this, in virtually every society of which we have knowledge, provision—however meager—is made for the indigent, and the requirement for contributing to its support is extended beyond the limits of the primary family. Whether rationalized as Christian charity or as a bribe to maintain public order in the face of food shortage, tax proceeds consistently have been used to blunt the impact of market forces upon the least affluent members of society. Clearly, both in RAP and in laissez-faire, something is missing: compassion.

For laissez-faire, the existence of compassion is a two-fold source of embarrassment. Arguing that the state has no business using tax proceeds to alleviate suffering, and should leave this task to private citizens, goes counter to a strong current of religious opinion and has alienated many potential sympathizers. Awareness of this fact has led some advocates of laissez-faire to propose schemes for the state to take steps to provide succor for the poor, even at the cost of ideological consistency.[23]

But, once it is conceded that the state may (must?) devote some resources to maintaining a minimum level of consumption for all within its purview, it becomes necessary to specify the minimum level. Opinions on this vary from one tax payer to another and, for any given taxpayer, with the consequences of the specified level for his own tax bill.

Yet a further complication arises once it is recognized that the state may have obligations to individuals whose identification with its sovereignty is uncertain. Increasingly, claims upon tax proceeds are made on behalf of illegal immigrants, and the poverty-stricken in other countries who have not (yet) migrated, as well. Once sympathy and compassion are admitted as a basis for determining the beneficiaries of public expenditure, laissez-faire offers no limit to the potential claimants to a share of the proceeds of taxation.

Surely, the laissez-faire concept of the state is incompatible with the use of tax power to redistribute wealth solely for the purpose of achieving

---

23. I interpret Milton Friedman's (1962, chap. 12) proposal of a negative income tax as a leading example.

a statistical target. However, once it is conceded that the minimum level of consumption at which the state should aim varies with what taxpayers are deemed able to tolerate, it becomes difficult to prevent the characteristics of the income distribution from becoming a criterion for judging the quality of the tax structure.

What this means is that, in order to maintain its relevance as a guide to social policy, laissez-faire must sharply limit the extent to which it permits concern for the social minimum to expand the share of resources filtered through the tax system. But, as we have just seen, this is not an easy task.

Externalities and the Environment

An externality exists whenever the lawful action of another party can reduce the value of an individual's property or the utility that can be derived from it. A paradigmatic example is the case where there is pollution of the air about one's property by smoke from a neighboring factory. Clearly, it would be desirable to suppress such externalities if it were possible to do so, and action by the state is an obvious means of suppression. But as such actions run counter to the intent of laissez-faire, its supporters must oppose them.

One simple line of defense against demands for such state action is to minimize the importance of externalities, that is, to argue that they are of infrequent occurrence and/or cause only negligible losses to the victims. Another line is to emphasize the availability of redress through the courts without (otherwise) involving the state.[24] While both of these arguments are widely used by laissez-faire defenders, their persuasiveness varies with the ideological commitment of the listener.

In general, laissez-faire supporters are disposed to recognize the existence of externalities that it might be appropriate to correct by use of state power. However, they are anxious to limit the frequency of such use and therefore would reserve it for the most egregious cases, and in any event would drastically limit the total quantity of resources used by the state for this purpose.[25]

The most difficult cases for laissez-faire supporters are presented by allegations of massive environmental damage caused by the action(s) of diverse parties. Global warming is a classic example. If a significant degree of global warming is occurring, and if it is the result of the fuel-using practices of much of the population of the planet, the transaction cost of

24. In this connection, the reader will recall the Coase theorem and its salience in modern economics.
25. See Friedman (1962), pp. 31–32.

inducing voluntary changes of behavior sufficient to effect a substantial reduction would be impossibly high. The obvious alternative, if one is available, is governmental action—probably on an international scale—to compel fairly drastic changes in individual behavior. But it would be hard to imagine a course of action more subversive of the objectives of laissez-faire.

Perceiving this supporters of government intervention, for any of a variety of reasons, are eager to piggyback on the alleged need for preventive action to prevent global warming. In particular, advocates of an international redistribution of wealth are given to arguing the need for use of bribes to elicit the cooperation of the large populations of impoverished countries in making the behavioral changes needed to abate the danger of global warming.

If valid, the predictions of global warming would constitute a social objective comparable with the need for adequate national defense that (at least some) laissez-faire supporters might consider to be justification for overriding the claims of individual rights. But as the existence of a warming trend is in dispute, with supporters and opponents of precautionary or preventive action by governments assessing the evidence in accordance with their prior beliefs, laissez-faire supporters are generally unwilling that governments should act in advance of the establishment of the facts.

Managing the Money Supply

While disagreeing about the means of achieving it, all economists agree that society would benefit appreciably from maintenance of full employment without inflation. Despite some disagreement as to whether a "properly managed" monetary supply would be sufficient for this purpose, no economist would deny that it would be necessary. The dispute(s) are about what would constitute proper management of the money supply, and whether achieving such management would constitute a valid social objective. Indeed, the need to maintain full employment has been probably the most salient single argument advanced in support of the welfare state.

The most convenient position for a laissez-faire supporter to take on this issue is to deny the competence of the state to improve on the unimpeded action of free markets. Thus some laissez-faire adherents argue that, by allowing individual transactors to issue promises to pay as they wish, an optimal supply of money or monies would emerge, just as the pursuit of individual gain generates optimal supplies of any good or service. The optimal monetary regime might include one or more commodities (e.g., gold or silver) and almost certainly fiduciary issues (i.e., promises to pay) of private parties. In principle, the market would value each proferred means of payment as efficiently as it values anything else, and the state need play no role in providing a medium of exchange.

Such a monetary system is usually termed "free banking," since in effect anyone would be legally free to issue bank notes without obtaining permission of the state. A minority of laissez-faire adherents argue for the adoption of free banking.[26] The efficiency of a free-banking system relative to that of one where the government has a monopoly on the issue of legal tender depends critically upon the information flows and expectations generated under the two systems, and no easy comparison of the two is possible at a purely formal level.

However, most laissez-faire supporters have followed Milton Friedman in rejecting free banking on what can be described as "practical grounds."[27] In its place, they propose a government monopoly of legal tender, subject to the monetary authority (treasury or central bank) following a fixed rule for increasing the money supply. Though the characteristics of such a rule have been a matter of much debate, it is generally agreed (among laissez-faire supporters) that the behavior of the money supply should be as insensitive as possible to the current state or recent history of any economic variable, especially the level of business activity.

Thus, although conceding a role to the state in providing a stable money supply, laissez-faire supporters would limit the power of the state to manipulate the money supply to what was permitted under a predetermined set of rules, that is, such rules would have the de facto status of a constitutional provision. If such rules were followed, the resulting monetary regime might well be judged as consistent with the spirit of laissez-faire. However, to believe that the state would consistently deny itself use of the monetary instrument in the face of political exigency is to ignore the insight that sparked the theory of regulatory takeover.

The question of how to manage the money supply is, of course, a major and confrontational interface of laissez-faire with RAP. The case for active manipulation of the monetary supply to assure full employment without inflation depends mainly upon the relative efficiency in achieving this

---

26. For excellent surveys of free banking, see David Laidler (1992) and L. H. White (1993).

27. Friedman (1962), chapter 3; also see Friedman (1959).

objective of a rule-based system with one or another specific program for adjusting the money supply in response to the recent behavior of the economy. Belief in the superiority of the former is implied by RAP and is highly congenial to laissez-faire ideology. The reverse belief makes it difficult to adhere either to the paradigm or to the ideology.

THE TENSION BETWEEN PURSUIT OF SOCIAL OBJECTIVES AND LAISSEZ-FAIRE

The doctrine of laissez-faire is most comfortable in the absence of social purposes that require the coordination of a plurality of individuals by means other than voluntary agreement. The fewer such goals, and the less their salience, the better for laissez-faire. Yet, laissez-faire adherents accept at least two such goals—defense and law enforcement—and possibly more. How are they to be reconciled with laissez-faire? Since, so far as I am aware, there has never been an explicit attempt at such reconciliation, the following must be considered as a speculative effort in that direction.

The benefits of free exchange within the private sector are reflected as gains in efficiency, i.e., Pareto improvements. Such gains are not considered commensurable with the benefits of achieving a social goal. Thus, in war, the value of victory is not considered translatable into what taxpayers might or might not be willing to pay to obtain it. In terms of a Bergson-Samuelson social-welfare function, achievement of victory is a constraint (additional to the resource constraint) upon the level of social welfare available to the community. The state takes what it needs to win the war, and the market is (or, in the view of a laissez-faire supporter, should be) left to optimize with what is left.

It might be possible to conceptualize such social goals as law enforcement, environmental protection, or full employment as capable of greater or less attainment, and therefore susceptible of comparison with the marginal tax cost that citizen-taxpayers would be willing to bear in order to effect a specified marginal improvement in the degree of approximation to a specified goal. But to attempt such comparisons would not be in the spirit of laissez-faire, but rather more in the style of an economist bent on implementing the goals of a Welfare State.

Laissez-faire economists are generally committed to ignoring the benefits of attaining social goals (other than defense and law enforcement) as insufficient to warrant the entailed expansion of the public sector. The existence of exceptions to this rule may be conceded, provided that the public-sector resource use entailed by all of them combined is small enough as to be considered negligible. Social goals requiring use of more than a negligible amount of resources (e.g., attainment of full employment or control of the environment) are rejected as not yielding sufficient benefit to warrant the required diversion of resources to the public sector.

Deciding whether attaining a proposed social goal would yield sufficient benefit, or whether state action would be adequate to attain it, is a matter of secondary importance to a laissez-faire supporter. The main point is that the state should not make such attempts. In short, acceptance of any social goal (other than the specified exceptions) is considered tantamount to abandonment of laissez-faire. Thus laissez-faire adherents are (properly) apprehensive that a societal committment to avert the consequences of alleged global warming might be used to justify large-scale action by state(s).

EFFICIENCY OF PUBLIC AND PRIVATE PRODUCTION

While they do not deny the existence of various sources of inefficiency in profit-seeking production, laissez-faire advocates minimize their salience. Although, when careful, they avoid claiming that the private sector of a capitalist economy yields a good approximation to Pareto optimality, they are prone to dispute specific allegations of market failure.

Thus, among laissez-faire adherents who are also economists there is a tendency to minimize the importance of network economies (discussed in chapter 14) in achieving productive efficiency. In RAP, such economies—resulting from facilitation of search, communication, and contract administration—are considered reductions of transaction cost. Laissez-faire adherents are prone to stress the strength of the survival-driven tendency of private firms and individuals to form networks when the entailed cost-savings warrant it.[28] Denial of the strength of this tendency provides one ground of opposition to laissez-faire, and a number of its opponents have stressed the inadequacy of this tendency to achieve Pareto optimality and the importance of the resulting opportunity for state action to improve upon the performance of the private sector.

A leading example of such alleged market failures arises when the ef-

---

28. This tendency can be considered as an implication of Coase's theory of the firm.

ficiency differences in alternative technologies in long-run steady state are swamped by the costs of obtaining acceptance of either.[29] Thus the state, by designating any one of the contending technologies as "champion," might effect net savings of resources over what would be used in a competitive selection process replete with duplication of both research and sales efforts.[30] If this argument is valid, and the resource savings significant, it constitutes an important debating point against laissez-faire. This point has been used to support adoption of industrial policies and/or otherwise abandoning free trade on grounds of efficiency.

The argument from network externalities is not only an attack on laissez-faire as policy, but also on RAP as paradigm. Thus the significant overlap of RAP adherents and laissez-faire supporters is doubly motivated to oppose it, though their grounds of opposition differ. The RAP adherent must oppose the argument on the grounds of its (lack of) empirical importance; this has already been discussed in chapter 3. Where the RAP defenders prevail, the task of defending laissez-faire from this attack becomes easier.

However, the defense of laissez-faire does not rest upon the validity of RAP in this context. One could concede, as a number of its defenders have, the validity of the network externalities argument in some circumstances while continuing to uphold the laissez-faire doctrine. The other support of laissez-faire is based on the alleged general malfeasance of the state. Although a wise and well-disposed state might be able to select technologies better than a private market that was unable to exploit network externalities, actual states are neither wise nor consistently well-disposed so that, it is contended, the conceivable social gains that might result from the actions of a wise and beneficent state would be more than offset by the losses caused by the departures of actual from ideal political processes.

The contrast between defense of laissez-faire and adherence to RAP is strikingly exhibited in debates over free trade. Non-economist opponents of free trade who are vaguely aware of arguments based on "gains from trade" are prone to assert that free trade is good in theory, but defective in practice. An economist, aware of market imperfections, network externalities, and the like, is likely to reply that it is just the opposite: it is

---

29. These costs (often categorized as adjustment costs) are inversely related to the efficiency of networks.

30. This possibility has been discussed above, in chapter 6.

easy to make a case against free trade in theory, but hard to defend it in the context of politically driven actions by the state. The laissez-faire argument for free trade may be rested more on the (alleged) malfeasance of the state than on the beneficence of the Invisible Hand.

IDEOLOGY, PARADIGMS, AND PERSUASION

An ideology is a set of beliefs. People can have ideologies of which they are unaware, or in any case cannot articulate. But the ideologues with whom this book is concerned are otherwise: their primary concern is to express their beliefs. Their avowed purpose is to persuade others to share these beliefs, and to act upon them.

A laissez-faire ideologue need not accept RAP. Aversion to the use of state power and/or dislike of political processes provide sufficient reason for a laissez-faire orientation. However, anyone interested in the functioning of society is likely to ask questions touching on decisions about production, distribution, and trade, the answers to which can lead to reinforcement of antistatist predilections by perception of the virtues of the Invisible Hand. But regardless of whether an individual comes to appreciate RAP because of a prior antistatist attitude, or develops an affinity for laissez-faire because of prior exposure to RAP, the two sets of beliefs are—up to a point—symbiotic.

Development and exploitation of such symbiotic relations among groups of concepts is a major function of ideology. Acceptance of RAP does not entail acceptance of laissez-faire, but if one can recognize the workings of the Invisible Hand in daily life she is primed to greet any perceived malfunction of supply with the query, "why isn't the market working?"

Appreciation of the Invisible Hand is not to be taken for granted. Varying with business conditions, complaints about the (lack of) "fairness" of selling prices, wages and employment conditions, and trading practices (especially of foreigners) recrudesce frequently in discussions of economic policy. Typically such complaints accompany an appeal for redress through government action. While belief in the Invisible Hand does not guarantee immunity to such appeals, it does serve to make potential listeners skeptical and receptive to rebuttal arguments.

In effect, acceptance of an ideology is usually paralleled by adoption of a supportive conceptual framework that filters experience and communication to protect against cognitive dissonance. Such a framework may be highlighted by various images and/or dicta that evoke stereotypical responses to various proposals for action. In the case of laissez-faire, examples of such evocative symbols would be the Invisible Hand, "there is no free lunch," and "the offer of alms increase the supply of beggars."

A critical facet of the relation of RAP to laissez-faire is that they share many salient elements of the same conceptual framework.[31] Because of this it is fair to say that to understand RAP is to understand the argument for laissez-faire, and conversely. But, as always, understanding of an argument does not imply acceptance.

Critical appraisal of laissez-faire requires sufficiently deep comprehension of RAP as to enable one to appreciate the distinction between RAP proper—to which the highlighted images do apply—and RAP as augmented in various ways to which the images may not apply, at least without amendment. But appreciation of this distinction is not a sufficient condition for an economist to reject laissez-faire: only a necessary one. Whether an economist goes from comprehension of RAP to acceptance or rejection of laissez-faire depends upon his judgment of the possibility of the state acting as a vehicle for achieving social objectives.

One's appraisal of laissez-faire reflects not only beliefs about the essential characteristics of the state, but also those about the importance of the social goals that the state might help to achieve. Economists who reject laissez-faire despite mastery of RAP are not necessarily naive about the pitfalls of politics. Rather they (may) feel that such aims as achieving full employment without too much inflation, obtaining a more just distribution of income, or halting global warming, are both possible and worth the cost, even while granting that the realities of the political process make that cost greater than it should be.

It is likely that an individual's judgment for or against use of state power to achieve social goals is heavily influenced by her perception of how she may share in the exercise of that power. Thus adherents of the Keynesian paradigm typically think of the government as something that can—under proper circumstances—be influenced to manipulate effective demand so as to move the economy closer to full employment. Similarly, (some) environmentalists believe that the trend of global warming will force politicians to take appropriate corrective steps, though possibly too few, too small, and too late. But all such individuals feel that their own efforts may be able to make a beneficial difference in the response of the state to an important social problem.

---

31. This conceptual framework influences, not only ideas about economic policy, but also the way in which personal relationships and institutions are conceived.

For individuals of this outlook, the state is an instrument of great potential for good or harm. To harness its power is a task that is both parlous and fascinating, but not impossible. For such persons the insights offered by laissez-faire and/or RAP serve mainly to impede needed action: in their view, this effect outweighs any virtues that such ideas may possess.

PART FOUR

ECONOMICS AND SOCIETY

ELEVEN

WHAT ECONOMICS
IS GOOD FOR

S
o far the thrust of this book has been negative. It has emphasized the limitations and shortcomings of economics so strongly that anyone persuaded by its argument might well ask why society at large pays heed to those whose claim to attention is based on its mastery. In this chapter I offer some answers to this question.

ESTABLISHING INSTITUTIONAL FACTS

One key to the expert status that the economics community demands for its members and which, by and large, the wider society accords them, rests on the role of the subject in the construction and interpretation of certain important institutional facts. To fix ideas, let me discuss one such "fact": others will be considered later. The fact in point is the cost-of-living index or, alternatively, the index of consumer prices.[1]

Movements of this index are used, inter alia, to determine the magnitude of required changes in payments of all kinds which amount to billions of dollars per annum. In legislative debates, in court proceedings, and in the negotiation of contracts, movements of this index are treated as "facts"—that is, determinative of action—by all concerned.[2] However, these facts are not records of any specific actions by specifiable individuals, nor do they even make reference to such records. Rather they refer to records of such behavior *after* they have been combined and manipulated by a variety of arithmetic operations. These operations consist of multiplications of recorded prices by combinations of variously selected recorded

1. There are valid reasons for the traditional reluctance of the U.S. Bureau of Labor Statistics (BLS), the organization responsible for the construction and calculation of this index, to identify the index of consumer prices as a cost-of-living index. However, as was recently stated by the commissioner of the Bureau, "the BLS has long said that the cost-of-living framework guides operational decisions about the construction of the index. . . . [I]f the BLS staff or other technical experts knew how to produce a true cost-of-living on a monthly production schedule, that would be what we would produce." Abraham et al. (1998).

2. The notion of institutional facts was introduced by John R. Searle (1995), chapters 4 and 5.

quantities, called weights. The "validity" of the resulting index depends upon the weights used in its construction.

The proper selection of weights to be used is the subject of much technical debate that does not concern us. Roughly, the object of the construction exercise is to find the smallest percentage change in total expenditure that would enable a choice maker to purchase the identical basket of goods and services on two different dates despite changes in the relative prices of the component items.[3] This percentage is then applied to the nominal payments that are to be "indexed" so as to make these payments just sufficient to buy the same market basket on both dates, despite the changes in relative prices.

The arithmetic involved in determining this percentage does not require any economic theory and throws no light on why one set of weights should be used rather than another.[4] But arithmetic alone will suffice for the exercise only so long as the list of items in the basket is unchanged and the possibility of variations in quality over time is excluded. These conditions are never completely satisfied, and typically it is the magnitude and significance of the violations that is at issue when the validity of such an index is debated.

Inevitably, discussion of the significance of variations in quality of "old" goods, and/or the significance of new ones, for a cost-of-living index requires some means for translating such variations of quality into variations in quantity. While it would be too much to say that such a translation *must* involve the effect of such variations on the utility levels of the choice makers, the availability of such a translation—together with the familiarity of the relevant concepts—has made "utility" the concept of choice among economists for explicating the theory of index numbers.

Thus the arcane calculations involved in estimating the magnitude of the under- or overstatement of change in the cost of living (i.e., cost of attaining a given level of utility) by the change in the cost of buying a given market basket have come to be directed by the need to satisfy the

3. More exactly, to purchase (possibly different) baskets on two different dates yielding identical levels of utility.

4. To move from the objective of finding a percentage change of expenditure that would enable a consumer to purchase identical baskets to finding the change that would enable her to buy baskets yielding the same utility is to move from arithmetic to economic analysis. Choice of weights that would accomplish the latter objective is a major topic of the theory of index numbers.

strictures of RAP.[5] As a result, debates about the accuracy of movements in a given index number as an indicator of movements in someone's cost of living come to be debates about the implications of RAP; a matter where the economist has a justified claim to expertise.

To illustrate the use of economic expertise in the application of cost-of-living indices, consider the following episode. In 1994 a presidential commission chaired by the economist Michael Boskin reported (in effect) that the Department of Labor's index of consumer prices (CPI)—used to adjust Social Security and other payments to offset the (alleged) effect of changes in consumer prices—tended to increase about 1.5 percent faster than an increase in the "true" cost of living of a representative household. Since the rationale for the annual adjustment in Social Security payments is that they serve to offset the effect of price changes on the "real value" of said payments, the implied policy recommendation was that the payment adjustments should be reduced. As can be imagined, the report provoked a bitter debate between those desiring such reductions in payments and those opposing them. Although the debate was really about how (post tax) income should be distributed, it was presented as a debate about the facts of movement in a "true" cost-of-living index.[6]

That is, the issue at stake was presented in terms that referred to a concept of economists' construction, and its resolution required invocation of their expertise. But why should politicians, whose understanding of the relevant conceptual issues was limited and whose interest in them even less, have permitted this to occur? There are two reasons: (1) need for a basis of compromise among contending interests, and (2) need for persuading "disinterested" members of the public to accept whatever "solution" was agreed upon.

1. Politics involves repeated struggles among contending parties about a variety of issues among which many can be resolved only through compromise. It is important to each party or faction that it should avoid both the appearance of being overly compliant, and of being so obdurate as to discourage offers of concessions made in hope of eliciting return offers. Recourse to an arbitration procedure is an obvious method of accomplish-

5. In addition to these strictures, there are the requirements of sampling theory, which is involved in estimating the actual quantities purchased by individuals, and the issue of how best to represent the choices of a multitude of choice makers of heterogeneous tastes by a single set of quantity weights. We shall, however, ignore these further complications.

6. See the *New York Times*, 27 September 1995, p. D-22 and 30 September 1995, p. 18.

ing both objectives and, in a variety of contexts, experts function as arbitrators. In such functioning it is not only expertise that requires certification, but also impartiality. To serve as an acceptable method of dispute settlement, expert fact finding must appear to all concerned parties, at a minimum, as not biased against them. This condition would appear to have been satisfied in the dispute about adjustments to Social Security payments, as is evidenced by the statement of House Speaker Newt Gingrich that the House of Representatives would not attempt to alter the application of the CPI to Social Security payments in which he remarked that "determination of the CPI should be left to the 'professionals'".[7]

2. Often in political negotiations there is a substantial number of disinterested parties who want merely "to do the right thing": in this case to save people from reduction in real income on account of inflation.[8] Lacking competence and inclination to choose among proposed solutions, they seek expert guidance. Obviously this objective dovetails neatly with arbitration by experts.

The net effect of this is to establish such notions as cost of living and real income as institutional facts over whose determination economists exercise a monopoly of expertise. This expertise is based upon recognized capability of certifying that proposed measurement procedures conform with the implications of RAP.

As John Searle (1995) describes them, many institutional facts are conceptually simple matters like treating pieces of paper with prescribed markings as money. To comprehend or interpret phenomena involving such simple facts requires no special expertise. But, as exemplified by changes in the cost of living, there are more complicated facts such that their comprehension does require special training. Typically, such facts become salient in the process of governing an organization, notably a state. The parties involved in the governing process need criteria and measures by which they can appraise performance and, where necessary, account for stewardship. Almost always such measures and criteria are complex, and can serve as subjects of discussion or debate only after they have been translated into a stylized format.

As such translations can usually be made in any of a number of ways, with differing consequences for the discussion in which they are to func-

7. Reported in the AARP *Bulletin* of 27 March 1996, p. 1.

8. The disinterested are joined by many interested individuals who, rationally or not, seek only what they were promised but no more, and who desire impartial and expert guidance as to what is their just due.

tion, it is necessary to justify the particular format selected. Such justification can be made best (only?) in terms of conformity with the implications of some paradigm: in practice, RAP is the only economic paradigm that is currently used for such purposes.

Establishment of such conformity, both in general and for particular applications, is the job of the economist. In short, it is the economist who constructs and directs the implementation of concepts that are staple elements of discussions of statecraft and administration generally. Examples of such concepts are: indices of the cost of living, and of aggregate production and resource productivity; measurements of gross and net output of nations, of local areas, and of the entire world; measurements of various aspects of the distribution of income and wealth among segments of population; and dating and measuring fluctuations in economic activity.

Quite apart from questions of prediction, to describe the current state of an economy in relation to where it recently had been, requires employment of concepts such as the above which are the constructs of economists and of which economists (successfully) claim to be custodians. In short, economists have the function of constructing and certifying the records of certain *institutional facts*.

In a sense, the social role of the economist is similar to that of the public accountant. Both are charged with responsibility for ensuring the availability and proper interpretation of records of economic performance relevant to decisions governing use of resources. In constructing social accounts and their various components in nominal terms, quite literally the economist performs the functions of an accountant. But in going beyond nominal records to infer changes in real magnitudes which are devices of their own construction, economists draw on propositions of economic theory that cannot be derived from accounting principles alone.

Another illustration of the role of the economist is the measurement of the money supply. Once there is agreement on the definition of money, measurement of changes in its nominal stock is entirely a matter of accounting, but experts at this measurement task are almost always economists. This is because the proper definition of money, for measurement purposes, has been subject to change over time and is the subject of continuing controversy among economists.

The reason for the sensitivity of economists to the definition of money is its central role in RAP. As was discussed in chapter 3, the quantity theory of money makes the behavior of the general price level dependent upon movements in the stock of money and in (real) aggregate production. Accordingly, the definitions of (all of) these magnitudes must be co-ordinated and otherwise chosen so as to satisfy the requirements of RAP. Manifestly, choice of a proper operational definition of money is a task requiring the highest order of professional expertise.[9]

Thus, in reporting on the recent behavior of the money supply as part of a description of the current state of the economy, a central banker or other quasi-public official is describing an institutional fact whose meaning and construction is the result of decisions made by economists. This remark applies, a fortiori, when a nation's money supply is partly dependent upon international factors not wholly under control of its government, for example, if it is on a gold standard or is otherwise constrained to maintain exchange parity with one or more foreign currencies.

Now let us turn to the critical evaluation of certain index numbers, the interpretation of which is generally left to economists. In the past two decades there has been great concern with the adequacy with which indices of factor productivity reflect increases in the capability of computers to perform a large and growing number of tasks per dollar of computer services purchased. Similar concerns have arisen as to the capability of conventional indices of the cost of health care to allow for the effects of improvements in drugs and technical equipment on the length and quality of life.[10]

The bearing of such indices upon political debate is fairly obvious. For example, debate about how large a fraction of a nation's resources should be devoted to providing health care turns in good part upon judgments of the effect of such expenditure upon the state of health of its population: such judgments must rest on appraisal of what—in real terms—can be obtained for an additional dollar devoted to health care. Unsatisfactory though the best available measures of health care productivity may be, they are obtainable only through the application of techniques falling within the purview of economics.[11]

9. For example, such choice involves deciding when or whether "money" is to include deposits in saving accounts, money-market funds, and unused borrowing capability on credit cards.

10. Such measures, like those incorporated in the CPI of the U.S. Department of Labor, have no way of reflecting the increased therapeutic potency of new drugs that have replaced older counterparts.

11. In this connection, the technique most commonly used is construction of a hedonic index which translates each of the goods in an index into quantities of underlying characteristics that it is alleged to incorporate, and to find implicit prices of these underlying characteristics. Arguably, therapeutic effects of medical care can be translated into such characteristics, and appropriate prices found. While this procedure is ingenious, it is of debated

Similar problems are encountered in devising an index number to allow for the growth of computing power obtainable for a dollar spent on computing service. But in the case of computers, estimation of the effect of gains in computing power upon overall growth in productivity was (in the 1980s) confounded by further conceptual (i.e., weighting) problems. As Edward Denison (1989) showed, inappropriate weighting procedures led to an incorrect appraisal of the relative slowdown (during the 1970s and 80s) of productivity growth in U.S. manufacturing and nonmanufacturing industries. In good part because of Denison's critique, the procedures and estimates have since been revised. However, for a number of years, the faulty weighting procedure led to a serious understatement of relative growth retardation in U.S. manufacturing during this period, and to a corresponding misconception of the causes of loss of U.S. competitiveness in world markets.

Appraisal of the consequences of this error for policy making is not to the present point. Our argument is simply that the perception of the state of the world, both by economists and by policy makers, was largely the result of measurement procedures created by economists and, as such, was sensitive to the outcome of technical discussion within their community. In short, when accepted by a consensus of the economics community, the data on productivity change functioned as an institutional fact.

Yet another example of an institutional fact created by economists is the dating of business cycles. The dating of business cycle phases, in particular the dating of cyclical peaks and troughs, is done by an official commission whose pronouncements are widely accepted as authoritative.[12]

The importance of the institutional facts of business-cycle dating derives from the background opinion that fluctuations in business activity are sometimes excessive, and that such excess could be avoided, or reduced, if wise monetary-fiscal policy were followed by the government and the central bank. Hence the dating of the turning points at business cycle peaks and troughs can become foci of (dubious) political debate as to the proper assignment of credit or blame for the course of subsequent economic events.

An extreme example of this is the persisting debate as to whether the

---

applicability to any given problem. But, however applied, the technique is an extension of RAP, and is comprehensible only to its initiates. For a brief introduction to the subject see Jack E. Triplett (1987).

12. While not directly associated with any particular paradigm, the characterization and measurement of business activity is a highly technical matter. For a brief history of the procedures used see K. Lahiri and G. H. Moore (1991), chapter 1.

bottom of the Great Depression of 1929–32 (or '33) occurred in the summer of 1932 (to the credit of Hoover) or in March 1933 (credit Roosevelt). The substance of this or similar debates about business-cycle dating does not concern us: our point is that establishment of the relevant institutional facts is delegated to the economics community.

Strictly speaking, the task of business-cycle dating is historical: it is undertaken to determine what happened and when, but without suggestion of what the determination might portend for the future. Nevertheless, one of the most important elements of the procedure is the behavior of "leading indicators." As their name would suggest, movements of these variables tend to precede those of the composite that is called business activity. Once again this raises the question of whether economics is, or can be, of any use in predicting behavior.

From the discussion of chapter 8 on financial markets it follows that, so far as the question relates to future behavior, the successful forecasting of which would enable one to turn a profit, the answer must be negative. (As used in the preceding sentence, "profit" should be interpreted broadly: it refers not only to personal financial gain, but also to any situation where it might be argued that the purposes of planned expenditure could be better achieved by utilizing and timing of the forecasts of the state of relevant economic variables.) This is because where adaptive adjustments to forecasts are feasible, as soon as an acceptable forecast becomes generally known, actual aggregate expenditure will deviate from what had been indicated by the forecasting instrument, thereby throwing the forecast off its mark. Thus any forecasting procedure that had been valid prior to some given date and was capable of inspiring adaptive behavior, will be rendered invalid (for any subsequent date) by publication, because publication would alter the behavior patterns (e.g., of expenditure) on which the forecasts had been based.[13]

QUASI-FORECASTING

Despite this caveat, there is a class of economic forecasts embodied in the leading indicators that is useful in prediction: for want of a better term, I shall call them quasi-forecasts.[14] These are short-term forecasts of aggre-

13. I shall ignore the possibility that a forecaster might anticipate the change in behavior resulting from publication of her forecast and make appropriate modifications of her forecasts. While such a possibility might be relevant to some forecasting instruments, it does not apply to leading indicators.

14. The distinction between a forecast and (what is here termed) a quasi-forecast is that the latter depends upon knowledge of a prior commitment of resources while the former

gate quantities. A leading example would be the prediction of aggregate expenditure on plant and equipment one or two quarters in advance. Such a quasi-forecast would be based on a survey of "planned" or "intended" expenditures by a sample (often large) of firms. The accuracy of the individual responses to the survey is due to the fact that the numbers reported are largely a reflection of commitments (e.g., orders) already made, and from which it would be costly to withdraw. Obviously, the extent to which responses to such a survey reflect commitments already made diminishes with the length of the forecast horizon; a three-month-ahead forecast is more dependable than one that is six months ahead, and so on. Increasingly, forecasts over longer horizons depend more upon plans, scenarios, and the like, which, though indicative of intentions, are less definite and would cost less to alter than actual commitments. Consequently, the accuracy of quasi forecasts diminishes, and rapidly, with the length of the forecast horizon.[15]

A quasi-forecast for an individual firm is simply a statement of its plans and/or commitments to a certain class of expenditures, and should be a by-product of its internal budgeting process. As such it is of no special interest to any outsider except the firm's actual or potential suppliers, or its close competitors in the product market. However, an economy-wide aggregate of such quasi-forecasts is an institutional fact that was not known prior to its publication, but is of concern to central banks, fiscal authorities, and generally to anyone affected by changes in the level of aggregate expenditure.

Once published, such quasi-forecasts cannot be a source of profitable speculation to anyone. However, this is not the case prior to publication. Prepublication knowledge of the quasi-forecast aside, skill in anticipating what the quasi-forecast will show—"forecasting the forecast"—can be of great value. And economists are prominent among those skilled in the making of forecasts of forecasts. This skill is derived from access to the returns of particular firms that can be interpreted as bellwethers of the aggregate or, more generally, in knowing how to use or devise proxies for related variables that can be obtained prior to publication of the relevant aggregate.

Examples of such proxies include data on new orders, on planned out-

---

does not. Put differently, a quasi-forecast involves exploitation of "private information," as that term is used in the finance literature.

15. For a careful and detailed discussion of business forecasting, see Victor Zarnowitz (1992), especially part 4. Also see the essays in Kahiri and Moore (1991).

lays by purchasing agents, on the volume of unfilled orders, on the length of delivery delays, and on the price behavior of purchased raw materials traded on organized exchanges. Integrated with explicit or implicit econometric models, prepublication clues as to the behavior of these variables can be a source of speculative profit. In a completely specialized world, the economist would have no comparative advantage in gathering such clues: for forecasting purposes, they could just as well be gathered by others and then integrated with econometric models constructed by economists. And, probably, such division of labor sometimes occurs.

However, as the economist is at no great disadvantage in gathering clues, it is not surprising that occasionally she will engage in "backward vertical integration" to combine the tasks of providing and analyzing information. Because the behavioral regularities on which the validity of clues depend are likely to be evanescent, the quasi-forecaster must be very sensitive to changes of structure within the information chains on which she relies.[16] Probably the need for such sensitivity increases the likelihood that frequently the economist will investigate the current reliability of forecasting clues, which will tend to reduce the salience of non-economist collaborators in this activity.

Nevertheless, in making quasi-forecasts the roles of the economist and of the knowledgeable (lay) industry or market specialist become blurred, so that the specific contribution of economics becomes conflated with the techniques of acquiring particular bits of information that are often of fleeting value. As a result, the salience of "practical knowledge" in quasi-forecasting is exaggerated—not least by economists possessing it—to the neglect of the role played by economics. This conflation is sometimes infelicitously described by (mis)application of the phrase, "it is an art rather than an exact science."

As a result of this conflation of tasks, many quasi-forecasters bear the label of economist—with propriety—and are so recognized.[17] And, despite frequently issued caveats, the comparative success of their short-horizon forecasts has a halo effect on their projections and scenarios over longer horizons. Surely, such projections and scenarios do not go unchallenged by non-economists who often flaunt the banner of "practical

16. It might be remarked that the better a particular clue has been in the past, the more likely it is that the pattern of behavior that it reflects will alter—adapt—as the information provided by the clue is increasingly exploited.

17. For some indication of the number and other characteristics of these economists see Zarnowitz (1992), pp. 387–89.

knowledge" or "broader vision" to offset the claims of scientific grounding that are—or might be—made for the competing entries of economists. Nevertheless, the views of economists are an important ingredient in public discussions about "the future" and how to plan for it.

CONSTRUCTING BELIEFS ABOUT "HOW THE WORLD WORKS"

Information Gathering

Plans to adapt to forecasts of the future begin with assessment of the present situation. And, so far as it concerns economic behavior, description of the present is the province of the economist. As already remarked, the very concepts employed in constructing variables reflecting the behavior of real magnitudes are chosen with regard to the strictures of RAP. But, even apart from this, the particular measurements of variables used in describing the "current economic situation" such as streams of payments, stocks of assets, quantities of work performed, numbers of individuals or households in specified states, and so on, are chosen mainly by economists guided by their relevance to economic theory.

They are able to do this because, on account of their research needs, economists are the major consumers of economic statistics and therefore constitute a major lobby on all matters pertaining to their gathering and organization. Their effectiveness as a lobby results from the fact that, on these matters, they are generally united and face virtually no opposition. Further, the nature of their interest in the gathering and organizing of data serves to produce both intensity and persistence of effort to promote adoption of their collective agenda.

The influence of economists in the selection and formatting of the data used to describe "the present situation" serves to give them a great advantage—if not a collective monopoly—in utilizing it. This serves further to enhance their collective influence in modifying and extending the statistical base used in the description of any economic situation. Indeed, an important characteristic that distinguishes the economist from the lay person is ability to interpret the statistical artifacts conventionally used to describe an economic situation.

However, taken literally, the situation as of a given moment is rarely of interest to anyone. It is the contrast of the present situation with that existing at some time in the past which is of concern, usually as a possible indicator of what is yet to come. The particular characteristics of the potential future that the economist wishes to emphasize direct the selection

of those features of the present that are to be contrasted with their counterparts in the relevant past. In constructing and estimating a model in
which there are "structural parameters," the economist implicitly is offering a contribution to a prevision of the future that is relevant to a projected course of action.

Presenting the Lessons of History

However designated, the shortcomings of such "previsions" are well
known both to economists and to the wider public. Nevertheless, discussions of prospective actions proceed by comparative assessment of alternative previsions, and economists' descriptions of the "present"—that is,
comparisons of the present with the recent past—are essential ingredients
of this process.

The economist's contribution to such previsions varies from case to
case. The remarks of the last few paragraphs refer to situations where the
economist's contribution is relatively modest: highlighting and interrelat-
ing some statistics that purport to show that recent economic events lend
credibility to a particular prevision of the future. But, as we shall see,
sometimes the economist's contribution to prevision is much larger than
this.

The layman's belief in a particular prevision of the future does not,
cannot, depend heavily upon commitment to a theory that is an integral
part of his beliefs about how the world works. Typically, his understanding
of a theory or a paradigm to which he may be practically committed is
shallow and in need of continued reinforcement from ongoing events, including reports of fresh research. His or her commitment to a paradigm,
while sometimes bordering on the fanatical, usually is sensitive to events
that would appear to invalidate its claim to prescience.

By contrast, as perceived by a member of the economics subculture an
economic paradigm incorporates both a conceptual organization and
some general beliefs about the structure of the empirical relationships
among them. Paradigms function as frameworks for her research, guiding
the selection of problems and framing the interpretation of evidence bearing upon specific hypotheses. This makes her attachment to a paradigm
much stronger than that of the lay adherent.

But although the economist's commitment to a paradigm rests far
more upon theoretical considerations than a lay person's, it is not impervious to "disturbing facts." While acceptance of a paradigm does not entail
acceptance of one story or another about particular historical episodes,

stories about certain key episodes are regarded as providing strong pieces of evidence for the paradigm's validity, and attacks upon them are (properly) regarded as attacks on the validity of the paradigm itself.

For example, as seen by Keynesians, the Great Depression of 1929–32/33 is a story of labor-market failure that was not—and, they claim could not have been—corrected by proper monetary policy or other measures compatible with a generally noninterventionist policy of the state.

A Keynesian need not deny the monetarist story that a sharp decline occurred in the real money stock in 1931, or even that it contributed to the subsequent decline in output: what is essential is that a sequence of events somehow resulted in a drastic reduction in aggregate demand and employment that could not be offset by the working of free labor markets. Accordingly, suggestions that a substantial contribution to the decline in employment resulted from reductions in aggregate labor supply à la Lucas-Rapping (see above, pp. 148–50) are resisted strongly.

In effect, the Great Depression functions as a historical exemplar of the Keynesian paradigm. Similarly, Marxists have tried to employ a few major revolutions (e.g., the French and Russian revolutions and the events of 1848) as exemplars of the paradigm of *The Communist Manifesto;* Malthusians were wont to point to the period of 1790–1825 in Britain as an example of the (alleged) deleterious effects of excessively accessible poor relief; neomercantilists present the fuel shortages and high gasoline prices of the 1970s as an illustration of the consequences of relying on free markets to supply raw materials; and RAP–laissez-faire advocates are given to pointing to queues, shortages, and deterioration of product quality during war and immediate postwar situations as illustrations of the consequences of price controls.

Typically, these and similar examples that could be cited offer "lessons of history" to induce adherence to paradigms. Given the weak empirical basis for acceptance of any economic paradigm, even for the professional economist belief in the (rough) factual accuracy of one or another exemplary cases constitutes an important support for continued adherence. Hence the events recounted in such stories as the above are focal points for research in economic history. And the evidence provided by such research is a significant part of what economics contributes to political economic discourse.

In addition to serving as reinforcement to the beliefs of professional economists, such evidence plays an even more important role in supporting the belief structures of lay participants in the process of policy making.

Generally, such persons are aware of the fragile bases of forecasts over horizons longer than one year and—unlike professional economists—are not deeply committed to a particular paradigm, so that their current beliefs about the consequences of policy actions depend greatly upon psychological reinforcement from recent events. In this context, recent events consist not only of reports about the recent past, i.e., the content of "new" statistical reports, but also, and importantly, of fresh revisions of stories about salient events in the more distant past.

Put differently, the beliefs of the lay participant—the educated lay person—in the policy-making process depend partly on acceptance of certain historical accounts as being factually accurate. While coherence of accepted historical accounts with the structure of a paradigm is very important to maintenance of a belief structure, the beliefs of most lay persons are not sensitive to currents of theoretical discussion, but respond more to what are perceived as factual reports.[18] Provision, interpretation, and critical analysis of such reports is a major part of what economics contributes to discourse about policy making.

Providing Ideological Support

Like experts, lay persons vary in the strength of their attachments to theoretical paradigms and/or to related views of history. The minority that is strongly attached both to a paradigm and an associated view of history is commonly described as having an ideology. For the moment let us accept this, and say that—for some persons—economics provides an ideology, or at least critical parts of one.[19] An ideology includes both a paradigm and a supporting set of historical accounts that serve as its exemplars. The effect of an ideology is to provide a frame for assimilation of experience (i.e., new evidence) such as to make it compatible with continued acceptance of the ideology. In Bayesian terms, an ideology provides a prior for events relevant to the validity of any member of the set of hypotheses that bear upon the acceptability of a paradigm.

As I conceive it, an economic ideology acts on the belief structure of policy makers in a manner analogous to a military doctrine. Both are based on stylized views of particular historical events conflated with theoretical arguments. A military doctrine is used to guide details of diplo-

18. As envisaged here, the operative beliefs of the lay person respond only to such shifts of theory as can be interpreted as reflecting a change in the consensus of expert opinion.

19. As I prefer to use the term, an ideology involves more than just a set of beliefs (see above, chapter 10).

matic policy, and of military tactics and strategy: an economic ideology is used to make choices of policy on a variety of matters, especially those related to monetary and fiscal policy.

While not sacrosanct, matters addressed by each set of beliefs are considered the special province of the designated experts, a consensus of whom normally is able to overbear contrary opinions among the laity. Often the messages of military doctrine and of economic ideology infiltrate both a community's folklore and its written history. In other words, whatever their scientific validity, military doctrine and ideology function in much the manner of a Sorelian myth. As such, they are able to generate powerful frames for interpreting experience and reconciling the flow of events with prior beliefs.[20]

Despite the similarities, I would avoid exaggerating the salience of the parallel between economic and military doctrines. Most economists, like most lay participants in the policy-making process, do not apply a unified ideology in all contexts. Rather, most of them have one or more networks of interrelated beliefs about the "way things work," together with some related exemplars that they apply in loosely defined sets of circumstances. Each of these belief networks provides a frame for analyzing the effects of policy proposals that fall within the relevant set of defined circumstances. Usually, the several belief networks of a given individual are more or less interrelated, though I have no useful generalization to offer on this point.[21]

Lay and Professional Opinion

Finally, the influence of economic ideas upon the body of lay opinion operates via two distinct channels: directly and through the respect accorded expert opinion. The argument of this section has been an attempt to describe the channel of direct influence, in contrast to the channel of expert opinion described in chapter 2.

In Western societies, policy makers feel pressured to abide by the consensus of judgments of recognized experts on matters within their ascribed domains. As already argued, the basis of such recognition is attribution of scientific competence. Thus, an economist can influence ideas

20. The role of legal doctrine, and the correlative influence of lawyers, on the beliefs and practices of a community provides yet another parallel to the role of ideology in economics.

21. At the limit, where the interrelation among the beliefs becomes so strong as to constitute a unified set, that set of beliefs becomes an ideology.

by persuading the bulk of his professional colleagues of their correctness, and thereby recruiting them to serve as his messengers.

As Keynes put it in the preface to *The General Theory* (1936, p. iv),

> if my explanations are right, it is my fellow economists, not the general public whom I must first convince. At this stage of the argument the general public, though welcome at the debate, are only eavesdroppers at an attempt by an economist to bring to an issue the deep divergences of opinion between fellow economists which have for the time being almost destroyed the practical influence of economic theory, and will, until they are resolved, continue to do so.

CREATING INSTITUTIONS
International Monetary Arrangements

One of the most prominent functions economists are called upon to perform is the determination of the rules under which exchange rates of various currencies are to be established. Considering the enormous stakes involved, it is not surprising that voices other than economists should "intrude" into such discussions. Nevertheless, the purely technical arguments of economists emanating from arcane theoretical debates within their own community are heard, and provide grist for the mills of political debate among policy makers.

Notoriously, the recommendations of experts on the conduct of international trade have sometimes been overruled by (often uncomprehending) political superiors when they entailed substantial near-term losses to an appreciable segment of their constituencies. Nevertheless, there are many cases where the prospective long-term advantages from better procedures for the setting of exchange rates, or the handling of customs duties, have carried the day against short-term considerations. And it is in these cases that the expertise of economists (in arguing for the importance of the long-term effects of trade provisions and spelling out their details) has been salient, so that often the design of institutional "details" has been left in their hands.

Organized Exchanges

As we saw in chapter 8, there is a large and rapidly growing market for synthetic assets (derivatives) which serve as vehicles to transfer risk from one party to another. In the creation of such assets, the application of the RAP-based theory of finance has played a major role, and economists have been major figures in the continuing development of the institutions involved.

The economist's architectural role in the creation of organized exchanges is but one illustration of how RAP has been used in the design of "transaction-facilitating" institutions: another example is the design of auction markets, both in the laboratory and in the "real world." I alluded briefly to laboratory models of auction markets in chapter 7; now let me elaborate a bit further.

Auction Rules

As Vernon L. Smith (1994, p. 115) claims, by varying the market rules of exchange in identical (experimental) environments it has been possible to establish the comparative properties of various sets of auction rules. These properties refer to the characteristics of price movements and the quantity of transactions. The sets of auction rules compared are described variously as English and Dutch auctions, first and second price sealed-bid auctions, or uniform and discriminative price multiple-unit auctions, to name but a few examples.

Students of laboratory behavior have studied in some detail the effect of different sets of auction rules on price-quantity behavior, such matters as the speed with which bids approach the final sale price, and the relation of prices realized and the quantities sold. Since in RAP models auction rules cannot affect equilibrium prices and quantities, any interesting results would seem to be artifacts of experimental procedure unless they can be presented as anomalies to RAP.

Because of this, it is tempting to regard such laboratory results as research curiosities, and without practical value. But this would be a mistake: the design of auction rules has become a matter of great moment to auction participants, especially governments, which often are in the position of monopoly sellers. Obviously, if the price-quantity combinations that result vary with the rules under which an auction is conducted, a monopoly seller will have an interest in the rules chosen. As a result, in the past three decades there has been a small stream of "real-world" experiments with alternative auction rules, conducted mainly by economists strongly motivated by theoretical interest in the problem.

The sponsors of such experiments include the U.S. Treasury, which has a continuing concern with maximizing the revenue from its recurrent auctions of government bonds. The Treasury's specific interest is to compare the revenue yielded by one-price auctions (where all successful bidders for units of a specific bond issue pay the same price) with those of a discriminatory sealed bid auction which the Treasury has long used. In the latter type of auction, each purchaser makes a sealed bid specifying the quantity desired and the (maximum) price he is willing to pay. The Treasury then allocates units on the principle of always choosing higher bids to lower ones, until the entire stock of units offered is exhausted. However, the purchasers were required to pay whatever price they had offered to pay in their sealed bid, with the result that some bidders paid more than others.

Economists, notably Milton Friedman, have argued that a one-price auction would generate greater revenue than the auction rules under which the Treasury had been operating, and laboratory experiments appear to confirm their speculations. These results aroused the Treasury's interest in the alternative one-price procedure. This interest has continued and has attracted the interest of other government bodies, and of private institutions as well. This has lead to experiments in the procedure for auctioning such items as emissions permits, and landing slots at airports.[22]

However, by far the most prominent case where economists have developed designed auction rules is the ongoing (as of 1996) government auction of licenses of sections of the electromagnetic (airwave) spectrum for commercial use.[23] The practical importance of these auctions is suggested by the amount of revenue they have raised: as of early 1996, this amount was about $9 billion, with a substantial fraction of the spectrum yet to be sold. The attention of the media to the occurrence of the auctions, to their novel characteristics, and to the role of economists in their design has been commensurate both with the dollar magnitudes involved and the evident gratification of the participants.[24]

The salience of economists in designing the auction rules was due not only to their monopoly of expertise in the theory of auctions but also to the inherent complexity of the auctions themselves. Each piece of the spectrum placed at auction had relations of substitution or complementarity with other pieces, so that the value of a given piece to a given bidder depended upon his success in obtaining certain other pieces. Thus an optimal bidding strategy for a bidder on spectrum piece A would vary with what he thought competitors would bid on other pieces, B, C, etc.

Even to design an optimal bidding strategy for a single bidder was a

22. See Smith (1994).

23. See McAfee and McMillan (1996) and Milgrom (1996). The following paragraphs have greatly benefited from discussion with Paul Milgrom.

24. See McAfee and McMillan (1996).

formidable task; to design rules for conducting the auction in which such bids were strategic moves was far more difficult. While it would have been possible to lay down rules arbitrarily, the government (acting through the Federal Communications Commission, or FCC) had in mind a number of desiderata that it wanted the rules to achieve. Though it was not prepared to specify an objective function in detail, the FCC had "the stated objective of putting licenses into the hands of those who value them most."[25] But in addition to this objective, and the obtaining of revenue for the Treasury, other objectives emerged in the design process, including means of avoiding payment defaults by bidders; ways to allow bidders to resubmit or alter bids, if it seemed advantageous to do so, while preventing the auction from dragging on for too long; and methods for screening out frivolous bids.

The rule design finally adopted was a compromise among various desiderata resulting from extended discussions among representatives of the FCC and potential bidders, most of whom were economist game-theorists who had been active contributors to the literature on auction theory.[26] The rules adopted specified a simultaneous, multiple-round auction. "Simultaneity" meant that participants could make bids on several pieces of the spectrum at once. "Multiple round" meant that after a set of bids from all interested parties had been made, the bids were revealed to all participants who could then revise their bids for a second round of bidding: this was to be repeated for as many rounds as was necessary to satisfy the auction termination rule. The termination rule adopted was intended to insure that no participant who wished to make a new bid for any license was prevented from doing so.[27]

The details of the auction rules are not important for our purpose. What matters is that the criteria by which the rules that were selected could be deemed to have performed well, or badly. As judged by remarks in the media and the comments of the auction participants, the auctions

25. Milgrom (1996), chapter 1, p. 3. The enabling legislation specified that "the primary objective of the process was to to insure the "efficient and intensive use of the spectrum" (ibid., p. 13). Milgrom points out that the FCC's interpretation of this is not identical with seeking an efficient license allocation (in the sense of a Pareto optimum) because of the absence of competition in product markets, but notes that the FCC believed that such absence would not cause serious losses of potential welfare.

26. These discussions are described vividly by participant-reporter Milgrom (1996), pp. 11–22.

27. The rules prescribed that a new bid for any license must be higher, and by a specified amount, than any previous bid for that license.

were successful. The economists involved appear to have been satisfied with the performance of their creation, and highly optimistic about the chances for further applications of the techniques developed.[28] Some of this satisfaction arose from comparison of the results of these auctions with those of earlier auctions of airways spectrum licenses in Australia and New Zealand. Indeed, design of the rules for the U.S. auctions was guided by the conscious desire to avoid certain unfavorable aspects of the outcomes experienced in the Antipodes.[29] Judged by this standard, the auction format adopted appears to have been a success.

However, this is a rather low standard, and I would doubt that the economists involved would claim much credit for meeting it. While revenue generation might have provided a more demanding performance criterion, revenue maximization was not an explicit objective of the exercise, and at least two of its avowed objectives were inconsistent with such pursuit.[30] So far as I am aware, no attempt has been made to estimate the maximum revenue obtainable from sale of the licenses, but the amount derived seems considerably to have exceeded what the FCC had anticipated.

Various quantitative performance indicators (mentioned both by McAfee and McMillan and by Milgrom) might be used to appraise the performance of a particular set of auction rules, but this is for the future. For the present, it is sufficient to note that the parties directly affected by the auctions have not offered any challenge to their design or suggested that some alternative procedure might have yielded better results.

Acceptance of the design procedure is remarkable testimony to the authority conceded to a scientific community to determine a matter of general concern by application of its own criteria of performance. The authority conceded to a small group of economist game-theorists was due partly to their prestige within the larger community of economists, which was reinforced by the advice of the expert consultants hired by each of the prospective bidders in the auction and by the FCC. Of course, the expert consultants themselves were members of the small community of

28. See the articles cited in McAfee and McMillan (1996), and the references contained therein.

29. See Milgrom (1996), pp. 4–11.

30. One of these was the deliberate favoring of bids submitted by small businesses, women, minorities and rural telephone companies; the other was the reservation of several choice pieces of the spectrum for allocation (on a noncompetitive basis) as rewards for technical innovation.

economist game-theorists which, no doubt, greatly facilitated the substantial degree of consensus arrived at. That each of the highly competitive bidders came to hire an individual from the same group of esoteric thinkers reflects the monopoly of relevant expertise possessed by this group. Prospective participants were able effectively to convey their desired input to the design process, and appraise the impact on their own interests of proposals from competing participants, only by means of the arcane procedures known to this group of experts.

Probably the initial validation of these procedures to the outsider-principals (mainly large telecommunications companies) came through the affiliation of leading members of the group of initiates with universities and research institutes from whose prestige they drew reflected luster, strongly reinforced by their collegial contact with natural scientists and mathematicians upon whose judgments corporate organizations had learned to rely. The support of the latter groups for the game theorists was probably enhanced by their common reliance upon use of sophisticated mathematical techniques. That the principals had qualms about their dependence on experts in a very new field is likely, but in attempting to assess the proposals of their own experts they could resort only to other experts; no one else had sufficient command of the relevant language or technique.[31]

In describing the body of theory applied in the design of the auction rules, the participants in the rule-designing process stress game theory rather than economic theory in general.[32] Briefly, the relation between these two bodies of theory is as follows. As is the case in RAP, in game theory decision makers (players) are conceived to be constrained utility maximizers. However, in game theory, the constraints include not only resources but the rules of the relevant game, with heavy emphasis on the latter.

The purpose of RAP is to find models that will explain price-quantity as movements between equilibrium positions, the equilibria requiring

31. Thus when Pacific Telesis attempted to validate the recommendations of their own experts (Paul Milgrom and Robert Wilson, of Stanford University) the best they could do was to hire Charles Plott (of the California Institute of Technology). See Milgrom, (1996), p. 16.

32. As Milgrom (ibid., p. 20) puts it, "Game Theory played a central role in the analysis of rules. . . . Ideas of Nash equilibrium, rationalizability, backward induction, and incomplete information, though rarely named explicitly, were the real basis of daily decisions about the details of the auction design."

both market clearing and constrained utility maximization by the decision makers. The focus of game theory is on the decision-making process of the individual participants, with emphasis on the calculation of the effect of contemplated actions upon the prospective behavior of other players as determined by the rules of the game and the specific assumptions made about the information available to each of the players. While significant both in RAP and in game theory, assumptions about information are generally more salient in the latter.

Though RAP may be extended by suitable paradigm adjuncts to cover noncompetitive situations, because of the salience of market clearing conditions (in RAP) such extensions have not led to very useful results. In contrast, game theory was designed specifically for analyzing games with small numbers of players, and contains no role for market clearing in the determination of an equilibrium, which makes it a more promising tool for the analysis of oligopoly. However, although attempts have been made to apply game theory to situations of oligopoly, and even to implement the results empirically, the difficulties have been such as to prevent more than limited success.[33]

While it is unlikely that the difficulties of constructing an empirically implementable theory of oligopoly will be overcome in the near future, this does not have adverse implications for such tasks as auction design. Although the spectrum auctions are oligopolistic games, and prey to their analytical difficulties, the task of designing rules for them does not require finding a solution to the resulting game—or even establishing that there is a solution—but only to establishing that the rules proposed make it impossible, or highly unlikely, that certain specified undesired outcomes of the auction will emerge.[34]

The modus operandi used to accomplish this was characteristic of game theory, though alien to RAP. That is, the analysts used theorems of game theory to deduce the strategic implications of each set of proposed rules for the behavior of each player, on the assumption that he would correctly deduce every implication of the rules for every other player and calculate an optimum strategy based on the assumption that every other player was behaving in a similar fashion. The theorists assumed that the actual behavior of each player would correspond to what had been deduced, and that the observed correspondence of deduced with observed

33. The problems of applying game theory to the analysis of oligopoly are analyzed in great detail by Lester G. Telser (1972). For an earlier treatment of the subject, see William J. Fellner (1949); a more recent discussion is Hugo Sonnenschein (1987).

34. Milgrom (1996), p. 22.

behavior was sufficiently good for their auction-rule designs to be considered successful.

In effect, the game theorists made successful, albeit limited, if-then predictions. They stated that if certain sets of auction rules were adopted, specified behaviors and outcomes of the auction would be avoided and, within acceptable limits of error, they appear to have been correct. But whether anyone can design rules that would meet a more demanding set of criteria remains to be seen. Also, one may suspect that the performance of the designed rules was assisted by the fact that, in these auctions, the formulation of a bid was so technically demanding that its details were, per force, left to the game-theoretic consultants of the corporate principal. Such players might be expected to exhibit a greater-than-normal tropism for theoretically correct moves. Still further, the effect of tightly specified rules of conduct prevailing in an auction (or on any organized exchange) probably exerted a constraining effect on behavior—thereby inducing predictability—that would be absent from oligopolistic competition in a more unstructured setting.

For a final contrast between game theory and RAP, in appraising the pedagogical value of the auction design, McAfee and Macmillan remark that "a lesson from this experience of theorists in policymaking is that the real value of the theory is in developing intuition." As applied to game theory, this is on the mark; but it is the reverse of what an RAP theory should and usually does attempt.

In designing auction rules, the analyst's concern is with remote and not readily perceived strategic possibilities that skilled and motivated players might discover after much search or experimental play. In making such searches, the theoretical results of game theory are likely to provide excellent guidance. But RAP is not designed to find possible but as yet unobserved patterns of behavior: its objective is to use intuition to find or construct theories that can be used to rationalize what has already been observed. In the former case, theory is used to anticipate potential but as yet unobserved behavior for the purpose of devising rules that will prevent its appearance; in the latter case, observation and intuition are used to devise RAP-compatible theories capable of reconciling observed behavior with the paradigm.

ECONOMIC ADVISING: A BRIEF COMMENT

In considering the practical functions that economists perform, thus far I have omitted their role in administering foreign loans and grants. While not previously unknown, it is in the period since 1945 that economists have become important figures in the design and execution of plans to improve economic conditions in particular parts of the world. Foreign aid had its inception in the efforts of the victors of World War II to direct the economies of the vanquished countries they were occupying. These efforts were concentrated in Western Europe and Japan, and were more-or-less completed by 1950. But they have been succeeded by efforts to promote economic development in Asia, Africa, and Latin America. Still later, in the late 1980s, efforts to help economies in the former Soviet Bloc convert from socialism to capitalism began. Often such efforts, undertaken in the same spirit of assistance cum tutelage that had infused reconstruction plans after World War II, were administered by the same personnel, many of whom bore the title of economist.

Variously, the provenors of this assistance were agencies of the United States government, the United Nations, private foundations, the World Bank, and the International Monetary Fund. Since about 1950, these organizations have been a major source of demand for persons bearing the credentials of economist. Recognition of this fact by training centers of economics has exercised a substantial influence on the curricula of such institutions, sometimes leading to struggles over the amount and quality of the training given to students intending to participate in the process of economic development.

Although interesting, the feedback from developmental aid upon the training of economists is not of concern here. Our present concern is with the effect of the discipline of economics upon the process of development, as this effect has been transmitted by economists. And this effect has not been a major one. Despite their number and the high quality of the contribution made by some of them, the effect of economists in promoting development has been varied and of uncertain relation to their core competence. Development economists have been utilized in a whole range of tasks from the design of banking systems to the upgrading of agricultural techniques, but rarely has the level of their technical skill been salient to the success or failure of their performance.

Overwhelmingly, the reports of participants and observers of the developmental process indicate that the effectiveness of an economist depends upon her ability to grasp the specifics of a situation and to adapt and/or modify the tools she brings so as to make them applicable. The emphasis is upon the facility with which a few relevant tools are applied rather than upon the number of tools brought to the job, or the technical quality of the tools. That is, often the on-the-job performance of broadly educated economists has surpassed that of otherwise comparable economists with superior technical training but less general knowledge. As a result, the contribution of the discipline of economics to economic development is very poorly gauged by the contribution of individuals bearing the title "economist."

In the context of development economics, the weak link of technical training to on-the-job performance is further weakened by ideological disagreements. That is, in this subfield, ideological division—between adherents of laissez-faire and those favoring an active role for the state in guiding economic activity—is far more salient in dividing the economics community than in other branches of the subject. Indeed, the divisions of opinion about the proper paradigm to apply and the associated disagreements about the quality of work performance are such as to create serious dispute as to who should be considered an economist.

SUMMARY

Economics creates institutional facts: that is, it creates concepts associated with measurements that policy makers accept as indicative of one or another aspect of the state of the world. These concepts are rooted in the conceptual framework of the subject, and their interpretation or application to particular situations is considered to lie within the domain of economic expertise.

Economics also contributes substantially to the creation of institutions that perform important functions in banking and finance, especially those operating in international trade. Further, it has played a major role in the creation of rules for the operation of organized exchanges and the conducting of auctions.

By allowing the community of economists to exercise as much authority as it has over these institutions and institutional facts, the larger community of policy makers has given de facto recognition to their expert status and permitted their technical concerns to influence the course of political and economic events in society as a whole. This de facto delegation of authority to economists parallels analogous delegations to (other) scientific communities, but is conditional upon the economics community conforming to the intellectual conventions generally accepted by other such communities.

The delegation of authority to the economics community enables its representatives to function as arbitrators of otherwise intractable disputes. Thus, when a disputed issue can be translated into a dispute about facts

that can best be accessed by means of procedures falling within the economist's domain, disputing parties can—and have—used their expert findings as support for agreements based on the "facts" of the matter. Similarly, as I argued in chapter 9, sometimes cost-benefit studies and other
applications of welfare economics are able to provide what are taken to
be subculturally sanctioned measurements of the effect of events and/or
government actions, already taken or contemplated, upon the general
welfare.

In addition to this, economic ideas add an important ingredient to the
belief structure of the larger community concerning its past, and the possibilities open to it in the future. This contribution is closely related to the
interface of paradigms and ideologies, discussed in chapter 10. In this
chapter and its predecessor I have argued that the contribution of economics to the wider community's belief structure, including what is transmitted through formal education, constitutes a significant part of its total
contribution to society.

The reader will note that in this summary I have not mentioned prediction and control. This is because that aspect of scientific performance,
despite its importance in discussions of scientific method, has played a
minimal role in the contribution of economics to society. This is not to say
that there is no possibility of future achievement in prediction and control: only that there has been a paucity of such achievement in the past.

TWELVE
WHAT IS GOOD ECONOMICS?

L et us begin by recalling Viner's definition of economics—"Economics is what economists do"—and adding a corollary: "Good economics is what good economists do." This corollary is not trivial: it suggests that the quality ascribed to a work depends not on its intrinsic properties but on its authorship. Obviously such a method of quality appraisal is incompatible with any conventional concept of scientific method. Nevertheless, the actual procedures of quality appraisal in economics, and indeed in any science, contain enough elements of deference to authority as to raise serious questions about their propriety.

The most important of these questions concerns the identity of the judges making the quality appraisal. Obviously, in a free society, anyone can make his own judgments on whatever criteria he chooses. But this is not what is meant by the question that constitutes the title of this chapter. As that question suggests, there may be some consensus on the matter: let us inquire into its formation.

Its claim to a monopoly of expertise implies that it is only bona fide members of the economics community who need be included in this consensus. As with physics, chemistry, biology, and the like, good economics is what recognized economists say it is, whenever they speak with one voice. And, despite some diversity of opinion, the generic characteristics of what is considered to be good work are sufficiently clear as to make it possible to describe the dominant view as a consensus. For purposes of discussion I shall consider serious objection to this view to be denial of the (economics) community's claim to expertness, rather than reflective of an alternative standard of quality.

An alternative basis for quality judgments of performance may, however, be found in the societal role of economics as a creator of institutions and institutional facts (as described in chapter 11). Non-economists might—and do—judge contributions to economics in terms of how they improve the performance of its societal functions rather than by the esoteric criteria of the economics culture.[1] As we shall see, these two sets of quality criteria do not coincide. And, because of the economics community's implicit recognition of the need to fulfill its societal functions, the interface of the two sets of criteria is a locus of ongoing debate about the proper characterization of good economics. Let us defer consideration of this debate until later in order to describe the criteria themselves.

These criteria fall under three headings: validity, importance, and intuitive appeal. As their interpretations differ for economists and outsiders, I shall discuss application of these criteria for each audience separately, but with primary attention devoted to those of the culture itself; the eso-teric criteria.

ESOTERIC INTERPRETATION: THE VIEW FROM WITHIN THE CULTURE

Validity

Every intellectual discipline must have some criterion or criteria by which it distinguishes valid statements from invalid ones. In any discipline that claims to be scientific, one major criterion of a statement's validity is that acceptable offers of proof conform with scientific method. While the precise meaning of the term has undergone numerous changes and continues to be a focal point of methodological debate, all definitions of scientific method have two common characteristics: (a) a valid statement must conform with the reported experience of "qualified" observers in circumstances where nonconformity would have been possible, and (b) a valid statement must conform with generally accepted rules of logic and/or mathematics.

Although most economists would agree both that valid statements must conform to the canons of scientific method and that these canons include the above two characteristics, during the past decade this view has been strongly challenged by D. N. McCloskey whose arguments have prompted numerous counterattacks and rejoinders.[2] While McCloskey

---

1. The sharp distinction between "inside" and "outside" opinion applies to large countries—primarily the United States and the United Kingdom—in the period since World War I. In small countries (e.g., Sweden or Australia) and prior to the twentieth century generally, the total number of interested persons was usually too small to justify this bifurcation of opinion.

2. See in particular D. N. McCloskey (1993), which contains an extensive summary of the controversial literature surrounding McCloskey's arguments on behalf of rhetoric as well as an extensive bibliography. Unless otherwise stated, reference to McCloskey's work is restricted to this publication.

does not deny that economics is a science, he insists that, like all sciences, economics employs a variety of rhetorical devices to persuade diverse audiences of the validity of what is being said. In particular, he disputes the propriety of demarcating classes of disciplines (e.g., humanities and sciences) by their conformity with the canons of scientific method. For McCloskey, all disciplines employ a variety of rhetorical devices of which adherence to scientific method is but one.

While accepting this contention, I would add that some rhetorical devices are preferred to others by particular audiences in particular circumstances. The external audience(s) that economics addresses strongly prefer (in fact, will accept nothing other than) arguments that purport to conform with scientific method. Acceptance of the discipline of economics as a source of societally recognized expertise is conditioned upon conformity of the economics community to the same code of validity determining procedures as what is perceived to be followed in other scientific communities. Failure to conform to this code would result in severe criticism that would endanger research support and inhibit recruitment of personnel. Further, the resulting hostility of other sciences would cause a loss of general public confidence that would undercut the status of economics as a source of expertise.[3]

In effect, to use McCloskey's terminology, conforming to canons of scientific method is a condition for effective use of rhetoric in communicating with other scientific communities. Moreover, the proscientific prejudices of the "policy-making class" are such as to make acceptance of the expert status of members of the economics community conditional upon acceptance of its scientific bona fides by other scientific communities.[4] But while McCloskey might accept adherence to scientific method as one type of rhetoric, he would reject the suggestion that observance of any specific

3. What is said of economics applies also, though in varying degree, to all sciences. The societal acceptability of any individual science depends its recognition by the others. However, as was already remarked, some sciences are more vulnerable than others to disapproval by collegial disciplines.

4. Remember that the alleged "proscientific prejudices" of the policy-making class are not shared by the population as a whole, or even by all members of the policy-making class. For example, Associate Justice (of the U.S. Supreme Court) Antonin Scalia recently asserted that the modern world dismisses Christians as fools for holding to their traditional beliefs, and urged Christians to "pray for the courage to endure the scorn of the sophisticated world." Among these traditional beliefs, Scalia explicitly included miracles (*San Francisco Chronicle,* 10 April 1996, p. A3). I take Scalia's "sophisticated world" to be roughly identical with what I term the policy making class.

code of research procedure, or style of exposition should serve as a precondition of validity.

McCloskey's argument has two variants, one general and the other specific. The general argument is a denial of the propriety of using conformity
with any preconceived criterion as a screening device to separate arguments to which one should attend from those which one may ignore. In
taking this stance, McCloskey joins Deconstructionists in a variety of disciplines, notably literary criticism, in rejecting the propriety of giving a
"privileged position" to any particular style of argument. All arguments,
and arguers, must start on an equal footing, with their merits allowed to
emerge from the resulting "conversation." The implication and intention
is to "delegitimize" claims to intellectual authority or expertise from any
source in order to promote an (initial) equality of all proposed ideas.

The difficulty with this position, to which an economist should be especially sensitive, is that it ignores the scarcity of attention.[5] In personal life,
as in the life of an intellectual community, more propositions are presented than it is possible to consider carefully. Consequently, a triage procedure of one kind or another must be established to decide which will
be considered carefully, and which rejected peremptorily. One such basis
of triage is research methodology employed: others are style of argument,
citations made, and personal characteristics of the arguer.

As this plays out in an intellectual discipline like economics, candidates
for scarce boons—journal space, jobs, honors, prizes—are given differential consideration in accordance with the decision maker's method of allocating attention. One way or another, some candidates will receive more
attention than others and this will be perceived as unfair by those who
are unfavored.

But to the decision maker, the procedure chosen is likely to appear
as a matter of efficiency in the allocation of time: efficiency in screening
eliminates no-chance candidates expeditiously, in order to save time for
more careful scrutiny of the rival claims of serious contenders, or for other
useful purposes. From the viewpoint of the decision maker, an efficient
screening procedure must balance the gain from "proper" rejections
against the loss from improper ones. An optimal loss function would reflect both the probabilities of proper and improper rejections, and the loss

5. It is "attention," which has other dimensions as well as time, that is scarce. However,
attention is a difficult notion to pin down, and the reader may without serious error use time
as a proxy for it.

of utility (to the decision maker) associated with each.[6] Only one feature of such a loss function is relevant to the present discussion: how proper rejections are to be distinguished from improper ones.

In the present context, a proper rejection is one that would be made by the decision maker after full examination of the matter. Thus a "perfect" screening procedure would reject all of the candidates that the decision maker would reject after full examination, and none of those that she would have accepted (after full examination). Accordingly, if a decision maker were certain of the validity of her triage procedure, rationality would require that she waste no time examining the case for rejects. However, McCloskey and sympathizers would (properly) object to such a decision-making procedure on the ground that it allows no opportunity for the argument of a candidate to alter the standards of the decision maker. That is, they would (or could) argue that the decision maker should not make up her mind in advance but should remain open to argument, at least on some points and to some degree.

The question then becomes a matter of "to what degree" and "on what points" should her mind be open. On such matters, McCloskey's argument offers no guidance. His general tone—that economists should listen more than they do, both to outsiders and to the heterodox within their own community—would suggest that he would favor a general reduction in the tightness of priors, though his remarks on "positivism" and related ideas suggest that he would be no slower than the next economist to push the reject button on a manuscript presenting the wrong view on an issue that he regarded as settled.

Surely, McCloskey is correct in arguing that an intellectual establishment can be too dismissive of unorthodox ideas. But it is at least as certain that refusing to consider the history of ideas, or the previous contributions of their proposers, in the treatment of new proposals would lead to an intolerable waste of time in sorting them out.[7] Indeed, the potential waste of an "all ideas are created equal" approach to journal editing, or an "all candidates should be treated equally" approach to personnel selection, is so obvious that it is never attempted literally. The practical question is whether the particular compromises between the extremes that any scien-

6. The idea of a statistical decision theory involving minimization of a (utility) loss function was first presented by Abraham Wald (1939). The reader will note the RAP inspiration of this theory.

7. To say nothing of the incentive effects on potential proposers of new ideas.

tific culture—in this case, economics—has adopted could be improved upon.

It is clear that the economics establishment is not, and has not been monolithic. The changes in fashion among once seemingly dominant ideas during the past half century provides evidence aplenty of the openness to challenge of contemporary orthodoxies. To mention a few examples, (1) the rise of Keynesianism in the late 1930s to 1950s, culminating in a period when it was often said "we are all Keynesians now"; (2) beginning in the late 1950s, the rise (or resurrection) of monetarism, and its subsequent partial decline dating from the late 1980s; (3) the revival of Keynesianism (New Keynesianism) in the late 1980s in the wake of policy problems posed by stagflation; (4) the half-century rise of mathematical economics from a position of scorned stepchild to luminary of the realm, alongside a still vocal opposition to its alleged predominance in the culture of the subject; and (5) the substantial amount of attention paid during the past decade to the "rhetorical approach," despite its highly critical attitude toward widely cherished doctrines (aka sacred cows) of economics.

Were it needed, much more evidence could be cited to rebut any across-the-board charge that the economics culture is completely closed to new ideas. But such a charge would be silly and, despite occasional bits of hyperbole to the contrary, I doubt that it is seriously made. What can be justly charged is that this culture has some priors (also known in some quarters as prejudices) on the characteristics of valid and important work, and that these priors operate to the disadvantage of those who ignore or defy them. But whether these priors are too tight, or even have the correct sign, is a matter that can be settled only—if at all—by the future history of the discipline.

Further to debate the general exhortation to greater tolerance and patience with dissenting ideas would be pointless. Such exhortations mainly target the particular screening practices of what is perceived—on the whole, correctly—to be the economics establishment. It is through these practices that the economics subculture distinguishes what it considers to be a valid contribution from what it does not. Let us consider some of these practices.

a. Behavior versus "Talk"

In addition to insistence upon adherence to scientific method, the economics subculture also exhibits a strong preference for observed behavior, as opposed to "talk," as a source of empirical evidence. In deprecating talk (e.g., statements of intention and/or purpose by prospective actors) as evidence for occurrence of the behavior foretold, economists are seeking to model their subject on the procedures of (some) natural sciences, where what is to be explained is the behavior of observable entities such as atomic particles or bits of organic matter. Obviously, such entities cannot communicate their intentions or purposes to human investigators, who are therefore compelled to seek theories that do not rely upon such communications. Even if atoms did begin to speak, it is not clear how the information they provided would alter the structure of physics. But, as it is now constituted, physics would have no way of incorporating whatever atoms might have to say concerning their own behavior.

By contrast, economics is blessed with a rich source of testimony from its elementary units about their own behavior. In adhering to a behavioristic methodology that refuses to use this source of information, economics has voluntarily adopted a restriction that nature imposed on the natural sciences. Although adoption of this laconic restriction was, no doubt, encouraged by the physics-envy that has plagued the economics culture from its inception, its acceptance was not entirely a matter of disciplinary psychopathology.

As we have seen, utilization of testimony is attended by serious difficulties. Often what people say about their intentions and motivations is at variance with what they do: for self-serving reasons, they may lie; they suffer from fallible memories; or they misinterpret questions. Evidence from experiments is compromised by the effect of the language filter on communication between experimenters and subjects.

In economics, however, the behaviorist tropism for the laconic is severely restrained by the need to use records of transactions as a source of evidence: such records can be no more than codified talk. In their preference for recorded behavior as a source of evidence, as opposed to (say) expressions of intention, economists reveal a preference for one kind of talk rather than another, but it does not lessen the vulnerability of their inferences to the frailties of human communication.

Despite the behaviorist vocabulary that some of them affect, and which few eschew explicitly, most economists would not be greatly bothered by learning that the "hard facts" to which they like to point ultimately depend upon talk. When they deprecate "talk" what they are inveighing against use (as evidence) of anecdotes of a small number of individuals selected in an uncontrolled (and usually unspecified) manner, in opposition to a good theory combined with recorded data on specific transactions. Often such anecdotes have been used by sociologists and anthropologists, and by disfavored economists, in lieu of price-quantity data.[8]

While economists differ in their willingness to accord credence to anecdotes, almost all prefer to rely on evidence from reports of price-quantity behavior when it is available. Occasionally, a strong (and desperate) partisan of a particular theory will defy convention and conflate theory with anecdote to reject the apparent verdict of available price-quantity data. However, such a mode of argument is considered methodologically unsound, and those who engage in it lose face within the profession.

Generally, anecdotes about the attitudes or dispositions of other people, especially aggregates of them, are heavily discounted when offered as evidence of behavior.[9] While this negative opinion carries over to responses to questionnaires, economists are compelled to rely on questionnaire responses for behavioral evidence on a variety of matters. A large part of all data on household behavior must be obtained from responses to questionnaires: data on household expenditures, quantities of labor supplied, and changes of household financial position are available only from questionnaires (or, occasionally, from tax returns).

While there is no formal protocol available to guide economists in attaching relative weights to data from different sources, the preferred practices are fairly clear. The closer a data source is to records of resources committed, the better;[10] the less incentive reporters have to misreport, the more reliable are the data; the more specific a question, the more reliable the answer.

b. Conceptual Coherence versus Quantitative Accuracy

Normally the keepers of records have purposes other than providing information for researchers. And often these purposes lead them to process the information that is encoded in the records so as to create a desired impression. Though this is not news to economists—or to any sophisticated user of statistics—it is a matter to which they devote relatively little

8. Such practices are sometimes termed, disparagingly, "man-who econometrics"—a contraction of "I know a man who—."

9. E.g., statements about the "state of opinion," "the general attitude toward price cutting," etc.

10. See the discussion of quasi-forecasting above in chapter 11.

concern.[11] In short, economics is more concerned with avoiding "errors of concept" than those of magnitude, a fact that is reflected in the payoff structure of the culture.[12]

The esteem in which a theory is held varies with the importance of the phenomena it purports to explain. As we have seen, the theories that are held in the highest esteem (and whose creators receive the highest rewards) are not quantitatively precise. Rather they are concerned with the signs of the interrelations among variables and/or, at most, with rough orders of magnitude. Thus, although care to measure accurately is appreciated, it is not considered to be of major importance unless it can be shown to make a difference to a proposition considered to be important. To bring kudos to an economist, making refinements in data must pass the "so what?" test. That is, to gain wide attention among economists, data improvement must invalidate some widely accepted proposition or, less frequently, shore up an important proposition whose empirical support had been under challenge. In making such an achievement, display of technical virtuosity that reflects credit on new or recently developed tools is likely to count for more than meticulous attention to quantitative detail. Even more, "mere" establishment of some facts showing that an accepted proposition is empirically false gains far less renown than a plausible, though unsubstantiated, argument suggesting that an alternative to that proposition might be true. To reiterate Paul Samuelson's remark, "It takes a theory to kill a theory: facts alone will never do it."

The effect of this on the incentive structure of the culture can be imagined readily. What pays off are theories that are robust to variations in empirical details, that is, theories that are resistant to new empirical findings though somehow managing to be (or seeming to be) practically relevant. The result of this is a relatively low valuation of efforts to improve the accuracy of the subject's database, a fact that has caused a lingering stream of unsuccessful complaint.

I venture to describe the rationale of the profession's posture on this issue as follows. In economics we have no prospect of being able to devise theories that can satisfy both the requirements of one or another of our paradigms and yet account for an appreciable part of the variety of empirical phenomena that such theories are called upon to explain. Improving

11. This point has been made in considerable detail by Oskar Morgenstern (1950).

12. An important exception to this statement should be noted. In matters relating to institutional facts for which they are societally responsible (see chapter 11 above) economists are very much concerned with numerical accuracy.

the quality of the data is not likely to improve this situation: indeed, it might be that better data would reveal even greater complexities of behavior than are yet recognized, thereby adding to the burden placed upon theory. Consequently, let us get the "gross facts" as straight as we can, but not worry too much about their details. Instead, let us focus attention on the construction of relatively simple theories that have some prospect of accounting for the gross facts while remaining valid regardless of how the details of these facts turn out.

So conceived, economics has hope of performing its limited societal functions even though its achievements are not comparable with those of the natural sciences where theories imply quantitatively precise predictions. Because of the quantitative precision of their predictions, determination of the validity of theories in the natural sciences requires a degree of care in scrutinizing empirical phenomena that is far greater than what is either possible or useful in economics.

c. Formalism

The obverse side of the economics culture's rather relaxed attitude toward matters of empirical detail is its close attention to fine points of logic. While the discipline has always known discord between "theorists" and "empiricists," the tension between these poles of emphasis has been greatly accentuated since the 1930s. Signaled, if not caused, by the formation of the Econometric Society in 1931, economics has steadily increased the salience of formal consistency as a criterion of validity. In economics, as in any science, logical consistency has always been a necessary condition for validity, but the emphasis upon insuring adherence to its requirements has differed over time and among branches of the subject. While credit has always been given for detection of logical error or ambiguity of meaning, it is only in the past few decades that framing and/or reframing economic theories for the sole purpose of uncovering logical errors or ambiguities, regardless of whether such blemishes had affected or might sometime affect empirical applications, has become an important task for economic theory.

To develop the formal properties of a theory it may not be necessary to use the notation of mathematics or resort to its techniques. But it has been found to be so much easier to use mathematics in such endeavors, and so much easier to avoid logical error if it is employed, that formalism and use of mathematics have become virtually synonymous in the economics culture. In addition to its intrinsic advantages, proper and effective use of mathematics has also helped to establish the scientific standing of economics among other disciplines.[13] Finally, because of its salience in the training process, superior command of mathematics is a source of prestige and status among neophyte economists, giving its possessors a head start in their professional careers and reinforcing belief in the association of mathematical elegance with superior quality of research.

Without gainsaying the above explanation for the ascendance of mathematics within the economics culture, I would suggest that an important additional reason for its present status is the "solidity" of the achievements of the formal branch of the subject as compared with those of the empirical. While the laws established in the natural sciences may not be eternal verities (their validity may be limited to only a small segment of space-time) their range of applicability encompasses the entire span of human experience. Moreover, while the laws of nature are not immune to change as empirical evidence accumulates, it is only rarely that the resulting modifications compel abandonment of previous findings of practical value. Thus, in the attempt to solve its jigsaw puzzle, a natural science receives reinforcement—often a great deal of it—from the application of its empirical findings.

By contrast, the empirical regularities that economics has been able to establish are quantitatively imprecise and restricted to particular decades and countries. Worse yet, the best empirical support that can be mustered on their behalf is very imperfect, and highly vulnerable to the revelations of new data sources. Finally, the few and fragile practical applications of its findings have been highly vulnerable both to theoretical innovation and to new empirical evidence. As a result, the doubts of collective self-worth to which economists are subject are little assuaged by the fruits of empirical research.

These doubts are dispelled more effectively by the achievements of the formal branch of the subject. The mathematical demonstrations of economists are as "solid" as the demonstrations employed in any other science. Moreover, they possess a certain aesthetic appeal, the importance of which should not be underestimated, especially in attracting recruits to the discipline. Even the best empirical work always concludes with wistful references to limitations of data, matters left unexamined, and the like. But a good mathematical demonstration is complete: QED. It satisfies explicit criteria that are carefully prescribed, and its elegance lies in the parsimony with which it performs its task.

13. Also, use of mathematics has alleviated the physics-envy that has long plagued economics.

In their often maligned concern to establish existence theorems, mathematical economists perform the distinctly useful task of demonstrating whether the concepts and relationships embodied in a specified class of models—or in a paradigm—are consistent with a posited equilibrium solution (or time path) and, if not, what changes might be required to make them so.

Since logical consistency is a necessary condition for validity, performance of this task may save research time and effort that would otherwise be spent on attempts to implement logically inadmissible models. A similar economy of effort may be achieved by showing that the assumptions required for (say) the existence of an equilibrium in a given model are intuitively implausible. To the chagrin of the empirically oriented, the professional kudos to those who establish that a widely accepted model has no equilibrium, or that it has one (or several) with specified characteristics, is likely to exceed what is accorded to those who attempt to implement the model empirically, or even to those who originally proposed it, if they had not also provided appropriate formal trimmings.[14]

The effect of this state of affairs is to pose an undesirable antinomy between the criterion of validity and that of importance. The concern of such critics of the "mathematization" of economics as Donald McCloskey (1993, pp. 127–45) and Thomas Mayer (1990) is that excessive concern with establishing the formal validity of a theoretical argument is clogging the channels of communication both within the economics community (i.e., the professional journals) and between that community and the broader public. Presumably, neither McCloskey nor Mayer nor others of their opinion would want to oppose correction of perceived logical errors. What they object to is the creation of elaborate mathematical schemata whose main (sole?) purpose is to uncover logical errors or ambiguities that otherwise would remain undetected. Implicitly, they are arguing that the expected loss of disciplinary payoff from failing to uncover an additional logical error by such means is less than the analogous gain to be expected from enhanced disciplinary attention to empirical investigation, or other desirable objectives, thereby made possible. As the notion of a loss function from logical errors is not well-defined, to say the least, the details of the argument (which I ascribe to them) have not been developed very carefully.

However, it has been noted that successful natural sciences proceed

---

14. This is in addition to the very important role played by formal analysis in the conceptualization and analysis of welfare economics.

without the degree of concern with mathematical conceptualization presently displayed in economics. As both McCloskey and Mayer point out, the mathematical style of economics is more akin to what is cultivated in mathematics departments than to what is used in physics or engineering. An appropriate reply to them would note that in the physical sciences theoretical formulations either receive reinforcement from experimental successes—often quickly—or are abandoned, while economists—often indefinitely—must take such comfort as they can from demonstrations of the logical purity of their constructions.

As will be discussed below this debate on the appropriate attention that economics should bestow upon formal developments of theory has further ramifications for the pedagogical aspect of the subject. For the moment, let me remark that I do not consider it to be the task of this book to resolve this debate.

Importance

In economics, as in any intellectual discipline, validity is a precondition of merit. But once an argument or contribution of any kind is accepted as valid, its worth depends upon its importance. However difficult it may be to determine, once the decision is made, validity is zero-one: importance is a matter of degree. Within economics, the importance of a contribution lies in the extent to which it alters the opinions of members of the community. This might be termed the "influence" of the contribution, but measuring influence is more difficult than naming it.

Influence is a multidimensional concept encompassing number of persons affected, the extent to which the opinion of each is altered, the importance of the individuals affected, the length of time during which the influence is manifested, and so on. The most common measure of disciplinary influence, number of citations listed in a citation index, reflects only some of these indicators, and these very imperfectly. Other indices are even more problematic. To avoid a problem I do not know how to solve, I shall make no attempt to measure influence, but simply discuss a few of the properties that characterize important work.

a. Origination of a Paradigm

If a graduate student were to ask how best to become a famous economist, a fairly safe answer would be, "invent a new paradigm." Unfortunately, this is not easy: negative paradigms aside, the only paradigm created during the twentieth century that has gained wide support has been the Keynesian. Acceptance of this paradigm within the profession was the result, not only of its intrinsic merit, but of the position of its author within the profession and in the larger society and the economic conditions and political atmosphere of the 1930s. Our ambitious graduate student would be well advised not to count on such a favorable conjuncture of circumstances.

While not easy, construction of a negative paradigm is a more promising avenue to fame among economists than construction of a new one from scratch. The recipe is simple: find an empirical phenomenon that is incompatible with a nontrivial implication of RAP and develop the implications of the resulting anomaly. Arguably, the case of increasing returns and "lock in" of an inferior technology, discussed in chapter 7, constitutes such an example. A widely applicable alternative to the assumption of rationality (in the analysis of choice behavior) that could account for the various anomalies discovered at the interface of economics and psychology might constitute another. However, thus far, none of the numerous and continuing attempts at this task has gained wide acceptance within the profession.

Although not constituting paradigms, negative or otherwise, let me offer a few examples of research contributions that I believe to have been widely accepted as "important" within the profession. In this selection I have tried to pick items that have received wide recognition and have made every effort to avoid personal favorites. While all of those included are very important, I have omitted other books and articles that have equal claim to merit. I have attempted to classify the various contributions mentioned by possession of a common characteristic indicated by the title of the subsection in which they are listed.

b. Concept Alteration

Descending from the heights of paradigm invention, we encounter the category of concept alteration. Contributions of this kind do not involve assertions about the world, but propose conceptual changes in the structure of existing paradigms, mainly RAP. I offer three examples.

1. Piero Sraffa (1926) showed, in a brief note, that the Marshallian notion of economies of scale "internal to an industry but external to a firm" was incompatible with the existence of a competitive equilibrium under the maintained hypothesis of rationality of all resource owners. This implied that a competitive equilibrium could not exist in an industry which had a negatively inclined supply curve and led to the abandonment of the assumption of (perfect) competition as the normal state of affairs in an "industry."

2. Albert O. Hirschman (1970) drew attention to the "obvious," but somehow neglected, point that the behavior of a rational individual was often critically affected by whether his best course of action, if aggrieved, was to abandon an affiliation (exit) or to maintain the connection and protest in the hope of rectifying matters (voice). The implications of this dichotomy have affected the manner in which economists regard the relation of principals and agents and the forms of both political and economic organization.

3. In chapter 9, I commented on Kenneth Arrow's impossibility theorem. The purpose and effect of this theorem is to show that the several intuitive notions of fairness and individual rationality underlying the institutions of majority voting may be mutually incompatible where there is more than one voter and more than two candidates (propositions). It is readily perceived that the strictures on voting procedures implied by this theorem also apply to societal choices among alternative possibilities of resource allocation and thus to the entire framework of welfare economics. Consequently the conceptual integrity of that branch of economics was brought into question, and its repair—i.e., finding ways of either avoiding or overcoming the strictures of the impossibility theorem—became a matter of primary importance for anyone concerned with the application of economics to the making of public policy.

The importance of the theorem was enhanced by two "incidental" facts. By its breadth of application—to voting and other procedures of group choice as well as to welfare economics—Arrow's theorem provided a common problem for economics, political science, and philosophy. This common problem has become the subject matter of a new cross-disciplinary subfield: Social Choice.

The substantive result of Arrow's work was greatly enhanced by the manner in which he presented his argument. Arrow established his results by rigorous deduction from a set of axioms, each member of which embodied one of the intuitive requirements of an acceptable mechanism for making social choices. Both its abstractness and the rigor with which the demonstration was performed served to illustrate what might be accomplished by use of advanced (for the time) mathematical techniques.

c. Discovering a Structural Characteristic of the Economy

The importance of the examples described under (b) is not a matter of serious dispute: however, the propositions they assert refer only to the properties of concepts. In this section, I give some examples of contributions that involved assertions about behavior.

1. *The permanent income hypothesis.* This hypothesis is the center-piece of Milton Friedman's (1957) *A Theory of the Consumption Function.* The hypothesis involves both a conceptual innovation and a statement about the structure of the economy. The conceptual innovation concerns the formation of expectations and the relation of expectations to behavior.

Friedman proposed that decision makers be considered as viewing changes in a time series (of prices, quantities or incomes) as consisting of both a permanent and a transitory component. Thus the behavioral response to an observed change in (say) a household's income would vary depending upon whether the change was expected to be "permanent" or "transitory" (i.e., temporary). If the change was expected to be only transitory, the response of consumption would be different, and generally smaller, than if it was expected to be permanent.[15]

The validity of the distinction between permanent and transitory changes in observed magnitudes has been generally accepted and constitutes a significant paradigm adjunct to RAP. In addition, the distinction implied the need for modification of the consumption function of KP. However, the particular applications of the permanent income hypothesis made by Friedman were and are matters of ongoing dispute.

2. *The Phillips curve.* I discussed the Phillips curve in chapter 8.[16] The original relationship discovered by Phillips was soon found to be defective in a number of ways, notably in its failure to take account of the influence of expectations of inflation. However, after augmenting it to take account of such expectations and (sometimes) to exogenously caused increases in total factor productivity, the Phillips curve has continued to play a prominent role in discussions of economic policy for well over a quarter century. That is, when augmented, the Phillips curve has continued to serve as a basis for defining a nonaccelerating inflationary rate of wage increase (NAIRU), which some economists consider a criterion for a sound monetary-fiscal policy.

Although the appropriateness of this policy criterion is a matter of professional debate, the continuing salience of the modified Phillips curve

15. If the change was expected to be partly transitory and partly permanent, the consumption response was hypothesized to be a weighted average of the components. However, the details of the argument are not of concern here.

16. See above, pp. 88–89, 106. As originally presented, the Phillips curve was a simple empirical relationship between levels of unemployment and changes in wage rates: the theoretical underpinnings were provided later by others.

as a focal point of discussion about the attendant issues ensures its place in the history of economic thought.[17]

3. *Technological progress and growth accounting.* Not the least of RAP's intuitive shortcomings is its treatment of technological change. Technological change is a dominant fact of economic life, and any acceptable conceptual organization must somehow permit consideration of its impact upon prices and quantities. But, in its original form, RAP assumed technology to be given: therefore it was necessary either to create an adjunct that enabled the paradigm to accommodate technical change or to leave it irrelevant to a major determinant of the behavior it purported to explain.

Robert M. Solow (1957) proposed such an adjunct. In essence he proposed augmenting the Cobb-Douglas production function by a variable to represent technology. His particular proposal was to represent the level of technology by the antilogarithm of time so that the logarithm of (aggregate) output could be represented as the sum of the weighted regression coefficients of technology (time), labor, and capital. In this framework the coefficient of output on time can be interpreted as an estimate of the effect of technological change on aggregate output, with the quantities of labor and capital held constant.

Solow's initial calculations generated empirical estimates that were neither intuitively unreasonable nor repugnant to RAP, and his simple accommodation of RAP to technical change continues to serve as a point of departure for estimation of the (cet. par.) contribution of technical change to growth of aggregate output. Attempts to improve on Solow's initial contribution have resulted in a substantial cottage industry aimed at allocating credit for economic growth among various "causal factors" such as population growth, growth of the capital stock, and, especially, technological progress. In these exercises in growth accounting, the objective has been to reduce, isolate, and pare down a residual in output growth that persists after imputations to growth of input quantities: a salient part of this residual is designated as technological progress.

Because there is no direct measurement of this variable, its magnitude must be somehow inferred from the tangled intertemporal variations of input and output quantities. The contribution of Solow's article was to provide a framework within which these interrelated quantity variations

17. As evidence for this assertion, see the symposium, "The Natural Rate of Unemployment," in *The Journal of Economic Perspectives* 11, no. 1, (Winter 1997): 3–108.

could be brought into contact with the body of theorems that constitutes the RAP theory of production.[18]

d. Establishing Facts

All of the examples presented in the last section are cases where a conceptual innovation has served as a focal point for empirical research. The examples of this section are cases where it was the empirical research itself that was important. The first of these is not a particular piece of work, but a whole body of research associated with one man: Simon Kuznets. A major part of Kuznets's work was concerned with developing measurements of various aspects of national and international income, production, and wealth. For the present illustrative purpose, selection of any one of a number of his studies would serve equally well.

Although making numerous nontrivial clarifications of concepts and measurement procedures along the way, none of his studies is notable for its contribution to economic theory. Nor is any of them distinguished for achieving, or striving to achieve, a state of perfection in the historical record that would defy efforts to effect further improvement. Rather, in each case, the work was conceived as a foundation for further efforts to fill lacunae to which he drew attention. What makes the totality of Kuznets's work an important contribution to economics is that it provides, first, a set of categories for organizing newly gathered data to supplement what Kuznets had already made available, and second, a set of rough procedures and assumptions for manipulating the new data so as to enable it to be combined with other records to produce a coherent historical picture.

In a nutshell, I would describe Kuznets as a kind of intellectual architect who designed a house with many interconnecting rooms, of which he filled an appreciable number through his own efforts. But without deprecating his own work, it is the architectural aspect of his achievement to which I am drawing attention, that is, his leadership in establishing the field of quantitative economic history.

While Kuznets provided essential tools for the study of economic history and sketched its broad outlines, he did not focus on the details of

18. Almost from the beginning, it was generally recognized that the framework of Solow's model was too simple to capture the essential aspects of technological change, especially the implication that such change is separable from the rate of growth of inputs (for a recent discussion of this point, see Richard Nelson (1997)). However, the discipline's need for the RAP framework has outweighed its concerns about descriptive inadequacy.

any particular aspect or period of history as Robert Fogel and Stanley Engerman (1974) did in *Time on the Cross*. This work provided a new history of slavery in the United States that treated the functioning of the "peculiar institution" as an exercise of economic rationality in an unfamiliar context. Its highly controversial results attracted much attention, both from "cliometricians" and from traditional historians, but the importance of the work for economics stems as much from its methodology as from its substance.[19]

What is essential to the cliometric approach is the intensive gathering of data on prices and quantities, and use of them to infer further facts and relationships among them. The validation of these inferences depends upon acceptance of the economic theory—generally RAP—used in their construction. Traditional economic historians and, a fortiori, general historians did not offer such acceptance, which made *Time on the Cross* a major testing ground for the new methodology. Despite the many quarrels over specific details, economists have generally recognized that the book established the fruitfulness of applying the tools of their trade to issues and materials previously considered beyond their purview. It is this recognition that makes *Time on the Cross* an important contribution to the culture of economics.

e. Where Importance Depends upon Validity

Until the previous subsection, (d), we had distinguished between two reasons for which a contribution to economics might be considered good: validity and importance. But as the discussion just above indicates, this dichotomy is not perfect; some propositions must be valid, if they are to be considered good. This raises, or should raise, a question as to how a proposition could be "good"—i.e., a valuable contribution to the subject—if it were invalid. A valid proposition may be trivial, but how can any proposition be important if it is invalid?

My answer to this question is as follows: a proposition that clearly is false—recognized as such by the overwhelming majority of the profession—is not important. Thus none of the arguments of the "brave army of heretics . . . who, following their intuitions, have preferred to see the

---

19. A good sample of the critical literature on this book is Paul A. David et al. (1976). The term "cliometrics" is the name adopted by a group of younger economic historians who were and are continuing to seek applications in economic history of the concepts and techniques used elsewhere in economics. Fogel and Engerman are among the leaders of this group, and discuss its program in the prologue to *Time on the Cross*.

truth obscurely and imperfectly rather than to maintain error"[20] are important in this sense. However, none of the sample of contributions cited in (c), nor of the population from which they were drawn, have been established as either valid or invalid. Rather, they have served as starting points for a series of successive modifications, most of which are themselves in a similar limbo.

In economics and in the social sciences generally, a significant category of contributions that are of unchallenged importance consists of propositions that are regarded neither as true nor false, but as "seminal ideas," "interesting mistakes," and the like. Such categories do not exist, or are far less salient, in the natural sciences where experiments perform a fairly quick triage on hypotheses, extracting what is considered valid from the rejected remainder. Recognition of its inability to perform in a comparable manner is the key to many of the distinctive features of the culture of economics.

But whatever the differences between economics and a natural science, they are similar in their functions as repositories of societally recognized expertise. And in performing this function, what is demanded is validity not insight. The non-economist is not interested in our "interesting mistakes": she needs correct answers and, whatever her misgivings, she relies upon us to deliver them. Hence in the creation of institutional facts, good economics must be (what is recognized as) valid economics. In measuring changes in the cost of living, good work is characterized by conformity of concept and measurement procedure with consensually accepted standards, and with manifest care for computational accuracy. Thus Edward Denison's (1989) criticism of productivity measurement qualifies as a piece of good economics, despite its lack of theoretical innovation or claim to discovery of a hitherto unperceived structural characteristic of the economy.

The same criteria apply to discoveries of economic trends or other basic characteristics of economies that are presented as "facts" without attempt at theoretical interpretation.[21] The value of such contributions depends upon the verisimilitude of what is alleged to be present in the data and what others later agree was present. Neither the interested public nor the economics profession finds reports of nonexistent trends to be

20. Keynes (1936), p. 371.

21. N.B.: Authors are not always careful, or able, to distinguish sharply between reports of trends and theoretical-speculative attempts to "explain" them. Often it is left to the critic to make the distinction as part of the appraisal of work.

"interesting mistakes": to earn that rubric an offering of fact must come wrapped in a theory.

Intuitive Appeal

As we have seen, economists consider intuitive appeal in evaluating arguments. Often, comments of journal referees or arguments in seminars are studded with remarks like "that argument is not believable." Although the criteria of "believability" are numerous and vague, they are powerful determinants of what a given individual will consider to be good or even acceptable economics. However, as this point has already been argued (in chapter 7), I shall not elaborate further.

EXOTERIC CRITERIA: THE VIEW FROM OUTSIDE THE PROFESSION

Non-economists, too, entertain ideas about economic phenomena and, like economists, they distinguish among them in respect of quality. While in making these distinctions they apply criteria that might be described under the same headings as those used by economists—validity, importance, and intuitive plausibility—their use of these criteria is so different that it would not be helpful to stress the parallelism. For our purpose, the importance of nonprofessional ideas arises from the permeability of the membrane that separates professional from nonprofessional opinion, combined with the concern of professionals about the state of outside opinion.

To nonspecialists, in any field, validity is all-important. Seminal ideas that stimulate research are not their concern: what they want is to "get the facts straight," and have them interpreted so that they can understand them. Their concern with understanding is pragmatic: they wish to understand ideas well enough to make correct decisions when called upon to do so. Understandably and appropriately, laymen are intellectually lazy about details and refinements. They are intolerant of numerical errors that might affect a decision, but impatient with attempts at greater accuracy than their purposes require. Similarly, they are quick to apply a "so what?" test to allegations of logical error or conceptual ambiguity in accepted ideas.

Indeed, to suggest that the layman consciously performs a triage on economic ideas is to exaggerate. More nearly, he accepts the "consensus of the qualified" whenever it can be identified, but otherwise attaches himself to ideas—preferably simple ones—that have been acquired somehow. Often these ideas will be associated with a particular spokesperson whose pronouncements are taken as gospel until events compel reconsideration.

For those non-economists who are relatively more sensitive to currents of ideas than the public at large, for example, practitioners of other social sciences, historians, intellectuals, or public policy wonks generally, unusual turbulence of ideas or research findings within a field may be sufficient to prompt reconsideration of previously accepted "basic notions." But for most people, such reconsideration occurs, if ever, only on the heels of a public catastrophe such as a major depression or a war. Occurrence of such events is likely to involve a change in beliefs about the way in which the world works, and/or has been working, and the identity of trustworthy guides to policy. Catastrophes are, to the non-economist, what a shift of paradigm would be to an economist.

For our purposes, it will be useful to restrict consideration of the views of non-economists to those whom we have identified as being "relatively sensitive" to currents of ideas. Regardless of whether they adhere to a particular economic paradigm, or are eclectic, such persons are not likely to appreciate innovations that are simply clarifications of concepts, or logical refinements. Whether they regard discovery of a structural characteristic of the economy or of a pattern in historical records as important will depend upon its impact on their attitude toward policy, and/or their belief as to how the world works. With rare exceptions they pay little heed to innovations whose impact is confined to the internal culture of economics.[22]

The effect of this difference in quality standards, as between the economics community and outsiders, is reflected most clearly in the differential standing of individual economists within the profession, and outside. The reputations of most economists, even the highly successful, are internal to the culture. Individuals who are widely known to the general public, such as economic journalists, are also well known among economists, but often are held in low esteem. Envy aside, the reason for the lack of esteem is the strong tendency of such "economists" to oversimplify arguments and exaggerate the importance of transitory events either to attract reader attention or (sometimes) in order to advocate particular policy positions. The negative attitude of economists toward their work is reinforced by the unorthodox and/or skimpy training of these interlopers, and (often) by their lack of proper credentials.

---

22. The exceptions are where ideas in other fields are affected by developments in economics. (See below, chapter 14.)

In short, the attitude of the economics community toward those at its fringe is more-or-less typical of any group trying both to protect its turf and to maintain its internal standards. What is of special interest to us are those cases where a member of the community in good—occasionally excellent—standing ventures to go beyond the pale to seek fame and fortune outside. The community's commitment to the general standards of openness common to all scientific communities, together with the ingrained scorn of its membership for guild restrictions, precludes the possibility of formal sanctions upon such individual actions. Nevertheless, writing that presumes to address the general public through nontechnical channels is subjected to careful scrutiny and to severe criticism when found derelict. What is most strongly proscribed is failure to respond to specific technical criticism, formal or empirical, in professionally recognized journals or books, while continuing to advance the challenged line of argument in nonprofessional channels.

The reason for the profession's resentment of such behavior is that it tends to undermine the salience of internal consensus as a criterion for certifying the validity of propositions lying within its domain of expertise. Such resentment is especially strong if the offender has an otherwise strong claim to professional distinction, and is heightened even further if his command of public attention is attributable to extraprofessional factors, especially political connections. Advocates of supply side economics such as Arthur Laffer would constitute a leading example of such economists.[23] Problematically, J. K. Galbraith and many of his admirers might be similarly categorized.[24]

The conflict of quality standards between the economics community and outsiders derives from the insistence of the latter on obtaining clear answers to questions relating to public policy that (most insiders believe) economics is not capable of delivering. Not surprisingly those who offer such answers are given high marks, especially by those who like the answers being offered. The offense to the mores of the economics community lies not in the offer of answers to practical questions, but in the claim that the answers reflect that community's expertise. As we shall see, the issue is rooted in a disagreement about the proper role of the profession in guiding opinion on public policy.

23. On supply side economics, see Krugman, (1994), chapter 3.

24. The problem with placing Galbraith in such a category is the esteem in which he is held by highly respected members of the economics community, including Paul Samuelson and Henry Rosovsky. For an idea of the ambiguous status of Galbraith within the economics community, the reader should consult S. Bowles et al. (1989), especially the preface.

The Formation of Public Opinion

It would be easy to say that, in order to satisfy internal standards of quality, a publication must be directed to a professional audience, and be "technical." But this would be false. Most economists recognize the existence of a professional responsibility to provide sound but nontechnical expositions of economic ideas and relevant facts. Where their standards differ from those of laymen is in the insistence upon "soundness": they will not accept arguments that "get the right answer for the wrong reasons." Typically, the layman places heavy weight on getting the right answer, and is prone to accept as "good" any well-written piece that supports a preconceived notion, and to overlook deficiencies in the supporting argument.

Operationally, the economist's criteria of good work require compatibility both with an accepted paradigm and with relevant facts. Very often, conformity to such criteria inhibits decisive judgment as to the significance of recent events, or the capability of proposed actions to accomplish desired results. This sharply limits the body of work that can both interest the educated public sufficiently to inform it, and still pass muster within the economics community. Nevertheless, there are some examples of work that have had considerable impact on the general public while being well regarded by economists.

Some Examples of Good, though Nontechnical, Economics

Each of the following works has contributed in one way or another to the mind-set of the educated public concerning important trends or events that had bearing on the condition of the economy, and on the possibility for beneficial public action.[25] While each of these has shaped public opinion upon an event or trend that had a significant impact upon the economy, none of them would have been acceptable as a Ph.D. dissertation in economics during the past half century.

1. A. A. Berle and G. C. Means (1932), *The Modern Corporation and Private Property*.

Although it did not invent the image of the "soulless corporation," this book clothed that image in vivid descriptive detail. By exposing the "separation of ownership from control" in American corporations, Berle and Means undermined the fiction that corporate managers were mere

---

25. "Mind-set" is shorthand for beliefs about historical trends, etc. discussed in chapter 11.

agents of dispersed stockholders, and promoted the belief that managers constituted (a major part of) a social network that exercised great influence over both political and economic events.[26] That the nature of this influence was exaggerated and misinterpreted is beside the point, as is the fact that the world they described has changed drastically since (say) 1970. For its time, roughly 1930 to 1965, *The Modern Corporation and Private Property* provided an insight into the sources of political and economic influence (power, if you prefer) that had wide acceptance among the educated public. That its relevance to post-1975 circumstances—where corporate takeovers occur frequently and stockholdings by large investment funds are commonplace—is highly questionable does not detract from its historical significance.

2. J. M. Keynes (1920), *The Economic Consequences of the Peace*

If awards were given for best-ever contribution to economic journalism, this book would be a very strong candidate. It was the result of an almost unique conjuncture of time, situation, and person. Keynes was a highly placed civil servant in the British Treasury who had been a key advisor to Prime Minister Lloyd George at the Versailles peace conference. Disgusted with the political intrigues he there observed, and greatly disturbed by their anticipated economic consequences, he resigned to write a trenchant critique that created a political sensation. It was at once an insider's report on how the treaty was made, and a highly competent economic analysis of its probable consequences. That it was the work of a highly regarded Cambridge don who was also the editor of the *Economic Journal* added both to the book's impact and the size of its audience.

The message of the book—that the reparations clauses of the treaty would severely hamper the process of rebuilding pre-1913 trading and financial relationships among European countries—became part of the "received wisdom" of policy makers both in Britain and throughout the world. It serves as a prime example of what can be accomplished by a talented person of good, broad education with an emphasis on economics, when that is seasoned by practical experience.

The Economic Consequences made no pretense of technical innovation, and some of its arguments on the details of the reparations process were flawed. Moreover, its strength lay in its timeliness. The coming of Adolf Hitler made the book's message irrelevant, and in the perspective of the late twentieth century it appears only as a tract for its time, and an

---

26. The influence of this work on Galbraith's view of economics is obvious.

incident in the career of a great economist. Although not a significant part of the culture of economics, it stands as a shining example of what economics can contribute to the general culture.

3. Gunnar Myrdal (1944), *An American Dilemma*

Before 1940, the literature on the general social condition of American blacks was scattered and lacking in a central focus; material on their economic condition was sparse. To ameliorate the resulting ignorance, and to focus public attention on some woefully neglected social problems, the Rockefeller Foundation launched a major research project. To avoid distortions of perspective that might result from closeness to the problem, the Foundation selected a non-American to head it.

Ignoring conventional disciplinary boundaries, they chose a Swedish economist, Gunnar Myrdal, to lead a project that drew more from, and had greater impact upon, sociology than upon economics. Nevertheless *An American Dilemma,* the major work that resulted from this project, was heavily concerned with the economic aspects of the situation of American blacks.

An American Dilemma offered no contribution to technical economics and its empirical work was more nearly a task of organizing, updating, and interpreting material from previous studies than of original research. Nevertheless, and despite the distraction caused by World War II, the overview of the socioeconomic conditions of American blacks that the book presented created a perception that became the common property of the educated American public. As such it served as the intellectual starting point for the Civil Rights Movement of the 1950s and 60s, as well as of the subsequent burst of research on its subject matter.

Like the other works in this list, *Dilemma* represents neither a contribution to a reading list for graduate students nor a classic for the ages. However, it did provide an important component of the intellectual baggage carried by an educated American in the middle of the twentieth century.

Some Reflections on the Diverse Criteria of Quality

Historians of thought and devotees of the exoteric criteria of quality are sometimes given to nostalgic longings for the days of giants such as Smith, Ricardo, Malthus, the Mills, and, for some, Marx. These heroes of thought contributed both to the technical development of their subject and to the general culture of society. Among the historians, the more perceptive recognize that it is the specialization and concomitant professionalization of the subject that has been responsible for the creation of the two sets of criteria, and often express regret at the mutual alienation that this reflects. Clearly, it would be a great achievement for an economic work to satisfy both the esoteric and the exoteric standards of quality, but—with the possible exception of *The General Theory*—none has.

The reason for this divergence of standards is the paradigm orientation of research in any science, including economics. To satisfy the esoteric criteria of quality, research must be oriented toward some paradigm which makes it very difficult to comprehend its significance without first understanding the paradigm. By the same token, to satisfy the exoteric criteria of quality research must avoid orientation toward a paradigm: but if this is done, the bearing of the research on a relevant paradigm will be unclear and its esoteric quality obscured. Thus, most economists must choose between one audience and the other. During the twentieth century, during which esoteric criteria developed and became distinct from the exoteric, I would judge that only two economists have managed to meet both sets of standards: Keynes and Milton Friedman.

A Brief Remark on the History of Economic Thought

At least since Kuhn remarked on the matter, it has been recognized that typically practitioners of a science have had little interest in the history of its development. Seventy-five years ago this statement would probably not have applied to economics, but since then economics has moved increasingly toward the modal pattern. Few economists would find this a matter for concern: to the extent that they are even aware of the trend, many would consider it to be but one aspect of the approach of their subject to the status of a mature science, and therefore approve of it. Although there is a continuing low level of interest in this topic sufficient to keep it in most graduate curricula, the topic is rarely considered to be of sufficient importance as to make it a degree requirement, and courses in it are never considered to be a major addition to the CV of a newly minted Ph.D.[27]

Disproportionately, it is left to the small minority of economists[28] who are devotees of dogmengeschicte to preserve the traditions of their culture. A few of these make this work their primary task, and they are joined by a somewhat larger number of part-timers—often of great professional stature but with a tendency to be long in the tooth—with a proclivity for

27. For a good recent discussion of the place of history of economic thought in the economics culture see Barber (1997).

28. Of which I would consider myself to be a member.

finding their own precursors. Within the culture, the fruit of this work is judged by the canons of conventional scholarship with special attention to technical proficiency. It is esteemed, but not considered the sort of work which one would recommend to her most promising graduate student.[29] As a result, and with regret, I have come to consider this aspect of the culture of economics to be of secondary importance to the argument of the book and to defer discussion of it to another occasion.

Teaching: The Creation of Opinion

Save for the brief introductory remarks in chapter 1, I have ignored a salient part of the culture of economics: the fact that a very large fraction of its members are, or have been, college teachers of the subject. This fraction includes almost all of the major contributors to the technical literature that is the primary focus of this book. In view of this, it would be very surprising if the esoteric criteria of quality did not somehow reflect the desiderata of the pedagogical process. However, such reflection is not easily reconciled with the quality standards of a scientific community.

In the natural sciences and in mathematics, the "substance" of a contribution and the date of its "creation" are all that are (supposed to be) relevant to appraisal of its quality. While facility of expression is recognized as desirable, in the distribution of kudos it is given distinctly less weight than substance and priority.

In idealized form, a research contribution is a report of a scientific discovery. Clarity of the reporting instrument is zero-one: either the report is judged to be clear enough to enable the claimed discovery to be replicated or otherwise substantiated, or the report is rejected as invalid. In practice, journal editors and/or colleagues readily assist in bringing the exposition of an otherwise valid contribution up to minimal standards of comprehensibility.[30]

In this hierarchy of research virtues there is no place reserved for qual-

29. For reinforcement of my perception of the dominant attitude of economists toward research in the history of their subject see Jacob Viner (1991). Viner, himself, was one of the great students of the subject.

30. Priority is determined by date of submission for publication, and is intended to distinguish "true discoverers" from imitators and/or plagiarists. To avoid disputes about priority arising from submissions to different journals, and to the vicissitudes of the refereeing process, many journals accompany publication of an article with a notice indicating its date of submission. This practice, which is standard in journals of mathematics and natural science, has been adopted by (some) economics journals only within the past twenty years or so, and may be taken as one indication of both an increased desire to conform to the practices of other sciences, and of a felt need for doing so.

ity of exposition. However, generally the members of scientific communities are highly educated people of conventional tastes. Among these is appreciation of good literary style and expository lucidity. Thus, often an unusually well-written research paper will receive an extra measure of praise from referees and book reviewers. While this may not count for much in the evaluation of submitted research papers, it is of considerable weight in appraising papers that survey or summarize a field, and is of even greater importance in appraising a textbook.

Although quality of exposition achieves its greatest salience in the writing of textbooks, it also has considerable importance in the presentation of new findings or techniques to the wider professional audience that is not directly engaged in using them.[31] An advanced expository text, not sharply distinguished from a treatise, has its greatest opportunity to contribute to the culture of a science in the period immediately after the initial publication of a major technical innovation. Thus the reputation of Sir John Hicks was greatly enhanced by his expository skill, most notably displayed in *Value and Capital* (1939) and in his famous IS-LM paper (Hicks 1937).

While McCloskey is surely correct in arguing that expository skill (a species of rhetoric) is used in all sciences, it is more salient in economics than in most others. This is because of the importance of conformity to a paradigm (mainly RAP) in establishing the validity of an argument. Though a natural science experiment does not "speak for itself," a careful account of how it was conducted goes a long way to persuading the relevant community of its validity: but this is much less the case in economics.

In economics, much of the weight of an argument rests on a showing that the reported behavior can be plausibly regarded as emerging from attempts at suitably constrained maximizing by the actors involved. Because of this, publications in a subfield of economics consist of otherwise disparate research reports, the validity of each depending critically upon its relation to a unifying principle. Hence the exposition of such principles (e.g., paradigms) and the ancillary procedures necessary to establish the validity of a proposed application becomes the essence of instruction in research.

However designated, in giving such instruction a research manual is a useful if not an essential tool. While many teachers prefer to construct

31. Thus both *The Journal of Economic Literature* and *The Journal of Economic Perspectives* (official publications of the American Economic Association) are primarily directed to publication of expository pieces for a professional audience, rather than original research contributions.

their own manuals, not all have the time or capability of doing so: hence the textbook. The utility of a textbook obviously depends upon the expository skill with which it is written: this is especially true where the course instructor is not the author. In this context, expository skill resides more in clarity and organization than in stylistic elegance. Keynes's epigrams conveyed both pleasure and insight, but it has never been suggested that *The General Theory* is a good textbook.

In principle, even a very good textbook should not gain great professional kudos for its author. And, in practice, it rarely does: typically, in addition to his royalties, the author of a successful textbook gains a reputation for being a good expositor, but this virtue is held to be distinctly inferior to being a producer of seminal ideas. Nevertheless, a textbook sometimes serves as the locus classicus of ideas and techniques which are original to the author, or to which the author has a colorable claim, with the result that the text becomes a "treatise," and its author a "leading authority," reflecting some combination of expository skill and research performance.

This blurring of the distinction between research inventiveness and skill in presenting its fruits is much more marked in economics and other social sciences than in the natural sciences, and is attributable to the importance attached to establishing an explicit relation of applied work to theoretical foundations, as discussed above. In the ethos of science, the distinction between the content of a theory or proposition and its vehicle of communication is sharp and, despite marginal problems, largely defensible in the natural sciences. But in economics, as the status of textbooks and their authors reminds us, the distinction is less sharp.

In economics the emphasis upon theoretical argument is related to the occupational composition of the members of its community. The main source of employment for economists is in the teaching of the subject, a fact that should—and does—influence the way in which they are trained. Though not usually recognized, the typical graduate curriculum is fashioned as much by concern with transmission of the correct style for presenting research findings as by desire to teach the technique of research. While economists are not instructed in how to teach, they are taught what they should teach. They are taught that they should present the subject matter of research as an economic problem susceptible to analysis by application of an appropriate paradigm, usually RAP.[32]

---

32. That insufficient attention is paid in graduate economics programs to the acquisition of teaching skills is an old and valid complaint, but I shall refrain from discussing it.

So viewed, a good graduate or advanced undergraduate textbook is one that expresses and applies the quality criteria of the esoteric culture. But the more important, and lucrative, market for textbooks is at the undergraduate level, especially in the beginning course in the subject. Here, the values of the esoteric culture collide with those of the exoteric culture. Judged by esoteric standards, a good undergraduate text or course is one in which students are taught the criteria for distinguishing valid research and/or reports of it that may be taken as credible from research with the opposite properties. To accomplish this, it is necessary somehow to provide the student, not only with an analytical apparatus, but also with a conceptual organization and related material that describe a real economy.

Here is where exoteric values enter: whatever its other virtues, a good text must arouse and maintain the interest of the student. To this end, the arts of exposition must be employed successfully, which generates obvious tension between the desiderata of simplicity and validity. But serious though this problem is for a textbook writer, it is less important for our argument than the problem of selecting a conceptual organization.

From the exoteric viewpoint, the principal quality of a text lies in the view it imparts of how the world works. For example, the functioning of an economy will appear very different if it is described as subject to marked fluctuations of aggregate output resulting from exogenous fluctuations in private investment regardless of the behavior of the money supply (Keynesian image) rather than as a collection of industries where adjustments of relative prices hold aggregate output more or less steady despite fluctuations in the outputs of individual industries, if only the money supply is kept on a proper course (monetarist/laissez-faire image).

From an exoteric standpoint, conveyance of a proper image of the economy outweighs almost any other virtue, or vice, that a textbook may possess. Although they would concede that it is better to be right for the right reasons, for exponents of the exoteric virtues being right takes precedence over the rationalization offered for being so. By contrast, in the esoteric culture it would be irresponsible, if not downright immoral, knowingly to use an invalid argument to make a valid point.[33] This conflict of values creates continuing problems for textbook writers and course designers.

Instructors who like the conceptual organization conveyed by a partic-

---

33. Such behavior would involve, inter alia, violation of the implicit trust placed in the expertise of a scientific community by the larger community.

ular text will be inclined to overlook or minimize the importance of skimpiness or sloppiness on matters that they consider to be of secondary importance. Conversely, those who dislike that conceptual organization will find the skimpiness of treatment—which is likely to be on matters that *they* consider to be of great importance—serves to convey a hopelessly unrealistic view of the economy that will cause students gravely to misunderstand how the world works, and how it might be improved. Thus, in conflicts about textbook adoptions both sides are in effect expressing concern with the contribution of the course to the formation of general (i.e., nonprofessional) opinion on economic matters.

This concern is very proper: it is in the teaching of their subject to undergraduates that economists exert most of such influence as they may have on the formation of public opinion. However, conflict over conceptual organizations is not the only source of disagreement about the teaching of economics.

The complaint discussed above about excessive concern with mathematical refinements, both in textbooks and journal articles, is also involved. As I interpret it, this conflict is as much about the salience of technical refinement in the distribution of prestige within the culture as it is about the use of mathematics itself. Mathematics enters the conflict because concern with technical issues is highly correlated with the use of mathematical tools—both in economic theory and econometrics—the employment of which is regarded as essential to their resolution. Those who deplore the salience of technical refinement are really urging that more of the loaves, fishes, and kudos at the disposal of the economics community should be directed toward those concerned with forming the economic opinions of non-economists, and less to those whose achievements can be appreciated only by those within the trade.

CONCLUSION: GOOD ECONOMICS AND USEFUL ECONOMICS

One of the main lessons of this chapter and its predecessor is that in economics there is no simple relation between the good and the useful. The culture of the subject and the nature of its subject matter combine to place great weight on logical refinement as a criterion of research quality. The principal reason for this is that it is much easier to ascertain the validity of a formal argument than of one that purports to explain empirical phenomena. But, unfortunately, many of the technical refinements that are highly esteemed within the economics culture make no direct contribution to fulfilling the social function of the economics community.

Nevertheless, there is a wide variety of empirical studies that have been recognized as "good" (e.g., by prize awards to their authors) because of the value of their conclusions either to the making of public policy or to the functioning of institutions that are in some way dependent upon the input of economics.

Yet a third type of good economics consists of teaching the subject properly, including the writing of textbooks that facilitate the teaching process. The teaching of economics, primarily at the college level, makes a major contribution to the creation of the informed public opinion that is a major source of the societal demand for economic expertise.

PRIZES, ESTABLISHMENTS, AND HEROES

A s is the case in other communities, the culture of a science is much concerned with the deeds of heroes. The deeds for which its heroes are renowned, and the qualities held to be exhibited in their doing, tell us much about the history and aspirations of a society, as well as the behavior it holds to be valuable and worthy of encouragement. By definition, heroes have high status: major status symbols for scientific heroes are receipt of a prize, an honorary degree, or membership in an honorary society.

Although in a general way emoluments are positively correlated with scientific status, the relationship is sufficiently loose that an important rationale for accompanying the award of a prize with a cash payment is to lessen the disparity of financial rewards of those successful in science or (some of) the arts with those who succeed in activities more strongly oriented toward the pecuniary.[1] Regardless of the relation of fame and riches among scientists, discussing the details of their monetary rewards would throw little light upon their activities or upon the culture in which they operate. Accordingly I shall speak of prizes, and the heroes who receive them, without much attention to the pecuniary rewards that are occasional by-products of scientific recognition.

The awarding of a prize implies the existence of a decision-making mechanism that selects its recipients. Typically, the decision is made by a committee—rarely, if ever, by an individual—the membership of which is appointed by an individual or by yet another committee chosen by the donor of the prize. Although it may be alienated, the ultimate power of appointment necessarily rests with the donor: alienation does not obliterate the appointment power, but merely transfers its locus.

---

1. Although some scientists and artists do extremely well financially, it is widely perceived that many scientific and artistic achievements of great social value receive relatively little pecuniary reward—because of the inappropriability of their product—and that it is important that this be rectified, so far as possible. The rationale for giving prizes for some kinds of outstanding performance, but not for others, is discussed at some length in William J. Goode (1978), chapter 7.

Only rarely is the power to make awards exerted directly by the donor. Generally, donors are anxious that the prizes they establish—which are often eponymous—should appear to be merited, and not an expression of personal favor. Although other reasons may be adduced to explain this tradition, for the present purpose a genetic explanation will suffice. Early prizes were awards made by the sovereign to acknowledge valuable services (to the crown) and to inspire more of them. By establishing the prize the sovereign attracted favorable personal attention as a patron-connoisseur and, in granting recipients of the prize recognition by the ultimate source of secular power, legitimized their own claims to preeminence.

With rare exceptions, kings neither pretended to extensive personal knowledge in the arts or sciences, nor needed it. What they sought was to make their courts, and more generally their realms, renowned as places where these things were appreciated. Consequently, in making awards they sought the advice of those recognized—in other courts—as qualified connoisseurs, and took pains to make known the identity of their advisors.

But how does an individual become identified as a qualified connoisseur? Obviously, by being recognized as such by other qualified connoisseurs. If this were the sole source of identification, however, the answer to the question would immediately degenerate into a chicken-and-egg problem. Fortunately, it is not our task to explore the many possible ways in which a self-confirming elite gets established, or identifies new members. For our purposes it is enough to note that such connoisseurial elites somehow get established, and consider the consequences of their existence.

Typically, in a precapitalist society patronage of the sovereign was the criterion for elite status. And to the present, elites welcome the reenforcement of their legitimacy that such patronage provides (e.g., presidential or congressional prizes and medals). However, symptomatic of the multiple sources of prestige in a modern Western democracy, patronage by a sovereign or sovereign surrogate is no longer essential to the prestige of an award.

The awards of private foundations or committees, established by wealthy individuals, often stand alone as sources of recognition, though their ability to do so depends upon the membership of the selection committees. In order for a prize to command prestige within a scientific field, its selection committee must include recognized experts from within the relevant community. And, indeed, some of the most prestigious scientific awards are those sponsored by the professional associations of the relevant scientific communities.

Although awards for scientific performance have a variety of sponsors, with rare exceptions they all reflect the criteria of a single professional establishment. This establishment has a symbiotic relation with the state, the (law) courts, and other loci of prestige and authority: for example, when a government agency wants scientific advice, it must seek it from a recognized member of the relevant scientific community on pain of being condemned for acting on incompetent advice. Conversely, recognition of a scientific community's monopoly of expertise in a given field by an external locus of power enhances the prestige conferred by membership in that community.

The force with which the remarks in the previous paragraph apply increases with the strength of the internal consensus on matters considered to be important. While no scientific community is monolithic in its beliefs, some more nearly approach this pole than others. Physics, chemistry, and biology would be nearest the unanimity pole, while (perhaps) sociology, anthropology, and political science would be closest to the opposite. Economics would be somewhere in the middle. The question is how to characterize the consensus that obtains in fields like economics where there are obvious disagreements about matters recognized to be important.

Despite sharp disagreements among the adherents of conflicting paradigms, the economics establishment accepts most, though not all, of the disputants. Even more, there is considerable agreement within the establishment as to the relative professional standing of its various members. (Such agreement sometimes puzzles practitioners of other social sciences where the consensus is much weaker.)[2] The bases for this consensus are of two sorts: doctrinal and institutional.

THE DOCTRINAL BASIS FOR CONSENSUS

As we have seen, the various paradigms having currency within the field of economics are not in conflict at all points of the terrain. There are substantial areas where their respective tenets do not conflict, and are often in explicit agreement. Thus, an economist who achieves recognition for a contribution to one of the uncontested areas normally is recognized as a "competent economist" or better—depending upon the magnitude

2. For an interesting illustration of this difference among the social sciences see George J. Stigler (1988), p. 86.

of her contributions—even among economists who dissent strongly from a particular paradigm which she advocates. For example, many of the early Keynesians, for example, Joan Robinson, Lerner, Kahn, Hicks, Lange, Kaldor, had made substantial contributions to price theory (RAP) and were recognized as "more than competent" members of the trade.

Though it does not depend upon it, this notion of an "uncontested area" within economics is strongly supported by the dominant position of RAP. For the past half century, every candidate for an advanced degree in economics has been required to learn a substantial amount of price theory and, increasingly, to apply it in his research as a mark of professional competence. Because of the near ubiquity of this requirement, mastery of price theory displayed in either theoretical or applied research is widely appreciated within the profession and serves as a litmus test for expertise.

Although somewhat less emphasized than price theory, econometric tools increasingly have become part of the analytical equipment required of professional economists. Accordingly, skill in the use of such tools is appreciated across the whole of the profession and its possession serves as a second basis for determining expertise. As both techniques (price theory and econometrics) are greatly dependent upon mathematical skill, their possession is highly correlated among economists and bears much of the responsibility for the emphasis placed on mathematical competence in training programs.

Yet a third basis for ascription of professional expertise is detailed knowledge of empirical materials useful in research. As the range of such materials is very wide, covering all of recorded history over all of the planet, no one scholar can be expected to know much about more than a very small fraction of the total. Hence there is little commonality of expertise, and recognition of experts about unfamiliar parts of the economic universe is accordingly difficult. In practice, attainment of expert status because of empirical knowledge comes by the "route of citation." Individuals whose work is cited as a source of empirical information used in research that displays noticeable expertise thereby gain recognition as experts. The degree of recognition, of course, varies with the frequency of such citations, the width of the field within such citations are made, and the degree of dependence of the citator's research upon the work cited.

The route of citation to professional recognition is not confined to empirical scholars, but is also used by economists whose claim to expertise rests upon their command of technical skill (i.e., theorists and econometricians). Indeed, citations are an important trace of professional reputation and evidence of the extent of a scientist's recognition by his peers within his profession. Accordingly, economists (like other scientists) are jealous of the quantity and quality of their citations and are gravely offended by failure to cite their work on an occasion that they consider appropriate.

Citation is a vehicle by which members of a scientific community extend recognition to the work of others in the community. Usually the reason for such recognition is the contribution made by the work cited to the research of the citer.[3] Although there is no generally applicable criterion for determining what may be considered as a contribution, establishment of new propositions in price theory or econometrics are leading examples. Such establishment may require—or at least provide an occasion—for recognition of an economist who adheres to a paradigm rejected by the citer. Thus, frequently, the work of Joan Robinson in price theory was cited approvingly by economists who would reject her Keynesianism and/ or her quasi Marxism. In similar fashion economists who would reject James Tobin's Keynesian views on monetary theory acknowledge (and make use of) his contribution to the statistical analysis of discontinuous variables, commonly termed Tobit. Again, economists who reject Milton Friedman's approach to monetary theory accept the importance of the distinction he introduced between permanent and transitory magnitudes.

It might well be asked what views would cause someone who writes on economic matters to be excluded from the economics establishment. While a categorical answer cannot be given—the banishment criteria differ from one part of the establishment to another and have changed over time—some illustrative examples might help.

Typically, cranks—especially monetary cranks—are excluded. Though the criteria for crankiness have shifted with the winds of admissible doctrine (consider Keynes's [1936, pp. 353–71] favorable remarks on "heretics" like Gesell, Hobson, and Major Douglas) exponents of ideas that attribute power to effect important changes in the behavior of real variables to specific institutional changes in the determinants of the supply of money are strong candidates for the label of crank. Unless excused by a display of technical skill or an institutional connection, Marxists have

3. Of course, citations can be negative, as when the citer comments adversely on the validity of the work cited. Nevertheless, even an adverse citation may serve as a backhanded recognition of the membership of the cited author in the scientific community: the reason for an adverse citation is to warn the audience against being misled, implying that the argument under attack has received some currency, and might have been sufficiently persuasive as to have the capability of misleading.

generally been excluded from the establishment. Similarly, barring countervailing considerations, adherents of Henry George's Single tax Doctrine or the ideas of Technocracy would be excluded.

In general, because of the plurality—and occasional inconsistency— of the paradigms accepted by impeccably credentialed members of their establishment, economists cannot be as rigid as (say) physicists in designating ideas as unsound or unscientific, thereby excluding them from consideration. For example, at present, the scientific credentials of "supply siders" are under vigorous attack by some members of the economics establishment.[4] While I consider the arguments of the supply side opponents to be very persuasive, their rhetorical style is noticeably different from that of members of a natural science establishment engaged in rejecting an unsound proposition; the latter will simply cite accepted laws or principles and show that the offending proposition is incompatible with them.

But the critics of supply-side economics do not proceed in this manner: instead they argue that the supply siders are advancing propositions that all competent members of the establishment reject—even those who agree with the supply siders' policy recommendations.[5] The reason for the rhetorical style of economists in situations such as this is the absence of applicable "laws" that are well established. It is this absence that compels resort to arguments of the form "even Milton Friedman would agree that—." (It should be observed that resort to this form of argument confers status recognition upon the cited individual from dissenting professional peers.)

To say the same thing differently, the continuing coexistence of conflicting paradigms reflects a failure of any of them to solve a common problem, or problems. But attempts of researchers operating from different paradigms to find a solution to what is recognized as a common problem generates cross-paradigmatic recognitions of skill and scientific competence that serve as an important basis for identifying and ranking members of a disciplinary establishment.

THE INSTITUTIONAL BASIS FOR CONSENSUS

While an individual may be recognized as a member of a scientific establishment by virtue of her contributions to the field, such recognition is normally reinforced by an institutional identification. Typically, such iden-

4. See Krugman (1994), chapter 3.
5. See Krugman (1994), especially pp. 89–95.

tification is provided by membership of the faculty of a college or university, or appointment to a recognized research institute, but it can also be provided by a high-ranking civil service appointment.

Although the institutional and doctrinal bases of professional recognition are supposed to be complementary, they can and have served as substitutes. Thus if someone were to challenge the credentials of a putative member of the establishment with "what has he ever written?," an answer satisfactory to the general public and to part of the establishment would be, "he is a professor at X university." The possibility of such a dialogue is well recognized, and much lamented, in scientific circles.

A related but less stringent requirement for establishment membership is possession of a higher degree from a recognized training center. In economics, this degree is usually a Ph.D. from a recognized university.[6] Receipt of an advanced degree is supposed to indicate a command of basic analytical tools (notably price theory and econometrics), and completion of a dissertation normally consisting of an article or two of sufficiently high quality as to be publishable in a technical journal. Obviously, the quality of technical skill varies substantially even among a given cohort of degree recipients of a specific training institution and, moreover, technical skill is subject to a fairly rapid rate of decay. Consequently, at any given time there is substantial variation in the technical proficiency of accepted members of the establishment, that is, among recognized experts.

Nevertheless, it is generally agreed that receipt of a Ph.D. from a reputable institution should be indicative of a (fairly high) minimum level of professional competence as demonstrated by performance on examinations and in the writing of a dissertation. While there are quarrels as to how high this required minimum should be set, and about what its components should include, there is sufficient agreement—especially among the large producers of Ph.D.s—as to permit entry of the graduates of all recognized training institutions into a national market (for positions in college teaching, research, and civil service) in which they are judged on their individual merits, but into which a non-Ph.D. finds it very difficult to enter.[7]

The content of the minimum level of training constitutes a major part of the culture that distinguishes economists from others. However, as this

6. This remark refers to the United States. The criterion in foreign countries varies, though the American model is spreading.

7. At the highest levels of research, this market is international rather than national, but that does not matter in this context.

content has undergone continuous change, there are distinguishing generational and even cohort characteristics reflected in the graduates of a single institution. And there are cultural differences among contemporaneous graduates of different institutions, e.g., between Harvard Ph.D.s and those of the University of Chicago. Though such differences are associated with differences of paradigms accepted, or at least seriously studied, the relationship between paradigm(s) of adherence and either date of degree or granting institution is very imprecise—and not germane to our purpose.

THE CHARACTERISTICS OF AN ESTABLISHMENT ECONOMIST

In the various fields of applied economics, detailed knowledge of relevant institutions, history, technical conditions of production, consumption, and transaction are highly regarded and even considered essential for expert status. However, the possessors of such knowledge are appreciated only within the confines of their relatively narrow subspecialty and, unless they receive a major award or a chair at a leading institution, remain largely unknown to most members of the profession.

The technical skills or contributions for which an economist gains renown throughout the culture are those in fields with which all economists are familiar: economic theory and econometrics. A major component of the doctoral examinations (prelims) that all degree candidates must pass are in economic theory (with heavy emphasis on price theory) and in econometrics. Unusual facility or ingenuity in utilizing the required techniques is widely appreciated both aesthetically and because of its instrumental value. It might be remarked that aesthetic appreciation of skill that is specific to a particular discipline is common among developed sciences, and serves as an indicator of proper training. Indeed, the presence of aesthetic criteria in the culture of a discipline serves as a support for its claim to scientific status.

The wide appreciation—within the profession—of technical virtuosity accounts for the status accorded to pure theory. It also explains the characteristics of contributions to "applied" fields (e.g., international trade, finance, or labor) that are considered to be outstanding. While substantive findings are valued, they are far more appreciated when they are rationalized (i.e., reconciled with a paradigm) by an ingenious application of existing theory or, even more, if a theoretical innovation can be shown to have suggested the findings and to have inspired the ancillary research.

Conversely, if unaccompanied by an acceptable theoretical rationale, substantive findings are unappreciated or even resisted. Resistance is especially likely if the findings appear to conflict with an accepted paradigm. Consequently, seekers of discipline-wide acclaim tend to stress the theoretical implications of their research and to take great pains with its formal underpinning. As I have argued throughout the book, the paucity of substantive empirical results in economics has led to the assignment of much heavier relative weight to theoretical elaboration than is customary in natural sciences.

Skill in theoretical elaboration, either of a set of axioms or of a rationale for empirical findings, is largely an extension of the technical skills imbued and displayed in doctoral training programs. Thus unusual technical facility is noted by teachers and fellow students alike fairly early in the training process, and those possessing it acquire professionwide renown at an early stage of their careers, sometimes before publication of any research. This is especially the case among students at leading training-research institutions.

Early manifestation of technical facility in economic theory is closely associated with mathematical aptitude; a fact of great importance for the culture of economics. This fact influences the choice of field for graduate training among college seniors. As presently constituted, economics has a great attraction for students with a taste and aptitude for mathematics, and much less appeal to those whose interest lies in art, literature, or history, or to those interested in careers involving direct service to a clientele, such as law or medicine, or in the public service. This biases the pool of applicants from which the graduate student body is drawn. Similarly, it biases the kind of curriculum, and style of presentation, that will be well-received by students. Students are sought who like formal, structured, and logically tight expositions and who deprecate courses and materials that fail to manifest these desiderata. The effect of such biases on the interests and characteristics desired of faculty recruits can be readily imagined.

This is not to suggest that the primary interest of all, or even of most, graduate students in economics is in formal theory. The demands of society for economic research on problems of practical interest generate a derived demand for economists trained to do such research and, in yet a further derivation, for (graduate) programs to provide such training. However, from early in the training program, the first class members of the culture are those with theoretical skill. Even those who are bent on careers in applied work find it essential to demonstrate theoretical competence, the more the better, while the many whose interests are not sharply focused are exposed to the full pressure of a cultural environment in which there is a hierarchy of talents with theoretical capability occupying the highest rank.

MATHEMATICS AND THEORETICAL COMPETENCE

Even in the mid-1990s, theoretical talent is not identical with mathematical facility, but the confluence of the two is far closer now than it was a half century ago. In the mid-1990s, command of a fair amount of mathematics—for example, differential calculus sufficient to cope with problems involving constrained maximization, integral calculus adequate for the statistics ancillary to econometrics, and the linear algebra required for either—is common among economists under (say) 40 years of age. The fact that such knowledge is widespread greatly influences the style of communication within the profession, and its hierarchies of prestige and reward. In this section I will attempt to describe the development of this state of affairs.

While there is no difficulty in finding traces of mathematical ideas in the writing of classical economists, before 1871 explicit mathematical formulations were very rare. Even after that date the accumulation of a literature of mathematical economics was slow, mainly related to the formulation of various aspects of RAP, and generally considered to be an esoteric development. Even where available, courses in mathematical economics were taken by very few aspiring economists and were not considered essential for the study of economic theory. In retrospect, one can discern a slow trend toward increased formalization from the latter part of the nineteenth century until the 1930s when the gradient increased sharply.

The founding of the Econometric Society in 1931 might be taken as a benchmark for the acceleration of the trend, but it is only one of several indicators. Despite Keynes's well-known dislike of mathematical economics, the controversy engendered by *The General Theory* increased the familiarity of economists with explicit closed models and the salience of such models for problems recognized as being of practical importance. This effect was greatly reinforced by contemporaneous developments within RAP, notably the theory of imperfect competition and the use of indifference curves, followed a few years later by the development of input-output analysis and linear programming.

Parallel developments in econometrics reinforced the salience of mathematics within the culture of economics. Starting in the early 1930s with Frisch's confluence analysis, the economic interpretation of multivariable regressions increasingly turned upon issues that could be comprehended only in mathematical terms. The major landmarks in this development (Haavelmo's simultaneous equations and the subsequent work on estimation of simultaneous economic relationships associated with the Cowles Commission), published in the late 40s, made command of matrix algebra and probability theory essential for quantitative empirical work.[8]

In effect, economic statistics as reflected in (say) the pre-1950 publications of the National Bureau of Economic Research was displaced by econometrics, whose hallmark is the estimation of the parameters of models which are derived as much as possible from economic theory and incorporate explicitly specified stochastic components. The interpretation of the results of such exercises requires reference to the concepts and procedures of mathematical statistics, notably the theories of estimation and hypothesis testing. The literature of these subjects was, and is, explicitly mathematical, and intelligent participation in discussions involving its use requires familiarity with the relevant concepts and procedures. Thus, willy-nilly, the economist seeking to do quantitiative work in an applied field has become enmeshed in the problems of applying econometric techniques properly, with her success critically dependent upon selection of the proper tools and their correct usage.

In economic theory, the tradition of stating the main argument entirely in words and diagrams, with mathematical appendices provided for a few initiates, began to dissolve about 1940. This tradition, exemplified by Marshall's *Principles* and Pigou's *Economics of Welfare,* lasted through Hicks's *Value and Capital* (1939), but thereafter began to lose adherents. Samuelson's *Foundations of Economic Analysis* (1947), whose text included a substantial amount of mathematics, may serve as a point of demarcation for the time when economic theorists ceased to apologize for explicit use of mathematics. It was around that time that explicitly mathematical articles—with a few paragraphs of verbal interpretation "to motivate the argument"—began to appear in the major professional journals, gradually elbowing out articles that were primarily verbal, or verbal-diagrammatic.

By the 1970s, the presumption that a theoretical argument was primarily verbal, with mathematical proofs added as a rhetorical flourish to persuade a few purists who needed reassurance that the logic was tight, had

8. Before the mid-1940s, mainstream statistical work in economics—as evidenced by the contents of publications of the National Bureau of Economic Research or the statistics requirement for doctoral candidates—required no mathematics beyond high school algebra. This state of affairs was only gradually relieved during the 1950s.

been completely reversed. To the contrary, it was assumed that what an author intended was a formal demonstration of one or more propositions, usually involving constrained maximization of something or other, and that it was up to her to present the argument in a format in which a reader could most readily appraise it: a mathematical one. If for some reason the argument was presented verbally, it was incumbent upon the author to show (somehow) that the argument was capable of mathematical translation, and that such translation would not impair its validity. Quite literally, readers and editors trained in the tradition that a theory is an expression of mathematical relationships do not trust arguments expressed in other terms. The effect has been such that, for the last decade or two, with rare exceptions, any article published in a major journal that pretends to have a theoretical underpinning will have the argument of one or more of its major sections expressed in mathematical terms.

Of course, this transformation did not occur overnight, and, as we shall see, being a laggard has not precluded receipt of a Nobel Prize. Nevertheless, the trend is unmistakable and, as of the early 1990s, the salience of mathematics in economics was firmly established. As was stated in the 1991 report of the Commission on Graduate Education in Economics (COGEE) "we believe the theoretical tools of economics to be central to the discipline and that mathematics is essential for grasping them."[9]

But, despite—or because of—its salience in the culture of economics, there remains a substantial residue of concern about the proper role of mathematics. The same COGEE report continues,

> Our concern is that, as each successive generation of economists becomes more skilled at mathematics, each demands more of the next. If this trend continues indefinitely . . . some might worry that this would lead to a fundamental change in the character of academic economists, as teaching shifted more and more to passing on the tools and not the questions. We might teach the language of mathematics but not the logic of economics, and end up valuing the grammar of the discipline, rather than its substance.[10]

The concerns that COGEE expresses moderately have been stated with much greater vehemence by others, notably Thomas Mayer (1990).

Much of the complaint about "too much mathematics" in economics

9. Kreuger et al. (1991), p. 1041.
10. Ibid.

fails to distinguish between two distinct aspects of the mathematization phenomenon. One is the general shift of economists from one of the two cultures distinguished by C. P. Snow (1959) to the other.[11] The second aspect is the development of a subculture within economics emphasizing mathematical elegance and ingenuity as criteria of scientific performance, regardless of substantive contribution.

There is little to say about the first aspect, which is simply a reflex to the spread of mathematical literacy among the educated public. The increasing insistence on mathematical formulation as a prerequisite for publication in professional journals may have the effect of excluding valuable articles formulated solely in words—the reverse of the situation existing prior to about 1940—but this means simply that the advantages of using a particular language may be partially offset by the sacrifice of communication with those who cannot use it.

The rise of the cult of mathematical elegance within economics is another matter. The literature to which I am referring generally exhibits far greater mathematical knowledge and sophistication than that generally displayed in articles in the major economic journals, and its subject matter is focused on a narrow range of topics whose common characteristic is a high degree of abstraction, for example, the conditions for the attainment of general equilibrium and/or Pareto optimality under very general conditions; specification of the axioms for choice functions (individual or social); and, recently, various applications of game theory to situations of incomplete information. While the most highly acclaimed contributions to this literature are those bearing directly upon major propositions of economic theory or public policy, such a focus is not essential for obtaining recognition. Display of mathematical virtuosity in proving or in making "minor" amendments to generally accepted theorems generates professional esteem that many consider disproportionate to the contribu-

---

11. One of Snow's two cultures is that of mathematics and the physical sciences; the other comprises literature, history, the arts, and (as of the time he wrote) most social sciences. This cultural divide was reflected in, and at least partially caused by, the presence of mathematics in the training of students seeking entry into the first culture and its near absence from the curricula of students intending to specialize in subjects belonging to the second. This difference was (alleged to be) manifested in different styles of thinking and expression, and even of alleged differences of personality, between typical members of the two cultures: concern with accuracy, literalness of statement, careful appraisal of evidence, and psychological rigidity among scientists as contrasted with imaginativeness, concern with feelings, and intellectual venturesomeness in the other culture.

tion made either to theory or to policy.[12] While there is considerable dispute, both as to how much recognition actually is given to mathematical esoterica, and over how much of its literature is substantively important, it is generally conceded that a substantial number of its contributors are not much concerned about the bearing of their work upon applied economics.

Why then is this literature so highly regarded in the profession, and its contributors so highly esteemed? The answer lies in the hierarchical structure of the culture, and in the characteristics of its heroes. While not all recent heroes of economics have belonged to the coterie of the highly mathematical, an appreciable number of them have. The example of their work and, even more, their patronage of the less-acclaimed members of the group—manifested most prominently in the making of faculty appointments—has provided an effective shield for the pursuit of mathematical refinement.

The prestige of mathematical economics, like that of mathematics itself, stems largely from the endorsements of the outstanding figures who have participated in its development and application. The position of these heroes derives at least partly from acclaim for their work outside of mathematical economics: indeed, it is acclaim for this "outside work" that provides the bully pulpit from which they induce respect for mathematical esoterica that would otherwise go unappreciated by most members of the culture.

A second reason for the respect accorded mathematical economics is that it treats the "classical" problems that have occupied the attention of leading economists for more than 200 years and which, accordingly, have a major place in the history of economic thought. These are the problems surrounding the "theory of value"—for example, the conditions for stable market equilibrium, the relation of demand to utility, of private to social cost, and of productive efficiency to information—which are formulated in very general terms[13] and whose solutions lie in conceptual innovations rather than empirical discoveries. As these problems are common to a

---

12. The counterargument to this assertion is that, until the proper mathematical demonstrations have been made, whatever is generally accepted may be false and/or seriously misleading. The heavy reliance of economics on sign restrictions derived from theoretical considerations (as distinguished from observation) lends weight to such arguments, but there is no consensus on the matter.

13. That is, the problems are stated so as to make them relevant to a very wide range of circumstances, both technological and institutional.

wide variety of times and places, interest in their solutions is accordingly widespread.

HEROES AND PRIZES

Obviously, to the heroes of a scientific subculture go its major prizes. Though the direction of causality is not unambiguous, I will stipulate that usually receipt of a major prize constitutes (additional) recognition of achievement(s) previously identified as "heroic." Receipt of the prize both confirms and enhances previous recognition. In marginal cases, award of a prize may serve to resolve debate about the heroic status of the recipient's work and, in some extreme cases, the prize may even create a colorable claim to status that would not otherwise be considered seriously. However, we are not concerned with the pathology of the awarding process, but with its normal results and what they reveal about the culture in which the awards are rooted.

The significance of prizes rests not only on their direct effect in molding the aspirations of ambitious members of the community but also on their relation to the research funding process. It would be only a slight exaggeration to say that every research grant is made in the hope that its product will be of such quality as to merit a prize. Granting agencies act as if their objective was to promote work that would be recognized by prize selection committees as of outstanding quality and importance. Hence what will be said of prizes as motivators of research can, with obvious small amendments, be applied to grants as well. Prizes guide researchers in the selection of projects to undertake, and also guide grantors in the type of projects to fund. Obviously, the two channels of influence are mutually reinforcing.

As in other fields of activity, there is more than one prize for achievement in economics. However, and especially in economics, the salience of the Nobel Prize is so marked as to make it an obvious and convenient proxy for the whole set of prizes that is offered. In discussing the effects of the "en-Nobeling" process I shall eschew speculation about the internal politics of the selection committees, and the alleged idiosyncrasies of their members, and assume that their objective has been to recognize and reward what they consider to be outstanding contributions to the field.

As I perceive it, the sequence of Nobel awards in Economics suggests that the criterion of merit used has been a mixture of the personal views of the selectors and their perception of the dominant views of the economics community, with distinctly heavier weight given to the latter. To a first approximation, the Nobel selection committees have behaved as though they were trying to maximize the prestige of their awards within the economics community.

Since that community contains many diverse groups, each with its own notions of comparative merit, it is very difficult to find a consensus, or even a heavy plurality, in support of any one prize nominee. Consequently, the committees have appeared to follow a strategy of recognizing and rewarding important (i.e., numerous and vocal) groups who support the claims of particular individuals, or of particular subfields, to a prize. The result has been a sequence of awards whose rationale has been minimization of the clamor from those whose nominations had previously been ignored.[14]

But, of course, a committee is always free to ignore clamor if it sees fit to do so. Here is where the personal predilections of the committee members enter the selection process, and one would suspect that quite consciously the committees do a triage to separate opinions that they will consider, from those that they intend to ignore.

It would be very surprising if the opinions of previous prize winners were not highly influential with selection committees, thus generating serial correlation among the characteristics of award recipients. Moreover, though hard to prove, it is very likely that the perceived standards of the selection committees exercise an appreciable influence on those upheld by the economics community. This is simply to reiterate that, as with all establishments, there is the strong possibility that the criteria of merit perceived to be utilized by official bodies whose decisions purport to reflect community standards tend to reinforce those standards.

The Nobel Prize in economics was not included in the original set of prizes established by Alfred Nobel and first awarded in 1887. It was not until more than 80 years later (in 1969) that the first award in economics was made to Ragnar Frisch and Jan Tinbergen jointly. In this case, the committee chose to honor two leading members of the group of founders of the Econometric Society (in 1931), both of whom were major contributors to the early development of econometrics. Without denigrating the substantive contributions of these pioneer laureates, their awards can be interpreted as due, in good part, to their role as initiators of a major change in the culture of economics: mathematization. Of the next six awards, three were made to economists whose major contributions were associated with the promotion of mathematical methods in economic the-

---

14. This is not to suggest that the selection committees consciously aim at this goal, but only that they have been acting *as if* this were their objective.

ory: Paul Samuelson (1970), Kenneth Arrow and John R. Hicks (1972), and Tjalling Koopmans and L. V. Kantorovich (1975).[15]

After 1975, relatively few awards (3 of 20) were made for contributions to the deployment of mathematical techniques in economic theory: De-breu (1983), Allais (1988) and (arguably) Harsanyi, Selten, and Nash (1994).[16] However, several other awards recognized origination of econo-metric techniques: Leontief (1973), Haavelmo (1987) and, in part, the awards to Koopmans (1975) and to Tobin (1981).

In the case of Haavelmo, the basis of the award is clear. His monograph on the estimation of simultaneous equations[17] laid the basis for modern econometric procedures, and far outweighs his other contributions. Simi-larly, Leontief is generally accepted as the originator of modern input-output analysis. In the case of Koopmans, the prize may in part have re-flected his contribution to the technique of estimating simultaneous equa-tions, but even more it resulted from his work on activity analysis and welfare economics.[18] While Tobin has made one well-known contribution to econometrics (i.e., Tobit),[19] it is a relatively minor part of his achieve-ments.

The main point to be made is that, unlike the practice in other sciences, in economics, Nobel prizes have not been awarded for specific discoveries, but have betokened recognition of a series of contributions, not always closely related to one another.[20] Despite some ambiguity, many of these

15. In the 1990s, and even as of the date of his award, Hicks's work would not have been considered by economists as "mathematical." However, his magnum opus, *Value and Capital* (1939) marked a distinct step in the formalization of price theory, for although the main argument was carried by a verbal text, the (implicitly inessential) mathematics was appended for those who could appreciate it. Samuelson's *Foundations of Economic Analysis* (1947) marked the turning point at which mathematics became an integral part of the textual expo-sition with no concession made to the undertrained.

16. The Harsanyi, Selten, and Nash award was made for their contributions to game theory. While these contributions are highly mathematical, in principle they are ancillary to hoped-for applications.

17. T. Haavelmo (1944).

18. The work on simultaneous equations is contained in W. C. Hood and T. C. Koop-mans (1953); the work on activity analysis is in T. C. Koopmans and S. Reiter (1951); and the work on welfare economics is in T. C. Koopmans (1957).

19. J. Tobin (1958).

20. This was written before the award for 1997 was made. That award (to Myron Scholes and Robert Merton) has been generally interpreted as recognition of a specific contribution, the Black-Scholes formula. However, one observation does not make a trend, though it militates against generalizations to the contrary.

awards can be placed under one of several broad headings: tool making, field establishment, concept innovation, and economic development. Tool making would cover the awards for contributions to pure theory and econometric techniques, for example, input-output analysis, linear programming, and, most recently, application of game theory to economics (Nash, Harsanyi and Selten, 1994).

Field establishment refers to the awards—usually but not always joint—to economists who are identified as making major contributions to the creation or advance of a particular field: international trade (Meade and Ohlin, 1977); public goods (Buchanan, 1986); finance (Markowitz, Sharpe, and Miller, 1990); economic history (Fogel and North, 1993).

The distinction between concept innovation and field establishment is not sharp: I would conjecture that, when feasible, the committee has preferred to make awards to innovations that have resulted in the creation of a field. Examples of such innovations would include Arrow's Impossibility Theorem and the field of Social Choice; Becker's work on choice theory and the field called "economics of the family," for which he received the 1992 award; and Solow's work on aggregate production functions that gave theoretical direction to Growth Accounting.

The awards committees seem also to have been inclined to recognize contributions to the application of economics to economic development, even when such contributions were not associated either with tool creation or concept innovation. Hence the awards to Myrdal (1974) and to Schultz and Lewis (1979).

Following the trend of professional opinion, the committees have made most of their awards in pure theory to mathematical work, but—still in accord with professional sentiment—the awards to Coase (1991) and Buchanan (1986) constitute notable exceptions to this tendency. As has already been noted, while conceptual innovations may be purely theoretical (i.e., involving no attempt at empirical implementation), a substantial number do. While varying in degree, the work of Friedman (1975), Simon (1978), Tobin (1981), Stigler (1982), Modigliani (1985), Becker (1992) and Lucas (1995) all include attempts to estimate quantitative relationships based upon their innovations.

That none of these efforts has found quantitative relationships that are generally accepted as valid within the economics community[21] is in sharp contrast to the reception of the conceptual innovations on which they

21. Again, an exception for the Scholes-Merton (1997) award should be noted.

rest. All represent innovations that have been widely recognized as valid and important, and subsequent research has generally been modified to take them into account. Nevertheless, such specific quantitative results as they have obtained are, without exception, subject to vigorous ongoing debate. This is to say that, in economics, the highest awards often are given for promising beginnings and/or improvements made, rather than for achieved results ready for practical application.

For this reason, more than in other subjects, the deeds for which heroism in economics is recognized extend well beyond specific research results obtained. The achievements of Simon Kuznets or Theodore Schultz or Milton Friedman go beyond what can be put into a citation for a prize. While each of these, and others, has done enough significant research to serve as rationalization for award of a prize, often it would be easier to explain an award as the symbiotic result of a number of disparate contributions of research and personal activity that do not fit readily into the categories of recognition designed for sciences where the criteria of success are more restrictive but satisfied more frequently.

FOURTEEN

THE BOUNDARIES
OF ECONOMICS

To identify economics with a specific culture is to assert that the boundaries of its subject matter are the result neither of accident nor of conscious choice. Obviously, the boundaries of any subject are influenced by its history and traditions and by the competencies generated through its training programs and sources of personnel. Despite some overlaps, economists, psychologists, sociologists, political scientists, and anthropologists learn different techniques, become familiar with different institutions, and read about different aspects of human history. This readily accounts for the distinctive characteristics of vocabulary, thought processes, and general knowledge associated with membership in one rather than another of these disciplinary cultures.

Such differences have not always been so marked as they have become during the past three-quarters of a century, and they are probably more salient in the United States than elsewhere. The separations among the various social sciences are both cause and result (I would emphasize the latter) of the fact that they are associated with distinct academic departments in institutions of higher education. Administrative separation, together with the existence of national and international disciplinary organizations, has fostered emphasis on the distinctive features of each discipline and encouraged appointment and promotion of those individuals whose work best exhibits these features.

In the appointment-promotion process, breadth of interest and competence is given less weight than disciplinarily focused skills, thus sending a message of specialization to students in training. I would be derelict in disciplinary duty if I failed to point out that this tendency toward specialization has been resisted by considerations of organizational size. For example, in small liberal arts colleges multidisciplinary competence is often demanded of job candidates, and combined departments of (say) economics and sociology are not unknown. But over time, as institutional size has grown, there has been a decline in the relative number of students who are taught undergraduate economics in departments not specialized to that discipline.

341

In an efficient world, a lesser degree of specialization would imply a sacrifice of output quality that would be accepted only because of the cost entailed in overcoming it. But, in the present context, such an implication might not be valid. Since Adam Smith, economists have warned (and been warned) on the adverse effects of excessive specialization on intellectual capability. And, more to the present point, there has been a continuing series of "border wars" between economics and other social sciences as to the proper limits to application of economic principles in the explanation of behavioral phenomena.

The attitude of economists to these border wars varies with the paradigm to which they adhere. Most of the shafts hurled at economics from other social sciences are directed at RAP, and are felt most strongly by its adherents; adherents of other paradigms react differently. For example, in the Marxian tradition there are no established boundaries between the subject matters of the various social sciences, and such de facto specialization as may have arisen has always been subordinated to the requirements of application.

Unlike RAP, the history of Marxism has been driven by political rather than intellectual developments, and the greatest prestige has accrued to authors of effective tracts on important political issues, not to burnishers of theoretical weapons. Hence aspiring Marxists have been encouraged to acquire the mixed bag of tools appropriate for political action rather than the more specialized collection needed for success in an academically defined discipline.

Because the Keynesian paradigm contains no implications about the relation of economics to other social sciences, its adherents have been free to adopt any of a variety of positions on the matter. Consequently, one finds considerable sympathy among Keynesians (including neo-Keynesians and New Keynesians) for including various institutional factors in explanations of the functioning of labor and product markets.

The common characteristic of such explanations is the incorporation of factors that cannot be accommodated within the framework of RAP, factors whose operation cannot be explained on the assumption that observed behavior is generated by utility maximizers constrained by fixed tastes and resources. Typically, the operation of such institutional factors incorporates assertions about behavior whose support involves propositions of some other social science. This leads to lack of resistance to, and even encouragement of, demands that economists learn about other social sciences and/or that they collaborate (more than they have) with their practitioners.[1]

What has been said of the attitude of Keynesians to the other social sciences applies, more or less, to adherents of the other non-RAP paradigms as well. This is because the interdisciplinary confrontations of economics with other social sciences occur mainly on the RAP section of the frontier. While non-RAP economists generally share the common disciplinary pride in their core competences and exhibit the same impatience with amateurish invaders of their traditional turf, they recognize limits to these competences and accept that there are borderlands which they might peacefully, and perhaps with mutual advantage, cohabit with disciplinary neighbors.

This attitude does not differ radically from that of many—perhaps most—RAP adherents concerning areas removed from their own specialty. Like most economists, the typical RAP adherent does not feel strongly about big methodological issues, but only about their application to his immediate area of expertise. However, despite case-to-case differences, in all specialties the basic RAP attitude is maintained. The preferred interpretation of phenomena must be compatible with RAP, which implies restricting the role of the other social sciences to the explanation of whatever might be encapsulated in the residuals of behavioral equations.[2]

In addition to the broad spectrum of economists who apply RAP in their work but are otherwise methodologically agnostic or indifferent, there is a prominent and recently growing group of RAP enthusiasts who have sought to expand the applications of their subject and paradigm beyond its traditional boundaries. Not improperly, these economists have been termed economic imperialists,[3] and they define economics, not in

1. Examples of demands for collaboration with (or even abdication of territory to) psychologists were presented above in chapters 6 and 8 (in explaining speculative bubbles). Examples to the same effect with regard to sociology were offered in chapter 8. For an argument to the same point in the context of ideology see John Lodewijks (1994).

2. Despite appearances, this statement is really a tautology. An economist whose beliefs did not conform to it in the context of his own work would not be classified as an RAP adherent.

3. Although the roots of economic imperialism extend back at least to the 1930s, it became prominent only in the 1960s. A good brief discussion of this movement is contained in the introduction to Richard Swedberg (1990), pp. 13ff. Ronald Coase (1994), chapter 3, presents a skeptical view of the prospects for a long-term takeover by economics of the

terms of subject matter, but in terms of a set of analytical procedures. With but slight exaggeration, these procedures can be identified with those sanctioned by RAP plus the associated econometric techniques.

Economic imperialists believe that RAP may be applied properly to any situation where either (1) a choice or decision-making entity is confronted with alternative uses for limited resources or (2) a set of the characteristics of a population can be described as the outcome of a selective process in which the criteria of "fitness" are set by the choices of resource owners. Going beyond traditional economic problems, attempts have been made to use RAP to explain, inter alia, demographic phenomena and characteristics of family structure,the occurrence of marriage, divorce and other forms of cohabitative relations, the incidence of various kinds of criminal activity, the development of legal doctrines and practices, the characteristics of organizational structures and the evolution of social institutions generally, and political behavior, particularly the behavior of voters, regulators, and legislators.

Each of these applications has generated a substantial literature and a cluster of leading authorities. Perhaps the leading figure in the entire movement has been Gary Becker, whose methodological position is succinctly stated as follows:

> The combined assumptions of maximizing behavior, market equilibrium, and stable preferences, used relentlessly and unflinchingly, form the heart of the economic approach as I see it. . . . The economic approach is clearly not restricted to material goods and wants, nor even to the market sector. Prices, be they the money prices of the market sector or the "shadow" imputed prices of the nonmarket sector, measure the opportunity cost of using scarce resources, and the economic approach predicts the same kind of response to shadow prices as to market prices.[4]

It is Becker's work in extending the field of application of what he has termed "the economic approach" that is responsible for his Nobel prize. But he is not the only Nobel laureate to emerge from the economic imperialism movement: Douglass North's (1993) prize was due largely to his

---

subject matter of other social science disciplines based on superiority of analytical technique or conceptual approach.

4. Becker (1976), pp. 5–6.

work on the application of RAP to explaining the evolution of economic institutions.[5] And it is quite possible that yet other Nobel prizes will accrue to creators of spokes to the hub of economic imperialism. For example, the burgeoning field of law and economics, which has centered on the application of RAP to the analysis of legal institutions, might well be a candidate for recognition by a future Nobel selection committee; in such case Richard Posner would be a salient candidate for an award.[6]

Such forays into the territories of other social sciences and law have met with a mixed reception from the native populations and some dissent from economists who reject the aspect of RAP that is being applied. In what follows I shall discuss the demarcation of economics from each of its neighboring disciplines. I have omitted anthropology because no methodological issues have arisen on its frontier that have not appeared elsewhere, and because its border with economics has been comparatively quiet in recent years.

The reception of economics in all of its neighboring disciplines stems from the essential characteristics of RAP (proper), which are substantially the same as Becker's description of "the economic approach." The price-quantity relations implied by RAP invite quantification of concepts and of the interrelations among them, with empirical implementation to follow as soon as possible, or even sooner. Once accepted as a conceptual framework, the web of price-quantity interrelations characteristic of RAP invites development of a variety of research programs, the implementation of which requires command of price theory.

Thus, where the economic approach is accepted, sociologists, political scientists, and others need to acquaint themselves with the intricacies of economics, and economists are given opportunity to move into neighboring disciplines. In all disciplines, the need for such movement across borders confers an obvious comparative advantage upon the young. This has the effect of making struggles between invaders from economics and

5. Douglass C. North (1981) and (1990).

6. Richard Posner is surely the leading figure in the law and economics movement which has had a major impact on both economics and jurisprudence during the past quarter century. However, despite an enormous scholarly output on law, economics, and other matters, Posner's principal employment has been as a federal judge (of the 7th Circuit of the U.S. Court of Appeals). Although his economic writings reveal him to be an enthusiastic adherent of RAP, probably he would be better identified as a lawyer than as an economist. How the issue of professional identification might affect a Nobel selection committee is an interesting question.

native turf defenders parallel with an intergenerational conflict among the defenders.

It is important to note that the large body of technical apparatus used in price theory and econometrics has no parallel in the other social sciences. This creates an asymmetry that precludes interchange among economists and other social scientists on a basis approaching equality, once the RAP framework is accepted. Economists know price theory and others must learn it. There is no comparable body of apparatus which practitioners of another social science might apply to "economic phenomena," thereby compelling economists to master an alien discipline in order to mount an effective response.

Together with the capability of making quantitative assertions about subject matter within the purview of other social sciences, this asymmetry is responsible for "the feeling among the economists that their science [is] clearly superior."[7] Though widespread, this feeling is not universal among economists. As we have seen, some economists believe RAP to be defective in one way or another and in need of serious amendment before being capable of proper application even within the traditional boundaries of its home subject. Often, to resist the advance of RAP, these economist critics of the paradigm have joined forces with the embattled turf defenders of other disciplines. Unfortunately, however, there is no generally applicable description of their arguments other than that they dispute one or another of the contentions of RAP. Let us now turn to the specifics of several of RAP's disciplinary aggressions.

SOCIOLOGY

Demography

One of the more prominent efforts to apply RAP outside the traditional territory of economics has been the attempt to explain the behavior of birthrates as the outcome of differences in family income and various prices (especially the shadow price of a woman's time) with "demand functions for children" fixed and unchanged. Opponents of this attempt, economists as well as demographically oriented sociologists, contend that differences in social values (reflected in differences of utility functions and/or in the "propensity to maximize") are at least as important as differ-

7. Swedberg (1990), p. 16. This feeling, among economists, of disciplinary superiority (to other social sciences) is well conveyed in Stigler's *Memoirs* (1988), pp. 191–205.

ences in the RAP variables stressed by Becker to explain differences (across time and location) in birthrates and associated demographic phenomena.[8]

It has not been seriously denied by any competent student that the decline in birthrates that typically accompanies "modernization" has been associated with changes in all of the following: contraceptive knowledge, availability of contraceptives and their relative cost, societal values regarding sexual and child rearing practices, and per capita family wealth. It is also generally agreed that definition and measurement of these variables is difficult, as is disentanglement of their interrelations by econometric procedures. What has been disputed is the attempt to encapsulate the effects of changes in societal values, especially as regards use of contraceptives and methods of child rearing, in variables labeled as changes of prices and per capita family wealth.

What is at stake in this dispute is use of the conceptual organization of RAP as opposed to some alternative formulation in which social customs and culturally prescribed attitudes toward sex and child rearing are not interpreted as proxies for RAP variables. In the RAP framework, changes in attitudes toward sex and child rearing are confounded with (such RAP variables as) changes in the price of women's time to the household (measured as their market wage net of foregone household production); the full price of contraceptives, including the time and trouble of obtaining them; the expected cost and returns from rearing a child; and so on. The RAP position is that whatever demographic phenomena can be explained at all, can best be captured by its own set of variables, with the remainder reflected in one or more disturbance terms.[9]

The anti-RAP position is to deny the applicability of RAP while offering an argument in support of the salience of one or another of the variables excluded by it. In principle, one would like to see the dispute pursued through presentation of two or more competing systems of regression equations. Were such a confrontation feasible, I conjecture that it would have been attempted already, but this has not occurred. The de-

8. For example see the review article by Yoram Ben Porath (1982).

9. This is due partly to the belief that the effect of relevant variables is captured in the price of time to the household and the associated wealth effect of improved opportunity for gainful employment outside the household. But it also reflects the difficulty of specifying and measuring relevant sociological variables so as to incorporate them in an explicit model alternative to RAP.

bate has been about the relative appropriateness of RAP and some (in-completely specified) alternative that incorporates one or more sociologi-cal variables.

A major stake in this debate is intellectual influence, that is, whether demographic experts are to be compelled to use the tools associated with RAP rather than those of sociology and (possibly) of some non-RAP eco-nomics. This aspect of intellectual influence is what most concerns the advocates of RAP.

However, public policy is also influenced by choice of the conceptual organization in terms of which the relevant causal relations are described. To think of demographic events in terms of RAP is to frame relevant policies in terms of wealth and relative prices which are conformable with taxes, subsidies, and pecuniary incentives: other conceptual frameworks suggest other types of policy instruments. Not surprisingly the conceptual organization of RAP appeals to individuals—economists and others—who prefer policies that can be implemented with pecuniary instruments to those that would require use of nonpecuniary instruments of persua-sion (or coercion) such as would be suggested by a model incorporating sociological variables.

Criminal Behavior

For a second example of economic imperialism directed at sociology con-sider the application of RAP categories to the explanation of criminal behavior. In this class of applications, criminal activity is considered as an industry the output of which is "produced" in response to an anticipated reward, and is impeded by its cost of production. This cost consists primar-ily of the value of the time spent in criminal activity (i.e., what the criminal could have earned had she used this time in a legal pursuit) plus the ex-pected loss of utility resulting from punishment for engaging in such ac-tivity.[10]

As might be imagined, the positive economic explanation of criminal activity runs in terms of its costs and returns, while policy proposals focus on the punishment of those convicted and the probability of detecting and convicting those engaged in the activity.[11] This contrasts with the domi-

10. This expected loss of utility is the expected disutility of punishment × the probabil-ity of being punished, given engagement in criminal activity.

11. The seminal paper on this subject is Gary S. Becker (1968). Also see Isaac Ehrlich (1973) and (1975). For a recent discussion see the symposium, "The Economics of Crime" in the *Journal of Economic Perspectives* 10, no. 1 (Winter 1996), pp. 3–67.

nant view among other social scientists working on problems of criminology (mainly sociologists and social psychologists) who stress factors influencing the social attitudes of potential criminals, especially their relative poverty. In particular, the non-economic approach views criminal behavior either as an expression of a more-or-less fixed disposition toward society, or as a transient response to anger and/or deprivation, but not as a rational response to (potentially variable) incentives.

This difference in the alternative frames for thinking about criminal activity leads to divergent approaches to the type of state action best able to curb it. Considering criminal activity to be a rational response to behavioral incentives suggests manipulation of those incentives, that is, increasing the penalties for convicted miscreants and/or devoting more resources to their detection and prosecution.

But if criminal behavior were thought to result from psychological malfunctioning or resentment at deprivation, manipulation of incentives would be ineffective. On this interpretation the appropriate response would consist of some combination of social work, counseling, psychiatric assistance, and poverty alleviation. All of such measures would involve increased use of resources by the public sector.

While debate about the proper framing of criminal behavior has covered the whole range of such activity, the most spectacular confrontation has arisen over the application of an economic model to estimating the effectiveness of capital punishment in deterring murder. This debate centered on several papers of Isaac Ehrlich (1973, 1975) which offered a variety of estimates of this effect, all purporting to show that "the rate of murders" varied inversely with the probability of execution. Although the resulting debate was inconclusive, Ehrlich's argument was strongly resisted by sociologists as well as by a number of economists.[12] The opposition was based both upon the (alleged) inappropriateness of framing acts of murder as rational choices (in the RAP sense) and on the sensitivity of the econometric results to the precise specification of the hypothesis to be tested. The details of this debate do not concern us except as they illustrate the issues involved in extending the boundaries of economics.

Networks

A third collision of economics with sociology occurs wherever it is proposed to use the concept of "network" in the explanation of empirical

---

12. For a critical appraisal of Ehrlich's argument and those of its critics see E. E. Leamer (1983).

phenomena. In general, a network is a set of connections among entities which are typically, though not necessarily, individuals. A connection between two or more entities may be any sort of relationship that induces a propensity (positive or negative) for one entity to interact with another entity with which it is "connected" rather than with an entity to which it is not so connected. A given entity may belong to many networks, and the fact of belonging to a plurality of particular networks may serve as the basis for yet another network. In sociology, an exemplar of a network is a sociogram.[13]

Membership in a network precludes anonymity. In the context of RAP, this preclusion is of considerable importance. A characteristic and much celebrated feature of "the market" is its impersonality. But this feature is incompatible with the existence of one or more networks among its transacting participants. The absence of networks from models compatible with RAP proper is reflected in the fact that an equilibrium determines the price and quantity of transactions, but says nothing about who transacts with whom. While such anonymity is well approximated in the functioning of an organized exchange where the objects of transaction are standardized, it does not obtain in markets where transactors seek partners with specific characteristics, for example, in labor or marriage markets.

In analyzing markets such as these, the assumption of impersonality must be either abandoned or amended to allow for qualitative search by potential transactors. The augmentation of RAP to accommodate the phenomena of search and selection constitutes a substantial part of the development of labor economics during the past 40 years, as is discussed in chapter 8. Moreover, extension of the formal structure of models initially developed for the analysis of job markets to the analysis of the "marriage market" is a prominent characteristic of Becker's (1976, chap. 11) theory of marriage.

Without going into details, the essence of what must be done to accommodate the fact of qualitative differences among units sold in the "same" market is to posit the existence of underlying (typically unobservable) characteristics which are treated as desiderata of the transactors (i.e., arguments of their utility functions) and related to the price variable in such a way that any given set of their values will fetch the same price regardless of the individual possessing them. Empirical implementation of such

13. Though having no place in RAP proper, the network concept has been widely used in economics, as is discussed above in chapter 6.

models requires that the unobservable characteristics be associated with observable proxies, and the success of the implementation will depend critically upon how well the behavior of the proxies reflects that of the underlying characteristics.

A successful search and selection model would leave no role for a network effect in the explanation of the behavior of any variable of interest. This is seemingly in conflict with the contention of sociologists such as Mark Granovetter, who contend that participation in a network is a prime determinant of success in finding and obtaining a job, a spouse, a lender, etc.[14] Participation in a network not only disseminates information about possible transaction partners but also (varying with the characteristics of the particular network) constitutes an indicator of character and reliability, and facilitates sanctions against defaulters on obligations or persons otherwise given to opportunistic behavior. In effect, participation in a network affects the information flows to a decision maker and the contract terms (e.g., prices) on which resources will be available to her, or whether they will be available at all.

Granovetter argues that many economic relationships are embedded in networks of personal relationships among the participants, and cannot be understood in abstraction from them. This, of course, is precisely what RAP denies. That descriptively pecuniary transactions are embedded in personal relationships need not, and should not, be disputed. Nor should the converse, that personal relations often serve as vehicles for promotion of pecuniary transactions, be denied. At issue is which set of variables and relationships—RAP, one or another network structures, or elements of both—should be used in constructing tools of analysis.

If the RAP structure were to be selected, membership in a network could be incorporated as an element of specific human capital.[15] But whether this would advance understanding of the phenomena to be studied depends upon the specifics of the particular problem. Indeed, specific human capital is sometimes little more than a label for the association of payoff with duration of a relationship. However, the fact that specific human capital is integrated with (an augmented) RAP gives it a salience far greater than what it derives from its explanatory power.

In effect, Granovetter et al. contend that attempting to collapse the particulars of network connections into amounts of specific human capital

14. See the interview of Swedberg with Granovetter in Swedberg (1990), chapter 5, and the associated bibliography.

15. See above, chapter 8, pp. 182–88.

would not improve explanations of variables of interest, but would impede understanding of network connections. They contend that the functioning of such networks varies from case to case and does not lend itself to useful abstraction—at least not in the form suggested by RAP. In this they are joined by the substantial minority of economists who argue for the salience of network externalities and other anomalies to RAP.

In the context of networks, it can readily be perceived that interdisciplinary aggression does not originate only in economics. The alleged inadequacies of RAP appear not only in "sociological" topics like marriage and murder, but also in "economic" topics like the functioning of labor markets and the organizational structure of industry. Indeed, in discussing Granovetter's work, Swedberg (1990, p. 107) speaks of a "new economic sociology," which is distinguished from an older one by its strong reservations about RAP as applied to certain parts of economics as well as to sociology.

In short, this particular conflict between economics and sociology closely parallels a conflict within economics between RAP adherents and dissenters who stress its limitations, especially those arising from network externalities. In both conflicts, a crucial issue concerns how network affiliations are acquired. To a sociologist, such affiliations are a matter of chance and propinquity; to an RAP adherent, they are a matter of rationally directed investment. That is, according to RAP one learns which networks it is advantageous to join and "invests" accordingly, for example, attends the right school, joins the right club, etc.

To make her point, the sociologist need not rule out the element of investment in network affiliations altogether. But she must insist on adding that some people are endowed with greater facility in making such affiliations, that is, some can buy into networks more cheaply than others. From this it would follow that proper employment of an RAP framework often will require that the givens of tastes, techniques, and resources be augmented with variables reflecting properties of social structure that determine access to valuable networks.

One criterion of the relative performance of sociological and RAP frameworks is their comparative success in "explaining" the behavior of variables of interest. However, on reading the remarks of Granovetter and other sociologists it becomes clear that—like some economists—they place as much (or more) weight on relative intuitive appeal.[16] That is, they

16. See Swedberg (1990).

find an explanation of behavior running in terms of resource-constrained rational choice not as informative as one that runs in terms of (say) the strong history of the particular phenomena under analysis.

As we have already considered the merits of such a position (in chapter 6), there is no need to discuss it again. However, it is appropriate to remark on the intuitive appeal of the RAP framework as applied to many problems outside the traditional domain of economics. For example, the image of a matrimonial market, with paucity of available alternatives influencing the quality of the match one might expect to obtain and hence the "reservation price" to set, bears a striking similarity to the image of a labor market, and suggests exploitation of the analogy. Such exploitation involves placing (forcing?) phenomena into RAP categories, and using the RAP framework to generate analogous relationships. Use of this framework directs the kinds of data that are to be considered as relevant and the kinds of expertise to be utilized in studying the phenomena.

Lack of such a framework places sociology at a great disadvantage in borderland competition with economics. The insights of sociologists and strong history economists must be developed case by case with only very limited transfer of common analytical tools. The common characteristic of their studies is rejection of one or another feature of RAP, and a (consequent) refusal to allow research to be directed by a seeking out of its implications. But for want of an alternative framework such research lacks a unifying principle, and partakes of a paradigm—either of economics or of sociology—only in a negative way, as a denial of the validity of RAP.

Networks and Transaction Costs

It is possible and often useful to think of a network as a source of differential transaction costs. That is, transacting with other members of a network involves lower transaction costs than transacting with nonmembers.[17] But whether it would be useful, or even feasible, to embark upon a wholesale translation of propositions about the properties of networks into propositions about transaction costs is problematic. In any case a systematic translation has not yet been attempted.

Whether the theory of organization, which may be thought of as a particular application of the theory of transaction costs, belongs to eco-

17. For example, the cost of acquiring information about potential transacting partners, of enforcing agreements, and of measures to inhibit opportunistic behavior by transacting partners is lower if transactions are restricted to members of an appropriate network.

nomics, to sociology, to political science, or to all three is clearly a matter for (not very important) dispute. Some organization theorists adhere more or less to RAP and explain the characteristics of organizations and related institutions as the outcome of a competitive process in which minimization of transaction costs is the criterion of survival. Others stress the importance of exogenously generated network connections, often combined with strong history effects, as a source of competitive advantage; still others are eclectic.[18]

An assessment of the relative contributions of economics and other social sciences to the theory of organization, and of institutions, is not necessary.[19] However, it should be clear that the claims to influence of the various disciplines are not claims about the salience of their conventional subject matters, but about the appropriateness and effectiveness of the conceptual apparati that they bring to bear.

Sociobiology

Economics has two interfaces with sociobiology: one metaphorical and the other substantive. The metaphorical interface is most prominent in the theory of the firm, where the spirit of RAP requires that if firms are to exist at all they must be as efficient as possible given the constraints of technology and equilibrium factor prices.[20] But while the requirements of a competitive equilibrium guarantee efficiency, they say nothing about how a system not already in equilibrium can be brought there.

Enter an evolutionary story running in terms of a selective tendency in the competitive environment that serves to generate lower profits (or losses) to all firms that fail to acquire the characteristics that generate maximum efficiency. While there is no way of precluding the possibility that dynamic processes other than natural selection might display a similar tropism for efficiency, none has yet presented itself. This has left RAP adherents free to exploit the isomorphism of models of biological selection with those of market competition to reinforce the efficiency metaphor of the Invisible Hand by conflating it with Survival of the Fittest.[21]

Such reinforcement is by no means redundant. Direct experience of

18. North (1990) is a leading example of an eclectic.

19. North argues (ibid.) that differential transaction costs are an important explanatory factor of the characteristics of organizations as well as of institutions generally.

20. The same type of argument is applied to develop efficiency oriented theories of organization and institutions.

21. A leading example is A. A. Alchian (1950).

the real world offers many examples that seem to conflict with the notion that the inefficient become extinct, while appeals to the long run require a leap of faith that is not always forthcoming. Survival of the fittest appeals to a deep and widespread Calvinist intuition of how the world "really is," independent of belief in the efficacy of the Invisible Hand. Social Darwinism is not identical with laissez-faire, but acceptance of either reinforces acceptance of the other, and therefore it is not surprising that their adherents have a large overlap, both with each other and with devotees of RAP.

Conversely, it is not surprising that economists and others who reject either RAP or laissez-faire should look askance at sociobiology. In their disapproval they join a faction of biologists and population geneticists who are highly critical of attempts to apply the results of biology to social phenomena in human populations.[22] However, beyond sharing the use of some formal apparatus, economics and sociobiology do not contribute much to one another's arguments on behalf of the salience of efficiency or fitness (the biological counterpart of efficiency) as a determinant of the structural characteristics either of organisms or of social institutions.[23]

In the economics of the family, arguments from sociobiology are exploited more extensively. RAP proper has nothing to say about the internal structure of decision-making units, which it treats as so many black boxes. In analyzing the family this will not do: biological survival of a family requires at least some degree of altruism of parents toward children, and the functioning of the family varies with the particular patterns of altruism that prevail. Thus Becker (1976, chap. 13) has drawn on sociobiology to develop a model of the family that allows for altruism and is driven by a tropism for genetic fitness.

The salience of the issues addressed by this model are such that the relevance of sociobiology to this part of economics cannot be disputed. However, the particular mix of social and biological factors that interact to determine which functions are performed by families, and which are left to extrafamilial social institutions, including extrafamilial altruism, is a matter of disagreement both among biologists and economists. In this

---

22. This dispute has generated a huge literature. For an introduction, see Arthur L. Caplan (1978). A more recent summary is to be found in Geoffrey M. Hodgson (1995), especially part 2.

23. As Becker (1976, 284n.6) puts it, "biological selection has not been integrated into and combined with the main body of economic analysis: it has been an occasional appendage rather than an integral part."

ongoing dispute, economists have, for the most part, been importers of ideas from sociobiology rather than imperialistic exporters. However, to the present these ideas have not greatly influenced the applications of RAP beyond the confines of the economics of the family.

POLITICAL SCIENCE

Economics has several interfaces with political science: on some of these economics is clearly the aggressor, but on others this is not the case. One locus of economic aggression is the interpretation of political behavior as an exercise of rational choice. Attempts to implement this interpretation have led to the creation of formal models that develop the implications of the hypothesis that candidates for office seek to position themselves in respect of various issues so as to maximize the votes obtainable from utility-maximizing ballot casters.[24]

In this connection, investigation of the properties of alternative voting rules and their evaluation in terms of criteria akin to Pareto optimality has been especially prominent. This work has resulted in the creation of the field of social choice, populated both by economists and political scientists, which has been briefly discussed in chapter 9. Specialists in this field are now well integrated into political science, yet I think it is fair to say that their roots and their sensitivity to theoretical developments in economics remain quite visible. While it is not necessary to label them as agents of economic imperialism, their expository style places heavy emphasis on formal demonstration and makes appeal to criteria of validity much closer to those prevailing in economics than to those of traditional political science.[25]

While the theory of social choice (or public choice, as some prefer) is the part of political science where formal theory is most salient, it is not the only area bearing the imprint of techniques of foreign origin. Within the past two decades there has developed a substantial literature on the development of political institutions as a response to the requirements of political transacting. This literature attempts to explain such institutions in terms of the need to monitor and enforce agreements, maintain the fidelity of agents, settle disputes about the interpretation of agreements expeditiously, and so on. The analysis runs in terms similar to those used in the study of business and labor contracts, with frequent appeal to the

---

24. The earliest work of this genre is Anthony Downs (1957). For a recent summary with an extensive bibliography see A. W. Finifter (1993), chapter 4.

25. An excellent example of this type of work is Peter C. Ordeshook (1986).

framework of game theory and resort to considerations of efficiency and survival as determinants of outcomes. North (1990) provides a good overview of this work, which he describes, not inappropriately, as "the new political economy."

The application of positive analysis of voting behavior, particularly in relation to the problems of implementing economic policy, is another interface of the two fields. The spirit of RAP would suggest that such analyses should begin by assuming the conventional resource endowment of each decision-making unit to be augmented with a quantum of political resources (e.g., command of votes), and postulating that each of these units allocates all of its resources in accordance with an integrated plan for maximizing its own utility.

If this were done, and a unique determinate equilibrium with positive prices and quantities obtained, there would be a price of political resources in terms of a numeraire, and each decision-making unit's wealth (as conventionally defined) would be augmented by the value of its political resources. The analysis could then proceed exactly as in a Walrasian model, with political resources allocated and priced like other inputs.

That this has not been done, or even seriously attempted, is due primarily to the inability to find either a suitable unit in which to measure quantities of political resources or their corresponding prices. While it is intuitively obvious that wealth in the ordinary sense can be used to buy political influence, and that the latter can be traded for wealth, conceptualizing the rate of exchange between them—and defining the ancillary unit of political influence—has not been attempted.[26]

A major reason for this omission is the difficulty of specifying the technology of producing and transferring political influence. Such a technology would need to be embedded in a model of the state conjugate with RAP, and no such model is on offer. As a result, attempts to explain political behavior as (rational) pursuit of pecuniary benefit typically explain voting behavior as an instrument in such a pursuit, but make little attempt to introduce cost factors, or even to show that the benefits obtained are commensurate with the costs incurred.[27]

For lack of a unifying theory, the various strands of research that at-

26. Put differently, there is no accepted procedure for estimating the pecuniary value of an individual's voting rights, or of his influence over the voting behavior of others.

27. That is, most of these studies treat the assumption that political action is simply "pursuit of wealth by nonstandard means" as a maintained hypothesis (i.e., they do not consider it subject to possible refutation).

tempt to utilize concepts and propositions of both economics and political science remain quite disparate. Thus discussions of such topics as political business cycles; the incidence and effectiveness of industrial regulation; the incidence of wars, revolutions and strikes; the generation of tariffs and other taxes; and the incidence of rent seeking, do not attempt to apply a common model, or even a family of related models, but go their separate ways, despite frequent obeisances to RAP.

In a nutshell, political science offers no general framework for analyzing the causes and effects of state action upon the economy; the framework suggested by RAP is a mirage that is dispelled as soon as it is attempted either to quantify or to price "political influence" or "political power." As a result, the borderland of economics and political science is contested territory where RAP adherents from economics make common cause with sympathizers from political science, and where economists who dissent from RAP find allies among political scientists congenial to their general outlook.[28]

PSYCHOLOGY

As we saw in chapter 6, the boundary of economics with psychology is very turbulent. Implicitly, RAP claims to be able to explain a wide section of all human behavior.[29] While in principle RAP adherents accept that RAP cannot explain all of human behavior, in practice they are reluctant to waive any particular parcel of behavioral turf and take delight in laying claim to fresh areas that had previously been considered beyond the reach of its conceptual apparatus.

Thus Becker and Murphy (1988) have attempted to show that addictive behavior can be reconciled with the postulate of rationality. In the same vein, Becker (1991) has attempted to reconcile the persistence of queuing with rationality and foresight of all parties concerned. The essential purpose of these and similar ventures is to demonstrate the flexibility of the RAP framework and to motivate the gathering of data that conform to its categories rather than to those offered by other social sciences.

It is not my purpose to judge the validity of these studies, each of which merits separate and careful appraisal, but to remark that they have

28. For an excellent discussion of the relation of economics to political science with particular reference to economic imperialism, see the article by Peter C. Ordeshook (1990).

29. Indeed, the claims are not limited to humans. As we have seen (above in chapter 7), experimental work with animals claims to have demonstrated that their choice behavior conforms to (at least some of) the axioms of RAP.

attracted both approval and dissent from both economists and psychologists.[30] As on the other boundaries of the subject, forays of RAP into the territory of psychology have met with resistance from its inhabitants. In the case of psychology, however, the identity of the aggressor is uncertain. Attacks on the concept of "the economic man" date from the early nineteenth century and, in various guises, have continued to the present. But it is only within the past quarter century that advocates of the "economic approach" à la Becker have taken the offensive to stake out new claims within the territory of psychology.[31]

On the psychology-economics interface, cross-disciplinary alliances and antagonisms similar to those found on the other boundaries of economics also emerge, though less prominently. Although in decrying RAP its opponents within economics join forces with critics of the rationality postulate in psychology, few active defenders of RAP can be found among psychologists. This is because, with the possible exception of social psychology, the problems of psychology make little contact with the implications of RAP.

THE GENERAL CULTURE

Without recourse to quantitative speculation, I will venture the timid conjecture that the impact of economic imperialism on the general culture may be even greater than on any of the other social sciences. This impact comes from the altered perception of social relationships that results from the suggestion that they might be thought of as implicit market transactions, rather than the consequence of a set of obligatory rules.

For example, the idea that a marriage contract is analogous to a commercial contract is quite different from what is suggested by "for richer, for poorer till death do ye part." The "present-value maximization" view of marriage leads spouses to take precautions to protect their separate titles to the assets they bring to the partnership, to provide nurturing services only to the extent that such provision is entailed by an ongoing bargain rather than as an expression of affection or obligation, and so on.

The "talk doesn't matter" branch of RAP adherents might argue that such changes in perceptions and behavior are a response to changes in prevailing behavior as observed, and thus can be explained without attributing influence to ideas. While such a contention would be debatable, and

30. Some of these studies have already been discussed in chapter 6.

31. This is not to suggest that there is any special virtue to quiet borders between disciplines: border raids are simply one manifestation of competition among disciplines.

is debated, I am inclined to side with those who, like McCloskey, ascribe to ideas some direct influence on behavior. Regardless of their direct effect on behavior, ideas are intrinsically important. This importance derives from their influence on what large segments of the population can be persuaded to believe (e.g., through advertising) either about political issues or consumer products.[32]

One very important manifestation of the impact of economics on the community's belief structure is its influence on the legal system. This influence is manifested partly through the growing use of RAP as a guide to the formulation of legal arguments and judicial decisions. But it is also manifested in what Margaret Jane Radin (1996) has termed the "commodification" of personal relations. That is, by providing an interpretation of personal relations (e.g., marriage and divorce, adoption and custody of children, transfer of body parts, rendering of personal services) as market transactions, RAP changes the way in which individuals regard other parties to the relationship. This may alter what they consider as their due and/or their obligations as a result of the relationship.

The interpretation that any individual places upon a relationship depends upon the interpretation that she believes others place upon it. Expression of a particular interpretation in a judicial decision is likely to promote adoption of similar interpretations in other courts and in the thinking of individuals. That is, the law is one of the channels through which economic ideas affect the general culture.

A second channel through which economic ideas enter the larger culture is in the formation of opinion as to what is credible. "What it is believed that people will believe" influences actual behavior in a wide variety of circumstances from trading on the stock market to governmental actions to increase the relative wages of one group of workers relative to those of some other group. For example, suppose that legislators believed that the public believed that relative wages were determined by market forces and that, therefore, legislation to alter them would be either futile or would adversely affect employment: i.e., the public believed that legislative action would not be a credible means of attaining the intended objective. Regardless of the facts, such a belief by legislators about the state of public belief would lead them to expect little public support for such efforts and would therefore inhibit the undertaking of them.

---

32. Whether the significance of a community's beliefs derives solely from their (indirect) effect on behavior, or is partly independent of the action(s) they prompt is a question that may be bypassed here.

Thus, by contributing to the public view of how the world works, economics influences its actual working. RAP contributes to one such view; KP contributes to a view that is, in some respects, contradictory. Other social sciences contribute still other views, some of which conflict with those of RAP, some of which do not. The impact of economics, especially RAP, upon the general culture depends upon the outcome of such conflicts of beliefs, which are influenced by the outcome of the disciplinary disputes as discussed above, and also by popular debates.

THE FUTURE OF THE CULTURE OF ECONOMICS

Economics is currently engaged in a bold attempt to expand the range of phenomena to which its expertise can be applied. This attempt has attracted much attention and has met with considerable success. However, it has also met with opposition from within its own culture as well as from other social sciences, and there have been counterattacks not only upon its claims to new territory, but also upon its competence within various parts of what had been traditionally regarded as its own turf.

While the outcome of these various struggles is uncertain, it is possible that one result will be a shift in the locus of expertise of economics and possibly of other social sciences as well. That is, the field of expertise of a social science may shift to follow the displayed applicability of the paradigms that it uses. Thus it is possible that economics will gain sovereignty over family organization and demography, but lose some territory in the field of industrial organization. However, the hold of economics on phenomena generated by the functioning of organized exchanges remains firm and, with the development of the theory of finance, is being exploited with increasing effectiveness.

One aspect of the theory of finance has been the creation of an array of synthetic assets—derivatives—to facilitate the transfer of risk. In the performance of this growing task, and in the creation of market institutions to implement the ancillary transactions, economics has created an expanding domain within which its expertise is largely unchallenged. Distinct from this, though related in conceptual framework, economics has also developed an analysis of the effect of bidding rules on the outcome of auctions which can and has been applied to the design of actual auctions.

A major virtue of market institutions is that they generate results—asset allocations and transaction terms—without residual dispute. This feature makes such institutions attractive to anyone interested in securing agreement among individuals having a conflict of interests without overt coercion of any of them, for example, by getting one party to purchase the agreement of the other(s). To do this requires that outstanding disputes be put into a form such that causes of offense can be made commensurate with dollars; if the result of the transformation can be made divisible into convenient units, so much the better. Thus, in devising transferable rights to pollute, the expertise of economics has made an appreciable contribution to statecraft in deciding who should be allowed to emit how much of a limited quantity of pollutants that it had been decided to tolerate. It is likely that this outlet for the economist's expertise will find increasing use.

Such use of a "commodified" concept of a social offense (emission of a noxious waste) encourages the development and application of further models in which the outcomes of seemingly nonmarket activities are transformed into quantities with correlative prices that can be paid (in the form of taxes or subsidies) to increase or decrease the quantity supplied. By extension, even when an activity cannot be commodified it often is possible to associate it with a shadow price that can be used to implement a cost-benefit analysis of its effect. Hence the burgeoning of welfare economics described in chapter 9.

Finally, the practice of statecraft necessarily involves consideration of the consequences of applying government resources to alternative uses. While the limitations of economics as a predictive science preclude us from forecasting a bright future for it in this pursuit, even here it is no less adequate than available alternatives: Arguments about the comparative merits of alternative proposals for use of public resources will continue to run in terms of their prospective consequences. Despite widespread reservations about the reliability of out-of-sample forecasts, faute de mieux, such arguments will continue to invoke the lessons of experience buttressed by appeals to what is intuitively plausible.

For the mobilization of such arguments, and despite disagreements among competing practitioners and caveats from all concerned, contemporary econometrics is an essential tool. At the very least, it is sufficiently well developed effectively to refute confident unconditional predictions, and thus to act as a check on wish thinking and unguided intuition. Such use rationalizes the continuing development of increasingly powerful statistical techniques that are ancillary to it. To paraphrase Bob Solow, "I know the wheel is crooked, but economics is still the best game in town."

BIBLIOGRAPHY

Abraham, Katharine G., John S. Greenlees, and Brent E. Moulton. 1998. "Working to Improve the Consumer Price Index." *Journal of Economic Perspectives* 12, no. 1 (Winter): 27–36.

Akerlof, George A. 1984. *An Economist's Book of Tales.* New York: Cambridge University Press.

Akerlof, George A., and William T. Dickens. 1982. "The Economic Consequences of Cognitive Dissonance." *American Economic Review* 72, no. 3 (June): 307–19.

Alchian, Armen A. 1950. "Uncertainty, Evolution and Economic Theory." *Journal of Political Economy* 58 (June): 211–21.

Alchian, Armen A., and Harold Demsetz. 1972. "Production, Information Costs and Economic Opportunity." *American Economic Review* 62, no. 5 (December): 777–95.

Allen, Helen, and Mark P. Taylor. 1992. "Chartist Analysis." *The New Palgrave Dictionary of Money and Finance,* 1:339–42. New York: The Stockton Press.

Alt, J. E., and K. A. Shepsle, eds. 1990. *Perspectives on Positive Political Economy.* New York: Cambridge University Press.

Argyrous, George. 1992. "Kuhn's Paradigms and Neoclassical Economics. *Economics and Philosophy* 8, no. 1 (October): 231–48.

———. 1994. "Kuhn's Paradigms and Neoclassical Economics: Reply to Dow." *Economics and Philosophy* 10, no. 1 (April): 123–26.

Arrow, Kenneth J. 1951. *Social Choice and Individual Values.* New York: John Wiley.

Arrow, Kenneth J., and Frank Hahn. 1971. *General Competitive Analysis.* San Francisco: Holden-Day.

Arthur, W. Brian. 1989. "Competing Technologies, Increasing Returns, and Lock-In by Historical Events." *Economic Journal* 99, no. 3 (March): 116–31.

Axelrod, Robert. 1984. *The Evolution of Cooperation.* New York: Basic Books.

Barber, William J. 1997. "Reconfigurations in American Academic Economics: A General Practitioner's Perspective." *Daedalus* 126, no. 1 (Winter): 87–103.

Becker, Gary S. 1964. *Human Capital.* New York: Columbia University Press, for the National Bureau of Economic Research.

Becker, Gary S. 1968. "Crime and Punishment: an Economic Approach." *Journal of Political Economy* 76, no. 2 (March–April): 169–217.

———. 1976. *The Economic Approach to Human Behavior.* Chicago: University of Chicago Press.

———. 1981. *A Treatise on the Family.* Chicago: University of Chicago Press.

———. 1991. "A Note on Restaurant Pricing and Other Examples of Social Influence on Prices." *Journal of Political Economy* 99, no. 5 (October): 1109–16.

Becker, Gary S., and Kevin Murphy. 1988. "A Theory of Rational Addiction." *Journal of Political Economy* 96, no. 4 (August): 675–700.

Becker, Gary S., and George J. Stigler. 1974. "Law Enforcement, Malfeasance and Compensation of Employers." *Journal of Legal Studies* 3, no. 1 (January): 1–18.

Ben Porath, Yoram. 1982. "Economics and the Family—Match or Mismatch? A Review of Becker's *A Treatise on the Family.*" *Journal of Economic Literature* 20, no. 1 (March): 53–64.

Berle, Adolf A., and Gardner C. Means. 1932. *The Modern Corporation and Private Property.* New York: Commerce Clearing House.

Black, Fischer, and Myron S. Scholes. 1973. "The Pricing of Options and Corporate Liabilities." *Journal of Political Economy* 81, no. 3 (May–June): 637–54.

Blaug, Mark. 1997. *Economic Theory in Retrospect.* 5th ed. New York: Cambridge University Press.

Blinder, Alan S. 1992. *Hard Heads, Soft Hearts.* New York: Addison-Wesley.

Boettke, Peter J., ed. 1994. *The Elgar Companion to Austrian Economics.* Brookfield, Vt.: Edward Elgar.

Bok, Derek. 1993. *The Cost of Talent.* New York: The Free Press.

Bowles, Samuel, and Herbert Gintis. 1986. *Democracy and Capitalism.* New York: Basic Books.

Bowles, S., R. C. Edwards, and W. G. Shepherd, eds. 1989. *Unconventional Wisdom.* Boston: Houghton, Mifflin.

Brickley, J. A., and J. J. McConnell. 1987. "Dividend Policy." In *The New Palgrave A Dictionary of Economics* 1:897–98. New York: The Stockton Press.

Buchanan, James M. 1986. *Liberty, Market and the State.* Brighton: Wheatsheaf Books.

Buchanan, James M., and Gordon Tullock. 1962. *The Calculus of Consent.* Ann Arbor: University of Michigan Press.

Burtless, Gary, ed. 1996. *Does Money Matter?* Washington, D.C.: Brookings Institution.

Caldwell, Bruce. 1982. *Beyond Positivism: Economic Methodology in the Twentieth Century.* London: George Allen and Unwin.

Caplan, Arthur L., ed. 1978. *The Sociobiology Debate.* New York: Harper and Row.

Card, David E., and Allen B. Krueger. 1995. "Myth and Measurement: The New Economics of the Minimum Wage." Princeton, N.J.: Princeton University Press.

Chakravarty, S. 1987. "Cost-Benefit Analysis." In *The New Palgrave A Dictionary of Economics* 1:687–90. New York: The Stockton Press.

Cheung, Steven N. S. 1969. *The Theory of Share Tenancy.* Chicago: University of Chicago Press.

Christie, William G., and Paul H. Schultz. 1994. "Why Do NASDAQ Market Makers Avoid Odd-Eighth Quotes?" *Journal of Finance* 49, no. 5 (December): 1813–60.

Clower, R. W. 1965. "The Keynesian Counterrevolution: A Theoretical Appraisal." In *The Theory of Interest Rates,* ed. F. H. Hahn and F. R. Brechling, 103–25. London: Macmillan.

Coase, Ronald H. 1960. "The Problem of Social Cost." *Journal of Law and Economics* 3, no. 1 (October): 1–44.

———. 1988. *The Firm, the Market and the Law.* Chicago: University of Chicago Press.

———. 1994. *Essays on Economics and Economists.* Chicago: University of Chicago Press.

Colander, David C. 1984. "Was Keynes a Keynesian or a Lernerian?" *Journal of Economic Literature* 22, no. 4 (December): 1572–75.

Colander, David C., and Arjo Klamer. 1987. "The Making of an Economist." *Journal of Economic Perspectives* 1, no. 2. (Spring): 95–111.

Conlisk, John. 1996. "Why Bounded Rationality?" *Journal of Economic Literature* 34, no. 2 (June): 669–700.

Cooter, Robert D. 1987. "Coase Theorem." In *The New Palgrave Dictionary of Money and Finance,* 1:457–59. New York: The Stockton Press.

Cootner, Paul, ed. 1964. *The Random Character of Stock Market Prices.* Cambridge, Mass.: MIT Press.

Cordato, Roy E. 1992. *Welfare Economics and Externalities in an Open Ended Universe: A Modern Austrian Perspective.* Boston: Kluwer Academic Publishers.

Coutts, K. J. 1987. "Average Cost Pricing". *The New Palgrave,* Vol.1. The Stockton Press. New York. pp. 138–9.

Dasgupta, Partha. 1993. *An Inquiry into Well-Being and Destitution.* New York: Oxford University Press.

David, Paul A. 1985. "Clio and the Economics of QWERTY." *American Economic Review* 75, no. 2 (May): 332–37.

David, Paul A., et al. 1976. *Reckoning with Slavery.* New York: Oxford University Press.

———. 1992. *A Paradigm for Historical Economics: Path Dependence and Predictability in Dynamic Systems with Local Network Externalities.* Center for Economic Policy Research. Stanford University, Stanford, Ca.

David, Paul A., and Shane Greenstein. 1990. "The Economics of Compatibility Standards: An Introduction to Recent Research." *Economic Innovations and New Technology* 1, no. 1: 3–41.

Deaton, Angus, and John Muellbauer. 1980. *Economics and Consumer Behavior.* Cambridge: Cambridge University Press.

De Long, J. B., A. Shleifer, L. H. Summers, and R. J. Waldmann. 1991. "The Survival of Noise Traders in Financial Markets." *Journal of Business* 64, no. 1 (January): 1–19.

Denison, Edward F. 1989. *Estimates of Productivity Change by Industries.* Washington, D.C.: Brookings Institution.

Douglas, Paul H. 1934. *The Theory of Wages.* New York: Macmillan.

———. 1948. "Are There Laws of Production?" *American Economic Review* 38, no. 1 (March): 1–41.

Dow, Sheila C. 1994. "Kuhn's Paradigms and Neoclassical Economics: A Comment." *Economics and Philosophy* 10, no. 1 (April): 119–22.

Downs, Anthony. 1957. *An Economic Theory of Democracy.* New York: Harper and Row.

Dunlop, John T. 1938. "The Movement of Real and Money Wage Rates." *Economic Journal* 48, no. 141 (September): 413–34.

Ehrlich, Isaac. 1973. "Participation in Illegitimate Activities: A Theoretical and Empirical Investigation." *Journal of Political Economy* 81, no. 3 (May–June): 521–65.

———. 1975. "Capital Punishment: A Case of Life or Death." *American Economic Review* 65, no. 3 (June): 397–417.

Einhorn, Hillel J., and Robin M. Hogarth. 1987. "Decision Making under Ambiguity." In *Rational Choice: The Contrast between Economics and Psychology,* ed. Robin M. Hogarth and Melvin W. Reder, pp. 41–66. Chicago: University of Chicago Press.

Epstein, Richard A. 1985. *Private Property and the Theory of Eminent Domain.* Cambridge, Mass.: Harvard University Press.

Feldstein, Martin, and P. Bacchetta. 1990. "National Savings and International Investment." In B. D. Bernheim, and J. Shoven, eds., *National Saving and Economic Performance.* Chicago: University of Chicago Press.

Feldstein, Martin, and Charles Horioka. 1980. "Domestic Saving and International Capital Flows." *Economic Journal* 90, no. 358 (June): 318–29.

Fellner, William J. 1949. *Competition Among the Few.* New York: Alfred A. Knopf.

Festinger, Leon. 1957. *A Theory of Cognitive Dissonance.* Stanford, Calif.: Stanford University Press.

Ferber, Marilyn A., and Julie A. Nelson, eds. 1993. *Beyond Economic Man.* Chicago: University of Chicago Press.

Finifter, A. W., ed. 1993. *Political Science: The State of the Discipline.* 2d ed. Washington, D.C.: The American Political Science Association.

Fishburn, Peter C. 1987. "Utility Theory and Decision Theory." In *The New Palgrave A Dictionary of Economics* 4:779–82. New York: The Stockton Press.

Fisher, Irving. 1930. *The Theory of Interest.* New York: Macmillan.

Fisher, Lloyd H. 1953. *The Harvest Labor Market in California.* Cambridge, Mass.: Harvard University Press.

Fogel, Robert W. 1964. *Railroads and American Economic Growth: Essays in American Economic History.* Baltimore, Md.: Johns Hopkins University Press.

Fogel, Robert W. and Stanley L. Engerman. 1974. *Time on the Cross: The Economics of American Negro Slavery.* Boston: Little, Brown.

Frank, Robert H. 1988. *Passions within Reason.* New York: W. W. Norton.

Frank, Robert H., Thomas Gilovich, and Dennis T. Regan. 1993. "Does Studying Economics Inhibit Cooperation?" *Journal of Economic Perspectives* 7, no. 2 (Spring): 159–71.

———. 1996. "Do Economists Make Bad Citizens?" *Journal of Economic Perspectives* 10, no. 1 (Winter): 187–92.

Frey, Bruno S. 1992. *Economics as a Science of Human Behavior.* Dordrecht: Kluwer.

Frey, Bruno, and Reiner E. Eichenberger. 1991. "Anomalies in Political Economy." *Public Choice* 68, nos. 1–3 (January): 71–89.

Friedman, Milton. 1953. "The Methodology of Positive Economics." Chapter 1 in *Essays in Positive Economics*. Chicago: University of Chicago Press.

———. 1956. *Studies in the Quantity Theory of Money*. Chicago: University of Chicago Press.

———. 1957. *A Theory of the Consumption Function*. Princeton, N.J.: Princeton University Press.

———. 1959. *A Program for Monetary Stability*. New York: Fordham University Press.

———. 1962. *Capitalism and Freedom*. Chicago: University of Chicago Press.

———. 1968. "The Role of Monetary Policy." *American Economic Review* 58, no. 1 (March): 1–17.

Friedman, Milton, and Anna J. Schwartz. 1982. *Monetary Trends in the United States and the United Kingdom*. Chicago: University of Chicago Press.

Goldfarb, Robert S. 1995. "The Economist-as-Audience Needs a Methodology of Plausible Inference." *Journal of Economic Methodology* 2, no. 2 (December): 221–22.

Goode, William J. 1978. *The Celebration of Heroes*. Berkeley and Los Angeles: University of California Press.

Greenwald, Bruce, and Joseph Stiglitz. 1993. "New and Old Keynesians." *Journal of Economic Perspectives* 7, no. 1 (Winter): 23–44.

Gordon, Robert J. 1990. "What is New Keynesian Economics?" *Journal of Economic Literature* 28, no. 3 (September): 1115–71.

Gurley, John G., and Edward S. Shaw. 1960. *Money in a Theory of Finance*. Washington, D.C.: The Brookings Institution.

Haavelmo, Trygve. 1944. "The Probability Approach to Econometrics." *Econometrica* Vol. 12 Supplement (July).

Hansen, W. Lee. 1991. "The Education and Training of Economics Doctorate." *Journal of Economic Literature* 29, no. 3 (September): 1054–87.

Harburger, Arnold C. 1964. "The Measurement of Waste." *American Economic Review Proceedings* (May) Vol. 54, pp. 68–76.

Hausman, Daniel M. 1992. *The inexact and Separate Science of Economics*. New York: Cambridge University Press.

Hawtrey, Ralph G. 1925. *The Economic Problem*. London: Longmans and Green.

Herrnstein, R. J., and Drazen Prelec. 1991. "Melioration: A Theory of Distributed Choice." *Journal of Economic Perspectives* 5, no. 3 (Summer): 137–56.

Hicks, John R. 1937. "Mr. Keynes and the Classics: A Suggested Interpretation." *Econometrica* 5, no. 2 (April): 147–59.

———. 1939. *Value and Capital*. New York: Oxford University Press.

Hirschman, Albert O. 1970. *Exit, Voice and Loyalty*. Cambridge, Mass.: The Belknap Press of Harvard University.

Hodgson, Geoffrey M., ed. 1995. *Economics and Biology*. Aldershot: Edgar Elgar.

Hogarth, Robin, and Melvin W. Reder, eds. 1986. *Rationality in Economics and Psychology*. Chicago: University of Chicago Press.

Hood, William C., and Tjalling C. Koopmans, eds. 1953. *Studies in Econometric Method.* Cowles Commission Monograph no. 14. New York: John Wiley.

Hoover, Kevin D. 1988. *The New Classical Macroeconomics.* Oxford: Basil Blackwell.

Kagel, John H., and Alvin E. Roth, eds. 1995. *The Handbook of Experimental Economics.* Princeton, N.J.: Princeton University Press.

Kahnemann, Daniel, Jack L. Knetsch, and Richard H. Thaler. 1987. "Fairness and the Assumptions of Economics." In *Rational Choice,* ed. R. M. Hogarth and M. W. Reder, pp. 101–16. Chicago: University of Chicago Press.

Kanbur, Ravi. 1987. "Shadow Pricing." In *The New Palgrave A Dictionary of Economics* 4:457–59. New York: The Stockton Press.

Katz, Michael L., and Carl Shapiro. 1985. "Network Externalities." *American Economic Review* 73, no. 3 (June): 424–40.

Kennan, John. 1995. "The Elusive Effects of Minimum Wages." *Journal of Economic Literature* 33, no. 4 (December): 1950–65.

Keynes, John M. 1920. *The Economic Consequences of the Peace.* New York: Macmillan.

———. 1936. *The General Theory of Employment, Interest and Money.* New York: Harcourt, Brace.

———. 1940. *How to Pay for the War.* New York: Harcourt, Brace.

Kirzner, Israel. 1987. "Austrian School of Economics." In *The New Palgrave A Dictionary of Economics* 1:145–50. New York: The Stockton Press.

Klamer, Arjo, and David C. Colander. 1990. *The Making of an Economist.* Boulder, Colo.: Westview Press.

Kleidon, Allen W. 1987. "Anomalies in Financial Economics: Blueprint for Change?" In *Rational Choice,* ed. R. M. Hogarth and M. W. Reder, pp. 285–316. Chicago: University of Chicago Press.

Klein, Lawrence R. 1983. *The Economics of Supply and Demand.* Oxford: Basil Blackwell.

Klein, Lawrence R., and Richard F. Kosobud. 1961. "Some Econometrics of Growth: Great Ratios of Economics." *Quarterly Journal of Economics* 75, no. 2 (May): 175–98.

Koopmans, Tjalling C. 1957. *Three Essays on the State of Economic Science.* New York: McGraw-Hill.

Koopmans, T. C., and S. Reiter, eds. 1951. *Activity Analysis of Production and Allocation.* Cowles Commission Monograph no. 13. New York: John Wiley.

Krueger, Anne O. 1974. "The Political Economy of the Rent Seeking Society." *American Economic Review* 64, no. 3: 291–303.

Krueger, Anne O., et al. 1991. "Report of the Commission on Graduate Education in Economics." *Journal of Economic Literature* Vol. XXIX, No. 3, pp. 1035–53.

Krugman, Paul. 1994. *Peddling Prosperity.* New York: W. W. Norton.

———. 1995a. "The Illusion of Conflict in International Trade." *Peace Economics, Peace Science and Public Policy* 2, no. 2: 9–18.

———. 1995b. *The Economist,* 25 April–5 May, 99–100.

Kuhn, Thomas S. 1970. *The Structure of Scientific Revolutions.* 2d ed. Chicago: University of Chicago Press.

———. 1977. "The Function of Measurement in Modern Physical Science." In *The Essential Tension: Selected Studies in Scientific Tradition and Change.* Chicago: University of Chicago Press.

Lahiri, K., and G. H. Moore, eds. 1991. *Leading Economic Indicators.* New York: Cambridge University Press.

Laidler, David. 1992. "Free Banking Theory." *The New Palgrave Dictionary of Money and Finance,* 2:196–98. New York: The Stockton Press.

Lange, Oscar. 1944. *Price Flexibility and Employment.* Cowles Commission Monograph no. 8. Bloomington, Ind.: The Principia Press.

Latsis, Spiro, ed. 1976. *Method and Appraisal in Economics.* New York: Cambridge University Press.

Lawson, Tony. 1996. *Economics and Reality.* New York: Cambridge University Press.

Lazear, Edward. 1979. "Why is There Mandatory Retirement?" *Journal of Political Economy* 87, no. 6 (December): 1261–84.

Leamer, Edward E. 1978. *Specification Searches.* New York: John Wiley.

———. 1983. "Let's Take the Con out of Econometrics." *American Economic Review* 73, no. 1 (March): 31–43.

Leijonhufvud, Axel. 1968. *On Keynesian Economics and the Economics of Keynes.* New York: Oxford University Press.

Lerner, Abba P. 1943. "Functional Finance and the Federal Debt." *Social Research* 10, no. 1 (February): 38–51.

———. 1944. *The Economics of Control.* New York: Macmillan.

———. 1973. *Flation.* Baltimore, Md.: Penguin Books.

Lewis, H. Gregg. 1963. *Unionism and Relative Wages in the United States.* Chicago: University of Chicago Press.

———. 1986. *Union Relative Wage Effects.* Chicago: University of Chicago Press.

Liebowitz, Stanley J., and Stephen Margolis. 1990. "The Fable of the Keys." *Journal of Law and Economics* 33, no. 1 (April): 1–26.

Lodewijks, John. 1994. "Anthropologists and economists: conflict and cooperation?" *Journal of Economic Methodology* 1, no. 1 (June): 81–104.

Lucas, Robert E., Jr. 1987. "Adaptive Behavior and Economic Theory." In *Rational Choice,* ed. R. M. Hogarth and M. W. Reder, pp. 217–42.

Lucas, Robert E., Jr., and Leonard A. Rapping. 1969. "Real Wages, Employment and Inflation." *Journal of Political Economy* 77, no. 5 (October): 721–54.

Machina, Mark J. 1987. "Expected Utility Hypothesis." *The New Palgrave A Dictionary of Economics* 2:232–38. New York: The Stockton Press.

———. 1989. "Dynamic Consistency and Non-Expected Utility Models of Choice under Uncertainty." *Journal of Economic Literature* 28, no. 4 (December): 1622–68.

———. 1990. "Preference Reversals." *Journal of Economic Perspectives* 4, no. 3 (Spring): 201–11.

Malkiel, Burton G. 1987. "Efficient Market Hypothesis." In *The New Palgrave A Dictionary of Economics* 2:322–36. New York: The Stockton Press.

Mankiw, N. Gregory. 1989. "Real Business Cycles: A New Keynesian Perspective." *Journal of Economic Perspectives* 3, no. 3 (Summer): 79–90.

Marshall, Alfred. 1948. *Principles of Economics.* 8th ed. New York: Macmillan.

Masterman, M. 1970. "The Nature of a Paradigm." In *Criticism and the Growth of Knowledge,* ed. I. Lakatos and A. Musgrave. New York: Cambridge University Press.

Mayer, Thomas. 1990. *Truth versus Precision in Economics.* Aldershot: Edward Elgar.

McAfee, R. Preston, and John McMillan. 1996. "Analyzing the Airways Auction." *Journal of Economic Perspectives* 10, no. 1 (Winter): 159–75.

McCloskey, D. N. 1993. *Knowledge and Persuasion in Economics.* New York: Cambridge University Press.

McElroy, Marjorie B., and Mary Jean Horney. 1981. "Nash-Bargained Household Decisions: Toward a Generalization of the Theory of Demand." *International Economic Review* 22, no. 2: 333–49.

Medema, Steven G. 1994. *Ronald H. Coase.* New York: St. Martin's Press.

Milgrom, Paul. 1996. "Auction Theory for Privatization." Churchill Lectures in Economics. Manuscript.

Miller, Merton H. 1987. "Behavioral Rationality in Finance; The Case of Dividends." In *Rational Choice,* ed. R. M. Hogarth and M. W. Reder, pp. 267–84. Chicago: University of Chicago Press.

Mincer, Jacob. 1974. *Schooling, Experience and Earnings.* New York: Columbia University Press, for the National Bureau of Economic Research.

Mirowski, Philip. 1989. *More Heat than Light.* New York: Cambridge University Press.

Modigliani, Franco, and Merton H. Miller. 1958. "The Cost of Capital, Corporation Finance and the Theory of Investment." *American Economic Review* 48, no. 3 (June): 261–97.

Morgenstern, Oskar. 1950. *On the Accuracy of Economic Observations.* Princeton, N.J.: Princeton University Press.

Myrdal, Gunnar. 1949. *An American Dilemma: The Negro Problem and Modern Democracy.* New York: Harper.

Nelson, Richard. 1997. "How New is New Growth Theory?" *Challenge* 40, no. 5 (September–October): 29–55.

Neumark, Daniel, and Paul Taubman. 1995. "Why Do Wage Profiles Slope Upward? Tests of the General Human Capital Model." *Journal of Labor Economics* 13, no. 4 (October): 736–61.

Noll, Roger G. 1989. *Handbook of Industrial Organization.* 2 vols. New York: North-Holland.

North, Douglass C. 1981. *Structure and Change in Economic History.* New York: W. W. Norton.

———. 1990. *Institutions, Institutional Change and Economic Performance.* New York: Cambridge University Press.

O'Driscoll, Gerald, and Mario J. Rizzo. 1985. *The Economics of Time and Ignorance.* Oxford: Basil Blackwood.

Okun, Arthur M. 1981. *Prices and Quantities.* Washington, D.C.: The Brookings Institution.

Olson, Mancur. 1965. *The Logic of Collective Action.* Cambridge, Mass.: Harvard University Press.

———. 1982. *The Rise and Decline of Nations.* New Haven: Yale University Press.

Ordeshook, Peter C. 1986. *Game Theory and Political Theory.* New York: Cambridge University Press.

———. 1990. "The Emerging Discipline of Political Economy." In *Perspectives on Positive Political Economy,* ed. J. E. Alt and K. A. Shepsle, 9–30. New York: Cambridge University Press.

Patinkin, Don. 1965. *Money, Interest, and Prices.* 2d ed. New York: Harper and Row.

Pencavel, John. 1991. *Labor Markets under Trade Unionism.* Oxford: Basil Blackwood.

Phelps, Edmund S. 1967. "Phillips Curves, Expectations of Inflation and Optimal Unemployment over Time." *Economica,* n.s., 34, no. 3: 254–81.

Phillips, A. W. 1958. "The Relation between Unemployment and the Rate of Change of Money Wage Rates in the United Kingdom, 1861–1957." *Economica,* n.s., 25, no. 2: 283–99.

Pigou, Arthur C. 1947. "Economic Progress in a Stable Environment". *Economica,* n.s., (August 1947): 180–88.

———. 1950. *the Economics of Welfare.* 4th ed. London: Macmillan.

Plott, Charles R. 1982. "Industrial Organization Theory." *Journal of Economic Literature* 20, no. 4 (December): 1485–1525.

Porter, Theodore W. 1995. *Trust in Numbers.* Princeton, N.J.: Princeton University Press.

Radin, Margaret Jane. 1996. *Contested Commodities.* Cambridge, Mass.: Harvard University Press.

Rawls, John. 1971. *A Theory of Justice.* Cambridge, Mass.: Harvard University Press.

Rebitzer, James B., and Lowell J. Taylor. 1995. "Efficiency Wages and Employment Rents." *Journal of Labor Economics* 13, no. 4 (October): 677–708.

Reder, Melvin W. 1982. "Chicago Economics: Permanence and Change." *Journal of Economic Literature* 20, no. 1 (March): 1–38.

———. 1959. "Alternative Theories of Labor's Share." In *The Allocation of Economic Resources,* ed. M. Abramovitz et al., pp. 180–206. Stanford, Calif.: Stanford University Press.

Regan, Donald T. 1988. *For The Record.* New York: Harcourt.

Robbins, Lionel C. 1935. *An Essay on the Nature and Significance of Economic Science.* 2d ed. New York: Macmillan.

Roemer, John E. 1986. *Value, Exploitation and Class.* New York: Harwood Academic Publishers.

Rogoff, Kenneth. 1996. "The Purchasing Power Parity Puzzle." *Journal of Economic Literature* 34, no. 2 (June): 647–88.

Romer, Paul M. 1994. "The Origins of Endogenous Growth." *Journal of Economic Perspectives* 8, no. 1 (Winter): 3–22.

Rosen, Sherwin. 1992. "Distinguished Fellow: Mincering Labor Economics." *Journal of Economic Perspectives* 6, no. 2 (Spring): 157–70.

Rosenberg, Alexander. 1992. *Economics: Mathematical Politics, or the Science of Diminishing Return?* Chicago: University of Chicago Press.

Ross, Stephen A. 1987. "Finance." In *The New Palgrave A Dictionary of Economics* 2:332–36. New York: The Stockton Press.

Roth, Alvin E. 1986. "Laboratory Experiments." *Economics and Philosophy* 2, no. 2 (October): 245–73.

Samuelson, Paul A. 1947. *Foundations of Economic Analysis.* Cambridge, Mass.: Harvard University Press.

———. 1979. "Paul Douglas's Measurement of Production Functions and Marginal Productivities." *Journal of Political Economy* 87, no. 5, part 1 (October): 923–37.

Sandor, Richard L. 1973. "Innovation by an Exchange: A Case Study of the Development of the Plywood Futures Contract." *Journal of Law and Economics* 16, no. 1 (April): 114–36.

Schoemaker, Paul J. H. 1984. "Optimality Principles in Science: Some Epistemological Issues." In *The Quest for Optimality,* ed. J. H. P. Paelinck and P. H. Vossen. Brookfield, Vt.: Gower.

Scitovsky, Tibor. 1951. *Welfare and Competition.* Chicago: Richard D. Irwin.

———. 1976. *The Joyless Economy.* New York: Oxford University Press.

Searle, John R. 1995. *The Construction of Social Reality.* New York: The Free Press.

Seator, John J. 1993. "Ricardian Equivalence." *Journal of Economic Literature* 31, no. 1 (March): 142–90.

Sen, Amartya. 1984. *Commodities and Capabilities.* New York: North-Holland.

———. 1987. "Social Choice." In *The New Palgrave A Dictionary of Economics* 4:687–90. New York: The Stockton Press.

Shiller, Robert J. 1981. "Do Stock Prices Move Too Much to be Explained by Subsequent Changes in Dividends?" *American Economic Review* 71, no. 3 (June): 421–36.

———. 1987. "Comments on Miller and Kleidon." In *Rational Choice,* ed. R. M. Hogarth and M. W. Reder, pp. 317–22. Chicago: University of Chicago Press.

Simon, Herbert A. 1957. "A Behavioral Model of Rational Choice." Chap. 14 in his *Models of Man.* New York: John Wiley.

———. 1991. *Models of my Life.* New York: Basic Books.

Simons, Henry C. 1934. "A Positive Program for Laissez-Faire." Public Policy Pamphlet no. 15; H. D. Gideonse, ed. Chicago: University of Chicago Press.

Simons, Henry C. 1938. *Personal Income Taxation.* Chicago: University of Chicago Press.

Skidelsky, Robert. 1992. "John Maynard Keynes" Vol. 2. Macmillan. London. pp. 604–5.

Smith, Vernon L. 1987. "Experimental Methods in Economics." In *The New Palgrave A Dictionary of Economics* 2:241–49. New York: The Stockton Press.

———. 1994. "Economics in the Laboratory." *Journal of Economic Perspectives* 8, no. 1 (Winter): 113–31.

Snow, Charles P. 1959. *The Two Cultures.* New York: Cambridge University Press.

Solow, Robert. 1957. "Technical Change and the Aggregate Production Function." *Review of Economics and Statistics* (August): 312–20.

———. 1986. "Economics: Is Something Missing?" In *Economic History and the Modern Economist,* ed. W. M. Parker, pp. 21–29. Oxford: Basil Blackwood.

Sonnenschein, Hugo. 1987. "Oligopoly and Game Theory." In *The New Palgrave A Dictionary of Economics* 3:705–8. New York: The Stockton Press.

Sraffa, Piero. 1926. "The Laws of Return under Competitive Conditions." *Economic Journal* 36, no. 144 (December): 535–50.

Stigler, George J. 1971. "The Theory of Economic Regulation." *Bell Journal of Economics* 2, no. 1 (Spring): 3–21.

———. 1988. *Memoirs of an Unregulated Economist.* New York: Basic Books.

Stiglitz, Joseph. 1997. "Reflections on the Natural Rate Hypothesis." *Journal of Economic Perspectives* 11, no. 1 (Winter): 3–10.

Swedberg, Richard, ed. 1990. *Economics and Sociology.* Princeton, N.J.: Princeton University Press.

Tarshis, Lorie. 1939. "Changes in Real and Money Wages." *Economic Journal* vol. 49 (March) pp. 50–4.

Telser, Lester. 1972. *Competition, Collusion and Game Theory.* Chicago: Aldine-Atherton.

Tobin, James. 1958. "Estimation of Relationships for Limited Dependent Variables." *Econometrica* 26, no. 1 (January): 24–36.

———. 1993. "Price Flexibility and Output Stability: An Old Keynesian View." *Journal of Economic Perspectives* 7, no. 1: 45–65.

Triplett, Jack E. 1987. "Hedonic Functions and Hedonic Indices." *The New Palgrave A Dictionary of Money and Finance,* 2:630–34. New York: The Stockton Press.

Tullock, Gordon. 1967. "The Welfare Cost of Tariffs, Monopolies and Theft." *Western Economic Journal* 5: 224–32.

———. 1987. "Rent Seeking." In *The New Palgrave A Dictionary of Economics* 4:147–49. New York: The Stockton Press.

Tversky, Amos, and Daniel Kahneman. 1987. "Rational Choice and the Framing of Decisions." In *Rational Choice: The Contrast between Economics and Psychology,* ed. Robin M. Hogarth and Melvin W. Reder, pp. 67–94. Chicago: University of Chicago Press.

Tversky, Amos, and Richard H. Thaler. 1990. "Preference Reversals." *Journal of Economic Perspectives* 4, no. 2 (Spring): 201–11.

Vaughn, Karen I. 1994. *Austrian Economics in America.* New York: Cambridge University Press.

Viner, Jacob. 1991. "A Modest Proposal for some Stress on Scholarship in Graduate Training." In *Essays on the Intellectual History of Economics,* ed. Douglas A. Irwin, pp. 385–95. Princeton, N.J.: Princeton University Press.

von Neumann, John, and Oskar Morgenstern. 1953. *The Theory of Games and Economic Behavior.* 3d ed. Princeton, N.J.: Princeton University Press.

Wald, Abraham. 1939. "Contributions to the Theory of Statistical Estimation and Testing of Hypotheses." *Annals of Mathematical Statistics* 10, no. 4 (December): 299–326.

Weber, Max. 1949. *The Methodology of the Social Sciences,* trans. and ed. E. A. Shils and H. B. Finch. New York: The Free Press.

Weinberg, Steven. 1992. *Dreams of a Final Theory.* New York: Pantheon Books.

Weintraub, E. Roy. 1985. *General Equilibrium Analysis.* New York: Cambridge University Press.

White, Lawrence H., ed. 1993. *Free Banking Theory.* Aldershot, Hants, England: Edgar Elgar.

Williamson, Oliver E., and Scott E. Masten, eds. 1995. *Transaction Cost Economics.* 2 vols. Brookfield, Vt.: Edgar Elgar.

Yezer, Anthony M., Robert S. Goldfarb, and Paul J. Poppen. 1996. "Does Studying Economics Discourage Cooperation? Watch What We Do, Not What We Say or How We Play." *Journal of Economic Perspectives* 10, no. 1 (Winter): 177–86.

Zarnowitz, Victor. 1992. *Business Cycles: Theory, History, Indicators and Forecasting.* Chicago: University of Chicago Press.

NAME INDEX

SUBJECT INDEX

accounts/accounting, 267
ad hoc/ad hocery, 157
adjunct. *See* paradigm, adjuncts
agent/principal, 239
aggregate: consumption, 68–72, 108; income (expenditure, demand), 68–72, 93–95, 108; investment, 68–72; output (production), 68–72
Alienation, 117
arbitrage, profits, 198, 201–6. *See also* risk, hedging
animal spirits. *See* investment
anomalies, 145, 160, 163, 176
antirationalist(s), 129–30, 132. *See also* rationality
Arrow-Debreu (A-D) world, 53–55, 137
aspiration level, 123
attention, scarcity of, 292–93
auction rules, 279–85, 361
Australia and New Zealand, 282
Austrian economists/paradigm, 136–38, 147, 151, 156

banks/banking, central, 101, 268; free banking, 253
behavior/behaviorist (vs. talk), 87, 294–96
Black-Scholes formula. *See* derivative(s)
bonds, 77–82; government, 93–107. *See also* debt
"border wars," among social sciences, 341–44
bottleneck(s), 72–73
bourgeoisie, 115–17
box diagram, 51
budget deficit, 107
Bureau of Labor Statistics, 263–66, 268
business cycles, 269–70. *See also* leading indicators
business economists, 11–12, 271–73
"buy and hold" strategy, 198–99. *See also* Index Fund

capabilities, 234. *See also* welfare economics
capital accumulation. *See* investment
CAPM (capital asset pricing model), 199. *See also* finance
cash balance (also money stock/supply), 57–59, 77–82
ceteris paribus, 143, 162
Chartism, 198–99
choice theory. *See* consumer choice, theory of
citation, as indicator of recognition, 325–26
Civil Rights Movement, 314
classical distribution paradigm, 110–15
classical economics/economists, 72, 110–15
class struggle, 115–17, 236
cliometrics/cliometricians, 307
Coasean(s), 223–30
Coase theorem, 223–27
Cobb-Douglas production function, 305–6
cognitive dissonance, 38–39, 130, 173–74, 257
commodification, 360
Communist Manifesto, The, 117, 275
Comparative Worth, 140
compassion, 250–51
compensation (*see also* earnings; wages), 178, 182–86; executive, 189–92; methods of, 182–86; principle (*see also* Pareto optimal), 217
concept alteration, 302–3
conceptual organization (CO), 16–17, 136, 166–71, 319–20
consensus, 212–19; bases of, 324–29
consumer choice, theory of, 44–50
consumer price index (CPI), 263, 265
consumption function (*see also* multiplier; permanent income hypothesis), 69–72, 82–84, 108, 169; unproductive, 112–15, 232